To Bishop Crispian, In hope that everything eventually in this will...

Humble aspir,

Vivian Flanagan

C000319860

THE ENCHANTMENT OF SOCIOLOGY
A STUDY OF THEOLOGY AND CULTURE

Also by Kieran Flanagan

SOCIOLOGY AND LITURGY: Re-presentations of the Holy
POSTMODERNITY, SOCIOLOGY AND RELIGION *(with Peter C. Jupp)*

The Enchantment of Sociology

A Study of Theology and Culture

Kieran Flanagan
Senior Lecturer in Sociology
University of Bristol

First published in Great Britain 1996 by
MACMILLAN PRESS LTD
Houndmills, Basingstoke, Hampshire RG21 6XS
and London
Companies and representatives
throughout the world

A catalogue record for this book is available
from the British Library.

ISBN 0–333–65167–7

First published in the United States of America 1996 by
ST. MARTIN'S PRESS, INC.,
Scholarly and Reference Division,
175 Fifth Avenue,
New York, N.Y. 10010

ISBN 0–312–12975–0

Library of Congress Cataloging-in-Publication Data
available from the Library of Congress

10   9   8   7   6   5   4   3   2   1
05   04   03   02   01   00   99   98   97   96

Printed and bound in Great Britain by
Antony Rowe Ltd, Chippenham, Wiltshire

To my mother

Maureen Flanagan

with love and many thanks

Contents

Preface

On the tomb of Robert Grosseteste, Bishop of Lincoln, 1175–1253, in the South transept of his Cathedral before the chapel of St Peter and Paul lies the manuscript of this book. It is placed there at a break from the annual conference of the British Sociological Association, Sociology of Religion Study Group Conference. It is the Wednesday before Holy Week as one fumbles to write the preface, rewritten on Good Friday evening and finished on Easter Sunday night.

For the reader, the introduction marks the beginning, the consideration of whether it is worth going further into this text; but for the writer it represents the epilogue, the ending of the book, the wonder as to what this private angst was about before its disinternment into the public domain and its departure into the publishing process.

This study is a reflection on an ambition to write the imperative for enchantment in sociology into the interface between culture and theology, a terrain of ambiguity where the discipline risks being propelled into a holy unexpected turn. Reflexivity, a self-awareness peculiar to sociology, raises issues of the self of the sociologist. If theology is faith seeking understanding, then in its reading of culture, sociology might be a novel strand to be added to theological thought. This forms a central theme of the study.

It examines the self-understandings of culture between theology and sociology to show their mutual and precarious relationship to secularisation. Whereas secularisation might signify the marginalisation of religious belief, it is argued that sociology finds metaphors of the sacred transferred to signify symbols, idols and icons within a commodified culture of postmodernity. But their vacuity within a religion without belief, combined with a sense of despiritualisation in a culture of postmodernity, can lead sociology to reconsider the originals of the metaphors of the sacred in a new light.

Sociology has its own domestic reasons for revolting against conditions of disenchantment and seeking enchantment. These derive from fear of imprisonment in Weber's iron cage. Because sociology fears what it enables, the capacity for limitless calculation in the realm of the social, it nurtures a nascent theological voice, an imperative for religious belief that becomes apparent in its understandings of culture. Enactment of religious belief within the cultural field links charisma with habitus, the disposition to believe and to act, that interlinks sociological understandings of culture

to those that belong to the tradition of theology. In this mutually implicated approach to culture, theology and sociology can begin to resolve the
common problems they face in dealing with postmodernity.

An ambition of the study is to reverse the seemingly fated unimaginative
sociological journey from Cathedral to cult. It seeks to make an intellectual pilgrimage back to the terrain of theology, Catholicism in this case.
In so travelling, it strives to retrieve what secular culture has misappropriated from the sacred. Much baggage that pertains to the distinctive cultural
nature of Catholicism has been stolen, dropped off, or has been discarded
naïvely by theologians in the past three decades. This study is less an
inquest on its dispersal than a sociological search for its restoration. In
addition, the study seeks to uncover impediments to religious belief as
related to readings of culture. It has a definite agenda of seeking to restore
to theology that which has been so misappropriated in a culture of
postmodernity. By the nature of its contextualisation in the secular university, academic theology neither understands the dangers of secularity, nor
the need to attend to a context where faith is realised in a detail of practice,
where habitus is to be cultivated if self-understandings of cultural enactments
are to be understood. The monastery is the exemplary site for this habitus,
but it also exemplifies the ideal field for re-enchantment and resistance to
postmodernity.

This study tries to escape from internal textual analyses of text, such as
those of the post-structuralists, and the ideological shibboleths of liberal
theologians. As far as one knows, there is no obvious equivalent to this
study, which partly accounts for its *ad hoc* properties, its idiosyncratic
concerns and its analytical, philosophical and theological shortcuts.

Sociology cannot accept that it is born to nihilism. This is an unreflected
tradition of the trade. Its opposite, a theological position, has gone by
convention and default. Secularisation reveals deeper dilemmas, unthought,
unconfronted theological issues, reflections which modernity partly disguised and which now postmodernity has resurrected. There is a nascent
theological position abroad in contemporary sociology in its dealings with
culture which this study tries to bring into critical focus. These are fragments of a theology but enough to uncover a mosaic that suggests belief
is not a sociological impossibility.

Catholic images hover near present dilemmas of postmodernity, its
concerns with the self, with ethics, aesthetics and appearances. These relate to interests of Baudelaire, Wilde and Huysmans. These pioneers of
modernity and decadence found their insights leading in a theological
direction which a secularised sociological tradition has ignored. There is a
Faustian property to sociological knowing, its limitless sceptical curiosity,

that begs questions about limits of knowing. The uncertainty postmodernity embodies relates to issues of choice, of judgement, which neither sociology nor theology can abdicate. A purpose of this study is to reflect on this issue of choice. Pascal's wager on the existence of God has sociological resonances in the context of postmodernity. But if sociology faces a wager in dealing with culture, even that of postmodernity, it reverts to the antinomy of Weber's wish to rescue enchantment from the fate of disenchantment. This fate points to charisma as the ameliorating solution to disenchantment, the routinisation of grace that proffers the prospect of enchantment. This is where the issue of choice lies between sociology and theology.

Clearly, this is a sociological work, primarily addressed to theologians, but also to sociologists as well. If space had permitted, one would have liked to have written two conclusions, one for sociologists, and the other for theologians, much in the manner of George Bernard Shaw's *John Bull's Other Island*. In many respect, the study is a venture into a no man's land, for sociologists do not see the need to refer to theology, and theologians might not grasp what self-understandings sociology offers them in their reading of culture and their effort to heal its disjunction with faith. The study is unlikely to offer theologians reflecting on culture what they *think* they want.

It is easier to say what the study is not about. It is not a study of why sociologists should become holy and seek God; nor is it a study of culture in terms of multicultural, multi-faith, liberation, feminist, ecological, New Age forms of theology; nor is it a study that seeks to anathematise liberal theologians by name and text; nor does it claim to typify sociology or to be exhaustive in its dealings with theology and culture. The study is none of these things, though they lurk in the background.

The aim of the study is to give expression to a sociological habitus and to link a reflexivity to theological reflection in understandings of culture. Its theological location is within the new Catholic Catechism. This provides an orthodox qualification to the unorthodoxies of sociological insights into the relationship between theology and culture. The study assumes religious belief; its problem is with disbelief and that which assists it. Liberal theology is the villain of this study. In an English setting, the study is a negative response to the polarities of a theological liberalism, exemplified in Anglicanism, in the form of the otiosely titled the 'Affirming Catholicism' Group, and in Catholicism, against the supposedly influential Catholic weekly *The Tablet*. Matters might be impoverished enough if these groups were innocent of sociology in their theological deliberations on culture. The trouble is that they unwittingly produce a deplorable sociology in their readings of culture that disables understanding of the viability and circumstances of belief in a culture of postmodernity. In sociological terms, their efforts are worse than useless.

There have been many reasons for writing this study. One incentive is to write out something new that transcends the tired split between theological progressives and conservatives, to sketch a sociology against theology, but for it. The cultural issues of Vatican II need to be rethought and reformulated. Few would resist the notion that if Vatican II had occurred in 1992 as against 1962, its cultural self-understandings and assumptions would have been much different. In Church history, the Council was highly unusual, in that it was called, not to confront a division of opinion over doctrine, faith and morals, but to repackage its relationships to the modern world. But these efforts have come seriously adrift and the division between faith and culture has become even more attenuated.

These reflections provide a context for this study written between June 1992–April 1995 against a crisis within English culture over community ties, morals and politics that form a gloomy agenda for politicians of both parties, Conservative and Labour. At a time when this culture looks to the theology of the main churches, they seem to have revealed a genius for shooting themselves in the foot. One cannot help feeling that the catastrophic drop in church attendance since the 1960s has been largely self-induced by a fatal misreading of culture by the churches and the theologians who supposedly service their needs. Instead of providing a cultural healing, a fragmentation has been imported into the churches who mirror the crises of the wider society. At a time when certainty is required, English churches blow the trumpet to sound divisions. As the disastrous implications of the ordination of women become apparent, one finds that Anglicans rarely sing from the same hymn sheet. Anglo-Catholicism has been smashed into pieces, leaving Anglicanism as a galaxy of sects ranged in a common warfare between Evangelical wings and liberal doubters tied together by the fiction of establishment and a growing financial crisis. Catholics engaged in ecumenical dialogue feel badly let down and now seek their own modus operandi within English culture. Theology has drifted into a mess that is disedifying. Against, this background, this study is a sociological effort to think a way out of the crisis in relationships between theology and culture. It works from the *Concilium* stable rather than that of *Communio*. The theologian who provides a sociological refuge is again Hans Urs von Balthasar, the late great Swiss theologian of aesthetics.

Many of the themes of the study echo those within the earlier work *Sociology and Liturgy: Re-representations of the Holy*. Instead of writing from within the Cathedral, the book represents a coming to it from without.

To some extent the journey of the book relates uncannily to that of J. K. Huysmans, as he moved from decadence and modernity to monasticism, from experience to a quest for innocence, for enchantment.

Reviews that enhance understanding of what one has written are greatly appreciated. Jean Séguy's discerning and astute review pointed to the self-implication of the sociologist in liturgical productions and wondered at its basis. To some extent the study is one of the wider implications of that question working through the issue of habitus and reflexivity to understand what enables and disables religious belief in a culture of postmodernity, where faith poses its own scandal of particularity. Instead of suspicion being turned against belief, it is turned against disbelief. A second influence on the book was a paper on 'Christian values and Benedictine Education' that was given to the staff of Downside Abbey in April 1991. It was an effort to think out the spiritual purpose and responsibilities for boys in a monastic boarding school. This accounts for a strand in the book, the issue of Pierre Bourdieu's notion of habitus, the theological implications of a term appropriated by sociology, but which, like other things, one seeks to return to the cultural field of Catholicism.

This study is not to be regarded as the final or indeed first word on a sociological reading of theology and culture. There are so many areas unwritten, unresearched, such as the reflexivity of those engaged in the reproduction of religious belief. This refers to actors devoted to seeking holiness in an unholy culture, such as monks, nuns, priests, novices, altar servers and choirboys. Self-understandings of their roles have no place within sociological research. Compared to the extent of study on vice, on the police, on medical sociology in relation to doctors and nurses, the absence of sociological research on the reproduction of virtue is truly astonishing. This study will have succeeded if it galvanises a debate, a redirection of sociological attention that moves from the narrow concerns of sociology of religion into the wider field of theology. It will also have succeeded if it forces theologians to look at the detail of the reproduction of belief in a cultural field and not to confuse generalised utterance with conceptual analyses that draw from sociology.

Although writing a book such as this is an isolated and isolating transaction, I have picked up many debts and much support in its writing. Again I wish to thank Mons. Gabriel Leyden and the assistant priests of Clifton Cathedral for many kindnesses. I also would like to thank Mother Catherine and the Little Sisters of the Poor, Cotham Hill, Bristol. The Cathedral and the convent have been my site of habitus and paideia. I have also gained much encouragement from the altar servers on both sites who cast doubt on Hebrews 13.2.

More secular debts are to my colleagues at the department of sociology at the University of Bristol, especially Professor Theo Nichols for squash, not talking about Durkheim, and for providing very much appreciated general encouragement. Likewise, I wish to thank Willie Watts Miller for support and for not mentioning religion too much in the pub. In this context, I thank *The Bell*, Alfred Place, Cotham who somehow managed to have a nightly pint on the counter between time of arrival at the door and the counter.

My colleague, Dr Rohit Barot, has been a source of infinite kindness, in providing sweets, encouragement, computer advice and academic support. I thank Professor Sylvia Walby for getting me a new computer and for pushing me along with the research rating exercise in mind. I owe a special debt to Mrs Jackie Bee, the departmental secretary, for labouring away past office hours on Holy Thursday to get the print out from the disks. My contemporary sociological theory course students, 1993–95, were patient and stimulating in helping me to cross from lecture notes into text and thought they ought to be mentioned. I do so with much gratitude.

I have two debts to readers of chapters of the study. Dr Gavin D'Costa, department of theology and religious studies at the University of Bristol, gave me some very useful comments on Chapter 3, and in its earlier draft, gave me some crucial encouragement. My colleague, Dr Tom Osborne provided me with some helpful comments on the overall draft and seemed to think the exercise was not entirely dotty.

My customary thanks go to John and Alix Farrell for long-standing friendship, support and Sunday lunches. I must thank their son-in-law, David Lowe, Deputy Headmaster of Douai Abbey School, who at a crowded Sunday lunch at the Farrells, managed to think up the title of the book.

My editor at Macmillan, Annabelle Buckley, has been extremely helpful and supportive of this venture and I give her my warm thanks. I would like to thank, again, my copy-editor, Keith Povey, for his care and attention to the detail of the manuscript. Any mistakes left are my fault! I would like to acknowledge the financial support of the Alumni Foundation of the University of Bristol for help with this large book.

I thank my brother Brian Flanagan, his wife Joan and the children for their interest in the book, again. Finally, I owe an enormous debt to my mother for many things, and dedicate this book to her accordingly.

Easter Sunday   KIERAN FLANAGAN
17 APRIL 1995

1 Sociology, Culture and Religious Belief: Some Reflections

To walk through a Cathedral is to journey in a labyrinth, a site of medieval conundrums. Promenading around Gloucester Cathedral on an Autumn evening, one goes up the lighted nave, on by the South transept and up the steps to pass by the side of the choir. Going around the back of the main altar, one comes before arches leading into the Lady Chapel. The unlit East stained glass windows loom in their leaden frames transmitting ghostly contours. Entering the chapel, one notices on the right a small door to another chapel. The shape of a window, the brass candles on a little altar can just be discerned. Sitting there, one feels enraptured in time, totally cut off from the twentieth century, somehow at one with those who sat there before. Leaving the dark, one goes back through the arches, seeing the lights of the choir dimly reflecting on the roof. Going down, hearing the organ intoning, one sees the choir moving steadfastly into evensong, their red cassocks and long white surplices rustling as they pass, to fill the medieval stones with a sound enigmatically produced by inhabitants of a culture of postmodernity.

This timeless ritual betokens witness to better theological times. The ritual speaks of an era when rites had rightly places in theology and culture. Now such rites seem decentred in a culture dominated by modernity. But if theology has collapsed as a belief system, it cannot be said that the bog into which it has disappeared, modernity, inspires much trust. As Berman notes, as modernisation has expanded, there has been a flatness, a dullness, an increased sense of futility which obscures the vision and sense of danger felt by earlier thinkers.[1] A belief in what theology signifies has been replaced by a sense of paradox that modernity offers much and delivers little. A sense of dullness has descended on contemporary culture, combined with a feeling of decay and a realisation that one is lost on the cultural map, but that it does not matter.

Clearly, some who go to the Cathedral are true believers. They are the proper pilgrims rather than the improper flâneurs who stroll to stake claims on the building for the heritage industry. But these flâneurs, seeking only to connect, live lives of oblivious disconnection. In this culture of postmodernity, their curiosity is dimmed. Their apathy masks their plight. Not for these idle flâneurs, the pilgrim's progress of the Norman knight, Richard de Godefroi, who constructed a flawless miz-maze, which he crossed on his knees, covering a hundred miles a year, out of disgust with the world and as a penance in lieu of not getting to Jerusalem.[2] Modernity does confuse, even in its highest refinements in academic culture. Some have come from its cloisters to the Cathedral as pilgrims. For instance, Schwehn draws attention to the wonderings over modernity in *The Education of Henry Adams* that stemmed from 'an intellectual inability to find order in learning or experience coupled with a political failure to secure power over a world seemingly spun out of control'.[3] Many of Adams' worries were derived from the modernising nineteenth-century university, Harvard in his case. But his quest for knowledge seemed complete when he confronted French Gothic Cathedrals. They presented a 'shock of recognition'. They mirrored what he had forgotten.[4]

Unfortunately, sociologists going around a Cathedral are unlikely to remember, for it is does not represent their notion of culture or their biography. It has no site in their literature, or so it seems. But some sociologists are aware their discipline is tainted with a Faustian property. If told that Faust was saved by the bell, some sociologist would think of their favourite tavern, of last orders nearly missed, rather than first calls heard from childhood in the Cathedral.

In his tragedy, Faust, unenlightened and disillusioned, sinks into despondency in his study. He reflects that

> knowing that knowledge tricks us beyond measure, That man's
> conversion is beyond my reach,
> Knowing the emptiness of what I teach.[5]

He contemplates poisoning himself, but stops when he hears bells and a solemn choir that

> lames my lifting of the fatal glass?
> Do bells already tell with vibrant drone
> The solemn opening of the Easter Mass,
> and choirs with comfort's anthem now resume
> The angelic breaking of the darkened tomb,
> The token of a compact comes to pass?

Now dispossessed from faith, the bells and anthem reminded Faust of his 'soul's indenture'. One cannot help wondering whether Faust was a former choirboy, for he muses:

> This melody the bliss of childhood taught me,
> The song of innocence, the joy of spring;

And thoughts of youth, this solemn hour, have brought me
In my last step a childlike wavering.[6]

Faust is the prototype of the sociologist dealing with modernity, where
choice is endless, but equally elusive. His plight has been resurrected in
recent sociological understandings of a culture of postmodernity.
As Newman might have said, sociologists also have souls. They are
weary and want to come home. But they know too much to go back and
not enough to go forward. They might echo the envy of Huysmans who
wondered at the privileges of Trappist monks 'who do not even know
what analysis is, but then they have not suffered the rotting effect of
literature for years on end'.[7] The occasion of these comments was the envy
and wonder Huysmans felt at the elderly Brother Simeon. He seemed
innocent in his knowing and 'knows that of which all others are ignorant'.[8]
This reflects a point of Weber that

> every genuinely devout religious faith brings about, directly or indi-
> rectly, that 'sacrifice of the intellect' in the interests of a trans-intellectual,
> distinctive religious quality of absolute surrender and utter trust which
> is expressed in the formula *credo non quod sed quia absurdum est.*[9]

The calling of the sociologist to know seems to preclude this 'sacrifice
of the intellect'. Yet, as the Faust legend would suggest, there are limits
to knowing, an inhibition that relates to a theological quest. Few sociologists think in terms of theology, so seldom face this dilemma. But what if
they do reflect in a manner that seeks to marry theology to sociology, what
tale is to be told? This invites the sociologist to think through issues of
culture in terms of their theological implications. Such a peculiar project
invites its own curiosity, for it is not part of the sociological tradition to
use the discipline to write an *apologia pro vitae sua*. Such an exercise is
as preposterous as it is presumptuous. The sociological vocation moves in
an analytical rather than a theological direction. Rethinking what it means
to believe, in this case Catholicism, through sociological means, portends
to be doomed to analytical failure. Sociologists will regard the task as
eccentric and theologians as unhelpful. The product risks falling between
the two disciplines. Anyhow, if there is a theological tradition in sociology, it relates to Judaism, not to Catholicism. Furthermore, theologians
have their own longstanding traditions of dealing with culture and will
regard sociological interventions as reinventions of the wheel.
Any exercise in sociological reflexivity about religious belief risks
producing themes, areas and concerns that seem as prejudicial as they
are idiosyncratic, as unsubstantiated as they are untenable especially to

progressive or liberal theologians, who will anathematise such a base exercise in apologetics. Such theologians might be aware, that for whatever domestic reasons, sociologists dealing with inequalities of distribution, of wealth and educational provision, present a pink face to society, but in dealing with mainstream theologies and misguided efforts to modernise, sociology offers a blue visage, a peculiar elective affinity with tradition and orthodoxy.

Sociologists do not live on analytical islands. Ultimately, they know, though it is not part of their discipline, that the bell tolls for them too and its peal in contemporary culture is dolorous. It communicates particularly to sociology effecting unexpected changes in its agenda.

Issues of risk, anxiety and de-spiritualisation now form part of sociological concerns in an agenda increasingly concerned with the quality of the meaning of life. Self and ethics loom large as conditions of trust become precarious. Anxiety emerges from intensified desires, a sense of being flooded with prospects in a culture that is increasingly becoming doom laden, nihilistic and emptying. A disbelief in consumer culture can be found amongst the young fed up with its price, the meaningless of life. An awareness that cripples is matched by a paralysis stemming from an incapacity to do much about it. The pessimism of sociology has passed into the wider culture and it refracts what the discipline discerns.

Everything seems to have become too malleable and in the pluralism that characterises postmodernity, any social convention can be commodified or overturned. To cope with these issues in postmodernity, sociology is increasingly falling back on metaphors that have a theological origin or root in its dealings with culture. It is not so much a matter of proving this change in use of metaphors that have theological overtones as noting their contemporary presence. Changes in sociological rhetoric point to shifts in sensibilities, in the ambitions entertained for dealing with culture. The application of sociology of knowledge to the domestic concerns of the discipline itself would indicate how contingent and shifting is its rhetoric and its expectations of what it seeks to understand.

As sociology is recasting its bearings, it is does so in a way that leads back to the earlier fin de siècle and the theological overhang to its activities, masked and forgotten. But as the modernity of Baudelaire, the sociology of culture of Simmel, and the mystical and angelic concerns of Benjamin have been rediscovered, so too have the theological packings surrounding their speculations. This theological aura attached to the ancestors of sociology of culture seems to pose an embarrassment, an aspect of their speculations that is best left unsignified. But the dilemmas which Marx, Weber and Nietzsche exposed have come to a fullness in contemporary culture.

Other thinkers in the nineteenth century were also feeling angst over modernity. If Baudelaire is credited with coining the notion of modernity that has become so central to sociology of culture, then links to Huysmans and Wilde, the pioneers of decadence, need also to be recast. Inconveniently for sociology, when the going got tough, they all took out the fire insurance that matters: Catholicism. Few sociologists refer much to that Catholicism, as if it was an aberration of their disciplinary biography and not something embedded in the implications of their interest in modernity which secularity masked and which postmodernity unmasks.

But if this theological root is recognised, it resolves some odd and arbitrary divisions within sociology, that sustain its misrecognition of the possibilities of religious belief within contemporary culture. Up to recently, sociology of religion has been concerned with sects and secularisation, the edges of theological failure of the main Churches. Sociology has cultivated a studied disinterest in studying the belief systems, the theologies of these Churches.

But what if sociology did wish to seek to find the theologies embodied in the Cathedral, the belief system of Christianity manifested in its architecture, what would it find? How would it speak to theology which has its own self-understandings of culture? Might theology affirm this disposition of the sociological trade or has it generated a shambles in its own house? Might theology have gone native in a culture that caused sociology to flee to hear the bell that saved Faust? If so, might theology make a muffled sound, one even the most pious of sociologists mishears?

In the new introduction to *A Rumour of Angels*, Peter Berger, in 1990, noted that 'the theological scene today is far more dismal than it was twenty years ago' when he wrote the book. Now some religious traditions have been reinterpreted so as to legitimate secular purposes, those of feminists and environmentalists, who sound loudest their prophecies in the theological marketplace and whose ideological divinations present irreproachable mandates to the dampest of theologians.[10]

Some theologians read secular culture in the light of a Gospel mandate in a way that seems immune to sociological redress. Thus, Rowan Williams argued that theologians should give 'some sort of critical identification with whatever political groupings speak for a serious and humane resistance to consumer pluralism and the administered society'. He had in mind those involved 'in ecological issues, feminism, civil rights and "peace" networks that have provided a new political language and a sense of the urgency and possibility of human unity'.[11] But these are movements of resistance rather than analysis, and certainly provide little space for sociology, other than to comment on some of their dysfunctional consequences, as in the case of liberation theology which has been a recruiting sergeant for the working class of South America, depositing unnecessary numbers into the clutches of right-wing Evangelical groups.[12]

These radical theological ventures that endorse passing ideological fashions, fail to confront the implications of Berger's comment that *'the "wisdom of the world" today always has a sociological address'*.[13] Every theological accommodation to the world can be rendered to sociological account for its consequences, for sociology aids in coining that which theologians seek to sanctify. Because of the intimate link between sociology and modernity, theologians try to read the masks of culture without reference to their sociological faces. Too often theologians seem to misread these signs, hence Berger's jaundiced comments on efforts to relate to modern culture, that 'recent Christian theology is well populated with bewildered and understandably resentful widowers'.[14]

Any sociological account of theology has to look at how it is represented in the mass media. In this context, Catholic theologians have to cope with what Jennings has termed the effortless superiority of English Anglicanism.[15] The incompetence of the mass media in dealing with Catholic theology is exemplified by the nugatory obituary in *The Times* for the great Swiss Catholic theologian, Hans Urs von Balthasar. It is inconceivable that the Archdeacon of Plumstead would have been allocated less.[16]

In a secular post-Christian society, Catholicism has to compete for media attention with cults, therapy groups and New Age religions. Because Catholicism is a religion of tradition, habit and routine, many of its activities seem unnewsworthy. Unfortunately, vice rather than virtue makes news about ecclesial culture. As a result, a distorted image of Catholicism emerges in English society. Its activities only become newsworthy when they constitute 'bad news'. A priest, who abandons his orders for marriage will receive public scrutiny to the degree to which the many, loyal to their vocation, are deemed inscrutable for the purposes of media attention. In sociology and as in the mass media, the 'successful' orthodox Catholic has no image and no place, within the culture constituted in the marketplace. Orthodox Catholics are deemed 'devout' and therefore incorrigibly dimwitted, or conservative, meaning fundamentalist, or in someway disembodied from English culture. They are in English culture but do not belong to it. But if their public image seems beyond redemption in the mass media and in popular culture, what can sociology say to reverse matters, if it so desires? How can it rethink the place of theology in the cultural field?

Following Pierre Bourdieu, in reference to philosophy, one wishes to see sociology as fieldwork in theology.[17] This notion points to the need to attend to the site of operation, the context of reproduction of belief, the cultural setting for theology and liturgical praxis. His notion of the field of cultural production, the site for symbol brokers, intellectuals and those who constitute culture, points to a form of analysis that can be tentatively applied to theologians. How is their discipline to be defined and in relation to what site, academic or ecclesial, and with what implications for their understandings of culture?

Although well versed in philosophy, Bourdieu is often regarded as being hostile to its unsociological basis. His comment that French philosophers 'cling in the manner of fallen aristocrats to the external signs of their endangered grandeur' could also apply to some liberal theologians. But earlier Bourdieu asserted that

far from leading to its destruction, a genuine sociological analysis of philosophy that replaces it in the field of cultural production and in historical social space is the only means of understanding philosophies and their succession and thus of *freeing philosophers from the unthought inscribed in their heritage.*[18]

In so claiming to free theologians from a history of the unthought (in relation to culture as conceived by sociologists) sociology might find itself being regarded as an instrument of revelation without grace. But the aim of sociology is more modest, of inducing into theology a reflexivity of the cultural implications of theological deliberations, lessening misattributions and enhancing a realisation of dysfunctions or unintended consequences that need to be understood.

This point arises in the confusion between modernisation and renewal in Catholicism since Vatican II that has had destructive effects, less due to the hostility of the surrounding culture and more to self-inflicted consequences only now being discerned. For instance, female religious orders were instructed to modernise their lifestyles, their habits, and their relationship to the world in the late sixties. The results were catastrophic, involving the virtual obliteration of many active orders of sisters and leading one prominent American sociologist, Andrew Greeley to describe the outcome as a form of collective suicide.[19]

Sociology has a dubious reputation in Catholicism for the unhelpful nature of its insights, customarily pessimistic in the wake of Vatican II. Responses can be hostile. Dismissing a gloomy sociological account of the demography of the priesthood in the United States, one bishop described the report as a 'great disservice' and added the future of the Church was shaped by 'God's design for his church – not by sociologists'.[20] Although recognising the significance of sociology of religion in other areas, John

Paul II indicated that its concern with statistics and the surface of matters, precluded it getting to the interior.[21] But again, sociology is more than about facts. It is about the interpretation of social forms operating within a culture and the elements that enable or disable belief that are peculiar to the social circumstances of a particular era. If Church statistics point to weaknesses, such as the fall in vocations, then a sociologist is correct to question the cultural formulations that might contribute to such an unintended decline. This trend might be the will of God, but it is presumptuous folly to use ignorance of the cultural insights of sociology as a method for discerning this.

In this study, one would wish to echo Berger's comment that 'the difficulties of religious belief in the pluralistic situation are not unique – not due to some mysterious fall from grace – but can be accounted for by clearly identifiable social processes'.[22] The examination of these forms a central strand of this study as it seeks a sociological understanding of the link between theology and culture. It is not that theologians are unaware of culture; it is that they do not conceive of it within a sociological remit and therefore their notion of accountability for its consequences is markedly different.

In his priestly past in 1963, Charles Davis wrote a much cited critique of a Catholic theology insulated from modern life. Entitled 'Theology in Seminary Confinement', this admittedly 'almost entirely negative' essay decried the isolation of English theology from modern knowledge. Davis argued that Catholic theology has always been influenced by its environment of gestation, whether episcopal or monastic, but now he felt strongly that this seminary version was operating in an intellectual vacuum. In short, it was not at 'the creative centre of modern culture'.[23] As will be argued later, his expectations were misplaced.

Davis's criticisms were answered partly in the documents of Vatican II, where theological relationships to culture and to the world were changed dramatically from the assumptions governing the Catholic Church since the Council of Trent (1545–63). The modern world was no longer regarded as a dangerous distraction. This change gave comfort to liberals and modernists who had long felt that the Church had resisted the modern world for too long. For many, it seemed as if Catholicism was frozen in time and had become dogmatic and irrelevant. Change and renewal were deemed necessary, almost theological imperatives, for ecclesial survival. Liberal theologians felt there was much to be learnt from the world in this opening of ecclesiastical windows to modern culture. Air and life had re-entered the Church and the quest for relevance took on a self-evident, self-conforming quality in the mid-1960s. But these expectations were naïve and self-deceiving. Confusion and chaos followed as the reforms were launched in a unique period of cultural instability that still unsettles theology.

In speaking of the place of the laity in the modern world, Vatican II failed to develop an adequate sociological means for consulting the faithful. The problem of the laity, that ran through so many of the documents of Vatican II, came from a clerical reading of their supposed position and this partly accounted for the confusions which followed. As von Balthasar asserted, the unrest which followed the Council came mainly from the clergy and religious.[24] A tension between the Church and the world was dissolved, so that paradox and signs of contradiction became indefensible. Somehow, the Church managed to endorse a mirror of the world that was inadequate as a means of telling the laity how to live in it. A condition of ecclesial anomie descended. Liberal theologians, influenced by existentialism, assumed that choice would generate a more informed, mature and authentic religion. Apart from exasperating an individualism which other parts of Vatican II sought to discount by affirming the communal nature of belief, theologians effected an embourgeoisement of the faith that marginalised the working class and sent the weak and indecisive to the wall.[25]

Since then, theology has become dominated by cultural issues it cannot seem to transcend or to control. The humanisation of theology has not been matched by a sanctification of culture. If anything the reverse, for modernity has made theology irrelevant in the cultural marketplace. Secularisation, a disengagement from the sacred, governs everyday reality. In its relationship to modern culture, theology seems to have lost its grip. The glue holding the Church has melted and the formula for a replacement seems unavailable. The 1980s was a uniquely grey period of theology. Despite dalliances with ideologies, little of substance has emerged.

In asserting pre-Nicence niceties, and abandoning its medieval cultural capital, after Vatican II, theology has become detached from its immediate ecclesial tradition, that prevailing just before the Council. English Catholic writers who pioneered efforts to engage with movements in France between 1900 and 1940 are now long forgotten. Many of these writers operated as gifted amateurs, who through lecture tours and royalties earned a precarious living. Few, if any had university posts. This meant that when Catholics were admitted to English academic culture, which was predominantly Anglican, only those sailing under liberal colours were likely to survive.

If theologians are to cope with contemporary culture, they have to find not only a point of connection but also a grammar with which to read its contours. Their efforts of late have not been very successful. For some theologians, feminism is *the* ideology to affirm in readings of culture, as it combines a quest for social justice with a synthesis that offers hope for a redeemed humanity.[26] There is a utopian cast to these formulations. The ordination of women in English Anglicanism, far from proclaiming a whole humanity, has split the Church of England into factions and sects, sinking Anglo-Catholicism and leaving the liberal and Evangelical wings to battle about new issues, such as homosexual clergy and lay presidencies of communion. The first anniversary of the ordination of women was marked in the mass media in a perfunctory manner that expressed a total indifference to the subject, illustrating pointedly the callowness of theological capitulation to passing ideological fashions. A more substantial means of reading culture has to be found.

In this failure to connect between theology and culture, a third of Catholic and Anglican Church attendance has come adrift since 1963. Now the disconnection between theology and culture is more pronounced. This institutional disconnection has been aptly characterised by Davie as believing but not belonging.[27]

Not only have adherents dropped in number, but also these Churches face a sense of irrelevance. The fruits of earlier efforts in the 1960s and the 1970s to be relevant have now gone sour. The creedally orthodox are a beleaguered minority as links with tradition are becoming more tenuous. The young, who lapsed into Eastern religions, new religious movements and sects in the 1960s, now use direct entry, bypassing traditional theologies altogether. Many, but not all the problems Churches now face have arisen over their self-defeating efforts to modernise and to engage with contemporary culture. The numbers cannot keep falling without the realisation that, since the 1960s, something seriously has gone wrong with the strategy for reading, understanding and engaging with culture.

Since Kelley's famous study, *Why Conservative Churches are Growing*, was published in 1972, it has been clear that evangelical Churches which make definite demands have been the hidden beneficiaries of the decline of liberalism.[28] In 1987, Roof and McKinney claimed that the study might have been called 'Why Liberal Churches Are Declining'.[29] They endorse Kelley's figures and point to a paradox, which sociologists have long noted, that since 1972, 'the large ecumenical bodies most comfortably allied with the culture were losing members'. Liberal Protestant Churches, with the highest socioeconomic status, that stressed individualism and pluralism in belief, that most affirmed American values, were in the 'throes of what can only be described as a serious religious depression'. Those who maintained a distance from culture, with distinctive life-styles, grew.[30]

There is no evidence that the liberal Churches gained from their progressive readings of culture. In their study of American religious trends, Roof and McKinney noted the way liberal Churches gained 2.2 per cent compared to the 8.00 per cent they lost. This led to an observation, which they felt went against popular wisdom, that 'the challenge to liberal Protestantism comes not so much from the conservative faiths as from the growing secular drift of many of their not-so-highly-committed members'.[31] Thus, despite their rhetoric, their appeals to reasoned credibility and the necessity for change, it seems as if far from halting a process of secularisation through concession, they seem to be accelerating it. Commenting on the Roof and McKinney study, Berger suggests that liberal Churches have now become *'schools for secularity'*.[32]

By endorsing the doubts of contemporary culture, liberal theologians pre-empted their capacity to confront what Lindbeck has termed the 'acids of modernity' and to seek definite forms of belief in communal enclaves that would be supportive for others rather than purely individual concerns with rights.[33] The whole strategy conceived in Vatican II, to open to the world, was fatally misconceived, as it misunderstood the basis upon which belief was secured within modern culture. It had no sociological means of asking, let alone answering this question.

McSweeney's study of Catholicism since Vatican II gave an earlier sociological indication of what has been borne out in the Roof and McKinney study, about the counterproductive nature of the theological pursuit of relevance in dealing with culture. In his chapter devoted to 'the victory of progressive theology', where its claims to tolerance and diversity seemed to have been won, McSweeney noted astutely that

theological pluralists rested their arguments about cultural diversity on the evidence of sociologists and anthropologists; they felt no need to create the sociological conditions which are necessary for consensus and without which any large group must divide and fragment.[34]

He went on to add that the vagueness of the notion of the culture so used without a regulating social mechanism has led to a condition of relativism.[35] Inadvertently, therefore, theologians in dealing with culture have thought themselves into a sociological field.

Any account of theology in a cultural setting has to attend to the historical and traditional circumstances surrounding its consumption and use. In the context of English society, one has to decipher the enigma of Anglicanism through slightly estranged Irish eyes. To a sociologist, and to others, English Anglicanism presents a property of mystery, less signifying the Divine, than a range of anomalies and contradictions that would sink any other organisation, sacred or profane. Anglicanism is linked to national identity in terms of its very Englishness – the Cathedrals, the village church at Granchester. English culture and sensibility seem defined in Anglican terms. Anglican ceremonials dignify state occasions; they are a focal point for loyalty; and they serve to legitimate the monarchy at its coronations. There is an element of mythology attached to this English-ness of Anglicanism, that makes it part of a reinvented twentieth-century tradition.[36] Colley's recent work on the British Nation shows the way the monarchy and patriotism became linked in a common Protestantism that regarded Catholicism as alien. As she suggests

> Protestantism was the dominant component of British religious life. Protestantism coloured the way that Britons approached and interpreted their material life. Protestantism determined how most Britons viewed their politics. And an uncompromising Protestantism was the founda-tion on which their state was explicitly and unapologetically based.[37]

In present society, English Catholics still have no ticket of exit from the pale into which history has deposited them since the Reformation. As strangers in the land, having to pass loyalty tests on a higher grade than others, Catholics live in a society still deeply Protestant in culture, a point exemplified in adherence to the Act of Succession. Since the Reformation and the overturning of a far more popular religion than has been hitherto realised,[38] Catholics have followed a process of assimilation into English Society. English-born Catholics have tried to conquer the notion that their Church is but the Italian mission to the Irish. Converts have pioneered a rapprochement with English sensibilities. Newman led the way. Cardinal Hume has given Catholicism a very definite Englishness. On the basis of Church attendance, it is the largest Christian group in the United King-dom, yet it is still disenfranchised from its official and civic culture. Dis-possessed from its own heritage, English Catholicism has always had an equivocal relationship to its surrounding culture. The Cathedrals it built stand alien and otherwise occupied; many of its monasteries that shaped English culture lie in ruins; and many of its customs have been transferred into what are often the mild civic demands of Anglicanism. The Reforma-tion still represents an unacknowledged wound in English society. But no sociologist looking at English society can ignore this disjunction, for Anglicanism is an instrument of secularisation a movement away from the enchantment this study seeks to affirm that represents the solution to the link between theology and culture. This makes this study a slight exercise in fiction, for the present cultural landscape, its tradition and practice preclude a realisation of the solution it seeks.

If, as Newman suggested 'the religion of a nation will ever partake of the peculiar faults of the national character',[39] Catholicism and Anglicanism confront a crisis in English society which sociology can but acknowledge, but cannot resolve. The back to basics campaign of the Tory party, launched in October 1993, however misconceived, caught a public mood of unease, malaise, and drift, a sense that trust had collapsed in a mass of indifference expressed in crime figures. Allied to this moral malaise was a collapse in confidence in public institutions, including the Established Church.

With the highest divorce rates in Europe and a religious practice rate that suggests a post-Christian society, the English feel a lack of moral direction, a drift which the Churches seem unable to stem. The situation of English society seems to embody Guardini's comment that 'without religion life becomes like a machine without oil; it runs hot; even if it functions, some part of it is always burning out'.[40] In such a society, the inhabitants have become spectators on the decline and disconnection from a tradition that would permit them a means of escape. A postmodern culture is increasingly post-Christian as Lindbeck has observed. A sense of bonding with a biblical culture is disappearing. Following an interest of this study, Lindbeck notes that forgetting rather than relearning the language of scripture is a major trend.[41]

In his striking Reith lectures, Jonathan Sacks, the Chief Rabbi of the United Kingdom, reflected on the idea of religion as a form of social and moral ecology, a perspective he derived from Robert Bellah. In criticising a supposedly inevitable link between modernity and secularisation, where religion lost its social significance and became a matter of private consumption, Sacks sought to rehabilitate the notion of community by reference to tradition. He also noted the unexpected prophetic character of writers in sociology and philosophy, such as MacIntyre, Taylor, Bell and Bellah, who equated the loss of religious tradition with the erosion of an environment 'within which alone a cohesive intellectual, social, political and moral life is possible'.[42] His use of ecology as a means of making a conservative argument might have perplexed liberal theologians expecting otherwise. But Sacks is quite clear, that within contemporary culture the sources of ills are due to the failure to service the social ecology of religion. Sacks criticises liberal theologies for breaking down traditions. Thus he argued

> liberal theologies, by conceding too much to passing moral fashion, have lost that sense of timelessness and transcendence which I believe to lie at the heart of the religious experience. They have had to shift their ground too often to give credence to claims to moral authority.[43]

If theologians have got lost in dealing with contemporary culture, why should sociologists care? They might have to, as sociology itself is uncovering aspects of culture that border on theological concerns. To clarify these, sociology might have to attend to what theologians *ought* to be saying.

There is an unsuspected resiting of sociological interests in theology that has not been given adequate focus, which this study explores further. Admittedly, these are straws in the wind, but they can be discerned and read in some unexpected quarters.

Thus, in the conclusion to a reflection on the implications of plastic sexuality for the transformation of intimacy in late modernity, Giddens suggested that

> a sexually addicted civilisation is one where death has become stripped of meaning; life politics at this point implies a renewal of spirituality. From this point of view, sexuality is not the antithesis of a civilisation dedicated to economic growth and technical control, but the embodiment of its failure.[44]

The issue of dehumanisation arises in a society whose culture is increasingly being penetrated by a spirit of calculation that despiritualises the ground of ideals and beliefs. The way many of these have become untenable disturbs sociological sensibilities as to what culture should be about. This worry is emerging increasingly as sociology, in the light of threats from postmodernity, is seeking to examine its own traditional understandings of culture. These are slightly different to what its tradition has hitherto affirmed. This reflects worries which sociology is starting to uncover in its own tradition as the issue of culture becomes recentred into its concerns.

In a recent work Scaff exposes Weber's debts to Nietzsche and more significantly to Georg Simmel. Scaff argues that Weber and Simmel shared a common interest in 'the metaphysics of modernity'. This indicates a concern with matters beyond the purely social, for Simmel regarded sociology as 'the instrument for coping with the unsettling fluidity of the world and the self'.[45] Scaff goes on to suggest that Simmel's 'special version of sociology might be understood as modern attempts to recover a lost unity to culture, to find a way of overcoming the paradoxical juxtaposition of life and form'.[46]

Unfortunately, sociology lacks the means to answer fully such a question about life and form without reference to the mysterious properties that transcend the paradox they pose. But if the site of belief can be found in culture, a field sociology can elect to occupy, equally the issue of disbelief can emerge from the same setting. Thus Scaff points to Weber's comment (to be understood in the context of Nietzsche's notion of the death of God) that 'today the routines of "everyday life" challenge religion and the "everyday" becomes "religious"'.[47] For sociology, the question of the self in relation to culture has become linked to issues of authenticity in the context of aesthetics and ethics. As Scaff aptly notes

> Weber's 'ghost of dead religious beliefs' haunts the 'culture of narcissism' of the critics at every turn. It inscribes the nightmare and cultural bad conscience otherwise known as the cultural contradictions of capitalist development.[48]

This points back to Faust's remembrance of what was, but which now cannot be.

The second strand, that points to a nascent rethinking in sociology about theological thoughts, relates to the increasing recognition the sociology of culture of Pierre Bourdieu poses as an alternative to the corrosive effects of postmodernism and postmodernity. In a philosophical form, postmodernity represents a deconstructive approach to culture, based either on power or linguistics. Derrida, Levinas and Foucault are the key figures identified with this very French movement that has come to dominate Anglo-American approaches to the humanities.[49] With the exception of Foucault, they have made remarkably little impact on sociology for it dealt with earlier post-structuralist Marxists, such as Althusser and Poultanzas in the mid and late seventies. Interest in Goffman was part of a sociological effort to offset the claims of structuralists and to effect what Touraine termed in his book the *Return of the Actor*.[50] But if the actor had been returned to the sociological stage, who is he to be? Is he a construct, a figment of the sociological imagination or is he an angst ridden flâneur, desperately seeking but not arriving, always rootless and ever restless. Again, in this shift, sociology seems to have stumbled on the edge of a theological question.

The third change relates to perceptions of the nature of culture and is linked to a realisation of the significance of reflexivity in sociology. Uncertainty derived from relativism, combined with an uncertainty of moral and political purpose after 1989, has caused sociology to recast moorings and to think introspectively about its language of purpose. The compass points for a mapping of culture have become unclear. A concern with risk and anxiety has emerged in a sociology of culture.[51]

It is not enough for sociology just to reflect passing cultural trends. Placing sociology within the nexus of culture in the marketplace can lead it to endorse everything, all commodities, idols and artifacts, indiscriminately, with a credulity. It also risks making sociology in the image and likeness of English cultural studies. Its status within sociology is low, for as Tester notes acidly, in his critique of the insubstantial nature of the mass media, 'cultural studies is a discipline that is morally cretinous because it is the bastard child of the media it claims to expose'.[52]

The notion of unmasking usually betrays a secular interest. In its ideological manifestation, culture is understood to disguise economic arrangements in a masking that sustains the hegemony of the ruling class. Power is enhanced in conditions where its basis is disguised. This masking amplifies the capacity to secure compliance by blurring or making indeterminate conditions of redress. In Bourdieu's writing, unmasking 'the real' basis of social arrangements is understood to have a freeing, emancipating aspect. Choice is believed to be enhanced when the ties that bind are disclosed and the structures which conceal are revealed. Thus, Bourdieu suggests that sociology unmasks

> self-deception, that collectively entertained and encouraged form of lying to oneself which, in every society, is at the basis of the most sacred values and, thereby, of all social existence. It teaches, with Marcel Mauss, that 'society always pays itself in the false coinage of its dreams'.[53]

But this unmasking is also the province of theology. It could be said that the ultimate deception is of the fool gazing at culture, who says in his heart there is no God. In *King Lear* (Act IV. Scene 1) the issue of seeing and not seeing emerges in Gloucester's exchange with the old man leading him. He states 'alack, sir, you cannot see your way', to which Gloucester replies 'I have no way, and therefore want no eyes; I stumbled when I saw'. Gazing, seeing without signifying, the visions of the blind, and the discerning ignoring the transparent, these are all biblical themes that complicate theological exchange with culture. Suspicion and deceit mix with issues of a fullness of sight, blind to what grace permits to be discerned. Such utterances hijack sociology into the realm of mystery but they also point to the issue of a fullness of understanding and the limiting theological implications of what might have been understood. But what is distinctive to sociological sight?

Seeing and not seeing relate to conundrums between theology and sociology. The failure of theology to scrutinise the cultural consequences of its transactions has become increasingly understood within sociology. This was a point Weber understood. He pointed to the dangers religions face of neglecting to service and scrutinise their social apparatus, lest it unwittingly imports counterproductive cultural assumptions that might enfeeble its basis. As Käsler has noted in the context of Weber's exploration of the link between ascetic Calvinism and capitalism, aggregates of subjective meanings can be detached from their original religious contexts so that the former is destroyed by the inexorable growth of a spirit of calculation.[54] Accretions unrecognised can effect a cultural judgement. A failure of attention to culmination might signify a pattern misread. It is presumptuous to ignore the sliding and shifting elective affinities between belief and disbelief, for as Marshall indicates, these express the way form and spirit collide.[55]

Within contemporary culture are processes that seem to signify the impossibility of religious belief. These cultural processes relate to the power to commodify, to manufacture images, to erect icons and to mark culture with an intensity in the marketplace that enfeebles. Religious belief seems to have sunk, less due to secularisation than to a failure to discern contemporary culture and to find a means of connecting to it. There is a fatalism in the disembodiment theology feels that is linked to a sense of disenchantment, as the spirit of calculation enters cultural deliberations. As theology seeks to engage with culture, it increasingly renders itself to sociological account in programmes, in monitoring of statistics and in its own forms of self-recognition.

If sociology is increasingly feeling unsettled in its relationships to culture, how does it become aware of itself? There is a distinctive sociological property of self-awareness, not so much in how it knows, but in its sense of knowing about the social. It sees too much to have ideals, but is experienced enough to know it needs them. This conundrum of sociology, as its knowing exceeds its capacity to assimilate what is known, lends a peculiarly Faustian property to the discipline and its calling. As a discipline, sociology is the hero of the tragedy of culture, but with what theological consequences?

2 'To be or not to be':
The Sociologist's Dilemma

To be a sociologist is to proclaim a property of definiteness. It is to be liked or disliked. There is something villainous about the role as cast in the 1980s in English society. Flattered by the dislike of Mrs Thatcher and misrepresented by Howard Kirk, being a sociologist is to occupy the fringe of public credibility. Yet, sociologists have a necessary role. They explore aspects of society such as the family, leisure, government and medicine to find shifts in their social arrangements, trends that signify social change, new understandings and structures that deserve rigorous systematic attention. With a welter of methods, theories and concepts, the sociologist seems well secured in the analytical weapons of his craft, whatever public and academic detractors might think. But behind the certainty lurks a sense of self-doubt seldom confronted. The sociological calling makes some unexpected biographical demands.

Being a sociologist involves bearing an analytical vigilance in all areas of life, private and public. Thus, confronted with incompetent undertakers at a funeral, private sensibilities of grief are violated by occupational worries about what Goffman might have written about these infelicities of impression management. Somehow, being a sociologist is inseparable from other mundane public and private roles. An occupational hazard of sociology is to see too much of the mechanism of reproduction that makes ordinary life predictable, routine and uneventful – for others. The sociologist is a necessary outsider on life, the ever present alien, the stranger, the heir apparent of the Persian visitor to English society in the eighteenth century who gazes at its unobvious social arrangements with scepticism. Thus, Bourdieu has suggested that 'to practice radical doubt, in sociology, is akin to becoming an outlaw'.[1] There is something definite about this metaphor for the sociologist's task, of making raids as an outsider on forms of cultural reproduction that conceal their basis of power. Doubt relates to suspicion about *all* social arrangements.

Yet, this notion of an Olympian heroism built on pursuing a sociological life of reflexive purity, disembodied from self and biography, should arouse suspicion. There is a dissimulation abroad, a concealing of flesh to this estrangement deemed necessary to see analytically further. Such a claim would be an incentive for sociologists as outlaws to make raids into other supposedly disinterested professions.

Some aspects of the basis of a sociologist's reflexivity can be rendered to account. Presumably there is a well-developed career, many publications, a lecturing post, all of which suggest peer testing and the certification of sociological competences. Likewise, the theories, concepts and methods used in a study can be relocated on to the sociological landscape to provide some form of critical redress. But with a biography so well concealed, one might assume that changes in theoretical emphases were the result of strict positivist logic, movements dictated by cumulative objective reasoning and explanation, rather than by shifts in subjective preferences in a biography that is well masked behind a professional facade. Intellectual shifts in theoretical interests, however, occur for other reasons.

For instance, many might wonder at the move of Giddens from a concern with time, space, historical materialism and structuration into issues of modernity, angst, anxiety and the self, in three of his recent books. Apparently, this shift of perspective arose from gazing around a Californian beach. It seemed a more realistic site, *the* place for a sociological imagination to stretch its contours of analytical awareness to engage with life as lived.[2] Doubtless, there are other more orthodox reasons governing choice of research topic that lie in the recesses of biography, or in the intrinsic interest particular topics animate. Equally, prosaic issues of accessibility, viability for grant application and ultimate publication could be significant. Academic politics also play a part. Deference to power and influence analysed in Bourdieu's *Homo Academicus* shapes the selection of theoretical perspectives and research topics. Yet something is still missing. Lying hidden is the self of the sociologist, his cultural context of enquiry and his relationship to that which he uncovers in his research.

Up to recently, these were not matters for sociological scrutiny. Masking enhanced methodological credibility, the disembodied, objective scientific gaze of the sociologist. But with a collapse of belief in science, the sociologist has had to rejoin the humanities, with all the disbeliefs and doubts that conveys. Society has changed in what it expects of the sociologist. Risk, anxiety, the body and self-identity have entered the sociological agenda, and with the fragmentation of the discipline which the term postmodernity signifies, sociology has taken an introspective turn. It has taken to reflect on the inward basis of its own activities, the self-awareness, or reflexivity of doing sociology. This relates to the disposition of the sociologist over what to study and how this becomes culturally constituted, itself a sociological question.

There has always been a problem over values and choice which foxed Weber. Even in the natural sciences, where issues of proof might seem to restrict movement between paradigms, and the puzzles they represent, shifts in theoretical affiliations have a property of conversion that suggest change moves almost by faith.[3]

These properties of belief and legitimacy can come attached to thinkers themselves in the humanities. French intellectuals, such as Baudrillard, Derrida, Levinas and Foucault, have legions of Anglo-American expositors and zealots, who read their text in an exegetical manner with a view to applying their insights to the minutiae of culture and literature. The writings of these heroes form the focal point for endorsement of life politics. They provide a rallying point for grouping issues and debates amongst a cognoscenti, a process that also applies to sociology.

Clegg has explored this social process of the elevation of a sociologist into a cultural icon, in this case Giddens, whose marketing flair, astuteness, productivity, and academic acumen have made him an social phenomenon in his right. He supplies an intellectual legitimation for what is to be constituted in the market. His ability to read the signs of the times and to be one step ahead, gives him a credibility and a capacity to shape the agenda of sociological response to contemporary culture.[4]

Most sociologists are aware of the risks of becoming canonised by the tribe they study after reading Alison Lurie's *Imaginary Friends*.[5] The implications of applying this process of canonisation to intellectuals also has its pitfalls. As with other cultural icons, fashion governs their rise and fall in the humanities more than one would expect. Often they can be revealed to have feet of clay, and seem to cannibalise themselves as in the case of the sadomasochism of Foucault, Heidegger's relationship to fascism and Althusser's murder of his wife. To refer to these tragic interruptions to lives of dedicated, disembodied analysis might seem to make a cheap disenchanting jibe, to confuse capacity to analyse with character. Yet, many of their critiques were based on charges of hypocrisy against organised religions. These thinkers, these formers of opinion in the humanities, the paradigm makers, fulfil a secular urge to find icons, rallying points for exegesis, belief and analysis. The aura and charisma surrounding the lives of these superheroes draw attention to a point increasingly being understood, that a sociologist is part of what he constitutes and accordingly has responsibilities that are exceptional and particular to his craft. The practice of sociology itself is a social process that bears reflection. This has given rise to an increased concern with the term reflexivity, a self-awareness peculiar to the sociological calling, one that increasingly characterises issues of postmodernity and the culture it seeks to clarify.

Hermeneutics has been employed to understand the problem of reconciling understandings. But it also applies to the process of reading a social transaction. Studying the customs of an alien tribe involves finding a grammar to read their practices, to appropriate that which has a property of distance. Social research is rather like the act of writing. It realises an enhancement of self-understanding that changes the self of the reader, in this case the sociologist. Little attention has been given to the reflexive basis of constructing sociological research, where like a rite of passage, the sociologist enters the terrain of an unfamiliar belief system.[6] As researchers grow into understanding in the passage of fieldwork, their reflexivity loses a certain property of innocence as appropriation of implications of what they discover increases.

Up to recently, little attention has been given to the untidy nature of how sociologists construct their insights in a relationship that changes with their subject matter. Occasionally, one gets reflections on the biography of fieldwork that suggest a reflexivity, a realisation that the formal research transaction gets in the way of understanding social relationships. This form of reflexivity can reflect a modesty, a realisation of not having fully grasped the actor's account in their ordinary lives.[7] Rarely does one find reflections on a sociological journey in the field equivalent to the very human encounters of Nigel Barley's *The Innocent Anthropologist*.[8] Most sociologists would be too insecure about breaching disciplinary conventions to write such an account. The notion that sociologists are in some way changed by their experience of research, that they become implicated in its findings in a way they have to recognise, is only recently gaining in recognition.

Any interesting research will unsettle the self of the sociologist who will seek compass points, either in the writings of others that seem pertinent, or in schools, concepts and theories that will help him to relocate his sociological sensibilities on an unfamiliar field of inquiry. Aldridge has drawn attention to this process of the social construction of the self as author in sociology. It bears on the credibility of what is to be reproduced as research. Certain producers are invoked to effect the production of what is deemed a sociological product, a text which can never be free of rhetoric.[9] The outcome of a piece of research has to be constructed in a manner that secures its credibility, but also its definition as a work of sociology. In journeying into unknown territory, Geertz suggests the anthropologist oscillates between being a pilgrim and a cartographer.[10] There is a sense of wager in entering unknown territory, a risk of being rebuffed by the occupants, or of succeeding by grasping fully the cultural basis of their lives in the field. Anthropologists and sociologists seldom refer to these reflexive changes in their research accounts, the processes of coming to hear the voice of their tribe in a way that resonates with their biography. Their research is usually presented in finished terms, in an objective fashion that masks the personal relationships, the changes in the self and biography wrought in the construction of the study. These matters are now deemed proper to sociology.

The issue of the accountability of the sociologist to his own belief system and the call to reflect in a sensitive manner on the aims of his clients, has very much arisen in feminism. It has managed to overturn conventions of uninvolvement in a way that has profound, but unexplored implications for sociology as a whole. There is a growing realisation that the role of being a sociologist, as a producer of knowledge, affects those represented in the study as well as having biographical implications for the researcher. The implication is that the sociologist *ought* to be changed by what is uncovered in fieldwork.

In her introduction to a recent collection, *Anthropology and autobiography*, Okely draws attention to a growth of interest in self-reflection in the late 1980s. Feminism is used to legitimate the need for consciousness of the moral implications of analysis for the subject matter. Thus, the reflexivity of the sociologist carries responsibilities for raising consciousness and awareness to rectify the marginality and invisibility which some women feel. A voice, a witness, is given to the underrepresented through the means of sociological analysis. In this context the self of the sociologist is not to be marginalised, but is to be implicated in the sociological act of understanding. In its fullest sense, Okely suggests that reflexivity 'forces us to think through the consequences of our relations with others, whether it be conditions of reciprocity, asymmetry or potential exploitation'. She goes on to add that 'if we insert the ethnographer's self as positioned subject into the text, we are obliged to confront the moral and political responsibility of our actions'.[11]

This notion of embodied knowledge offers an added dimension to Ricoeur's notion of the text as action. It suggests that issues about reflexivity and biography belong to ethnomethodology but also to hermeneutics. The sociologist's account, his fieldwork, and his intervention involve a distinctive process of distanciation and appropriation in the production of his research text. The sociologist adds his own reading to other versions of the text as action, those manifest in his field of inquiry. In so constructing, the sociologist refers to his own grammar, his rules of engagement, to read and to guess the meanings disclosed in *their* texts. The purpose of such reading relates to the power of the text to disclose a world. With such disclosure, Ricoeur argues that 'we are not allowed to exclude the final act of personal commitment from the whole of objective and explanatory procedures which mediate it'.[12]

The presence of the anthropologist as author in his text has been elegantly explored by Geertz. He suggests that styles of rhetoric are related

to notions of credibility of being there. This involves a quality of reflec-
tiveness that often seems masked, where the signature is in someways
disguised. Geertz points to the disappearance of one of the major assumptions of anthropological writing, the separation and moral disconnection of
its subjects and audience, where the first is described and the second
informed but not implicated.[13] In this tradition, the anthropologist was involved in a form of 'ethnographic ventriloquism', to use Geertz's apt phrase,
of claiming to speak not only about another form of life, but also from
within it.[14] The anthropologist has to speak in a way that resonates with
what the tribe will recognise. In so speaking, the anthropologist has to
utter from within, from his own self to begin with, for the research question is his but not necessarily theirs. To speak, he has to listen, but also
has to find in himself what to say. This relates to Cohen's notion of a 'self-
conscious anthropology' where the self is bound into the anthropological act
and is led to ask 'who am I?'.[15] This lends a property of self-recognition
to his deliberations in the image he conjures up of the tribe. Such processes
relate to a biography of sociological reflection.

This theme has been pursued by Stanley, who has drawn attention to the
way Merton has revolutionised the notion of sociological autobiography.
Perspectives, ideas, concepts, findings and analytical procedures reflect a
history written into the larger tale of the times. She argues that reflexivity
points to a lived experience, a 'consciousness raising'. Thus, reflexivity
involves 'treating one's self as subject for intellectual inquiry and it encapsulates the socialised, non-unitary and changing self posited in feminist
social thought'.[16] Whatever else feminism has accomplished within sociology, it has freed the discipline from the fiction that it can produce texts
about society without reference to the self of the sociologist. This breakage
of convention might seem acceptable within the contours of feminist
discourse where justification of ruptures might seem self-evident but it
increasingly applies within the wider discipline of sociology. One can
agree with Bourdieu that

> ordinary sociology, which bypasses the radical questioning of its own
> operations and of its own instruments of thinking, and which would no
> doubt consider such a *reflexive intention* the relic of a philosophic men-
> tality, and thus a survival from a prescientific age, is thoroughly suf-
> fused with the object it claims to know, and which it cannot really
> know, because it does not know itself. A scientific practice that fails to
> question itself does not, properly speaking, know what it does.[17]

A sensitive sociologist permits himself to be redefined by that which
seems alien in the conventional lives of others. This can have a profound effect on what the sociologist constitutes as being of analytical

significance. Baum astutely reminds us that these problems of self and anthropology have echoes back into the origins of sociology itself, in the writings of Troeltsch. The mind of the sociologist belongs to a certain world, a culture and a biography, that risks being changed by what it encounters. For Troeltsch, there was no division between science and commitment.[18]

Gouldner claims that sociology has become part of popular culture between 1940–60 and that it is increasingly implicated in what it seeks to analyse.[19] This raises an endless issue of the nature of sociology's dialogue with itself, its moral responsibilities, its analytical biases, but above all what it is conventional to say. As part of the humanities and influenced by the Romantic movement, Gouldner argues that sociology has sought to increase its knowledge, its self-awareness of what it is possible to know. This leads him to conclude that the inquiring subject and the object are mutually constituted.

Growth in awareness entails a relationship between persons and information with implications for values, and this leads Gouldner to propose his famous programme for a reflexive sociology. This involves finding a new praxis that transforms the person of the sociologist, in his personality, and in his relationship to society. It demands a persistent commitment to that awareness. The self is implicated in this process so that vision and practice combine to produce a fuller and more human sociologist.[20] Gouldner's sensibilities of the reflexive potential of sociology were formulated against a need to connect to moral imperatives, the striving to link ideals with praxis that governed the student radicalism in the late 1960s. But he pointed also to higher responsibilities of sociology in dealing with culture, which a recent tradition seeking a scientific status for the discipline had obscured. This relates to a comment of Tenbruck that sociology, within the culture it seeks to constitute, must

> critically review the tacit assumptions about its *raison d'être* and legitimation. It was Max Weber's idea that sociology, unable to become a strict theory anyway, had a very limited capacity for technical advice. For him, it was the foremost office of sociology to discover in the social phenomena their human meaning and cultural significance in order to assist us in becoming aware of our ultimate standards of values. What is ultimately at stake in the issue over culture, is the concept and office of sociology.[21]

The relationship of the sociologist to his subject matter depends on what is being sought in the account. Detachment is related to the pursuit of explanation, but engagement or empathy is the necessary instrument of understanding, one that assumes a degree of attachment. The issue of question and answer is of less significance as a methodological imperative for sociology than for history, yet both disciplines in relating to the humanities come under the hermeneutic remit this dialectic suggests.[22] In the debate on the significance of reflexivity, this hermeneutic dimension has not been adequately explored. There is a fear of unmasking the sociologist. But the most interesting defence of the connection between sociology and autobiography comes from Merton himself. He argues that the issue belongs to sociology of knowledge and tells how the product of sociological understandings emerges. It involves the interplay

> between the active agent and the social structure, the interplay between one's sequences of status-sets and role-sets on the one hand and one's intellectual development on the other, with its succession of theoretical commitments, foci of scientific attention, planned or serendipitous choices of problems and choices of strategic research sites for their investigation.[23]

In short, Merton turns back a question on to the sociologist more familiarly directed to his subject-matter – how does he come to know in relation to his field of inquiry; what are the steps of interrogation; and how is a grammar chosen to listen best and to speak for his clients with a fullness of authentic understanding they deserve?

Clearly, such questions belong to philosophy, to the methodological principles of enquiry governing sociological forms of knowing. But they also relate to the sensibilities of sociology as to what is credible in links with their subject matter.

One can readily understand why sociologists are loath to explore this area of biography and reflexivity. Firstly, the area opens up risks of reductionism to personal and subjective preferences in what are supposed to be objective public accounts of social transactions. Secondly, reflexivity becomes an instrument for incorporating relativism into the sociological gaze. Additionally, sociological accounts become subject to psychological accountability and biographical preferences. Sociological conventions dictate that public findings should speak for themselves without reference to the private dispositions of the sociologist. Thirdly, an issue is raised as to how far the sociologist needs to know his self to become worthy of sociological analysis. If he does not know himself privately, how can he exercise a reflexivity over what filters into his public sociological account? The knowing of the self in terms of sensitivity and availability to a topic requires systematic cultivation. Although not going so far as to suggest the need for psycho-analysis, Nadel has argued for psychological testing to increase awareness of the self of the anthropologist.[24] But what does the sociologist need to know of the self in the circumstances of a culture of postmodernity? The sociologist's fieldwork seldom takes him anywhere exotic that might risk rupturing his professional and personal sense of self. Any sense of estrangement necessary to suggest the need for analytical distance has to be found within the self of the sociologist. Being there in the tribe, to follow Geertz, involves the anthropologist in living within a cultural ethos self-evidently alien in the way the culture of modernity is not. In this culture, of English society, signifying being there often involves an inward journeying into estrangement, if for no other reason than to effect an analytical distance. It involves seeking differences, artificial and arbitrary to some, that mark a passage into an inward culture, a sensibility embodied in a reflexivity necessary to find a sociological voice. A sense of unsettlement needs to be cultivated if reflexivity is to be accomplished.

Reflexivity and modernity are interlinked in terms of the growth of self-awareness within contemporary culture, itself a cultural phenomenon from which the sociologist is hardly exempt. There is a confusion of knowing that operates in a world where globalisation renders all traditions insecure even that of the sociologist. Reflexivity takes on many properties of belief, ecological, cognitive and aesthetic, to name a few, that always present the sociologist with risks of engulfment. The issue arises over what tests reflexivity, what draws attention to this necessary but untidy concept? In his notion of an aesthetic reflexivity, which contains a mimetic property in dealing with culture, Lash argues that it only becomes critical when subject to bureaucratic forces that systematise.[25]

Reflexivity is a term with a potential. Lash links it with Bourdieu's term habitus (discussed later). The term, in this setting, relates to the unthought, dispositions that might be changed on sociological reflection. But Lash points to a wider meaning that embodies issues raised by ethnomethodology. In its reflexive circumstances, sociology faces often acute problems of translation, of situating analysis in the life-worlds of the subjects of inquiry. This relates to a hermeneutic dimension of suspicion, but also of trust sufficient to appropriate. By linking ethnomethodology to reflexivity, Lash points to a recognition of careers in transition, such as the ambitions for gender reassignment of 'Agnes', that involve the covert learning of a new role.[26] But this opens out an issue of what is understood by *being* in a role and how the actor reflects and adjusts to it.

Although a vague term, reflexivity denotes procedures of access to a subject matter. For Bourdieu, it has a particular objectifying function. It contains an ethical imperative that guides research practice by affirming the need to preserve sociological integrity and distance from the field. Bourdieu wishes to fence the sociological transaction within objectivity rather than subjectivity, so that the former facilitates cultivating awareness of the position of the interrogator on the field. As Wacquant indicates, Bourdieu's notion of reflexivity relates to the organisational and cognitive structure of the discipline, its epistemological unconsciousness and its place within contemporary culture. It involves recognition that the sociologist is himself a cultural producer and has an analytical place on the landscape he maps.[27] In his enquiry, he has to render himself to account as much as his subject matter. A degree of self-interrogation is required that depends on the questions that emerge from a particular field. Reflexivity has become of prime importance in sociology because it is a property that shapes self-understandings of culture. To understand, the sociologist has to become reflexive if the condition of a culture of postmodernity is to be understood.

But what are the implications for reflexivity and biography if the sociologist is dealing with a religious field, perhaps one that involves liturgical transactions? What happens if reflexivity contains an elective affinity for the sociologist with theological values? These generate a sense of marginalisation within the cultural field that is likely to cause a sociological reflexivity to query the power of secularity to exclude and to distort authentic religious sentiments. If a critical self-interrogation is given a theological voice, then the sociologist has to redirect questions against the conventional tide, to ask why cultural processes reproduce disbelief rather than belief. Clearly, this is an issue of grace, but it is also a matter of sociological analysis that raises other matters. What implications does reflexivity have for the issue of believing and belonging when dealing with religious fields such as their rituals?

If reflexivity is to be cultivated, it admits recognition of the arbitrary conventions that sustain a sociological bias in the discipline *against* religious belief. In this context, the issue of reflexivity relates to what is or is not on the sociological agenda, a point that has particular implications for theological issues in relation to readings of culture.

In his workshop on reflexive sociology, Bourdieu hands down advice, some of which is admirable, such as the necessity of taking risks, and the incremental and hazardous manner of research, where there is a need to cultivate a capacity to translate the mundane in to the realm of scientific interest. To pursue a sociological reflexivity, Bourdieu sees the necessity to develop a break with common sense and to reflect on presuppositions that relate to the cultivation of his notion of participation objectivation. This embodies a denial of interest in the object expressed in bracketing of the representations it sustains.[28]

If Bourdieu is referring to the need to find an artificial distance to gain access to a familiar entity, an aspect of social reality, one can accept this temporary necessity. But distance can become estranging so that one is doomed to remain outside, never connecting sufficiently to understand, to hear authentically what is being proclaimed in a transaction, a point that relates to religious rituals. At this juncture sociology faces an ambiguity in reflexivity. To grasp the language of purpose of the rite means contextualising it to the beliefs of the actors. But they can make a claim of grace that governs an understanding of what is seen. A demand is placed on the sociologist to seek what constitutes understanding in *their* terms of reference. It requires the sociologist to be implicated in the fullness of *their* transaction, if a completeness of understanding is authentically to be achieved. This would relate to Slesinski's insight that the liturgical moment brings out

the necessary *experiential* character of the faith which theology only endeavours to articulate. Without this primary experiential contact with the data of revelation, something liturgy engenders, there can be no theology. A non-praying theologian is a contradiction in terms.[29]

In studying liturgy in a fullness, it might be said that a non-praying sociologist is equally a contradiction in terms. Inadvertently, he commits a symbolic violence against the actor's assumptions by making definite the indefinite, the mysterious, that which is concealed, by imputing to it a hidden agenda of power, which might be denied. The problem reflexivity faces in dealing with liturgical transactions is that it risks sinking sociological insight into a quagmire of counterfactuals over belief and disbelief, which is likely to end up as a dialogue of the deaf.

If ethnomethodology is to be linked to hermeneutics and to reflexivity, then it is difficult to preclude understanding changes in careers of religiosity and the demands these signify to the actor. A young woman who becomes a nun receives a habit that redefines her. It does not make her a nun, but it conserves her and makes a demand for her self-adjustment, to fulfil a social and a spiritual ambition to be as she appears. In her habit, her biography takes on selective properties as she grows in self-understanding of what it is to be a nun, to authentically be as she appears so that self is bonded into the role. Reflexivity can point to understanding that career in sociological terms, but it also has to recognise the object of the transition, the deepening of relations with God. But this shifts reflexivity into theology, into a language of grace, that effects, sustains and makes possible this transition. It gives the career a point, one that rises above issues of self-interest and deception which might form the initial stages of reflexivity of a suspicious sociological gaze.

The problem of seeing to understand religious belief places sociology in a liminal relationship with theology, a grey area that is a matter of sight. One can understand the rite, but to grasp its fullness of significance from a property of verstehen is inadequate. Only grace gets below the surface of the performance to find hidden depths concealed from the graceless. Reflexivity becomes entwined in contemplation to signify a journey that moves out of sociology into theology. How far does the sociologist need to go to understand rituals accountable to theology?

Reflexivity is a subject and object of sociological study, not only of the internal dispositions of the sociologist but also of the actor under study. In a theological setting, reflexivity bears implications that take sociology outside its imperative to decipher social arrangements into an issue of what it is to believe, to be theologically reflexive, and in social terms, to occupy its own notion of awareness. This points to an intricate biography of understanding, of being implicated in a role, how it is constructed and self-constituted. This argument arises in the teaching of sociology of religion as a reflective enterprise, which McNamara has recently explored. He points to the way the reflexivity of students studying sociology of religion in terms of practice, of attending church as analytical adults, exposes a sense of deficiency of spirit for them which complements wider worries of its lack within American higher education.[30] McNamara is correct, that reflexivity in sociology is the beginning of things in matters of religion. It opens out issues scarcely begun to be considered. To reflect on religious belief is to risk becoming more deeply involved in it. The risk relates to Winch's point that some form of religious feeling is required to gain access to what has been understood by the actors and participants in the rite.[31]

Without this disposition, misunderstandings of the basis of a ritual act, such as a liturgy, the public ceremonial form of worship of Catholicism are inevitable. The disposition of the actors who regulate the rite presented, the monks, servers and choir, is to increase a disinterest, not an interest in the social basis of the liturgy.[32] Altruism forms the basis of a disinterested gift. As Marion notes, in the eucharistic present

> all presence is deduced from the charity of the gift; all the rest in it becomes appearance for a gaze without charity; the perceptible species, the metaphysical conception of time, the reduction to consciousness, all are degraded to one figure (or caricature) of charity.[33]

The more liturgical actors cultivate a disposition towards this mystery, the more they are likely to become aware of what they need to signify in enacting performance, a reflexivity enjoined on all, from the youngest choirboy to the oldest monk.

Not to utilise a theology to discern might mean missing the obvious point of the religious arrangement under study. Hillery faced this dilemma in his extended study of a Cistercian monastery. He moved from an initial interest in the monastery, as an unexplored facet of community studies, to a fuller understanding of the values of love which gave a purpose to life in this total institution. Without reference to this enriching virtue, the life made no sense, either in sociology or theology. Love ameliorated the harsh demands of the monk's daily round and supplied a harmony that transcended the imperfections of an organisation useless for any other purpose.[34]

There is a fine line between reflexivity as the cultivation of a sociological awareness and reflection as it relates to spirituality, to contemplation of the theological implications of what is seen and heard. At one level a reflexivity proper to sociology is acceptable, but somehow that lacks the completeness of meaning which the pursuit of religious belief might yield. A spiritual eye, which is a matter of grace, is required to complement that which is subject to sociological scrutiny in the game of rite. This is an area of limit proper to reflexivity that can turn into spiritual contemplation, the awareness of that which is beyond limit, of what *is* a matter of grace.

Ethnomethodology, feminism, the debates on rationality and relativism and of course, the writings of Simmel and Bourdieu have developed a climate of radical contextualisation, where an autonomy of form is admitted with its own internal moral and cultural circumstance. A climate of agnosticism has developed about selection from this array of topics. The need for an individualistic approach to their study is accepted. But this variability of topic generates the possibility of an equivalent pliability in the relationship between the sociologist and his subject matter of inquiry. Some topics make greater demands than others on personal judgement and on the self of the sociologist. Conditions of reflexivity will vary according to the subject, so that even demography, which is often purely statistical, will have a sub-text of fertility and infertility buried within. The sociology of organisation, which appears to be purely descriptive, has a hidden agenda of power and management of resources that enables and disables and that calls for a sociological judgement as to which side the analysis ought to be tilted. Each of these topics presupposes a disposition on the part of the sociologist, where moral and cultural resources of his self are tapped in a biographical manner that can appear to be unreflexive, but which contains a potential to be reflexive.

The study of religion demands a price of understanding which other belief systems and ideologies do not require. To understand the significance of a religious object or ritual is to contemplate an implication that can be transformative. Knowing what to see and what to read involves a grace of enlightenment, a point illustrated in the case of Phillip and the eunuch. This man had great secular authority, but could not understand the reference in scripture to a prophet being like a sheep led to the slaughter. Phillip was asked did the reference refer to the prophet himself or to some other man? Having understood from Phillip, the eunuch was baptised and went on his way. (Acts 8: 26–39) Grasping the point of a religious activity involves fine distinctions unfamiliar and hazardous to sociology which faces limits of characterisation, a point Winch understood. For him, the idea of prayer involves a religious question. Deciding between the prayer of the Pharisee and the Publican means 'the sociologist of religion will be confronted with an answer to the question: Do these two acts belong to the same kind of activity?; and this answer is given according to criteria which are not taken from sociology, but from religion itself'.[35] In this adjudication, the sociologist faces his own elective affinity between reason and revelation.

This relates to a point that left Shils puzzled. Noting that sociology needed to take steps forward to appreciate 'religious phenomena and the diversity of their manifestations', Shils felt that the sociologist, unlike Weber, could become more 'religiously musical'. But one area where sociology could not make peace was in the area of revelation, for this was outside sociological remit.[36] This presents sociology with a difficulty, for being a Catholic involves a career of grace and self-understanding that shapes what is to be understood. This constrains the reflexivity of the sociologist. It points to areas inaccessible, but of cultural significance in understanding the basis of religious belief. This was a point Evans-Pritchard understood when he cited Schmidt who had noted that

> if religion is essentially of the inner life, it follows that it can be truly grasped only from within. But beyond doubt, this can be better done by one in whose inward consciousness an experience of religion plays a part. There is but too much danger that the other [the non-believer] will talk of religion as a blind man might of colours, or one totally devoid of ear, of a beautiful musical composition.[37]

Many sociologists are wilfully colour blind to issues of religious belief in a manner that seems a matter of professional pride. This seems to follow an ignoble section of anthropological tradition which Evans-Pritchard noted. He suggested that many who studied primitive religion rarely had an understanding of Christian theology, history, exegesis, symbolic thought and ritual and the meanings these had for the beliefs of ordinary worshippers.[38] Theology, as a term seldom appears in any sociological index

The Enchantment of Sociology

in the mainstream of the discipline. One cannot help feeling that its expulsion from a sociological frame of reference reflects less its intrinsic worth than an unspoken reflexivity that nurtures a sensibility of disbelief.

To delineate and to describe without grasping the point can have tragic implications, such as arose in Peter Greenaway's film, *The Draughtsman's Contract*. This vain draughtsman, who prided himself on his capacity to sketch exactly rather than to embellish, recorded scenes of polite intercourse in a seventeenth-century formal garden. By not attending to the pattern emerging in his drawings, being a draughtsman rather than an artist, he witnessed a murder, and is murdered because the murderers cannot believe that anybody could record without signifying what was going on. His professional pride in not interpreting, but in just refracting, led to his tragic downfall.

Providing a clear explanation, where everything is in place, can represent a failure to understand, to grasp the point of what is observed. If sociology is realising that the self of the sociologist is changed in the research act, if it is to yield reflexive results, then in the case of religious rituals a fullness of understanding can come very close to conversion. A number of conversions have occurred through the beauty of Church music. For instance, that prototypal flâneur, J. K. Huysmans, was drawn into Catholicism through the beauty of plain-chant sung in an enclosed Benedictine convent in Paris.[39] He followed others such as Paul Claudel and Simone Weil.

The reflexive basis of sociology has been changed and compromised by a concern with the issue of virtue in a world of postmodernity and the problems of finding an authentic self within it. Two Catholic philosophers, Alasdair MacIntyre[40] and Charles Taylor[41] have inserted these elements on to the philosophical agenda. The relationship between morality, self and society focuses on a problem of trust. In a cosmopolitan postmodern order, where images are real and unreal, and where pastiche rules in a deceiving and ambiguous manner, issues of risk and trust have emerged. Detachment and attachment to the social order is increasingly a matter of investment of the self. A notion is presented in the politics of lifestyle, that self-creation is an endless possibility. But appearances can deceive. A self that is manufactured is inauthentic and there is always the possibility of a sociologist being fooled by misreading an ambiguous condition. The self is a place of illusions but also dilemmas. If there are wagers in sociology, these are to be located in the issue of the self and the culture within which it operates. The issue of roles and identity are central to the sociological tradition, but they also bear theological implications.

In believing that man had freed himself from mediaeval accretions and other impediments to finding himself, Guardini felt that the 'modern world deceived itself'. In a way which postmodernity seems to have come to affirm, he argued that man has failed to find the basis for a final judgement on the human condition. Disciplines such as sociology can only handle the accidents of man – his attributes, his relations, and his forms, but can 'never take man simply as he is'.[42] Guardini also understood the way modernisation gave birth to a culture that accentuated insecurities of the self, which could find no solution in the artifices of civilisation. In a prescient insight that betrays his interests in Pascal, and one which has come to haunt debates on postmodernity, Guardini claimed that the bourgeois superstition

> of relying upon 'progress' has been shattered. Many men now suspect that 'culture' is not all what the modern age thought it to be; many suspect that culture is not a realm of beautiful security but a game of dice. Its stakes are life and death, but nobody knows how the last die will be cast.[43]

He also noted the way cultures had moved from being about security to being marked with properties of danger, a quality that arises from the increased and intensified exercise of power.[44]

Forty years later these insights came to be recognised independently by two sociologists, Giddens and Beck. Neither referred to Guardini, but both were seeking to construct a sociology that would clarify contemporary worries about anxiety and risk. In *Modernity and Self-Identity*, Giddens explores reflexive aspects of modernity in the context of what he terms risk and ontological security. These involve the self in dealing with 'life politics', such as feminism. Anxiety, trust and the quest for ontological security are discussed in the context of the tribulations of the self. Lifestyle is married to the structuring of self-identity and a reflexive sociology has become implicated in its worries. The quality of social relationships as they oscillate between opportunity and danger leads to an increased reliance on experts who aid in the reconstruction of self-identity. The issue of the self, hitherto a question for philosophers and theologians, has been intensified into a cultural crisis with few available and viable forms of relief. A decline in ritual and the sequestration of experience from the public realm generates a worry, which Giddens shares with other sociologists, that existential and moral issues have been institutionally excluded in the context of modernity. Worries about a spiritual crisis in modernity are no longer the sole preserve of traditional Catholic theologians, such as Guardini and von Balthasar, who sought to engage theology with contemporary culture.

The quest for 'authenticity' that characterises self-actualisation has come to represent a morally stunted process, that involves an emptying rather than a filling. Thus, perhaps unexpectedly, Giddens asserts that 'personal meaninglessness – the feeling that life has nothing worthwhile to offer – becomes a fundamental psychic problem in the circumstances of late modernity'.[45] Giddens makes brief reference to religion, noting that it has failed to disappear. Indeed, he argues 'new forms of religion and spirituality represent in a most basic sense a return of the repressed, since they directly address issues of the moral meaning of existence which modern institutions so thoroughly tend to dissolve'.[46] Despite dealing only peripherally with religion, this study has profound implications for theology. Not only does it treat of the masking of the spiritual in culture in a climate of risk and distrust, but it also conveys a sense of the inadequacy of what is available to cope in a culture increasingly characterised by a reflexivity that entraps sociology. Any present crisis in self-reflexivity does not suffer from a shortage of solutions and opportunities. In what Giddens has referred to as an 'emotional democracy', a surprising number of possible options are available on the marketplace that all offer to re-order and to free biography. Wilde's notion that 'self-culture is the true ideal of man' has become democratised and commodified as a service for exploration and liberation.[47]

The self of the social actor is increasingly being made accountable in advertising, in the mass media, to fit the body it occupies to desired contemporary images of perfection. The self is also under scrutiny to place itself in a coherent biographical order. To enable this to occur with the minimum of emotional complications, the self is presented with many alternative forms of repackaging, whose price is its commodification and its placement in the cash nexus. Numerous techniques for self-improvement are on sale.

Heelas has explored this process of sacralisation of culture in relation to the self in the context of what he terms 'New Age Capitalism'. Since the 1960s, and influenced by the expressivism of the counterculture, the self has become a focal point for sacralisation. Self-religiosity is embodied in the phrase 'we are God. This is the essence of enlightenment'.[48] Heelas views this growth in the sacralisation of the self as a means of coping with the failure of mainstream institutions, which no longer bind or satisfy. Self-religionists, as he terms them, have become part of management and business training programmes used by mainstream companies. Thus, Heelas indicates, New Age self-religionists have become capitalist enterprises displaying their wares on the cultural marketplace. They supply an ethical basis for acquisitiveness, a form of legitimation at a time when image matters. In a climate where perfection seems endlessly possible, in computer games, in consumer satisfactions, why should the self be exempt? Heelas, slightly wearily concludes

> what has been called 'designer' religion will continue to cater for 'me first in every way' people. 'Religion for yuppies' is with us for the foreseeable future.[49]

Technology has become an increasingly important instrument in the context of globalisation, a term linked with late modernity. Increasingly symbol experts, such as those in public relations and marketing, seem to have the power to shape lifestyles through multichannel satellite television. Computer games offer endless prospects of the fulfilment of fantasy uncluttered by the untidiness of social relationship. Sources of gratification are available without moral struggle through the miracle of technology. This amplification of options is characteristic of a late modernity and involves a distinctive process which Giddens has noted, of a disembedding in social systems, the '"lifting out" of social relations from local contexts of interaction and their restructuring across indefinite spans of time-space'.[50]

The actor is left in a continued state of ambivalence, hovering between a choice that is 'real', as a consumer in the marketplace, but 'unreal'. As Giddens suggests, modernity is enigmatic at its core. This enigma of modernity cannot be overcome, thus 'we are left with questions where once there appeared to be answers'.[51]

In a striking comment, Taylor points to the existence of a selective blindness in the contemporary cultural order when he asks do we have to 'choose between various kinds of spiritual lobotomy and self-inflicted wounds?'.[52] Certain aspects of modernisation have facilitated this spiritual lobotomy at points where the self and the body are frail, where theological issues could be confronted, but which the medical model manages to mask or to have postponed. Illich has pointed to this metaphysical price to medical progress in the mid-seventies in a famous study riddled with theological metaphors that betray its Catholic origins. The capacity to postpone death and to relieve pain through medical technology has made many actors spectators on their own selves.[53] Yet, despite these medical advances, some diseases attract theological metaphors. They generate issues of risk and anxiety that seem to be associated with Divine retribution in ways difficult to exorcise from contemporary sensibilities. These diseases form the unwanted fruit of a culture of desire that has no moral limits. Despite despising notions of virtue that belong to traditional theology, these diseases bear their own portents of fate and tragedy. They have their own metaphors to express an inexpressible suffering.[54]

Interest in the self has to be offset by the recent emergence of the sociology of the body.[55] This has generated its own form of dualism in a culture of postmodernity. Their availability to commodification has accentuated a sense of living on the surface of social reality. Anxiety, worry about the future, awareness of ecological disaster have all led to a climate which bears sociological inspection. In a study that sold widely in Germany outside the confines of usual sociological outlets, and which has had considerable influence within the discipline, Beck sought to encapsulate these public and private worries. This study, entitled *Risk Society* tries to attend to post-Marxist considerations about the risks and worries that stem from affluence, from ecology, but also from the link between lifestyle and identity in the changing circumstances of a privatised culture, where the issue of 'I am I' is a unique question in an era detached from tradition. This issue of identity, of 'who am I' arises in von Balthasar's theology of aesthetics. Beck's tautology 'I am I' involves a secular play on the question of the identity of God in Exodus, where He states 'I am that I am' (Exodus 3: 14).

His use of the phrase relates to Steiner's comment that 'God clings to our culture, to our routines of discourse, He is a phantom of grammar, a fossil embedded in the childhood of rational speech'. This reflects a position Steiner seeks to reverse.[56] Neither Beck nor Giddens conceive of the notion of risk and anxiety in terms of belief or disbelief in God. Theological and metaphysical anxieties receive little attention in their work. Many of the problems encountered in discussion of modernity, reflexivity and risk, relate to earlier notions of the homeless mind and the migratory nature of a self suffering a 'metaphysical loss of home'.[57] Rootlessness, dispossession and the generation of a sense of anxiety and risk emerge in cultural circumstances that conspire against the self realising a sense of authenticity. It cannot be rooted or committed sufficiently to secure an adequate sense of who it is.

The difficulty with Beck's work is that risk is located in two different constituencies: ecological and cultural. The issue of ecological risk is clear-cut, but that embodied in cultural forms is less fleshed out. Beck presupposes that modernity frees from tradition, leading to an intensification of individualisation. Stable compass points have been upset. Increasingly choice dictates biography and life style. Thus, he argues that 'the reflexive conduct of life, the planning of one's own biography and social relations, gives rise to a new inequality, the *inequality of dealing with insecurity and reflexivity*'.[58] Issues of identity are located in changes in family structure. Beck's discussion of the resolution of issues of identity is largely set within gender relationships. He assumes that as tradition becomes progressively diluted, relationships become more important. God has departed, or rather has been displaced by cultural idols. With His apparent demise, confession has also vanished, the ritual where guilt and shame could be absolved.[59] Against this background, biography becomes an accomplishment, an entity constructed from the marketplace, from commodities and lifestyle politics, that mobilise focal points for collective identities. In this freedom, the self can elect to be enhanced, but at a price of standardisation that subtracts from a sense of individuality. These new responsibilities, to commodify the self to best advantage, greatly increase sensibilities of risk and anxiety, of making the 'wrong' choice. A failure of reflexivity, to be adequately informed, to calibrate authentically the social consequences of the commodification of self, emerges with concomitant risks that the results might be discrediting. Fatalism has now been transferred from God to a cultural climate of postmodernity thus precluding a theological solution either to the issue of identity or the self and its domain where lies the question 'I am I'. In a pivotal passage, Beck suggests that

> one even has to choose one's social identity and group membership, in this way managing one's own self, changing its *image*. In the individualized society, risks do not just increase, quantitatively, qualitatively new types of personal risk arise, the risk of the chosen and changed personal identity. And what is an additional burden, new forms of 'guilt ascription' come into being. Sooner or later, these constraints to a personal and reflexive handling planning and production of biography will produce new demands on education, care-giving, therapy and politics.[60]

Unfortunately, Beck's approach to risk tells us little about the spiritual or social effects of misjudgement. In his approach to faith and modernity, Beck gives little attention to the notion that the gods of science have failed.[61]

A further problem, is that a spiritual lobotomy renders one insensitive to the harm of transgression and blasphemy. Late modernity dooms one to a condition of misrecognition, to see without a sense of risk. Thus, images hitherto embedded in a sacred tradition, in a climate of late modernity, are open to being disembedded and reconstructed with impunity in another setting, that inverts and de-sacralises their basis. For instance, one sees a television commercial for jeans, with a scantily dressed woman so clad, prancing in to a Church, supposedly to pray, but there to exhibit before some distracted and giggling choirboys. The focus of worship has been shifted from the sacred to sensuality.

Reflexive modernisation is a conceptual means of capturing the excess of social awareness arising from an expert knowledge that unsettles and

which lodges a sense of pessimism into contemporary culture.[62] The self
has become causality of this intensification arising from privatisation of
emotions, loss of tradition, and difficulties in finding compass points in
what Lash and Urry term an economy of signs and symbols.[63] But at some
point in the clutter of reflexive modernisation the social processes surrounding the social construction of self have to be examined. How does
the self relate to sociological concerns and to what purpose?

For George Herbert Mead, the self emerges in social experience, where
it has a capacity to become an object to itself for the purposes of interaction. This reflexive idea of the self enables it to calibrate its effects in
social intercourse. Mead is pointing to a process of self-realisation that
affirms the symbolic, the tacit and the indeterminate in conditions that
bind the sociologist, who wishes to know, to the actor estimating what can
be known in social interaction.[64] There is a mirroring quality involved in
the display of social images that catches the actor and the sociologist in
discerning what is reflected. Any sociological understanding of the self is
likely to be caught between the issue of an inward growth, a reflexivity on
its roots and identity, that can be spiritual or psychological, or a concern with
cultural understandings of self-actualisation and manifestation that might
lead into philosophy and theology. This is an artificial distinction, because
within culture both inward and outward quests for self-authentication are
mutually implicated.

Taylor has fruitfully explored the moral sources and bases of the construction of the self, as it moves from a theological form of knowing and
identity to one increasingly lodged in the world where it is governed by
secularised philosophical considerations. Issues of trust, morality and identity arise as the self seeks powers to overcome and to authenticate its
sensibilities of being. Taylor argues that the pursuit of the self, either
based on reason or within nature, never quite escapes from theology. Secular
humanism, he asserts, has its roots in Judaeo-Christian faith and even in
an age of modernity, it is still dependent on this source. In this study, one
shares with Taylor a concern with the issue of the need to rediscover
spiritual roots in a culture that seems to have stifled the spirit. This form
of stifling is part of the price of secularisation.[65]

Postmodernity presents a price of masking deeper issues by enabling the
individual to live on the surface of life. As Nietzsche suggested 'the phenomenon of modern man has become wholly appearance; he is not visible
in what he represents, but rather concealed by it'.[66] Even more importantly, as Tester argues, 'post-modern relationships play a part in hiding the
problem of immortality'.[67] In postmodernity, the self is offered an eternal
present that masks the precariousness of such a false assumption. In

American society, the absence of a consensus on moral values means that
'one's own idiosyncratic preferences are their own justification, because
they define the true self'.[68] But in such a climate of postmodernity, it is
not so much God becoming dead as the self. Postmodernity proffers a
pliability that allows the self to squeeze past dilemmas of identity and
authenticity without facing a metaphysical bill. But the price of escaping
the hound of heaven is confinement in an iron cage lodged in a cultural
slum. As Bellah and his fellow authors conclude,

> much of the thinking about the self of educated Americans, thinking
> that has become almost hegemonic in our universities and much of the
> middle class, is based on inadequate social science, impoverished philo-
> sophy and vacuous theology.[69]

Endless openings are available for the self to float along on the surface of
life with moral impunity without facing any deep inspection of character
or identity. The self can deceive and be deceived through the ambiguities
of appearance in a culture where monetary rather than moral credit dictates what is to be esteemed. But as Finkelstein notes, 'in the process of
shopping for a self, we have unwittingly bypassed its origins in the experience of subjectivity'.[70] This has led to a cult of the superficial for she
argues tellingly

> the self as assemblage demonstrates time and time again how little we
> value the contemplative and how much we value the performative. This
> view shows the modern self is contingent, that in the authenticating
> narrative of the contemporary epoch, it has no enduring substance, it is
> simply treated as an icon.[71]

This *character redux*, to use her term, deceived in the act of realisation
from confronting the anomalies and alienation that wrought its basis, is
oddly blind to religious sensibilities. It echoes a property of self-oblivion
which Paul noted when he stated

> this I say therefore and testify in the Lord that ye henceforth walk not
> as other Gentiles walk,
> in the vanity of their mind.
> Having the understanding darkened, being alienated from the life of
> God through the ignorance that is in them, because of the blindness of
> their heart. (Ephesians. 4: 17–18)

A self that can be reconstructed through technology, that can find a thera-
pist to realise any autonomous claims, is unlikely to put off 'the old man,
which is corrupt according to the deceitful lusts'. Nor will it see the

necessity of putting on 'the new man, which after God is created in right-eousness and true holiness' (Ephesians 4: 22–4).

In a secular culture, the self is caught in a dilemma, which a reflexive sociology is implicated in, of being unable to discern what is worth losing in a culture that disguises the paucity of what is gained in life on the surface. As Pascal asserted, 'Christian piety destroys the human self and human civility conceals and suppresses it'.[72]

The illusion that the self can manufacture its own conditions of self-actualisation has become embedded in the culture of organisation. Nietzsche's notion of self-empowerment has become part of the currency of the marketplace, in social work, universities and in bureaucratic culture. Psychoanalysis, body technology and New Age religions proffer endless solutions to self-identity and to the resolution of its conflicts. The prospect of a more enabling authenticated self is now on view and can be pur-chased. The process of self-improvement has become commodified. Bellah and his fellow authors argue that the manufacture of the therapeutic self is defined according to wants and needs that increasingly belong to the cash nexus, and have become issues of cost-benefit calculation.[73] This re-centring of the self into sociology occurs as an awareness of the privatised nature of the actor and the link between ethics and appearance has come to the fore. The manufacture of self links modernity with the issue of decadence, but also to evil and redemption for there are theological issues abroad in this issue of artifice and appearance.

Finkelstein has explored the link between character and problems of judgement of authenticity and inauthenticity. She shows the way physiogno-mists who judged character by physical appearance have been replaced by plastic surgeons who mask through the miracle of technology what has been always regarded as a superstition, the belief the face tells all. Moral credit is now given to those who seek a face lift to redeem infelicities of character. In her account, beauty has become skin deep. Appearance and moral worth are interrelated in an unambiguous manner that suggests the authentic inner self can be changed without spiritual struggle. Plastic surgery offers the self the prospect of endless reinvention, but it is also a means of abolishing the ambiguity between the inner self and out-ward appearance.[74] But the risks of reductionism, of the cultivation of a narcissism, already abroad in American culture are greatly increased.[75] The notion that a self-produced self can produce an authentic image is a polite fiction.[76]

Appearances require a property of ambiguity, for without the curiosity they engender, a mystery is taken out of manners. Curiosity enables the self to attract, an incitement for character to be explored. But for others, the mystery works the other way. For the stigmatised, there is a mystery about the way their flawed appearance dooms them to social discredit, to a spoiled identity without relief. Flaws in character are inferred from those of appearance, so that there is no incentive to explore a character doomed to be discredited. The stigmatised actor lacks the resources of face work to manipulate contrary impressions of credit.[77] Finkelstein is concerned with the illusory shortcuts which a commodified culture presents, of rectifying what is believed to be an appearance deemed in someway as discreditable. Goffman and Finkelstein are critical of any mechanical relationship between self and appearance.

There is a Faustian quality to such efforts to render unambiguous that which of its nature is ambiguous. With the application of technology to beautify the face, a belief is made that age can be postponed. As aging does occur, the face becomes faceless, adorned by a mask whose technological basis becomes more apparent with time. If everything in modernity is about image and appearance, then as Finkelstein suggests, we come back to the dilemma raised by Wilde in *The Picture of Dorian Gray*.[78]

Gray achieved a capacity discernible in Goffman's actor, of enabling a problematic self to slide untested through an unfettered life, where through a lie, appearance mattered, but character did not. By making a Faustian wager, he transcended the ambiguous link between character and appearance. In the area of appearance, where face, role and clothing count, the ingredients sociology is comfortable in dealing with, greater truths lie hidden, which the discipline can elect to consider or to discard. As Wilde indicated 'the truths of metaphysics are the truths of masks'.[79]

The Picture of Dorian Grey is a parable about a young man 'who sold himself to the devil for a pretty face'. This apparently ageless youth bore a mask of innocence that rebuked the suspicious but experienced. The effect of his wager was that the sins of his life were not borne on his everyday public visage, but on his portrait, which nobody could see except himself. The relationship between body and soul was detached in this exercise in deception and self-deception. Gray deceived in his mask of innocence, but those who were experienced in vice were also taken in, not knowing of his Faustian wager. This is also a study in the ambiguity of appearance, between public image and private reality, where the self becomes spiritually dead and can only murder to survive. The effect of this descent into an unaccountable practice of dissimulation is an insensitivity to tragedy which is also one of the trademarks of a culture of postmodernity. In the end Gray is forced to kill the thing he loves, the image of himself in the painting, which portrays the truth of his self, unavailable to others, but to God. In the killing of conscience, Dorian Gray also dies.[80] This is an old fashioned story where the sinful and those who try to deceive God are punished.

The tale can be understood at many levels. It is partly about the tragedy of a man, a painter, who wished to frame beauty in a painting, but was murdered. Like the draughtsman in Greenaway's film, he failed to grasp the implications of that which he etched. As the painter of the picture of Dorian Gray observed, 'every portrait that is painted with feeling is a portrait of the artist, not of the sitter. The sitter is merely the accident, the occasion. It is not he who is revealed by the painter; it is rather the painter who on the coloured canvas, reveals himself'.[81] Likewise, the sociologist is implicated in that which he portrays.

In feigning innocence, Dorian Gray was killed in the experience. His spiritual sensibilities were blunted in a way that precluded him from realising how far he had gone in a journey into evil. Too late, Dorian Gray reflected, 'he would never again tempt innocence'.[82] He had developed a conceit, a fascination, over the discrepancy between his appearance of innocence in public and the sinful experience that marked his face seen privately in the portrait. By using a mirror in the attic, he sees both. By having access to both, Gray becomes removed from the social realm, for he can only achieve self-recognition before the painting, but not in the responses of others who are deceived by how he appears. Gray's tragedy is that he cannot escape the claims of the gaze on the painting – he cannot live with it and he cannot live without it. But he has another dilemma: the more he knows, the more he desires to know.[83]

As his narcissism deepens, so does his fascination with evil. Unlike Adam, who was merely tempted to such ambitions, Gray appeared to live with a knowledge of good *and* evil. He had found the power to transcend antinomial forms of knowing fuelling his desire to know even more. It is this achievement of a transcendence of ambiguity, the failure to realise the tragedy of his situation and the limitless satisfaction of all his desires, that gives him a recognisable place in a culture of postmodernity that suffers similar ambitions. The theological nexus of his tragedy is clear, even if it has become obscured in the present culture of postmodernity. But there are other Catholic elements to the story, not least in the fate of the model of Dorian Gray. His name was John. Like Huysmans, he accomplished a singular movement that reversed the theme of the tale of Dorian. He moved from a concern with decadence into a life that sought innocence, a revolt against modernity, so inexplicable as to be a matter of grace.

In her subtle biography, McCormack presents John Gray as a bright handsome man of working class background who managed to continually reinvent himself. As she indicates, Gray's 'real achievement was of a self in its own terms as perfect and as laboriously constructed as a work of art'.[84] Thus '"Dorian" Gray was not born, but made'. A minor poet, and like Huysmans also a civil servant, Gray allowed himself to be invented, to be recreated, first by Charles Ricketts and then Wilde. This process of construction of the self, as poet and poseur, came to form the basis for the model for Dorian Gray.

With the trial of Wilde and the death of Beardsley, Gray reconverted to Catholicism. The first time he had converted, in France, was as a result of attendance at a profoundly unaesthetic mass.[85] Desperation drove him back to the Church the second time, when he was on the brink of madness. Revolt against the mask of Dorian Gray led him to reinvent himself in another self, as a Catholic priest. To understand why Gray became a dedicated priest, who seldom referred to his past and died well worthy of his vocation, one has to understand what he was escaping from. Unlike most who deal with modernity, Gray was fleeing from the destructive effects of living with a self that had become stuck to the mask of decadence which Wilde had invented for him to wear and within which he had become trapped.[86] For Gray, reaching sanctity involved an escape from the brink, a rescue from a 'wilful self-preoccupation that had once led him into a nearly disastrous pursuit of pleasure'. In short, he was saved from his self.[87]

When Gray reached a certain stage of deception and interest in playing with evil, his mentor sent him a yellow book to read that fascinated him. He felt 'it was a poisonous book. The heavy odour of incense seemed to cling about its pages and to trouble the brain'.[88] The book was *Against Nature* by J. K. Huysmans. It carried forward the modernity conceived by Baudelaire into what we now regard as postmodernity.

Des Esseintes, its hero, sought to maximise all his desires in a life of total selfishness as a dandy, who would permit nothing to intrude on his notions of pleasure – however perverse. He considered artifice to be the distinctive mark of human genius.[89] Unlike Gray, Des Esseintes pursued a dedicated career of not being seen. Following an almost monastic career, this was a flâneur who retreated from the street and surrounded himself with objects of pleasure such as books, jewels, and perfumes. These objects were for use in the privacy of his chambers. Contact with the public violated Des Esseintes' aesthetic sensibilities. His life was a retreat from the social into the self, where only it could be pleased. Even the servants had to have their faces covered to preclude sight of their ugliness which marred the aesthete's view. Des Esseintes was the prototype of the computer addict, who in the privacy of his room, can make pictures of life without the discomforts of having to live it. But this pursuit of pleasure led to a certain weariness, a discovery of emptiness at the limits of sensuality. The career of the creator of Des Esseintes was if anything even more bizarre. As with Baudelaire, Huysmans' excursions into the limits of modernity led him to face a choice, between the cross and the revolver.[90]

Like Gray, fact and fiction became intermingled in the life of Huysmans. After *Against Nature*, he wrote *La Bas*. This most peculiar study centred on its hero, Durtal, another front for Huysmans himself, writing a life of Gilles de Rais, 'the Des Esseintes of the fifteenth century' who had 'an ardent, a mad curiosity concerning the forbidden sciences'[91] that led him into alchemy, satanism, and infamy as a notorious child murderer. Imitating the curiosity that drove de Rais, Huysmans wished to get the detail of this movement into evil correct. His fieldwork necessitated finding priests who said black masses, one of which he attended, an ethnographic account of which appears at the end of *La Bas*. Huysmans was so disturbed by this fieldwork exercise into hearing and seeing satanic verses, that he fled to a Trappist monastery for cleansing, a graphic account of which appears in *En Route*.

For him, naturalism, and positivism generated conditions of boredom. While positivism offered the prospects of limitless explanation, decadence proffered the making of a self without limit in mimetic art. The result was a vacuity that passed all understanding. Satanism offered a means of escape, but it demanded a price which positivism had no means of understanding. The descent of Huysmans into grace, virtually a digestive process rather than a conversion experience, led him to seek a life of piety as a Benedictine oblate. He sought a monastic solution to the dilemmas of modernity, starting from the medieval world of de Rais in *La Bas* and then moved into *The Cathedral*, Chartres, to find a theology of symbolism, one compatible with artistic sensibilities. The medievalism, which Smart sees as lurking around the fringes postmodernity, has a root in Huysmans.[92]

Running from Comte, who sought to invert Catholicism into a positivist religion of humanity, to Baudelaire, who coined the notion of modernity and the flâneur, to Georg Simmel who was to become the archetypical sociologist of culture, but also the chronicler of its tragedy, to Huysmans who foresaw postmodernity and fled, there is an unacknowledged theological strand passing through sociology as the thinnest of threads, but one that links its birth to its present orphan-like status in contemporary culture.

Too many of those who developed this movement of modernity and decadence in the first fin de siècle fell into Catholicism to be coincidental. They all seemed to have different reasons for ending up in the Church in a manner which suggests that there was some theological agenda haunting their flirtations with modernity and decadence. Their conversion to Catholicism hardly constitutes a collective movement as their biographical reasons for passing over were too diverse and individual. They were, however, the first to perceive the limits of modernity but also to chose to escape from it. Baudelaire received the last rites[93] as did Wilde, who claimed that much of his moral obliquity was due to his father not permitting him to become a Catholic. Ever concerned with style, Wilde felt rather snobbishly that 'Catholicism is the only religion to die in'.[94]

Heaven and hell seem matters inconvenient in a postmodern culture, issues which secularisation has long masked and discarded. Satanism might also seem equally a matter of triteness, a folk panic invented by Evangelical fundamentalists. But an inconvenient fact remains for sociology. If it is to explore further its Faustian roots in the metaphorical tale that governs its notion of modernity, it has to realise the game *was* played with the devil.

All of those who engaged with decadence and modernity in this tragic fin de siècle had a profound sense of evil. Baudelaire was fascinated with the works of Edgar Allan Poe and Huysmans' dalliance with Satanists led him in pursuit of God. Modernity was conceived when theological distinctions *did* matter, but such is the comfort of its masking that these have become matters of indifference. The commodification of belief in the second understanding of fin de siècle contrasts oddly with the experience of its first version dealing with early rather than late modernity.

There are obvious differences between the two periods. In the first, modernity was related to decadence, to the aesthete, who despised the public in a studied manner and who sought to convert art into life, so that pose mattered more than substance. Self-consciously theatrical, flamboyant and endeavouring to exceed the frontiers of bourgeois taste, decadence, as McCormack indicates, was a wilful confusion of art and life embodied in an image virtually defined by Wilde and Beardsley.[95] This notion portrays a certain wit in the dying in the mask absent in Nietzsche whose interest in decadence related to an empty shell of convention and appearance. His interest seems only too well to characterise the present concern with fin de siècle. It represents a more intensified, a more abundant, but more emptying form of reflexivity, facing diminishing prospects of achieving a newness amidst the eternal and the transient, which Baudelaire conceived as characterising modernity in its incipient stage.[96] In its fullness, a modernity has evolved into a condition of postmodernity, where in transit, the eternal has been terminated by belief in the instant.

The condition of postmodernity is losing a capacity to reinvent itself. Elegance, style, appearance are all part of a career of self-invention in an increasing plethora of images commodified into life styles that beg questions about the relationship between symbol and surface, mask and morality.[97] Postmodernity seems to have become an art of shifting the scenery on a stage in a way that denies sight of the tragedy of culture and the theological issues it portends. Unfortunately, with the growth of postmodernity, which is the fruit of a secularised modernity, a sense of evil has become disguised, and indeed, within certain limits has become a matter of taste in the pluralism of lifestyle and the tolerance which this diversity proclaims. In whatever form, the actor in sociology struts in a secular paradise, basking in the mirrors of what can be commodified, living still in life but somehow not of it. But who is this flâneur?

Gilloch draws attention to Benjamin's understanding of the flâneur as an actor on the stage of the city, a hero seeking to avoid boredom, but also engagement. In the end all is display, as he wanders noticed but there to be unnoticed. His tragedy is to become a victim of his own boredom. For Benjamin, 'the sandwichman is the last incarnation of the flâneur'.[98] There is a tragic fate in pursuing limitless choice, to always parade with impunity as the eternal outsider on a life in transience, journeying, but never arriving. The flâneur seems to follow the fate of Nietzsche's hero, whose self-will and self-consciousness reflects the exercise of a choice to overcome fate and to make his own idols of pleasure. But as de Huszar notes, Nietzsche 'saw in the murder of God, the prerequisite for the utmost development of self. He was pleased neither with God nor with man, and as an alternative invented the superman'.[99] But the hero so invented seems to stand outside the sociological realm. He is neither implicated in the collective nor does he seem to live outside it.[100]

In its dealings with modernity, now into extra-time with postmodernity, the traditional bias of sociology is to play a losing game with Mephistopheles. The plight of sociology might seem to be embodied in Faust's question to Mephistopheles as to 'where lies the way?' and be less than comforted with his reply

> There *is* none. Way to the Unreachable,
> Never for treading, to those Unbeeschable,
> Never besought! Is your soul then ready?
> Not locks or bolts are there, no barrier crude,
> But lonely drift, far, lone estrangement's eddy.
> What sense have you of waste and solitude?[101]

The Faustian wager that lingers in the relationship between sociology and modernity lies in the area of knowledge, power and the capacity to see what others do not. Pride is linked to the exercise of a curiosity unfettered by inhibitions in its exercise. In Marlowe's *Doctor Faustus*, the good angel tells him to 'lay that damned book aside and gaze not on it, lest it tempt thy soul', whereas the evil angel urges him go forward into 'that famous art wherein all nature's treasury is contained'. Faustus groans 'how am I glutted with conceit of this! shall I make spirits fetch me what I please, resolve me of all ambiguities'.[102] But in gaining such magic, that satisfies all curiosity, Faustus realises 'the god thou servest is thine own appetite'.[103] The Faustian wager embodied in modernity is unfettered knowledge. There are other wagers.

Tillich argues that 'the risk of faith is not arbitrariness; it is a unity of fate and decision'. It involves an existential risk, a risk in dealing with symbols, in the making manifest matters of faith, and of surviving the prospect of failure when confronting the unconditional aspects of belief.[104] But the pride lodged in modernity is a curiosity related to a right to know. The regulation of curiosity, of wishing to see in another mode, perhaps theological, is not one of the strengths of postmodernity, nor are self-denial and reverence. The distinction between wisdom and curiosity can become lost. This might seem an odd point in an age where there is a democratic right to know and in a culture that claims to be able to satisfy any curiosity at a price. Mystery and curiosity are interlinked in that what becomes apparent and clear can become uninteresting. There is a distinction between a curiosity to know, the need to cultivate a self-awareness, and the failure to respect the proper limits of what can be known in theological terms. A certain tact is required in dealing with tacit knowledge, such as in the case of the terrain of innocence and experience and the dilemmas this poses, which can be traced back to the problem of pride and the Fall.[105] In Kempis' *The Imitation of Christ* there is a warning against the cultivation of spiritually useless knowledge. Thus it is written

he whom I teach will swiftly gain wisdom and advance far in the life of the spirit. But those who seek curious knowledge from men, and care nothing for My service, will only discover sorrow.[106]

The limits of secular learning and culture caused others earlier in the medieval past to flee their books for lives of quiet contemplation.[107] But for Huysmans, as for many flâneurs gone holy, such a retreat did not seem possible, for like Benjamin's angel, going back was not possible and the way forward seemed mysteriously blocked. Thus, at the end of *En Route*, Huysmans declared wearily 'I am still too much of a man of letters to become a monk, and yet I am already too much a monk to remain among men of letters'.[108]

Cultural politics in the mass media deal with issues of the power to redress unfavourable images. This struggle achieves its legitimacy through efforts to recast the link between the past and the present. It can involve a wish to go back, that is more than an exercise in nostalgia. It can reflect an imperative to retreat, to relocate, that will accomplish an authenticity for the self, estranged and alienated by forces of modernity it cannot control. This movement back can disclose a romantic response to ethnic roots, an attempt to recover what is perceived as a primeval innocence before the fall into civilised experience. But beneath these layers of pos- sibility that inhere in a prized original culture, which offer the estranged routes for escape, dangerous currents operate that can lead to inconvenient ethical considerations. Some of these emerge in Alice Walker's painfully honest book, *Possessing the Secret of Joy*.

This is a tale of an Afro-American women attempting to return to her cultural roots, to rejoin the tribe which the enslavement of her ancestors had effected her expulsion from, to wander in the rootlessness of a modern alien American culture on whose field she had no place. She wished to return to its customs and to possess its full criteria of membership. But the price demanded for authentic belonging involved the woman accepting an operation of self-mutilation, female circumcision. This custom embodied more than access to a way of life. It offered a redefinition of the body, but with tragic and ambiguous results. At one level, the operation offered release from the alien definitions of American culture and an authentic assimilation into the customs of the tribe, but at another level, it destroyed her womanhood and led to a descent into madness, psychoanalysis, mur- der and execution. The woman saw too much to want to stay in American culture and too little in the African culture to which she took flight that would have warned her of the tragedy in store, another tale of innocence and experience.[109]

If religion has become secularised, then what is left, for retreat seems blocked, and the way forward seems equally impossible. This point wor- ried Turner at the end of his appendix on 'What is religion?'. He wrote

> in so far as this study has accepted the secularisation of religion, the de- finition of religion in modern society is particularly problematic. Although social-class positions remain important in our experience of modern society, in general we are exposed to the material world of commodities, objects and bodies without the intervening shield of religious meanings. The death of God has left us literally and culturally naked.[110]

It is no wonder that the issue of leisure and travel has now come to embody the eternal and the transient, but also has come to be understood in terms of escape.[111] But the vocation of the sociologist cannot have come to be the escape artist of the culture of postmodernity always fleeing but never arriving. Reflecting on the calling of the sociologist, Weber was definite about the need for the disinterested pursuit of knowing that bordered on the heroic. It seemed to admit of no weakness, save in terms of lapsing into religion. Thus Weber wrote

> to the person who cannot bear the fate of the times like a man, one must say: may he rather return silently, without the usual publicity build-up of renegades, but simply and plainly. The arms of the old churches are opened widely and compassionately for him. After all, they do not make it hard for him. One way or another he has to bring his 'intellectual sacrifice' – that is inevitable. If he can really do it, we shall not rebuke him.

It would be easy to read the above as suggesting the Church represents a rest home for sociological casualties injured in the quest for intellectual integrity.

But Weber is reproving those who lack the intellectual courage to clarify their own ultimate stand-point. He claimed that a religious return stands higher than academic prophecy. Citing Isaiah's oracles, who ask the watchman 'what of the night?', Weber goes on to add that for two millennia people have tarried and 'we are shaken when we realize its fate'. In the final lines of 'science as vocation', he asserts the need to set to work to meet 'the "demands of the day", in human relations as well as in our vocation. This, however, is plain and simple, if each finds and obeys the demon who holds the fibers of his very life'.[112]

The burden of reflexivity lies in uncovering the thrall to this demon, but it is also about the seeking of a redemptive solution which the religiously tone deaf Weber might have understood. The descent into vacuity which a culture of postmodernity realises affects the reflexivity of a sociology seeking only to connect but in changed circumstances to earlier concerns. Just three decades ago, a critical relevance emerged in a humanistically cast sociology seeking to refract the twin demands of relevance and idealism embodied in the argot of protest and the spongy rhetoric of the romanticism of the counterculture. By degrees, drifting through the seventies and eighties, from the selfish idealism of the Thatcher generation, to a concentration on life politics, of ecology and feminism, to eating disorders, one can track through the self-selected dissertation topics of two generations of undergraduate sociology students at the University of Bristol, their worries and what they sought to understand. One cannot speak for the present intake, but one gets the impression that the issues that concern, that draw their critical wits are less to do with lifestyles than issues of meaning and understanding.

As Melanie Phillips has aptly indicated, the Jews are the song birds of the mines, the first to notice the dangers of modernity. A similar occupational prescience affects sociologists, not so much of the dangers of modernity, now descended into postmodernity but of a slow turn of the tide on Dover beach. For this, there is no hard evidence, bar a certain dampness of the occasional religious practitioner. Yet, one feels within that things are changing sufficient to listen harder, for reflexivity can reflect an inward turning. This echoes a comment of Cooley that

> a true sociology is systematic autobiography. The whole organization and process of society exists in my mind, and I and others like me can understand it only as we learn what it means to us.[113]

Reflexivity relates to an enhancement of appreciation, the recognition of an implication, the attending to what has been neglected within the culture. In post-1989, there is a movement towards wanting to believe, for only emptiness beckons. To some extent it would seem as if we are back to the end of the first fin de siècle, but the quest for the spiritual has now moved more widely into culture in its second incarnation. Perhaps in 1994, as against 1964, one can better recognise the poignancy of the final lines of *Against Nature*, which Huysmans only came to understand later. The hero, the emptied prototype of the flâneur, Des Esseintes, reflected

> Well, it is all over now. Like a tide-race, the waves of human mediocrity are rising to the heavens and will engulf this refuge, for I am opening the flood-gates myself, against my will. Ah! but my courage fails me, and my heart is sick within me! – Lord, take pity on the Christian who doubts, on the unbeliever who would fain believe, on the galley-slave of life who puts out to sea alone, in the night, beneath a firmament no longer lit by the consoling beacon-fires of the ancient hope![114]

Sociology suffers its own theodicy in circumstances that are not of its own choosing. The reflexivity of the sociologist faces strange hazards when cast in a theological direction. The self might deal in religious issues, but in their sociological shape, they are stamped with disbelief, empty forms where faith has departed. But the religious awareness deriving from reflexivity risks the question: what if these religious forms were to be grace filled, how would they seem? Thinking such unthought thoughts, if only to enhance reflexivity, is to risk being surprised by grace. It is to risk a change in awareness. It is to seek a reflexivity that implicates believing and belonging in a distinctive sociological witness to understand theological matters better.

But this would be to ask what is the sociological nature of the link between theology and culture. If this had not been so misunderstood, then sociology would not feel the urge to find its own understandings to provide its own distinctive witness.

3 Theology and Culture: An Ambiguous Encounter

The issue of reflexivity for the sociologist denotes an accountability for a form of knowing of the social, for a heightened analytical sensibility of its detail and its implications that might lie unseen and unsignified. The reflexivity of the sociologist embodies a career of learning, a sense of expectation of what to read, that draws from a conceptual arsenal forged in academic rites of passage from vivas to fieldwork. The completion of an apprenticeship yields an enhanced awareness of subtleties indiscernible to the uninitiated. This peculiar sense of connection and disconnection shapes the hermeneutic task, not so much in terms of an endemic suspicion as a continual quest to articulate what has not been understood concerning the contingency of social arrangements. From these potential discrepancies comes the curiosity of the sociologist always seeking to bridge the gap between the argot of the discipline and the ever expanding contours of a culture, increasingly commodified and opaque. There is a property of prophecy, of revelation, in the sociological vocation that seems to endow it with theological properties. Settled matters become unsettled and the obvious is converted into the unobvious.

This calling, of articulating that which lies hidden in conditions of communicative hazard, might seem to give to sociology a sense of kinship with theology, which, superficially faces similar problems of articulation and communication in a culture of postmodernity. In its conditions of fragmentation and individualisation, theology also faces threats, not so much over the sacredness of the social bond, which sociology affirms, but over the status of the sacred itself. Theological reflexivity relates to different considerations, to those arising in sociological use. Its version points to a property of relationship in the reflection, in the self-awareness its use generates. But it is also a movement against the grain, against the assumptions of postmodernity and against the forces of secularisation that have placed the issue of the self in what Turner terms 'a profound process of social disenchantment of belief'. For him, this secularisation of faith occurs not purely at an intellectual or academic level, but as a steady erosion within 'transformations of everyday life which make belief either irrelevant or impossible'.[1] The passage of everyday life marks religious sensibility as incredible, irrelevant and as an unnecessary artificiality.

Resiting a sociological reflexivity into a theological field widens and engulfs what was originally a methodological form of accountability. The issue of awareness embodied in a sociological reflexivity becomes almost infinitely expanded and incomprehensible if placed in a frame of accountability to the whole gamut of Catholic spirituality, its theology and its own traditions for dealing with culture. Although not its term, theological reflexivity relates to a discernment that is spiritual yielded in meditation that embodies a journeying into a relationship of faith. The sense of belonging this occasions points to a quest, a searching for the Divine, that relates to a notion of grace and transformation. It also points to the differing frames of accountability between these two forms of reflexivity, accountable to theology and sociology, analytically separate, but on a theological agenda, mutually implicated. For instance, in sociology the paradoxical nature of liturgical transactions relates to ritual, to symbol, conceptual notions of a body of secondary literature that shapes a disciplinary consensus as to what to seek. But to a believer, these social games command a searching for a truth. The social wrappings of the rite, which give rise to sociological curiosity, require unpacking in a theological frame of reference, if their significance is to be properly understood. For true believers, this social fabric of rite gives a clothing to the unmanifest; it supplies a basis for credulity by giving to the intangible properties of the definite; and it supplies a communicative medium that enables a collective sense of the private to be understood in public. These rites supply a means of credibility for belief, a focus for confidence within which to refract back a sense of God.[2]

In dealing with issues of religious belief, sociology faces numerous problems, not least that its traditional biases are stacked towards disbelief. But assuming that imputations of disbelief are arbitrary, reductionist and mistranslations that effect a symbolic violence against those who do believe, for instance in the tenets of Catholicism in a fullness of its orthodoxy, how is sociology to approach the issue of the viability of belief? If, as Turner has indicated, the artificiality of everyday life propels actors in a secularised direction, there are exceptions. Religious orders still draw recruits; some of the young still go to church; and despite issues of modernity, materialism and passing ideological fads, theological issues still arouse interest and debate. But sociology has not much noticed these exceptions, these believers who persist in inconvenient witness despite the artificiality of everyday life. Likewise, sociological reflexivity has paid little attention to the social construction of their beliefs.

Finney's study supplies some insights into the randomness involved in finding religious belief, a searching within in which social relations play a crucial part. Coming to faith, for the majority of the sample, was a gradual negotiated journey of discovery in a variety of cultural settings. Within these can be found a property of contamination, an effecting of an elective affinity towards religious belief, that points to a social process of imitation and self-appropriation.[3] In contemporary culture, pockets of resistance operate against its dominant disabling artificial aspects, a conspiracy to secure disbelief.

Reasons for turning to belief are always complex and subjective. The factors that trigger a change of heart are multitudinous and relative. As James notes the phrase 'man's extremity is God's opportunity' very much arises in instances of conversion and this can lead to the self-surrender that is a crucial part of faith.[4] There is an incalculable property attached to the limits of disbelief, that can point to the necessity of turning to belief. Often this is a matter of grace.

Cultural circumstances supply a ground for faith, a setting in which theological and sociological forms of reflexivity merge. These make manifest the imperative to believe, through music, in skills of architecture, in styles of communal and ritual forms that seek to wrest the holy from the mundane and to provide a frame within which to refract the glory of God. Culture enhances sensibilities of belonging, of a shared intimation of the holy, of acting and being acted on in a mysterious Epiphany. But this is a language of belief that is estranging to sociology, yet one it has to assimilate if it is to achieve any understanding of what theology wishes to signify in culture.

The language of belief is equally strange and elusive to theologians. For them, faith is a gift of grace, a mysterious outcome, often unasked. It relates to a capacity to affirm in confidence a truth that embodies a sense of belonging. For a believer, not to belong, due to sin, marital difficulties or incapacity to get to Church, can be deeply wounding in a way nonbelievers might find hard to grasp. But where believing and belonging merge, the effects can be intense, again pointing to a combination of reflexivities between theology and sociology. Habits of belief relate to a biographical sense of journey, private intimations of grace difficult to articulate, yet not to be disowned because they are tacit.[5] The biography of the believer points to a career of affiliation, one where survival matters and where 'successes' are difficult to understand for outsiders. It could be the first sense of a prayer 'really' being answered; it could be affirmation through recognition of spiritual worth; or it could be the first witness to faith of a young person, where free from parents, teachers and clergy, a belief was expressed in his or her own terms. Theology makes its own demands for understanding its distinctive problematic, but it also has its own problems.

Louth has referred to the dissociation of sensibility between knowledge and understanding that haunts theology and that influences expectations of its use and significance. Prayer, worship and theological reflection are interconnected in a way that has recently become obscured. There is a reflexivity in theology, but one that relates to the cultivation of spiritual sensibilities and a notion of mystery and wonder in a searching for a truth that rises above the calculative and is beyond what belongs to the narrowly conceived social sciences.[6] This sense of engagement in a mystery of understanding points to a distinctive characteristic of theology, as an activity, that it seeks *interested* reflection and not disembodied analytical scrutiny. This point can be understood in relation to the use of icons, and their potential claims for their beholders. To contemplate the face of Christ in Rubliov's icon is to discern a profound spiritual experience in the gaze that is both deep and mysterious. A sensibility of the Divine is realised in the reflexive response to a window on heaven.[7]

Theological understandings are often best gained through contemplation. Thus, monks are advised to give themselves over 'assiduously, or rather continuously, to sacred reading, until continual meditation fills your heart, and fashions you so to speak after its own likeness'.[8] Theological reflection seeks an experience of the Divine, an intimation of presence that makes it something more than academic study, for properly understood it seeks to quicken the spirit to taste and see the intangible and the invisible in reflection on the living word. As an activity of the mind and heart, theology involves the self in a quest for spiritual understanding, contemplation and prayer in a chain that gives a wider significance to its reflexivity than sociology alone could yield.

Academic theology seems to have obscured the spiritual roots of its focus of study. The disjunction between theology and spiritual has had devastating consequences on the life of the Church, a separation which von Balthasar deplored.[9] For him, theology had to be related to the search for a sense of the experience of God. He asserted that 'it is only experience which allows us to understand the meaning of the text; to the unexperienced it means nothing'.[10] 'True theology', he suggested, 'begins only at the point where "exact historical science" passes over into the science of faith proper – a "science" which presupposes the act of faith as its locus of understanding'.[11] Theology is a conditional form of knowing, and this property of faith qualifies sociological interventions into its discourse in relation to culture.

But it could be argued that the reflexive nature of sociological bears a confessional quality that causes it to seek an engaged contemplative form of theology. After all, sociology is seeking a dialogue with theology from a spiritual aridness, one which emerges as values, ethics and morals form an increasingly central part of its agenda in dealings with culture. In seeking a definite difference, the prospect of spiritual enchantment, the last thing sociology wishes to couple with is a disembodied academic version of theology, grounded in a secular culture that represents everything the sociological mind wishes to escape from.

This begs a question as to what theology is and what is sociology seeking from it? Interrogating theology is a presumptuous sociological task, one that seems to have more to do with dispute than dialogue. The terms of reference between both are riddled with difficulties and misunderstandings. In a point that still applies, Mills, in his preface to the collection of essays, based on symposia held at Oxford, 1978–79, on the links between the two disciplines, stated that 'the most important point for the theologian to realize is that, in terms of *practical day-to-day working*, he and the sociologist are now further apart than they have ever been, but not because of disputes over God'.[12]

The most succinct expression of constructive hopes for the link between theology and sociology, that seems to express this effort to find a language of grace within postmodernity and culture, comes from the English Dominican, Timothy Radcliffe. He sees two contributions:

> first of all, the sociological exploration of the relationship between language and social structures can liberate the theologian from a false understanding of his own tradition. Second, the theologian should recognize that sociology is not merely explanatory. It is one valid way in which man attempts to make sense of himself and his experience. And so sociology can itself provide a locus for the encounter of gospel and world. This encounter would take place not through the theologian importing a particular 'theological perspective', but rather by the internal transformation of sociology itself.[13]

It is this internal transformation of sociology into a form of theology that governs this study. Clearly, the idea of sociology 'inventing' its own theology in the manner of feminism or ecology is preposterous. Such quasi-ecclesial ambitions can be dismissed in the light of the positivist efforts of Comte to found sociology in its own Church, one that would replace Catholicism.

Explicit efforts to link sociology to a belief in Christianity have come recently from Evangelical Protestants. The Christian origins of sociology are reclaimed for the kingdom from a strictly evangelical view, but one in which Catholicism is either marginalised or, more likely, ignored. An integrity of witness is sought in the blending of 'biblical truth' with sociology. The result is often a worthy, but unpersuasive intermingling of Christianity and sociology. A considerable number of theological shortcuts are made. For instance, one can accept the first line of the foreword of a recent American work, *Sociology Through the Eyes of Faith*, that 'sociology . . . is modernity struggling to come to self-understanding', but not the mishmash which follows. A fundamentalism in two chapters on God and culture and on 'learning to speak with a biblical accent' marks the theology of this work, which seems to jettison Catholicism from Christianity, to pretend that medieval thought never existed, and never quite tells us how faith can be deepened in seeking social understanding. One might be encouraged by the end of the book which speaks of 'The Christian Sociological Society' which includes hundreds of North American sociologists, which exists to 'give witness to Jesus Christ in sociological areas'.[14]

Relationships between theology and sociology are laden with mutual suspicion. If sociology goes too far into theology it loses its identity as a discipline. Likewise, some theologians think sociology is a profoundly unsafe intellectual neighbour to have any dealings with. Some sociologists occupy traditional theological positions difficult to characterise; others berate theologians for short-selling the sacred and the invisible in the interests of relevance; whilst others feel there is little difference between theology and sociology as both are dealing with the plight of the human condition in the context of a culture of postmodernity.

One of the few credible efforts to assimilate theology to sociological understandings, without misunderstanding its basis, has been accomplished by the Lutheran German sociologist Niklas Luhmann. His work is increasingly being translated and forms part of a prolific amount of sociological theory dealing with law, ecology, the professions and morality, to name a few areas. He is specifically concerned with a revised version of functionalism that operates in the context of systems and self-reference.

In a valuable overview of his significance, Green draws attention to a number of themes that bear on this study. Firstly, Luhmann, pointing to the social location of theology, is trying to formulate 'a new kind of theory independent of metaphysical and ontological presuppositions'.[15] Secondly, his formulations accept a notion of relativism, but like, Berger, he is also concerned with an issue of choice. Grounding theology in sociology is the beginning not the end of a sociological question. Thirdly, he suggests that religion functions to transform the indeterminable into the determinable, a sacramental function which can be found in other sociological writings, and particularly relates to an understanding of the basis of reproduction of liturgy.[16] The theology, or religious dogmatics, Luhmann is dealing with, serves as an antidote to the secularisation of society expressed in terms of

functional differentiation. This gives theology an autonomy which socio-
logy recognises in terms of its focus on dealing with the mysterious and
Divine. But this autonomy is granted on conditions of qualification, as
Luhmann regards faith as the personal precondition for the theologian.
The Christological basis of his effort to link sociology to theology needs
to be taken into account.

His approach to theology has to be understood in the context of self-
reference systems. These are distinctive closed networks that reproduce
and have specific means of dealing with paradox, differentiation and communication. Having to cope with its own paradoxes differentiates religion
from other fields. Religion has different degrees of sensibility that need to
be observed and described. Other activities function instead of religion,
but to a lesser degree of paradox. Different degrees of sensibility arise in
observing and describing religion. Thus, he suggests that 'it may become
the job of divine detectives to find out what can be observed and described
as referring to religion in the paradoxes of art and love, or sovereign
power, or making money or of recognising the conditions of cognition'.[17]
The admission of paradox to culture links theology to sociology but in a
way that secures the autonomy of the former against incursion by forces
of secularisation, which seek to imperialise and to dilute that which is
distinctive to religion. Like other sociologists, Luhmann feels progressive
and liberal theologians have sold their calling short.

In its endeavour to make theology relevant to the world, the cultural
trappings of reward and damnation in the next world have been marginalised
and treated as impediments to belief.[18] But in so veiling terrors of antinomies
between good and evil and lessening a sense of paradox to make for
credibility for the modern mind, matters have become incredible in theological terms for some sociologists for whom the need to make wagers to
the ultimate has been neutered. As Luhmann asks

> was it a good idea, this being perhaps the most important of all these
> semantical changes, to drop the notion of *Hell*, to renounce terror and
> fear in religion, to present it as pure love and thereby lose the distinction
> between salvation and damnation, the only binary schematism for the
> religious system?[19]

Given the disarray within contemporary sociology, it might wish to
believe in something definite that might be theological. Sociologists might
see in theology a risk of it secularising and becoming an imitation of their
discipline. This relates back to the earlier point of Weber, of sociology seeking to escape its endless analytical disputes into a safer more tranquil world
of theology. As Bauman suggests, sociology is internally ambiguous, 'a

schizophrenic discipline, organically dual, at war with itself'.[20] Yet in its wish to seek redemption from such internal strife, sociology might face hostile responses from theologians unwilling to receive such an imperialising discipline, however penitent. The relativising tendencies of sociology suggest an unsafe house guest for theologians to admit, one hardly pliant and grateful. In a point that could apply to relationships to theology, Bauman notes

> philosophy inspired by legislative reason left sociology a choice between the role of a handmaiden, keeping clean the analytical cutlery in the home of good knowledge owned by philosophers, or facing the prospect of dishonourable discharge without references.[21]

This worry over the safety of sociological interventions arises very much in Milbank's vast widely discussed *Theology and Social Theory*. A wealth of intellectual history is ingeniously used to reach an Augustinian vision of order, harmony and charity out of a secular chaos. In this journeying, theology is treated as a social science. In contradiction to the imperialising threats of sociology, a discipline treated as unsafe in dealing with secular thought, Milbank argues unequivocally that '*all* theology has to reconceive itself as a kind of "Christian sociology"'.[22] In the context of postmodernity, sociology has been abolished. Its capacity to explain and to reason has been tried and found wanting. The discipline has been sentenced for having over reached itself in sociology of religion, for having neglected its formative Catholic French incarnation, and for having deceived theologians with its fraudulent secularising. Prohibited from entering the field in its secular grandeur, a tame pious version, termed 'a Christian sociology' is given ticket of entry, under charity, to the suburbs of Milbank's vision of a *Civitas Dei*. Its duty is to tell a holy tale from the perspective of the society of its location.

His work is a tour de force and Roberts is correct to describe it as 'perhaps the most brilliant, ambitious – and yet questionable – work to have emerged in English theology since the Second World War'. Yet Roberts points to a paradox, that despite the warmth of its reception by English theologians, and having special issues of *New Blackfriars* and *Modern Theology* devoted to evaluating its significance, it has been virtually ignored by sociologists. Roberts feels this should arouse concern.[23]

The difficulty is that Milbank makes, with great intellectual persuasion, a false dichotomy between theology and sociology, dooming the latter to a functionalism, a concern with reason and explanation, which it is given no permission to deny and which is the basis of a hanging sentence. In this denial of the autonomy of sociology, but also the cultural permutations it

seeks to represent, a vacancy is left open for who is to explore those
elements which might lay siege to his reinvented *Civitas Dei*? A neutered
sociology is presented as a theological figment incapable of being released
to seek and find the enemies of charity and harmony. But his most important misunderstanding is his failure to realise that sociology has its own
theological reasons for fleeing secular reason. All Milbank has done is
tried to block its flight into theology and has misread the reasons for this
escape from the ambiguities of the culture that threaten to ensnare it in the
context of postmodernity. As Roberts suggests, realising the significance
of Bourdieu, Milbank fails to grasp the significance of a 'critical reflexivity, the capacity of the self to understand and depict the conditions
of production of its own knowledge'.[24] Such contextualisation returns
theology to a site, one where sociology does have something to say. A
catalogue of the history of ideas is no substitute for actual analysis of the
cultural circumstances within which theology reproduces its distinctive
form of knowledge.

With Milbank, the only option for the sociologist is to respectfully pass
on, as Bauman would say, discharged without references, except those it
can find elsewhere from other theologians on its pilgrim way. This involves journeying to other sites on the cultural way. But the seeking of
God through sociological instruments generates domestic disquiet over
methodological proprieties from within the discipline, from sources one
might have thought would be friendly. Strict demarcations between what
is proper to sociology, dealing in scientific evaluation of social connections, in verifiable and falsifiable statements, might affirm Martin's point
that 'a sociologist has no remit to talk about God. If he were to talk
directly about God, he would immediately convert himself into a theologian or a philosopher of history or a prophet'.[25] Likewise, Berger sees the
speaking of God as being beyond sociological remit. In Appendix II to
The Social Reality of Religion, Berger claims his work stands as an enterprise of sociological theorising in dealing with an issue of human projection. In a move that echoes his relativising the relativiser, in dealing with
Feurbach, the prospect of anthropology being collapsed into theology and
vica versa is noted. Dealing with empirical matters generates a methodological atheism, but Berger is using this notion in a defensive manner to
limit sociology from entering terrains in which it has no legitimate expertise. In short he is trying to keep wagers open.[26] Anyhow, as Gill argues,
theology and sociology have become intermingled as both disciplines face
a disciplinary uncertainty about demarcation lines. Their strands of concern have become intermingled.[27]

Sociologists have long argued that theology, as an academic activity, is implicated in sociology because of its social contextualisation. If theology deals in knowledge that is a product of social circumstance, it has to take into account the context of its production, otherwise it is engaged in the formulation of insights that are based on an illusion, the notion that by fiat these elements can be bracketed or expelled and that promulgations can be issued that are disembodied from a particular cultural nexus. Recognition of the contextualisation of theological reflection suggests that it is implicated in some form of sociological reflexivity. In the last analysis, man has to judge himself, but in so doing, he has to take all manner of circumstance into account if his wager is to be correct.[28]

To find a more familiar view of sociology and the issue of the secularisation of theology, one needs to turn to an early paper of Berger, delivered in 1966, when the issue of the death of God had crept into theological fashion and the realisation was dawning that Vatican II had opened up a vast new field of confusion. The point Milbank misses is that from early stages, sociologists such as Berger pointed to the unwitting secularisation liberal theology itself effected in its pursuit of pluralism and modernisation. The damage sociology might have done to religious belief, that makes it a scapegoat for secularisation, in Milbank's eyes, is as nothing to the internal demolition job accomplished by liberal and progressive theologians.

In this essay, Berger indicated that it does not occur to liberal theologians that those concepts to which they make appeal, embodied in secularisation, are themselves subject to processes of relativism. If the culture that forms the ground of belief for sociologists has become unsettled, a similar instability applies to liberal theologians who seek to open belief uncritically to what they perceive to be cultural imperatives. In dealing with this culture, sociology has become only too well aware of this process within postmodernity.

The cognitive validity which theologians granted to contemporary culture, that effected a pastoral process of modernisation, hence secularisation and dismantlement of sacerdotal bonds, that has had such fracturing effects three decades later, is untenable and has become more so in the context of postmodernity. With an uncanny inerrancy that admits few exceptions, many aspects of sociology and strands of philosophy are poised against the liberal agenda of theologians, not out of disciplinary spite, or rivalry, but because their claims to openness and tolerance in dealing with culture are based on an illusion. What is a solution to theology is the beginning of a sociological problematic one all the more apparent in the culture of postmodernity. Openness disguises agnosticism, pluralism veils indifference, and the pursuit of individual rights conceals fragmentation.

As Berger argued the movement that sought to secularise theology was

> emerging from a situation in which the traditional religious certitudes have become progressively less credible, not necessarily because modern man has some intrinsically superior access to the truth, but because he exists in a socio-cultural situation which itself undermines religious certitude.[29]

Because sociology is reflexive on matters of detail it often confronts a theology blind to the implications of what it enacts. Liberal theologians confuse rhetoric with analysis of consequences. Often these relate to trivial matters with significant consequences, which to the sociologist seem to uncouple boundaries and to undermine forms of representation and identity. Thus, the abolition of the Friday fast, female altar servers, the defence of the book of common prayer, matters which anthropologists and sociologists have descended on as signifying analytical matters of importance, elicit a scarcely veiled contempt from liberal theologians that these items could be of any cultural or social consequence. It is this arrogance of indifference that generates a sociological venom in dealing with liberal theologians. Liberal theologians do not think like sociologists. Conservatives and traditionalists do and they can relate to sociology. Unexpectedly, in matters of culture they think in its ways. They understand a sociological point that discarding apparently trivial aspects of religious belief and its social manifestation accelerates secularisation in an incremental manner, in consequence, increasing pluralism, fragmentation and indifference. As Berger notes

> the fierce opposition to concessions of even a minor sort among ultraorthodox elements in the religious institutions may thus be said to rest upon a rather sound sociological instinct, which is frequently absent in their more 'open-minded' opponents.[30]

Berger suggests that modernism posed a problem to Catholicism of a pandora's box of relativism that it has not been able to confront nor resolve. Theologians still do not understand this point, even thought second thoughts are now emerging about modernisation. The quest for modernisation has simply assimilated this relativising process to within theology.

Contrary to Milbank, sociology is a necessity if for no other reason than that it can account for the shifts in the sites of the production of theology itself. Theology is itself a victim of secularisation in its academic settings. This is reflected in its changing relationships and status with other disciplines. But as Dulles observes, if theology has been displaced from courses on religious phenomena by secular disciplines such as sociology and anthropology, then theologians might have to look to these disciplines to reverse the trend, to return belief back to issues of faith it cannot resolve.[31] One would agree that theology needs to reconstitute its tradition, to re-spiritualise itself, to re-build a culture of belief.[32]

Again this moves theology into an expectation of dealings with sociology. One can agree with Frei's comment that theology as a grammar of faith is closer to the social sciences, and to sociology in particular, than to philosophy. Frei sees Christianity as a a community with its own enduring structures, practices and institutions. Sociology is regarded as an agent that assists in its self-description.[33] But sociology can be an ambiguous agent. Returning theology to sociology risks rehabilitating Feurbach where belief is a projection of human needs from within culture. In dealing with modernity, sociology is the gatekeeper for theologians. As Berger suggested, today

> the sociological perspective constitutes the 'fiery brook' through which the theologian must pass – or, perhaps, more accurately, ought to pass. It is sociological thought, and most acutely the sociology of knowledge, that offers the specifically contemporary challenge to theology.[34]

Most sociologists would be demolished by the scholarly weight of patristics, biblical knowledge, and textual intimacy theologians bring to debate. But from this intimate scholarly knowledge has come a galaxy of ideological and cultural positions, all of which share one point – an innocence of sociological knowing, one which is slowly changing. When they impute to culture particular positions, which are sanctified, as in the case of feminism, ecology and liberation versions of theology, then sociology can respond, not so much in terms of relativising these stances, but of contextualising them and asking of the rules for such restrictive readings made outside their trade. This might involve pushing back theologians into the confines of their discipline, with sociology drawing the boundaries from outside the pale, but it does draw attention to the cerebral way theologians impute to culture readings removed from sociological accountability for understanding transactions in context of enactment. But who are these theologians and what is their cultural setting?

Theologians work from a bewildering variety of contexts of production. English Catholic theologians tend to operate outside secular academic theology, being in seminaries, or working with monastic orders. Non-Catholic theologians usually work within departments of theology and religious studies in the secular universities. Some combine pastoral duties with a considerable amount of theological writing. This variety of settings makes generalisations about theologians and their cultural circumstances difficult. For sociologists, academic theology is difficult to define. In a recent exchange between two Oxford professors, Richard Dawkin, who felt rightly that theology should not be taught in universities and Keith Ward who disagreed, a notion of academic theology emerged. Ward presented it as the academic study of texts, the history, sociology and psychology of religious traditions, which lent it a comparative disinterested aspect. To Hugh Montefiore, this presented an image of the study of religion, without reference to theology or indeed revelation.[35]

There is considerable worry about the way academic theology has become detached from spirituality and formation and has become too lodged in secular culture and thought. In so capitulating, it is felt that theology has compromised its identity as a discipline based on faith seeking to understand God. These worries are by no means confined to supposedly reactionary Catholics. The Anglican theologian Alister McGrath sees a lost generation in the 1990s coping with the wreckage left by the liberal theologians of the 1960s, who grounded their theology in the culture of the period. A sense of transcendence was lost and in the theological vacuum, where many theologians lost their credibility, New Age movements arose to fill the space.[36] A high price was paid for this cultural accommodation that was tied into a notion of theological credibility. Theology became a stalking horse for legitimising secular fashions and in the process lost its capacity to innovate and to lead. McGrath suggests liberal theology has become the addresser rather than the addressee of secular culture.[37] In the present climate of post-liberalism, McGrath is seeking a theology much in the mode of Lindbeck[38] that bases its 'theological programme upon a return to religious traditions, whose values are inwardly appropriated'.[39] Post-liberal theology accepts that it is socially mediated. It is an unusual example of a theology in search of a sociology to assist in the rehabilitation of belief.

In seeking to restore the initiative to theology in dealing with Western secular culture, McGrath argues that academic theology is too far disembodied from experience and ecclesial accountability. It is even more removed from pastoral practice, from communities of nurture, which operate on the interface with secular culture. The professionalisation of the discipline of theology has failed and with it the notion that it 'should be an academically neutral discipline conducted in isolation from the church'.[40]

This sense of being assimilated into academic culture, but also of being lost within it, has been caught by David Lodge, an astute observer of English Catholicism. In *Paradise News*, Bernard Walsh, teaches theology at a College founded to train Free Church ministers. It provided a sort of religious supermarket, within which Bernard, a sceptical theologian, could find employment. It offered courses on

> phenomenology and faith, situational ethics, the theory and practice of charism, early Christian heresies, feminist theology, black theology, negative theology, hermeneutics, homiletics, church management, ecclesiastical architecture, sacred dance, and many other things.

Reflecting on the complexities of process theology, Bernard wondered who cared, for it seemed to him that

> the discourse of much modern radical theology was just as implausible and unfounded as the orthodoxy it had displaced, but nobody had noticed because nobody read it except those with a professional stake in its continuation.[41]

Some understanding of theology and its genesis is necessary, however arbitrary and sketchy it might be, for this study to proceed. Following Anselm, who refines the insights of Augustine, one can suggest that theology is faith seeking understanding. It is both an academic discipline and a way of life, where reason and revelation are intermingled with grace that gives a capacity to discern the relationship of God to man in any culture. It provides a history of religious belief, of changes in creedal formulations, ecclesial life and strife, the nature of doctrine, eschatology and theodicy. In short, theology is a body of knowledge operating under ecclesial authority and revelation that is available as a resource to be mobilised for characterising and understanding present mysterious relationships to God. Theology affirms a mystery, within a deposit of tradition and assent, which, with faith and grace, can be discerned in the passing fields of culture.

In the light of earlier comments, Aquinas offers some solace to sociologists in the foreword to his dialogue on Christian theology when he observed that

> we have considered how newcomers to this teaching are greatly hindered by various writings on the subject, partly because of the swarm of pointless questions, articles and arguments, partly because essential information is given according to the requirements of textual commentary or the occasions of academic debate, not to a sound educational method, partly because repetitiousness has bred boredom and muddle in their thinking.[42]

Aquinas deals with theology in terms of a capacity to reason that moves beyond limits in faith. His theology reflects a capacity to engage with sympathy, through grace, the notion of a provident God. This 'divine

science' embodies theoretical and practical qualities. Because its aim is
eternal happiness, it excels all other sciences. Apart from dealing with
matters of ultimate concern, theology has a task of witness, of making
explicit what is contained in the deposit of faith so as to be able to defend
and to recommend interpretations of truth to half-believers and nonbelievers. Decipherment is another task of theology, for 'Holy Scripture
fittingly delivers divine and spiritual realities under bodily guises'. Dealing in metaphors is a necessary aspect of theological reflection. Aquinas
suggests that metaphors permit transference of ideas between places (and
presumably also forms of thought). This requires reason and discernment
as skills of the theologian, the former coming from training and the latter
from grace and prayer. Hidden dimensions to belief fulfil a protective
function, of putting an onus on the theologian to search for meanings in
the world which can be made manifest.[43]

Efforts to respond to revelation lead also to the cultivation of theological virtues. These virtues surpass the nature of man by enabling him to
partake in the Divine. Leaving aside the issue of precedence, charity, faith
and hope are the main theological virtues, properties that denote a relationship to the Divine. Aquinas suggests that

> faith and hope imply an element of imperfection, since faith is of things
> unseen, and hope of things not yet possessed. Hence to have faith and
> hope regarding things within human competence falls short of the na-
> ture of virtue. Yet faith and hope in things beyond our powers surpass
> all virtue that is in proportion to human nature. 1 *Corinthians* is to the
> point, *the weakness of God is stronger than men.*[44]

Aquinas treats the issue of religion separately in a manner that provides
a useful antidote to reductionist accounts in sociology or religious studies.
His approach to religion forms part of a wider theological tradition. Within
it, in the necessity of re-doing and re-reading, can be found a notion of
reflection, theological in intention, but bearing on and bound into sociological notions of reflexivity.

Religion is a moral and a theological virtue denoting the worship of
God. It signifies an ordering of a relationship to God, an arrangement that
needs to be re-made. There is a sacramental quality to this act of rearranging and re-doing, itself a form of grace. Thus, the social shape of a
rite embodies a property of grace conferred on those who act in adoration,
such as the priest, the servers, the choir and the congregation who are the
worshipping community. For Aquinas, the term 'religious' has a restricted
use, referring to those 'who dedicate their whole life to divine worship by
withdrawing from human affairs'.[45] In this setting, religious images serve

to draw man to God 'by means of the sensible world, since *the hidden things of God are manifested by those things that are made'*. External and internal actions are needed to worship God, thus

> in divine worship the use of corporeal things is necessary so that by using signs, man's mind may be aroused to the spiritual acts which join him to God. Therefore, the internal acts of religion are principal and essential, while the exterior acts are secondary and subordinate to the internal acts.[46]

The ritual transactions embodied in worship, the material resources used and the images so generated, serve only one purpose, to arouse a sense of God in the act and to enable the actor to be available, to be sensible of the possibility of a Divine response. Thus, for Aquinas, religion and sanctity are interlinked in a search for purity. Man, the temple and sacred things are said to be sanctified if they are devoted to divine worship. They should have no other purpose, and, indeed, they are useless for any other task. Thus in worship, 'the bodily signs of humility which we perform increase our desire of submitting ourselves to God, because we naturally proceed from things of sense to things of mind'.[47] Through sensible signs, man is urged to seek God. These insights, that link action to spiritual responsibilities, religion to theology, point to a fine line that unites a sociological reflexivity with a theological mode of reflection essential to its nature of faith seeking understanding. It also relates to a property of culture, of enchantment achieved through the cultivation of disposition located in Bourdieu's habitus, where an elective affinity can be wagered in a social transaction geared to yield the holy.

The issue of disposition, to utilise what belongs to religion and to harmonise it with matters proper to theology can relate to sociological considerations. Dispositions necessitate a selectivity in the use of culture, a wish to link action to sensibility of a self open to change. But in so changing, there is the risk that the disposition might be misguided. Certifying a disposition as reliable and true belongs to the judgement of ecclesial authority, but also to a question of conscience, which sociology might have no grounds to question, it being beyond its remit. This being the case, sociology has to defer to a theological context of argument and to use ecclesial definitions and the official expectations of authority that govern their activities. In *Veritatis Splendor*, theologians are charged with using reason in relation to revelation within two settings, that of the Church and that of the world. In a comment, progressives and liberals misunderstand, but which sociologists do understand, the moral theologian must therefore exercise careful discernment in the context of today's prevalently scientific and technical culture, exposed as it is to the dangers of relativism, pragmatism and positivism.[48]

Reflecting on the twentieth anniversary of the foundation of *Communio*, Ratzinger referred to the distortions to the truth in the supposed name of the spirit of Vatican II where people 'were sold goods from the old liberal flea market as if they were new Catholic theology'.[49] Oddly, Nichols notes that Vatican II had little to say on the role of theologians, and the crisis over their contribution to Catholic thought, which only became apparent later.[50] There are deep divisions between progressive and traditional theologians. Deploring the former, Lamb notes the activities of some 'Catholic theologians who simply cannot tell the difference between doctrinal differentiations and a process of hellenizing the Christian faith'.[51] Unlike, other academics, theologians operate under the ambit of an ecclesial authority, that gives them an aura of credibility in their pronouncements but at the same time they claim a right to roam free without accountability. Apart from reference to the credibility of their arguments in matters of theology and culture, sociologists face an acute problem of redress. What are these theologians accountable to in their pronouncements?

In the *Instruction on the Ecclesial Vocation of the Theologian*, his central task is defined in terms of seeking reasons for faith, communicating these and understanding the meaning of revelation. This 'commitment to theology, its distinctive vocation, requires a spiritual effort to grow in virtue and holiness'. More significantly, the instruction asserts that

> a consultation of the 'human sciences' is also necessary to understand better the revealed truth about man and the moral norms for his conduct, setting these in relation to the sound findings of such sciences. It is the theologian's task in this perspective to draw from the surrounding culture those elements which will allow him better to illumine one or other aspect of the mysteries of faith. This is certainly an arduous task that has its risks, but it is legitimate in itself and should be encouraged.[52]

The reference to risks in the light of later concerns with the term in a culture of postmodernity is of interest.

Theology has always had an ambiguous relationship to culture. It has a career of continual dispute and engagement with culture. Its advance into surrounding culture in the first four centuries of Christianity was based on unfashionable and untenable values, at least in worldly terms, of ascetics, virginity, and the folly of the cross, *the* scandal to the pagans as Paul observed. Christianity was founded in hostile circumstances of having to deal with the alien assumptions of a sophisticated Greek and Roman culture. It had to read the times, but in a way that somehow misread them. It has always tried to refine and to purify a fallen culture. The Benedictine monastic contribution and the missionary activities of the Irish between 400–1100 in civilising European culture are familiar. There has always been a tension between the centre and the periphery over liturgical matters, over custom, accommodation and representation as in the controversy in the eighteenth century over Chinese rites. This tension between culture and theological formulations bound into tradition is endemic in Church history. If theology has always had mixed feelings about culture, what has changed in the mid-twentieth century that suggests the need to make reference to sociology?

What has changed is the self-understanding of theology itself in relation to culture. Modern culture has changed expectations of theology, its form and its task. As Wicker observed in 1963, the incarnation of Christ within the world is related to issues of the quality of social and political relationship. But these aspects of manifestation in culture are tied in to questions of reception and recognition that pose a theological problem which Wicker sees as relating to an issue of effectiveness. The terms mission and credibility might be added. Wicker suggests that

> the struggle to create a Christian society is simply the struggle to make the presentation, to society at large, of the mystery of Christ, by the 'community of the faithful', adequate in a particular place and time.[53]

The need to modernise, to accord with contemporary social sentiment, but at the same time, to protect belief and doctrine from the corrosive effects of the Enlightenment, left theology divided against itself. If it did not modernise, its message would pass ungrasped and unnoticed; but if it did modernise, there was the risk of abandoning or corrupting the tradition upon which belief was formulated and founded. Modernism, the effort to adapt the Church's teaching to the world, denoted an effort to accommodate, that was marked as heretical in 1907, but seems to have been assimilated and endorsed in Vatican II. Since then, has followed a crisis of legitimacy and authority which has bedevilled relationships between theology and culture. The terms of reference have never been properly understood, as realisation dawns as to how inchoate were the initial efforts of Vatican II.

The difficulties sociology experiences in handling theology's dealings with culture are exemplified in *Gaudium et Spes*, 1965. It expressed the need to engage, to evangelise in an opening to the world, as far as possible unrestricted by tradition, but bound by revelation. Ecclesial structures were to be opened in culture so that no impediments existed in the spread of the Good News to a world that could only want to hear it. There was a self-evident property to the connection between renewal and modernisation that gave it a fated logic, that suggested its progress was inevitable and that theology was subservient to progressive readings of the spirit of the times, if it were to survive. But this posed a difficulty for sociology, and a division with theology over the issue of self-fulfilling prophecy in matters of progress, over whether the outcome reflected the will of God or was it a mechanism of cultural reproduction that was unscrutinised and which could be given a different reading? It was not an issue of authority but one of credibility. How authentic were these theological readings of culture that made no use of sociological insights?

With Vatican II, the Church dramatically changed its relationship to the world, placing its mission firmly in a modern context. Instead of the Church appearing to condemn the world, to be entrenched in a ghetto, theological rhetoric changed this relationship to affirm tolerance, dignity and modern values.

Unfortunately, and for understandable reasons, the document never formulated the terms of this dialogue in a way that would permit a socio-logical intervention. As indicated later, the issue of culture only became of central consideration for theology and sociology two decades later. Anyhow, the document was pastoral rather than analytical. It sought to affirm and to recognise modern culture in terms of a mutual benefit be-tween it and the Church. Chapter II, on the proper development of culture, gave a liberal theological reading of its basis. The section on difficulties and duties indicates some of the questioning felt over deciphering modern culture.[54] Harmony and rights, dialogue and tolerance in the context of pluralism were affirmed. The issue of culture was only part of a wider concern with economics, family, work, war and peace. In its sections on pastoral care, the document noted that beside theological principles, the findings of the secular sciences, especially psychology and sociology were to be used.[55] At this stage, sociology was an ingredient in the dialogue with culture. Its role was pastoral, descriptive and analytical of ecclesial consequences.

The document set in train some misunderstandings, fatal in any other organisation. Few of those who wrote the document could have realised the revolution in culture that occurred in its period of reception between 1965–8 and the ecclesial instability that followed. In a manner difficult to reverse, curiosity had been taken out of Catholicism. It has lost its social magic to more profane rivals, who offer instant idealism and the prospects of self-actualisation through idols of silver and gold and other commodities best not named. Catholicism became ungripping. The countries that tried to pioneer what was termed the Spirit of Vatican II, such as Holland, France and parts of Germany, experienced a remarkable fall in ecclesial influence, attendance and strength in the decades which followed. *Gaudium et Spes* exemplified a fault in the assumptions of the Council as these related to the means of deciphering the signs of the times. Its tragedy was that it sought to address culture without nurturing sociological instruments to arbitrate on its distinctions, those intended and those unintended that had theological implications.

But most importantly, the document launched an unanswerable sociological question without realising it. In seeking dialogue, it placed theological discourse itself under the rules of a sociology of knowledge. The contextualisation of theology and its siting within culture beg questions about the assumptions used to define its basis of reproduction. The more theology penetrates into culture the more it becomes immersed in sociological forms of knowing. A reflexivity follows of implications and unintended consequences. This has arisen especially in liturgy, in debates after Vatican II. Issues of bureaucratisation arose in relation to the translation of texts in the case of ICEL products in the early seventies. The purpose of the vernacular, of enchanting understandings of liturgical language became subject to sentiments of disenchantment at the bureaucratic products of a liturgical committee seeking Anglo-American forms of standardisation. The language of the rite permits a recontextualisation into the frame of sociology itself, thus begging questions about the authority and accountability of ritual experts, those who reflect on rites on behalf of a laity.[56] Newman's idea of consulting the laity and his notion of reception take on markedly different properties in an era of sociological expectation. He could never have envisaged the potential sociological agenda to consulting the faithful, the bureaucracy, the cultural rights, and the typicality of delegates that this process would involve. Again, the idea might resolve a theological dilemma, but it generates enormous difficulties for sociology, for consultation presupposes an authentic notion of culture upon which to base the notion of reception. As sociology is used more and more, it comes to constitute the culture theology seek to discern.

Gaudium et Spes offered an uncritical, philosophically based endorsement of a culture that concealed its more nefarious aspects. Understandings of culture became darker and more threatening after 1965. Ambiguity rather than clarity entered sociological understandings. The problem sociology faces in retrospect in dealing with *Gaudium et Spes* is that it failed to give sufficient attention to the tragic aspects of culture it had so optimistically endorsed. It had ground a theological solution down into a sociological problem. This denied sociology the relief of an exit point, a theology that was fitting for what sociologists conceived was the tragedy of culture, which Simmel had uncovered a century ago. A dialogue with science and the Enlightenment, where the fear and suspicion of the past 400 years were overturned, seems misplaced when almost two decades later the crisis of disbelief in these has come to pass in the debate on postmodernism.[57] Catholicism started to assimilate understandings of the Enlightenment, the need for reason and modernisation, just at the point when sociology moved into a post-Enlightenment era. Thus, as Lane notes, it is ironical that

> at the very moment in history when the Catholic Church is reaching to embrace the culture of modernity with all its promises, we are discovering at the same time that there is a dark menacing side to modernity.[58]

But this has not been the only 'near miss', where theologians failed to grasp the significance of how they *might* think in fruitful terms within contemporary culture. In 1973, the Anglican theologian, Urban Holmes, noticed a 'near miss' between a turning point in the anthropology of religion, its discovery of the significance of ritual and symbol in terms of understanding and the liturgical breakthrough of Vatican II, which came a decade too early.[59]

There are signs of reconsiderations about that suggest a near miss between theology and postmodernity is less definite than might be assumed. It is on the more 'conservative' wing of theology, centred around the journal *Communio* which reflects current papal thought, that the implications of postmodernity are being understood and rapidly assimilated. Certainly, a decade after *Gaudium et Spes*, changes in rhetoric were abroad as a revisioning of its basis was occurring. As Hollis notes, what Paul VI saw as 'the drama of our time', the divergence between Christian faith and contemporary culture, is perhaps better described as a form of tragedy.[60] But from a sociological perspective, the tragedy lay in what theologians could not discern in culture that effected the reproduction of faith. The problems were half understood because no sociological dimension to theology for dealing with culture was envisaged.

If postmodernity is about a condition of ambiguity, then it could be said that within *Gaudium et Spes* there was a nascent recognition of this point. Thus, Lambert draws attention to the ambivalence the Church becomes witness to in the modern world where choice is a necessary imperative. Thus he argues 'every secular value, no matter how authentic ontologically, is always ambivalent when we confront it in man himself, as a divided being, an enigma to himself'.[61] The introduction to *Gaudium et Spes* points to the ambiguity of man's freedom, that which constitutes the modern dilemma, that 'man is growing conscious that the forces he has unleashed are in his own hands and that it is up to him to control them or be enslaved by them'.[62] This bleak approach to culture, discernible in *Gaudium et Spes* and amplified by Paul VI, has come to characterise the distinctive concerns of the papacy of John Paul II. He is concerned with the issue of spirituality within a culture that has a self-destructive relationship to materialism. Holland notes that for John Paul II 'modern culture is revealing itself as a mechanistic civilization of Faustian destruction'. The self is increasing a victim of cultural seduction into a consumer ideology. In short, in a terminology which could be from a critical theorist, John Paul II, in Holland's words, sees Western societies as fabricating 'a shallow, plastic, even destructive culture of manipulative instrumentalization, whose artifacts it then hedonistically worships'.[63] Few sociologists influenced by critical theory would disagree with this comment.

Contrary to his apparently conservative teaching on sexual ethics, and on doctrine, such as the ordination of women, John Paul II steers debate far more in a radical direction than many might realise. Certainly, he seems attuned to sociological resonances in his pronouncements in a manner unequalled by any other pope. Thus, Baum notes the way the pope has criticised forms of commodification operating in a culture dominated by consumerism.[64] Religious urges, if not steered in the direction of God, make money and consumer values idols to be fought over in the marketplace.

In his address to the first meeting of the Pontifical Council for Culture, in January 1983, John Paul II noted that Vatican II committed

> the whole Church *to listen to modern man* in order to understand him and to invent a new kind of dialogue which would permit the originality of the Gospel message to be carried to the heart of contemporary mentalities.[65]

In a concluding reflection to his edited work on the Church and culture, Gremillion claimed that 'culture will become a core concern of ecclesial consciousness, scholarship and ministry for the 1990s and beyond – within the Church in general, not only among theologians'.[66] Certainly, there has been an important change in the self-understanding of theology. For example, in his entry in the supplement to the *New Catholic Encyclopedia*, Hill felt that, as a discipline, theology, like faith, 'has entered a period of crisis in which negatively its own identity is called into question and positively it faces the challenge of creative renewal'. He goes on to add that 'the approach to God has shifted from the objectivity of the cosmos, to an anthropocentric emphasis upon the immanence of thought and thence to radical historicality and *praxis*'.[67]

In his encyclical, *Centesimus Annus*, 1991, a reflection on the centenary of *Rerum Novarum*, John Paul II dealt widely with issues of the economic and political order in a critique of capitalism and socialism. Important as these elements are, it is Chapters 5 and 6 on state and culture and 'man is the way of the Church' that are most germane to this study. Familiar warnings on the commodification of the individual, a denial of his transcendence, mix with an interest in changes in 'established life-styles'.[68] This elusive comment is given a more direct focus, one that recognises sociological interests in Chapter 6. The place of man in 'the complex network of relationships within modern societies' is linked to the help offered by the human sciences and philosophy in interpreting the properties that constitute a 'social being'. The tasks of clarification differ between sociology and theology for the Church is concerned with assisting man on the path to salvation and with witnessing to man's full identity realised within faith. This shift into an interest in interdisciplinary dialogue marks an important recognition of the context in which man, as actor, operates. Thus the Church's social teaching

> assimilates what these disciplines have to contribute, and helps them to open themselves to a broader horizon, aimed at serving the individual person who is acknowledged and loved in the fullness of his or her vocation.[69]

This clarification of an enabling relationship between theology and sociology represents a significant rehabilitation of the latter, when Comte was placed on the Index in 1864. It also gives expression to a concern of this study, of an understanding of the site of reflexivity, the field within which the actor operates within a culture of postmodernity. Before moving to the issue of sociology's domestic relationship to religious belief and its own understanding of culture, some attention needs to be given to theology's own cultural understandings and that opaque term 'inculturation'. From this one can move to the issue of the cultural field theology operates within.

Apart from Michael Hornsby-Smith's important series of studies of English Catholicism, few major works come to mind that should force British theologians to attend to what the sociologists have to say.[70] Certainly, there are no equivalent studies to Potel's *L'Église Catholique en France. Approches Sociologique*, 1994, which draws from a wealth of research publications of high calibre.[71] The absence of a sociological dimension to theology in English society is itself a sociological question. A vast amount of self-monitoring needs to be undertaken in English Catholicism, which is prereflexive in its attitudes to sociology and in consequence, is incapable of authentically monitoring its current position within the society it operates.

Up to recently, the issue of culture related to a theological ambition expressed in the term inculturation. This term recognised a pastoral necessity of integrating the Church into the local culture of the people and of transforming and infusing them with the Gospel message. Inculturation recognises the necessity of an open and nonjudgemental approach to contextualisation and a sensitivity to local cultural needs. Principles of liberation and pluralism are embodied in the term which arose in a missionary context in dealings with non-European cultures. The term, originally conceived in 1979 by the John Paul II, was refined in the mid-eighties, but seems out of favour if the new Catholic Catechism is any indication of changes in theological position.[72]

The genesis of the term inculturation is itself a sociological issue. Inculturation seeks to represent the culture surrounding local churches in the Gospel message. This sanctification of indigenous cultural practices is deemed to facilitate reception of the Word of God. Inculturation also seeks to ameliorate the impact of a European ecclesial cultural ethos and its potentially alienating image in local cultures. The term denotes the admission of contextualisation of culture into theological reflection and a recognition of indigenous forms and styles of representation in worship. Assimilation through the symbols and customs of a people points to a sensitivity in accommodation to the Christian message. Inculturation is a post-colonial term that tries to establish a place for the local church and its distinctive cultural self-understandings within the Universal Church whilst at the same time apologising for the arrogance of a colonialism that was linked to more traditional forms of missionary work. But Collet argues that this can be equally patronising, for advocates of the term, often European missionaries, concerned with liberation theology, seem to speak on behalf of local communities in a way that obscures their indigenous voice. He feels that 'inculturation cannot succeed without repentance in the sense of a radical renunciation of knowing better and asserting oneself, with the sole aim of reproducing one's own previous identity'. In his comments, a virtual acceptance of an uncritical contextuality is admitted that would be untenable in contemporary anthropology.[73] There are sociological ambitions in the notion of inculturation that are defeated by sociology's own understandings of dealing with culture.

There is an inescapable call to judgement in the term inculturation. Webster suggests that the post-liberal theologian will develop a 'descriptive or catechetical role as the skilled grammarian of community usage', but he then goes on to add that this can lead to the loss of 'a lively self-critical awareness of its own limits and of what lies outside them'.[74] Inculturation risks institutionalising the marginality of the local church and condemning it to theological life on the edge of ecclesial culture.

There are some similarities between Catholicism and sociology in their approach to culture in the 1970s. For both, the issue of culture arose on the margins, from Third World countries (or elementary societies). Neither dealt with culture directly within a European context. This reflected custom and disciplinary demarcation. For sociology, the study of culture belonged to ethnography and anthropology. The legacy Simmel left to sociology of a concern with culture and modernity, was only begun to be understood in Britain in the late 1970s as his works were being translated most notably by David Frisby. For theology, culture belonged either to histories of civilisation or to abstract anthropological notions of man. Anthropological studies linked both disciplines together into a realisation of the complexities of culture, but in Third World societies.

Practical problems in fieldwork, either missionary or anthropological, exposed the complexity of dealing with small scale alien cultures, of either converting or of analysing them. For Catholicism, the issue arose from missionary work, from the task of translating faith into context, to plant it on alien soil. Contextualisation was related to rights, not to difficulties of analysis. Anthropology and in turn sociology, faced equal problems of translation, but not of planting an alien belief system, but of translating indigenous practices that were estranging into Western notions of commonsense. For these fieldworkers, contextualisation generated an agnosticism that pointed less to an ethic of non-judgement in the interests of sensitivity than to an irresolvable set of puzzles over incommensurable meanings that straddled the inquirer and his object of inquiry, leading anthropology, and sociology by default, into a hermeneutic circle. The agnosticism which inculturation raised for theologians was voluntary, a property proclaimed as a virtue, but involuntary for sociologists and anthropologists, a vice, a trap of misunderstandings in disciplines that should seek otherwise. Delivering alien messages in foreign fields forced theologians to reflect on culture. For sociologists, the issues raised in the rationality and relativity debate, about deciphering practices at odds with disciplinary Western scientific assumptions, effected an unsettlement, an uncertainty, over translation. But this puzzle about dealing with the cultural fringe, with its alien assumptions, disguised theological and sociological failures of confronting their own domestic European cultures and the issue of their characterisation. Both ignored the issue of what it meant to contextualise within a

European society, but also the question of what each discipline was to say about culture in the context of contextualisation. For different reasons, both disciplines came to their domestic cultures from a position of weakness. For theology, this stemmed from a secularisation accelerated by efforts to modernise, and for sociology, an uncertain tradition in relation to academic culture, combined with a fragmentation in disciplinary effort signified by the growing, but reluctant, recognition of the import of the term postmodernity.

A crucial weakness of inculturation is that in its resistance to judgement it postpones the issue as to which culture it wishes to affirm and to sanctify. A homogeneity of cultural style is assumed, but this holistic notion collapses in the face of rival claims to define. In a culture of postmodernity, there is an anarchy of definition. The notion of inculturation 'works' when the definition of culture is uncontested and unproblematic. The endemic vagueness of the term also masks its equivocal relationship to Western culture and simply begs questions. As Baum astutely asks, 'if Catholicism itself is a culture, how can it be "inculturated" in the diverse cultural traditions of the world? Furthermore, the issue of inculturation in Third World countries distracts attention from a crucial point that 'Catholicism as an ecclesiastical culture has not been able to incarnate itself in the modern, Western democracies'.[75] This shifts the ground of the argument. It leads back to the issue of the degree to which Catholicism, with its rich heritage of tradition, in European terms, is a culture itself, but one apparently disembodied from the society within which it operates.

There is a subtle movement in the new Catholic Catechism in its dealings with the term inculturation. Treated in the context of the mission of the Church, inculturation refers to a process whereby the Gospel takes 'flesh in each people's culture'.[76] Significantly, the term is not used in the section in the Catechism on the relationship between liturgy and culture. It is suggested that the celebration of the liturgy 'should correspond to the genius and culture of different peoples'.[77] A criteria of transformation is inserted into notions of culture that begs a question of judgement, if the notion of correspondence is amplified in terms of consequences and tradition. If correspondence is too closely sought, so that voluntarism, democracy and popular sentiment become the criteria for engagement, then bad taste, de-ritualization and a mendacious populism can follow, where the liturgical form comes to reflect the worst of tastes.[78] But the issue of correspondence carries echoes of relativism, of an ambiguity, which liberal exponents of inculturation scarcely conceived. It places the issue of culture in two contexts, ecclesial and secular and asks for a judgement of effect that echoes problems of hermeneutics. Contextualisation might seem a pastoral solution, but for sociology it opens up a range of problems of judgement, distinction and taste. If one argues that inculturation should reflect recognition of a fullness of cultural ability, then in the English context matters become Gothic, for as Pugin found, this style expresses a genius of a people, as did the Sarum Rite for ceremonial finesse. If culture relates to skills of sensibility, then an excellence is signified in these movements of tradition. But this is not what the advocates of inculturation had in mind. A democratic principle is embodied in their assumptions, which begs questions as to what they define as culture, apart from the relationship between the centre and fringe.

Clearly, the term inculturation is remarkably undertheorised. Lamb has speculated recently on the application of inculturation to American domestic circumstances. He wishes to resolve the dilemma of how to inculturate the Catholic faith in an American culture, which is as alien as any missionary field that necessitated the conception of the term. Lamb is concerned with a post-Enlightenment culture which has lost its institutional quest for wisdom. In an emptying culture, increasingly fragmented, Lamb sees theology as having a transformative task, a healing duty that involves the restoration of a sense of community. A rebuilding of institutions to secure a sense of vision is required especially in universities and seminaries.[79]

Various responses to the culture of postmodernity are open to theology, from seeking to escape its nihilistic qualities, to endorsing its basis. The latter strategy is sought in Matthew Fox's press release, on abandoning Catholicism for Anglicanism, where he notes with approval English young people who are reinventing forms of Christian worship through rave music, dance, techno-art and electronic music. He hopes such a movement will contribute substantially to 'an awakening and renewal in our culture and it is fitting that the young lead in such a resurrection from the modern to the post-modern age'.[80]

The questions generated by postmodernity require reference to theorists who dealt with modernity and civilisation in the earlier part of the twentieth century. Unfortunately, many of these thinkers, such as Christopher Dawson, were well aware of the precariousness of the link between religion and culture. They sought to rethink firmer foundations in medieval culture, in notions of civilisation and progress that gave reverence to continuities with tradition. The ground was cut under their feet with Vatican II. They became marked as traditionalists, who sought to warn about the rush to modernise and to renew. Dawson was deeply attached to the old Roman mass and found in latin an effective means of reversing the curse of Babel, which the introduction of the vernacular was about to resurrect.[81]

In seeking to accommodate to contemporary cultural circumstances and to reinvent a new definition of the past in relation to its liturgy and ecclesial form of culture, English Catholicism in the wake of Vatican II discounted its immediate tradition, the nascent efforts of Romanticism to cope with modernity through the neo-Gothic movements. These efforts reflected a deeper more imaginative form of response to cultural change that fought modern culture on a terrain it could not handle. By appealing to manifestations of the medieval, to the hidden language of its symbols and rituals, a powerful antidote was available to cope with the emptying of culture. In denying its immediate past, that of the Victorian era, Catholicism between 1960–90 became present bound and disembodied from its own tradition. This accentuated another tradition, of Catholics being strangers in the land. The Reformation was the civil means of their ejection from medieval culture and Vatican II blessed the notion that it was irrelevant. Catholics could wander around medieval Cathedrals as tourists to gaze at buildings which now belonged to the State Church. For them, the ecclesial past is increasingly a foreign country and cultural memory of belief relates to issues best not confronted.[82]

For the present younger generation, the excitement of the Council is now part of history. They are now indifferent to the boundaries the Council overturned, not least, because they live in an ecclesial wasteland, where traditional beliefs are also history. If they return to tradition, it is now to reinvent, to use the past again as a source of innovation, as a form of resistance to modernity, a strategy postmodernity signifies. The issue now is how to re-think theology in the context of culture, but in a markedly different way to what went before.

In a deceptively entitled work, *Introductory Theology*, two professors from the Gregorian University in Rome point to issues that relate to concerns at the beginning of the chapter. They suggest that liturgy has a quality of self-implication (which would relate to earlier considerations of sociological reflexivity).[83] Community is the real subject of their theological hermeneutics.[84] This notion carries a quality of accountability, but also a self-consciousness of the implications of belief, of what it means to assent in faith in the context of a contemporary culture which suggests otherwise. Thus, they argue that 'the task of theology is to deepen the understanding of faith for the people who must live it today'.[85] To accomplish this task, theology needs a 'body', a form of thought, a mentality within which the Word of God must be read, proclaimed and applied. But theology is now dealing in a culture where a 'profane reality' dominates. Theology also faces a crisis of synthesis of its subdivisions. No longer is theology 'the soul of a culture of fascinating unity'.[86] This fall into disunity of knowing can be understood by reference to the postmodernism of Lyotard, but it also relates to the marginalisation of theology within contemporary culture signified by the notion of the term secularisation. Understanding this shift belongs to the history of ideas.[87] But it also relates to the movement of theological matters into the ambit of sociological reflexivity, which some theologians now recognise. Thus, Alszeghy and Flick accept that an ecclesial culture which forms a visible community is subject to the laws of sociology. They argue that it is an absurdity to suggest that a community movement with such a history does not have some forms of socialisation, processes of typification of experiences, facts and persons, modes of constitution of roles and processes of legitimation.[88] But how far does theology have to move into sociological expectations before it becomes reconstituted as a sociological problem? Clearly, theology is not a form of sociology. Yet, as theology becomes implicated in efforts to inculturate (rehabilitating the term in the context of a culture of postmodernity) how far does it risk being drawn too far into the expectations of a sociological reflexivity?

Other understandings of the link between theology and culture exist in the writings of Tillich and Niebuhr. Neither dealt with sociological understandings of culture, which were themselves ill-conceived at the time they wrote their theologies of culture. Niebuhr does take into account Malinowski and does make reference to anthropology. Tillich argued that 'religion is the substance of culture, culture is the form of religion'. One being implicated in the other, he went on to suggest that 'he who can read the style of a culture can discover its ultimate concern, its religious substance'.[89] Although he does not state it, again this indicates where sociology has a potential ancillary theological role.

Many of Tillich's points on culture relate to earlier reflections. He argues that social reality has lost its inner transcendence, its transparent sense of the eternal. The pursuit of clarity and relevance in culture has made man less a mystery to himself, but in so doing has left him in an alienated state, disembodied from the mysterious within which his self could find completion. Far from being neutral and benign, culture masks dangers that need to be understood if theology is not to be corrupted by legitimising that for which it has no mandate in tradition, in revelation, or indeed, in sociology. This point takes on a particular force in the light of Tillich's argument that religion is embodied in culture.

An important strand of Tillich's approach to culture, one which complements newer anthropological and sociological approaches, is his stress on symbols. These are seen as double-edged, opening up reality but also the soul. They have an integrity 'which is just *it* and cannot be replaced by more or less adequate symbols'.[90] Because they are indirect in that which they embody and represent, symbols are at risk of misappropriation within culture. In addition, symbols have an ambiguous quality, a property of vulnerability that arises from their indirect manner of speaking of that which they represent. In a point that applies to culture, as well as to religion, Tillich suggests that 'religion, as everything in life, stands under the law of ambiguity, "ambiguity" meaning that it is creative and destructive at the same time'. But, he adds, symbols pose a further danger of becoming ultimate in themselves rather than representing it.[91] A culture of postmodernity accelerates risks of this danger in a process of commodification of symbols that makes them predictable, unambiguous and less prone to risk of failure. This flattening tendency accelerates secularisation within contemporary culture. Through commodification, the process is disguised by emphasis on allure and artificial forms of enchantment realised through marketing and advertising.

In his invaluable book *Christ and Culture*, Niebuhr offers some different insights into the dilemmas theology faces in dealing with culture. It is a rich work difficult to encapsulate briefly, but the quandaries it poses are clear. Niebuhr deals with the inescapable significance culture has in existential terms for making choices and decisions where faith might be weak. In his conclusion, he points to the 'fragmentary and frail measure' of faith as it is relative to culture. Clearly, his notion of relativity does not point to the destructive version wrought in complexity that assails a sociology now dealing with a culture of postmodernity. Rather it points to a solution to the endemic relativity of culture in a theological sphere. A faith that is absolute in its belief in Christ, is posited against a relativity that is both a symptom, but also a cure within contemporary culture. But most importantly, he wishes to widen the notion of choice into what he terms a social existentialism, one that is collective, that embodies a sharing, a concern with the 'we' rather than the 'I'. Widening choice from the individualistic existentialism of Kierkegaard into the social begs questions that can be taken forward by sociology in its effort to understand the link between theology and culture.[92]

The belief that culture is inherently corrupting has attractions in justifying a retreatism. But this represents an escape from the gift of self-realisation through culture, the means through which humanity is to be realised. It also points to a flight from stewardship, from an accountability for the use or misuse of cultural gifts that might convert evil into good, to fulfil redemptive plans. Thus, Niebuhr argues that 'Christ claims no man purely as a natural being, but always as one who has become human in a culture; who is not only in culture, but into whom culture has penetrated'.[93] There is an inescapable context to belief, that it is bound into

immediate cultural circumstances. This leads Niebuhr to give three possible readings of the place of Christ in culture, that have sociological
implications.

The first relates to a risk, which embodies Gnosticism, of lodging the
notion of Christ too far into culture. This relates also to nineteenth-century
liberal perspectives of a cultural Protestantism that dilute Christ and risk
turning Him into a chameleon fit for the times. His Divinity becomes
masked as he becomes a mere Man amongst others. Revelation and the
scandal of particularity become casualties of this approach which renders
theology innocuous. But more importantly, it fails to realise the way Christ
exceeds culture. It makes confession of this seem unnecessary.[94]

The second option is to place Christ above culture. This has implications for the cultivation of virtue. In this theological position, culture
embodies an ethic, a basis of imitation. This points to a synthesis of reason
and revelation, of a culture related to Gospel values, of converting an
imperfection of life into one of the pursuit of perfection through gifts of
grace. In this reading, 'culture discerns the rules for culture, because culture is the work of God-given reason in God-given nature'.[95] Niebuhr finds
this Thomistic synthesis attractive and a distinctive achievement of Catholicism in its dealings with culture.

Finally, Niebuhr examines Christ and culture in terms of paradox, a
more Protestant reading heavily influenced by reference to Luther. This
dualist position relates to notions of conflict, of sin and grace and the risks
of corruption by a culture within which a believer has to live. In a section
on the transformative notions of culture, which owes much to St Augustine, Niebuhr draws attention to the social sinfulness of man.[96] Again, this
illustrates the way sociology and theology can make arguments in parallel,
but which belong to different universes. Disorder relates to the notion of
a social pathology, a normlessness in Durkheim's account, but the same
phenomena could be related to the fallen nature of man, a denial of grace
for a more generalised spiritual failure. Both sociology and theology would
converge on the undesirable effects of egoism, or self-love.[97]

It might be thought that Neibuhr's characterisations of Christ and culture are unrealistically removed from sociology. But this would be to
overlook Weber's study of the Protestant Ethic and the Spirit of Capitalism. This study is concerned with the social and cultural consequences of
worldly and other-worldly strategies for salvation. For those for whom
salvation is to be found in the world, the vocation of seeking validation for
election derives from a salvation anxiety which provides the basis for an
elective affinity between Calvinism and the Spirit of Capitalism. Attitudes
to culture relate to forms of relief, sacramental in the case of Catholics, for

whom other worldly values matter most. For Weber, coming near a popular notion, it could be said that the 'greater other-worldliness of Catholicism, the ascetic character of its highest ideals, must have brought up its adherents to a greater indifference toward the good things of the world'. This relates to an equivocal reading of how Catholics relate to the world, which still haunts sociology itself.[98]

The issue of engaging and disengaging with culture points to complex theological issues that are far from clear-cut. Theology points to transformative possibilities within culture that are its moments of grace. As Dulles indicates 'the divine self-communication, therefore, has a social and symbolic dimension'.[99] Grace lies outside the realm of the social, but yet is embodied in it. It can transform the mundane the routine and the everyday. As Berger suggests, most of us do not have visits by angels nor are we transmuted routinely by mystical ecstasies. Transcendence, he suggests, for most, comes second hand in signals embedded in the moments of grace of everyday life.[100] These moments of self-recognition are fleeting, unprovable subjective insights that effect subtle change in biography. They pave the hidden ground of being where faith is to be found. Often these manifestations of grace are noted within the social, in appearances, in roles that transmit unexpected insights, that just happen to be noticed. They change the way one views the ambiguity of culture as it links to theology. But such change of sight, of seeing and believing, requires a cultural site for cultivation, where the spiritual eye is nurtured to see. The issue of seeing without believing provides a theological complement to the notion of believing without belonging. Both presuppose that faith is possible without grace or institutional form of attachment.

There has been considerable public debate in England on how to teach religion in a post-Christian society, where few believe never mind belong. Worries are expressed about education and a spiritual crisis in schools. Religious education is presented as comparative, multi-faith, multicultural and as oddly sociological in the common themes it covers. The desire for racial pluralism and tolerance has the effect of forcing Christianity to muffle its exclusive claims in the interests of securing cultural and political harmony. More importantly, religious affiliation has become attached to ethnicity and minority rights so that validation of belief forms part of claims for cultural recognition.[101] Some might feel that this debate hijacks a theological argument into the realm of cultural and ethnic politics, so that apologetics becomes transmogrified into apologies for the definiteness of one's belief. As religious education becomes more concerned with comparison, the issue of what it is to believe becomes marginalised. If all religions are the same, sharing common features, then believing without belonging is affirmed. Affiliation to one belief becomes eccentric and is deemed antisocial.

But the issue of tolerance and the desire for cultural harmony carries a price for all true believers, whatever their faith. This strategy of accommodation risks accelerating counterproductive notions of indifference and a secularisation which all religious groups fear. The price of liberal tolerance for Jews has been elegantly explored by Morris who points to the masking effect it has on religious belief, of removing it from the public sphere and confirming it in the realm of the private. Thus tolerance becomes an important instrument of secularisation. By removing religious belief from the public sphere, theology becomes detached from civility, from social accountability for the cultivation of virtue. Morris pleads for a genuine pluralism *within* religious traditions one that will allow these to flourish in their own terms.[102] The ironic implication of Morris' argument is that a rigourous pursuit of tolerance leads to intolerance, to a disabling climate that sacrifices authentic religious belief, one of commitment to one's tradition, on the altar of a public secular notion of liberality.

This issue of choice has become embedded in public debate on religious education. Advocates of comparison of differing forms of belief point to the tolerance of ethnic differences it facilitates that is so necessary in a multicultural society. But their critics claim that the result is a religious illiteracy that renders the young incapable of understanding what it is to believe, to judge, and to select in seeking to incarnate a sensibility of faith in the self. An understanding of religious belief that stresses its external manifestation in social forms but pays no attention to the reflexivity faith embodies is a theological and a sociological nonsense. The cultivation of such belief, the nurture of a reflexivity, amongst the young is seen by liberals to be a form of indoctrination, an unacceptable and corrupting proselytisation that commits the child to a fundamentalism, as almost any form of serious belief is now described. In this muddle, it is scarcely surprising that Muslims and Jews wish to have their own schools, where belief is nurtured and fostered as in Catholic tradition of education.

But debate over religious education at the secondary school level has concealed a fledgling and more fundamental controversy on the question of believing and belonging in relation to the study of theology within the university. In this debate, more advanced in the USA than in the UK, it is suggested that the siting of theology within the secular university and the growth of religious studies have masked and distorted the realisation of religious belief.

In a brave, brief and controversial paper, D'Costa argues that theology and religious studies are misleading in their tasks and need to be renamed and reset within academic culture. He claims that the incorporation of theology into the secular university, a movement stemming from the Enlightenment, has reduced Christianity to one tale amongst many to be taught at the court of reason. No virtues are assumed to gain admission and no excellence in the practice of theology is promised. The price of incorporation into the secularised and bureaucratic academy is teaching on the basis of a denial of commitment to the legitimate tasks of theology (the cultivation of faith and grace) either by teacher or student. To seek an understanding in faith is to disbelieve in the premises of academic theology, that it is a textual form of knowledge disembodied from personal commitment, bar adherence to the canons of disinterested scholarship. This nonconfessional property in a cultural milieu facilitated the rise of religious studies in the late 1960s. Elsewhere religious studies has been described as a minor parasite on theology.[103]

Religious studies is a sub-discipline of many branches, an amalgam of other disciplines such as sociology, anthropology and philosophy, which affirms that religion can and should be studied without either believing or belonging. It has grown into an ideology that now dominates theology. Indeed, D'Costa argues that religious studies has now killed the theology that facilitated its admission to the academy. Seeking a Christian theology that resists the secularisation of theological understanding, D'Costa echoing Morris, wishes for a return to the issue of the fidelity of tradition, a sectarian property in its best sense, but one where understanding can be secured in terms of its own narratives without reference to some supposed neutral court of judgement.[104] In seeking an engaged, confessional form of theology whose understanding is contextualised within its own tradition, D'Costa, also at the University of Bristol, has formulated a view independently but similar to the one being pursued in this study.

As presently constituted, no serious believing Catholic ought to consider reading for a degree in theology and religious studies in a British University. If one seeks tolerance in inquiry regarding religion, a sociology department is a far safer site. If there is a faith abroad in academic theology, it lies in the cultivation of a neutered detachment, a disinterested scholarship that legitimises a place in the secular academy, one that will embarrass few by wishing to connect believing to the obligations of ecclesial belonging. In their liberal and progressive hues, academic theologians seeking a recasting of orthodoxies, beg a sociological disbelief at their efforts. The more theologians are pushed back on to the site of their operations, the field of a secularised academic culture, the more they are forced under the sociological gaze and its notions of accountability. What they present becomes material *for* sociological reflexivity, for its appropriation

into its disciplinary paradigms. This generates an issue of a divided authority that splits academic theological speculation. It generates a question
as to what it is accountable to in its deliberations about culture.

Academic theologians might not worry as they are the beneficiaries of
this opaque division of accountability both to the academy and the Church.
But sociology does worry, because when it tries to redress supposed insights
derived from academic theological readings of culture, it becomes the
victim of this unresolved accountability. Sociology becomes disadvantaged
because its insights regarding culture and belief come from outside the
canons and traditions of theology. Theologians can appeal to the Holy
Ghost when all the sociologist can invoke is the ghost of Weber. But more
significantly, sociologists face acute problems of defining what theology is
as an academic discipline, what is its purpose and what assumptions does
it embody. Even to begin to ask this question risks sinking sociology into
a tradition of scholarship and learning that engulfs its tentative efforts to
understand the link between theology and culture in the context of
postmodernity. Rather than seek an elusive definition of theology, sociology can play to its strengths by looking at changes in its contextual basis.
This issue is bound into changes in cultural expectations of theology and
how it understands itself.

Nichols has provided a valuable but brief account of the history of
theology. Earliest theology involved interpretative responses to the revelation of the mystery of Christ. During the Patristic period, theology was
largely concerned with relating understandings of the mysteries of revelation to classical Greek culture and philosophy. This was the period of the
appropriation of the Gospel to the minds of the Gentiles, to produce their
own indigenous rhetoric and a literature that would bear critical scrutiny
The early Middle Ages saw theology being formulated within a monastic
setting. This institutionalisation of theology, for teaching, for the production of a corpus of knowledge, was related to a revival of interest in Latin,
and the linking of culture to civilisation. It was a period of reflection,
contemplation, the purification of resources and the readying of theology
for authentic transmission.

During the high medieval period, the study of theology evolved from
the setting of the Cathedral school into the university. This generated a
change in the teaching style of theology and sowed the seeds for a later
separation between the cultivation of reason and the certification of moral
and spiritual character. The teaching style and functions of theology changed
as it gained a place on an academic curriculum where a capacity to reason
was of prime importance. Theology became the queen of the sciences and
the centre of academic activity. In the medieval period, theological

knowledge became concerned with generating skills, with questioning within formal and ritual styles of public disputation and with the cultivation of a capacity to reason that increasingly linked theology to philosophy.[105]

This movement of theology from the monastery to the university has profound implications for understanding culture. In the medieval monastery, theology linked order to belief and grammar to spirituality in a way that had a practical purpose of seeking God through study and contemplation. The medieval monastery was what Aelred of Rievaulx has described as 'a spiritual wrestling-school'[106] where theological study enabled a young monk to grapple with sacred texts, to live an angelic life, but also to realise an understanding of his studies in his prayer life and in liturgical enactments. Virtue and practice were interlinked to make a complete demand on the self, so that reflexivity and reflection were mutually implicated.[107] Wisdom, grace and virtue were combined in the pursuit of a transcendent vision that linked sensibilities of culture to the notion of theology as an interested search for God. In monastic theology, aesthetics was given an institutional location, a social setting, a form of manifestation that came to characterise the medieval age. Thought became embodied in images, in a richness of symbolism, where, for Huizinga, 'religion penetrating all relations in life means a constant blending of the spheres of holy and profane thought'.[108]

This concern with richness of symbols in the late medieval period reached back to the theology of the Pseudo-Denys who integrated what belonged to the cultural in the liturgical form. Beauty and holiness converged in linking the visible with the invisible in a notion of culture that transformed in a manner whose vision now has become obscured.[109] Efforts to recover this sense of integration of belief and aesthetics can be found in Huysmans.[110]

Nichols characterises the period between 1500–1700 as one where there was a brave effort to put spirituality and theology back together. But most importantly for our purposes it was the beginning of a shift into a subjective or anthropocentric style of theology, one affected by humanism and the claims of the Reformation. Nichols suggests that the most important effect of this period was theological specialisation in areas such as dogmatic, moral or mystical theology. By the eighteenth century, for Nichols, the least creative period of theology, an arid interest in the production of manuals and encyclopedias was dominant.[111] This insulation and aridness could not survive forces of the Enlightenment that changed political and social attitudes to reason, civil rights and authority in a society increasingly moving from rural traditional values to those of urban and industrial life. The increased dominance of reason in terms of interests in science overflowed into the assumptions of the academy where disinterested scholarship made theology a subject, a department amongst many, one that formed part of a growing professional style of study that combined disinterest with a scientific vocation. This form was pioneered in Berlin and in German liberal theology in the early nineteenth century. The interests of a committed theology were an embarrassment to a university adjusting to relationships with the state and seeking from it confirmation of the professional nature of the calling of the academic. This movement in the nineteenth century towards state and civic accountability involved the bureaucratisation of the academy but also its effective secularisation. Academic freedom permitted theology a place in the university, but at the price of making unfree its relationship to conditions of practice where faith was joined to a seeking of understanding.

Although knowledge was presented in a disinterested manner, in the secular university it had to be given some symbolic and traditional lineages if this academic ethos was to be given civic recognition. It had to find a cultural form to represent its ambitions and to manifest the legitimacy of its claims. These it borrowed freely from theology. A process of architectural plagiarism was apparent in the secularised use of the Gothic in architectural styles, such as at the former Queen's Colleges in Ireland and at the University of Bristol, for example. This lent a quasi-monastic property to the civic university, one exemplified in the academic robes, the titles of its officers, such as dean and chancellor. This appropriation of symbolic capital, from the realm of the sacred to the secular, made academic theology the agent of a symbolic violence against the Catholic and monastic origins of the university.

A theology of faith and grace is expelled but its rhetoric is retained in a secular form to signify a consecration of learning and the construction of an aura of enchantment for the academy. Disembodied scholarship needs a symbolic wrapping, a means of expressing its values. This means that some forms of knowledge are more profane than others. Thus, within the university structure itself, subjects vary in importance in the production of academic knowledge. This can have a profound effect on spheres of influence, the operations of academic power to define and to include, but also to marginalise and to exclude. The ranking of subjects has a cultural agenda that masks interests of power that operate concealed behind incalculable values of disinterested scholarship.

Bourdieu has examined this hierarchy of knowledge in terms of fields of struggle within the university structure for access to symbolic resources that are unequally distributed but which form the basis of power and influence. He finds this process of allocation akin to 'social magic, which, as in initiation ceremonies, tends to consecrate a competence which is inextricably social and technical'.[112] This unique French study has no British equivalent. In his effort to entrap *Homo Academicus*, Bourdieu uses theological metaphors to characterise the consecration of learning, its ritual and symbolic power to disguise unequal allocations of status and influence. A cultural layer is added to bureaucracy to endow it with properties of the intangible. This layer has a protective function, one that suggests forms of knowledge do not speak for themselves, but have to be spoken for through the manipulation and regulation of cultural resources. Theology itself is not exempt from this proposition. In secular academic culture, the Divine mandate of theology is uninvoked, for in this setting it is accepted on the basis of reason and its membership of the humanities.

In the context of the issue of theology and academic culture the effect of Bourdieu's form of analysis is ironic. The secularisation that gave rise to academic culture, that legitimised the right to bureaucratise and to standardise knowledge according to principles of reason, that in consequence effected a redefinition of a theology detached from faith, requires reference to its metaphors, its supposedly discounted style of argument, to understand the unequal allocation of power within the marketplace of the university, and the varying status of disciplines and the symbolic capital they can claim. To understand the hidden basis of power within academic culture, requires reference by Bourdieu to the principles of sacramental economy. Thus, one finds the notion of a theology, subservient to these principles of disinterested rationalisation of knowledge, being transposed to a wider analytical context where what has been jettisoned as a principle of entry to the bureaucratised academy is resurrected as a principle of understanding by one of the disciplines, sociology, that displaced it as the queen of the sciences.

Academic culture has its own reasons for reverting to the principles embodied in a secularised theology in the present political context in Britain. Contrary to Bourdieu, present concerns require an effort to find principles of revitalisation of ideals, some form of enchantment to redress the sense of disenchantment into which the academic community is sinking rapidly. This has led to reflections that border on the theological, relating to a crisis of identity and purpose less over funding than the goals of the institution, which need to be reformulated in changed political circumstances. Worries exist about the purpose of university scholarship, the issue of the integral truth of what it proclaims in original and critical thought, and the separation of teaching and research.[113] Universities face what Weber feared, an irresistible growth of bureaucratisation that undermines their capacity to cultivate the notion of disinterested scholarship. To resist these pressures of a state which has taken over the civic realm of academic culture, universities have to conserve their symbolic capital, the resources for resistance to bureaucracy. They have to reinvent traditions that suggest enchantment rather than disenchantment.

Bureaucracy, accountancy and management styles have placed at risk speculative forms of knowledge, those that cannot be packaged into grant formats, where outcomes are known in advance and which are safe options for funding in the humanities. Yet, the universities have to cultivate an aura of mystery, of engagement with scholarship that requires cultural wrappings suffice to generate an image, one endowed with a mysterious property of allure. This cultural image requires regulation and policing to gain donations from alumni and from foundations.[114] This process of reinvention paradoxically leads to a rehabilitation of tradition, to a stress on elements that relate to a theological lineage, but which are repackaged in secular wrappings.

Because academic theology has engaged in a symbolic violence against theology itself, few would look for leadership to its departments. There is a price to the liberalism of the position of academic theologians and their concern with the disinterested study of religion. They are often forced into a liberal etiquette of marginalising or downplaying positions of faith, which are deemed presumptuous in a multi-faith, multicultural department devoted to comparison, dialogue and tolerance. Born again evangelical students pose a particular and embarrassing threat to this etiquette of availability to all, but unavailable to some. They present inconvenient fodder to academic theology of true believers seeking to enhance the basis of their spiritual reflection. The idea that prayer and spirituality should be associated with particular sets of lectures generates acute embarrassment, a phobia equivalent to responses of academics to the issue of sex and their students some decades ago.[115] Academic theology is like studying music, but with some mysterious injunction that indicates its basis of enchantment cannot be found by playing it.

Academic theologians have insulated themselves from significant changes in their own universities in two ways. The issue of the cultivation of faith is left to the chaplains with the result that the student body is structurally disconnected from the services of a theology department. This disconnection is unfortunate not least because of the very high church going rates amongst university students, far above that of the national age cohort. Secondly, many university staff, especially in science and engineering, but also in the arts, and indeed, sociology itself, feel their own practice of faith is patronised by the supposed enlightened views of progressive and liberal theologians. Many academics lack the critical means of redress to some of the views presented and tend to marginalise and isolate academic theology accordingly.

But academic theology faces other problems of a structural nature that undermine its credibility. In secularising itself and marrying religious studies academic theology has rendered itself, with some exceptions, unaccountable to any ecclesial body. This detachment of ecclesial interest in theology varies in the United Kingdom. Theology is taught in seminaries outside the university system, where belief and belonging do merge. Some chairs in Durham, Oxford and London are there by statute but are confined in effect to Anglicans.

Catholic theology, however, is mainly done outside English universities, by religious orders, such as the Benedictines, Jesuits and Dominicans, who publish a number of important journals in Britain. This displacement of Catholic theologians resolves a potential problem. The civic and secular charter of many British universities precludes confessional positions which are arbitrarily deemed to be sectarian.[116] But the effect of this exclusion of confessional positions in theology is damaging and misrepresents the discipline to the academic community. In error, it assumes it is dealing with an authentic package, as conceived by the Churches, to whom theology is supposedly accountable. Exclusion of a confessional position means that academic theology operates in a way that is removed from its conditions of practice, from faith and spirituality. It becomes an artificial exercise, a speculative exercise, a shell without substance that appeals to general academic virtues.

There are suspicions of the motives of those who have sought to disconnect theology from faith and to insert religious studies in its place. This relates to an impression of Marsden, one that deserves sociological study, which applies to academic theology and to religious studies, certainly in the USA, and possibly in the United Kingdom, that many of its academics have lost their faith. They are immigrants from belief who transmit disillusion and disbelief to students naïve enough to join such courses seeking to have their faith affirmed, but not demolished.[117] It is also clear in this study of the secularisation of American Universities that Protestant foundations have been hit far harder than their Catholic counterparts.[118]

Religious studies entered through Protestant theology, and quickly sought to secularise and to professionalise its host, converting it into a strict non-confessional, multi-denominational discipline where a positivist methodology lent it a scientific status. The strict adherence to texts, such as in the case of Buddhist studies, gave it a property of scholarship. But it is inconceivable that a case could have been made for the recognition of religious studies, given the lack of consensus as to its supposed distinctive subject-matter – religion. As a subject it excites disillusion and hostility, for it seeks to replace interested faith with disinterested study, somehow conveying the notion that believers are parochial, superstitious and in some way, are unprofessional in their treatment of belief. But for some, religious studies is itself an academic myth. Speaking for many, Hart cites a participant at a conference on the state of graduate religious studies, that as a field it has 'no identifiable frame of discourse', that the discipline is an 'in-house concoction' and that there is no '"cogent legitimation" for the academic study of religion'.[119] Religious studies presupposed the existence of theology to gain entrance to the academy. It offered to release theology from its ghetto. But in turn, religious studies has been 'ghettoised', to use Smart's term, for it sought links with sociology and anthropology to overcome its marginality, to supply it with a language of purpose, now that theology was assassinated.[120] As religious studies becomes increasingly concerned with contemporary issues, it seeks to move from textual and philosophical matters into those that belong to sociology.[121] Whereas theology might claim to transcend sociology, religious studies is but a creature of it. It deals with issues of ethnicity, gender, economic and communal factors that are proper to sociological concerns.

But as religious studies increasingly seeks links with sociology, its stance of non-confessional disinterest that effected the expulsion of theology, is itself untenable in the context of a reflexive sociology that is becoming positively confessional. Reflexivity pushes sociology into an issue of moral commitment, a hairline away from religious belief and commitment which religious studies spurns. The more religious studies seeks to relate to sociology, the more it is dragged back to its theological debts, denial of which formed the basis of its claims for autonomy. It is the moral obligation a subject makes on sociology and the biographical implications of this that renders the discounting of values unsustainable. This has changed sociological expectations of how religion is to be understood, thus making sociology more compatible with theology rather than with religious studies. Sociology forces an issue of choice which religious studies denies.

The university is a site for contemporary debate on postmodernity. All its disciplines are affected by the relativism, and the nihilism this embodies. Cere suggests that Nietzsche's proclamation of the 'death of God' paved the way for the displacement of theology by religious studies, so that the particular is contextualised but without universal truth issues being available. This issue of agnosticism over rules for arbitration between contexts that embody conflicting belief systems is endemic in the shift in sociology into hermeneutic considerations. It is also an issue that lies at the root of postmodernity, over how to cope with pluralism, fragmentation and the tyranny of ambiguities and antinomies. Cere criticises Bloom's controversial study on *The Closing of the American Mind* for failing to refer to theology for the resolution of universal values, such as good and evil.[122] Again, the failure of theology to engage emerges. Cere indicates that 'theology must involve more than a learned attunement of theological categories in secular discourses'. Significantly, he goes on to add that although 'deistic reconstructions attempt to address the concerns of culture . . . it is often secularists who are most critical of the theologically impoverished character of these approaches'.[123] It is clear that academic theology is not meeting the expectations of sociology or its needs.

Catholic universities have a string of problems coping with modernisation and secularisation. Gleason sees American Catholic higher education as moving from a ghetto state based on a discernment of a crisis in culture in the 1940s and 1950s. Many of the discernments of the need to respiritualise culture, conceived in this period, have simply rolled on unresolved into the culture of postmodernity of the 1990s. The rebellion of the late 1960s, when everything seemed to fall apart in Catholicism was a tragic distraction, a period of self-immolation, whose destructive effects still persist. The question of how to re-spiritualise culture became forgotten by a generation concerned with relevance and a misunderstanding of what modernisation meant. This period of unsettlement generated a crisis of academic freedom in many cases, placing universities against the episcopacy and led to a crisis in identity over what was Catholic about higher education.[124] Efforts to change the agenda of the university in terms of theology are getting underway.

There are signs that the Vatican is realising the need to recover an initiative. A recent document noted that

> university culture is one of the most promising, but also one of the most difficult. This particular milieu has so great an influence on the social and cultural life of nations, and on it depends to a great extent the future of the church and that of society.[125]

There is a property of urgency in the document, where it sees the university as a fundamental area in which faith and culture meet in a reflective context. Among many considerations, such as the increased professionalisation and specialisation of the modern university, the document refers to the scepticism and indifference wrought by the prevailing secularism which can be contrasted to a 'new and ill-defined searching of a religious kind'.[126]

One concern central to the document is the issue of human formation, an opening to spiritual values within academic culture. This issue relates to the question of the responsibilities of theology as a witness to spiritual values within the wider academic community, a problem that seems to justify its existence. Some of these issues were also raised by David Ford in his inaugural lecture at Cambridge in 1992. Defining theology as seeking wisdom, Ford sought for the discipline a public duty of a vigil covering long traditions of testimony.[127] Yet, this lecture seems unpersuasive, if not vague in a liberal Anglican way. The denominational responsibilities of such a theology and the issue of its authority are hardly sketched. Little attention is given to the issue of the way an academic theology disembodied from spiritual practice and ecclesial accountability is a contradiction in terms.[128]

There is little doubt but that academic theology has lost its way. If so, this forms part of a wider crisis in the university, one where the issue of moral character has been detached from the purpose of academic study. Victorians understood this relationship between moral endeavour and study in a secular context. This underlay the Northcote–Trevelyan reforms of the civil service.[129] A concern with credentials, with professional certification has masked this moral dimension to learning. Disinterested study has given way to interested advancement, a utilitarianism Newman deplored. Equally, the lives of students are treated with moral indifference, save for issues that come through counselling. It is not part of the contemporary university to form moral character. Students are treated as adults. Bar stipulated disciplinary offences, the secular university has few powers of intervention in their private lives. To this state of affairs needs to be added the bureaucratic ethos of the modern university, where research rather than teaching forms the basis of academic advancement. The Quality Assessment of Teaching, started in 1993, of the Higher Education Funding Council for England marks a public change of interest and concern. Moral formation is not an issue its documentation recognises.

This underlines the inimical grounds upon which theology operates in the secular academy. Even if it did wish to connect faith and prayer to its reflexive basis, theology would be operating such values in alien cultural circumstances. In the USA, however, the basis of teaching theology is subject to radical reconsideration.

Some of these difficulties have been brought together by Kelsey, an American liberal Protestant theologian. Reflecting on an extensive debate on the functions of theological education in the USA, Kelsey illustrates some of the difficulties academic theology faces. The issue of accountability emerges again. Affirming spiritual qualities incompatible often in the secular university, theology has a problem of accreditation that shapes its interests and concerns. Academic theology can justify its basis by reference to the need to professionalise the training of ministers, but this has to be offset against the academic culture to which these theologians are accountable. This culture shapes promotion prospects and funding, elements that are part of milieu of the sociology of theology and the practical culture that governs its credibility and relationship to power. But this accountability to the norms of the wider academic community carries a price. It marginalises theology from parochial and pastoral contexts that legitimise its significance for the Churches on whose behalf it speaks. Reference to academic necessities is masked in the public facade of credibility academic theologians present to the main Churches and to wider society. The diversity of interests and subjects to be covered within theology make it inherently fragmented and at risk from rival subjects in the academy.

These internal disputes about the nature of theology might seem far removed from questions of the dubious legacy of secularisation for sociology. But they do relate in terms of the divisions theology represents within the culture of the academy that have sociological implications. Kelsey shows theology divided against itself in terms of two models which he denotes as Athens and Berlin. The latter model relates to the pursuit of orderly, disciplined critical research and also the professionalisation of the education of ministers. In this model one finds the normative properties of the modern university, with its bureaucratisation and professionalisation but also its proneness to secularisation. But, it is the Athens model that has the most potent implications for sociology in its effort to understand culture. It offers a possible antidote to the secularisation embodied in a modernity that seems fatal both to the academy and to sociology.

The Athens model points to a theological education dealing with morality, with character formation and personal appropriation. Kelsey suggests that this model relates to what the Greek regarded as paideia – the process of culturing the soul – that leads to the cultivation of a virtue. For Kelsey, this moral virtue 'is a *habitus*, a settled disposition of the will to act habitually in a morally excellent way – courageously, faithfully, honestly, prudently, etc.'.[130] In this context, the term habitus is important for three reasons. Firstly, it points to an issue of disposition, an elective property that links theology with sociology in a cultural setting. It signifies a process of the will to engage, to become that which a theology promises. Secondly, its refers to a hermeneutic consideration in terms of appropriation. It points to a property which hermeneutics can assist sociology in understanding. Thirdly, and most importantly, it is a central aspect of Bourdieu's approach to culture and one that is developed later.

Many of the current debates on theology in the university and its relationship to culture belong to the history of the academy. It might be forgotten how innovative was Newman's idea of university and his plea for the place of theology within it. His own university faced immense problems over secular rivals in Ireland in the mid-nineteenth century.[131]

On the basis of tradition, Newman sought to defend the place of theology
in the university, where it risked expulsion by secular forces. Newman's
defence of theology as a form of knowledge took little account of the
specific moral and spiritual properties necessary for its contemplation. For
Newman, theology was the science of God and the truths about His basis.[132]
Newman's ambitions were for theology, the queen of the sciences, to be
embedded in all forms of knowledge within the academy. The truth claims
of theology were absolute and complete. Given that theology was a form of
knowledge, a university with universal claims to explore all facets had no
means of excluding theology from its portals. But Newman assumed theology would defend a distinctive territory, one characterised by faith and
revelation from the intrusions of other disciplines.[133] He could never have
envisaged the symbolic violence which contemporary academic theology,
neutered by religious studies, has effected in this domain. Theology has
transmogrified itself into being a humanity amongst others. Its links with
religious studies deny the possibility of paideia (whatever the wider con-
straints of the secular academy). Thus, the discipline that might have provided a witness to the spiritual values of the university, to which sociology
might have gazed respectfully, seems to have abdicated its distinctive
resources, those derived from belief, from grace, faith, and prayer. How
could and should matters be otherwise? Again one must turn to Kelsey to
see the way matters might move ahead.

The subtitle of his earlier book on understanding God asks 'what's
theological about a theological school?'. Again set against two models,
Athens, where paideia is cultivated and Berlin, where professionalisation
and research dominate and where there is no over-arching notion of truth,
Kelsey tries to rethink the social and communal nature of theology, but
above all its responsibilities to these properties in relation to its students.
Admitting that his ideas are utopian, Kelsey works against a context of
fragmentation within theology and suggests that faith is a property that
unites and transcends these academic divisions. Theology is defined as a
common seeking and enhancing of an understanding of God. His central
wish for theology is for the Christian thing it embodies. This involves a
seeking 'in concrete reality *in and as various Christian or worshipping
communities in all their radical pluralism'*.[134] This gives a definite focus
to theology, of operating in a context, a field, a site, where belief is reproduced. This would relate to the earlier ambition for sociology as the
fieldwork of theology.

It is in the setting of the congregation that theology needs to operate.
Each congregation has its distinctive social form and space. Kelsey is
concerned with the public bodily expression of communal practice that

belongs to a congregation in its activity of worship. A pastoral strategy is not envisaged. It will arise as a result of the siting of theology in a field of practice. Kelsey is pointing to the way theology has to take on a property of reflexivity if it is to understand how belief is reproduced against the odds in a culture of postmodernity. He wants theology to understand how a sensus fidelium is constructed often against the odds on a particular site, and for theological students to understand this point. Faith partly arises from inductive circumstances and sociology can clarify this point. This returns theology to the issue of liturgy, its exemplary site of practice and reproduction. It also generates an issue about how faith is formed amongst the young. The issue of grounding theology on a site gives added significance to the monastery, for it begs a question as to how far one should delimit the ambition to seek God? After all, monasticism is the original theological site for seeking. Habitus is linked to learning, and theology to liturgy in a way that admits no division. The culture of the monastery gives witness to this point.

Kelsey notes the scandal of particularity attached to congregations, the field for the theological seeking of God. It poses an offence, an embarrassment that baffles.[135] But university students of theology are amateurs compared to the professionals who consecrate their lives to a similar task. These university students have to face the scandal of particularity of their colleagues. In France, contemplative orders that make deep demands of commitment are attracting many novices and young monks and nuns. These form their own scandal of particularity. The young wimpled nun and the shaven young monk should not be there. Society states they belong on the beach, in the cafe, in a culture of drugs, sex and what is supposed to interest. Their consecration to chastity, poverty and obedience in a life of prayer and discipline makes a total demand on the self in time, habit, habitus and belief, all of which are a scandal to society, a waste that affronts images of youth doing other things. These young professionals give too much, seek too much, but understand too much to be understood by a society that can merely mock their efforts, or be indifferent to their theological basis. But a sociology seeking that elusive link between theology and culture might just have a glimmer of recognition, the possibility of a slight understanding.

Kelsey's utopian vision for theology might meet sociological resistance. As he indicates, feminists, and radical groups have revolted against the narrow constrictions of academic theology. But this movement of revolt is familiar. It echoes the stress on biography and reflexivity discussed earlier to escape the clutches of an uninvolved sociology. Clearly, this presents sociology with a dilemma. In escaping from the pluralism wrought in postmodernity, sociology is seeking something definite in theology, not a licence to make matters indefinite, which is where the discipline started from in its dealing with culture.

Mapping out the relationship between theology and culture is fraught with sociological perils. Suspicion about academic theology, its soul selling to the bureaucratised academy forms part of a generalised worry as to how culture is read by theologians, whatever their affiliation whether to the Church or to the academy. The virtual absence of any citable research in this area in English society suggests numerous difficulties. It is difficult to reach behind the rhetoric of liberal theologians, who believe in the ordination of women, who are tolerant and open on sexual matters, to ask what is their cultural agenda as understood in sociological terms? The absence of this agenda points to the failure of the Anglican decade of Evangelism in England. There are few if any signs that the significance for theologians of sociology in relation to culture has even vaguely been understood.

It might be said that one set of generalities about the link between theology and culture has been replaced by another set – those derived from sociological speculation. Yet sociological worries about theological understandings of culture have a real basis. The link between theology and culture in English is hopelessly undertheorised. The issues generated by inculturation have not even begun to be thought about in relation to English culture. Theologians seem to have a curious inability to recognise that the problem of belief lies in their ill-formulated understandings of culture. The much vaunted *Faith in the City* produced a lamentable theology (its understanding of liturgy was patronising and farcical) that was married to an adequate social policy document. There is a sense that theologians do not know how to think in relation to culture in terms sociologists would recognise. They might say this does not matter. But it does, given the crisis of culture they are surrounded by, with numbers falling and an entropy and disillusion settling into traditional Christianity. The happy clappy solutions of Evangelicals simply buy off younger middle class zealots, who either burn out, or realise theological ambitions and drift upwards and into Catholicism.

This study could stop at this point, and say matters are dreadful and join with the many to say that it is all the fault of liberal theologians. But it is necessary to go further, to think through impediments to belief that a sociologist notices. What reading of culture might permit an escape from disbelief if the sociologist had a free theological hand, unfettered by the deadweight of liberal thought of the past three decades?

Not unexpectedly, sociology has it own problems in relation to belief. Understanding these clears a way for discerning what might seem some theological solutions to its dilemmas. The issue goes back to a weakness of sociology that it can simply point to mechanisms of reproduction. It cannot certify their content. But it can adapt values, however perverse, to these ambiguous mechanisms that permit the insertion of any value. Instead of thinking of the marginalisation of religion in a culture of postmodernity from the centre, what if one thinks from the margins? Instead of assuming forms of cultural reproduction effect the persistence of disbelief, why not examine these in terms of how they might produce belief? Clearly, this is an artificial exercise that reflects the constricted theological vision of sociology but it does illustrate how it might like to think of such matters in terms of its own theological self-understandings, however atypical these might be.

Anyhow, sociology has to deal with its own hound of heaven, its own condition of secularity and misrecognition within its domestic circumstances. This returns to the issue of how sociology comes to understand belief and disbelief. If theology is grounded in culture, then what are the issues that effect the misrecognition of belief? Why does sociology need to believe in something beyond the mere characterisation of religion as a social arrangement? What is so limited about that? What was structured within sociology to marginalise religious belief, to make it seem so alien? Again, one wishes to return to a question that haunts this study: how does one find an apologetics through the unexpected medium of sociological efforts to understand the link between theology and culture? For theologians, this might seem a ridiculous route to ask such a question; for the vast majority of sociologists it is one that is fatuous to ask. But again, what in the circumstances of sociology point to an imperative to seek religious faith, Catholicism in this case, and in what terms can this be expressed?

4 The Disappearance of God: The Secularisation of Sociology

Even the sociological flâneur needs to seek bread. Gazing into the window of the local wholefood corner shop provokes mixed feelings, food for thought before the purchase of a loaf. The window displays a galaxy of advertisements for wholesome living, a panorama of fieldwork possibilities, such as a course on 'transformative dreamwork' or an expedition to London for Earth Alignment Day – clearly a feastday for some at the ecological end of New Age Religions. But inspection of the campscene directory for the year in the window discloses something more unsettling. Listed is the Merrymeet women's camp in Devon, offering

> weaving life stories * ritual dance * song * creating a sacred space in nature.

What might attract a gimlet gaze is not the event, but its presenting rhetoric. It seems rather sociological. Clearly, sociology does not own terms such as 'ritual dance' or 'sacred space' and 'life stories', but they do have a sociological ring. It might be that many sociology graduates are attracted to these alternative lifestyle movements and import the rhetoric of the discipline into their new religions, a curious and ironic reversal of Comte's endeavours. But New Age movements are not alone in appropriating a sociological rhetoric. Evangelical groups close to the market place where the churched and unchurched intersect also advertise in ways that incorporate a sociological rhetoric in their proclamation. For instance, the Willow Creek Community Church mission to England offers 'keys to building an effective culturally relevant local church' – its meeting schedule carries the waver that it is 'subject to change based on God's leading!'. So much belief yet a hankering for disbelief, the breadshop window seems to frame the dilemmas of a culture of postmodernity.

All things have changed greatly in the cultural milieu since 1989 and sociology cannot but be affected by these changes in sensibility. Issues of self-improvement, anxiety, identity, cultural politics, New Age religions all form a galaxy of possibility in the marketplace. Even the sociological gaze notices how ironic it is that in one of the main academic bookshops on the Left Bank in Paris, the amount of shelf space devoted to astrology,

tarot cards, Zen Buddhism and some exotic New Age religions is vast compared to that allocated to sociology. Theology has no section at all in this
supermarket of intellectual ideas. Superstition seems to be dancing on the
grave of positivism. The Queen of Reason crowned in Notre Dame Cathedral, Paris, has taken up semi-detached residence with the queen of spades.

The kingdom of sociology now deals in gambles not in enlightened
reasoned outcomes. Sociology plays in a new game, what has become
known as postmodernity. For Bauman and Tester this involves a pilgrimage without a map, without rules for journeying or arriving, where desti-
nations are unmarked.[1] The landscape is post-Christian and the God of the
tribe has been declared dead. The advent of modernity comes in train with
secularisation and with it the removal of public communal manifestations
of religious belief that might impede the pursuit of pleasure. If belief does
pertain, it is a private matter, indeed, for many an enigma and an embarrassment to those affirming the need for self-actualisation in a culture that
promises to manufacture all dreams. But this freedom leaves sociology
with an ambiguity, one which is embodied in the notion of postmodernity.
Bauman has encapsulated this dilemma when he observed of postmodernity
that it

> proclaims all restrictions on freedom illegal, at the same time doing
> away with social certainty and legalizing ethical uncertainty. Existential
> insecurity – ontological contingency of being – is the result.[2]

A young Catholic seeking cultural roots for belief might feel that the
landscape has never been so inimical. He might flinch before the fickle
blasphemies of his peers and wonder if God *has* gone. He might feel the
lament for the ruined temple in psalm 73 where it is written:

Turn your steps to these places that are utterly ruined!
The enemy has laid waste the whole of the sanctuary. Your foes have
made uproar in your houses of prayer:
they have set up their emblems, their foreign emblems,
high above the entrance to the sanctuary.

Something more than the ebbing of the influence of traditional religions
and the weakening appeal of the sacred is embodied in arguments on
secularisation. It seems to have delivered new beliefs that sow doubt. As
Lyon suggests 'ambiguity and paradox lie near the core of secularization
studies'.[3] Secularisation was never a safe topic confined to sociology of
religion, to plot the ebbing of church attendance, the marginalisation of
belief and the loosening of the grip of traditional religions. It has been
embedded in the roots of sociology. But in the context of postmodernity

these have taken a destructive turn. The pluralism and autonomy that characterised modernity, that fractured religious belief, that gave rise to sociology, have now been imported into the discipline in what has become known as postmodernity. The destructive forces of fracture and disbelief embodied in postmodernity leave sociology unprotected. There is no tradition, no God to turn to, for these illusory projections have been unmasked. All that is left is a nihilism, unchosen, a condition rather than an articulated belief, but one that seems have a naturalised link with modernity. Secularisation has spread a dry rot through culture which even the most religiously stone deaf sociologist can notice. The effect of postmodernity, where all is pastiche, ambiguity and game, seems to have conspired to reduce sociological ventures to wagers where the indeterminate has invaded ambitions to be determinate. Postmodernity seems to have rehabilitated Pascal's wager. Even in a culture of secularity, the game goes on, and the coin keeps spinning, even on the sociologist's turf. This wager was expressed as follows:

> 'Either God is or he is not'. But to which view shall we be inclined?
> Reason cannot decide this question. Infinite chaos separates us. At the
> far end of this infinite distance a coin is being spun which will come
> down heads or tails. How will you wager? Reason cannot make you
> choose either, reason cannot prove either wrong.[4]

This seems to capture the sociologist's dilemma in handling the issue of God in a culture of postmodernity.

In seeking to reflect on who killed God, it is a case of rounding up the texts of the usual suspects to give them a good grilling to find heresies all too well known. Nietzsche, Freud, Foucault and Durkheim, to name a few, come to mind. But this study is an exercise in sociology, not the history of ideas. Like the parade of theologians whose text might be read, such as Barth, Bultmann, and Rahner, that should have been displayed in the last chapter, here, these thinkers are also by-passed. Again, this might seem arbitrary. In defence, one can say there are lots of texts available elsewhere on all their writings. One wants to avoid the condition which Steiner has so aptly criticised, of becoming embedded in endless commentary that is secondary and parasitic, which offers an escape from direct confrontation with culture through textual exegesis.[5] It might confirm the prejudices of the Milbanks of theology as to the illusory basis of sociology, as being all explanation, but of no scholarly account. It might also invoke the telling anecdote which Bauman notes regarding the scandal felt by Popper at the response of an anthropologist to a deep scientific debate, where he was asked to comment. The anthropologist refused, saying he was not interested in the views, but in the movement of the debate, the forms of interventions and how it was enacted, by implication the scientists being to him one tribe amongst many he studied.[6]

Texts that relate to secularisation have been well explored elsewhere and are far too numerous to cite. A rather more interesting question, one that involves a sociology of sociology, is to ask what in the discipline's own traditions and arrangements of knowledge effected the disappearance of God? This involves reference to a history unwritten, of how sociology poisoned the hound of heaven on its trail. As implied earlier, the history of sociology militates against the pursuit of such a question. Usually, such histories are chronological, the accounts of a progress from classification to contextualisation.[7] Up to very recently, little attention was given to the issue of biography, to the circumstances of reflexivity of great sociologists and the culture milieu within which they operated. Matters are changing with growing and substantial interest in the biographies of Comte, Durkheim, Weber and Simmel. This is not to suggest that these were closet believers, but that they were aware of religious sensibilities and incorporated these in their sociological reflections.

Modernity is related to ideas of progress, but also to the demise of traditional forms of religion, the two being considered incompatible. This formed a central worry for classical sociologists concerned with the ebbing of its influence and with finding a secular substitute equivalent to the power of religion to enforce ethics and to provide a basis of cultural support. Marx, Weber, Simmel and Durkheim all considered religion to be of central importance. Reflecting on its contemporary isolation, Beckford notes that in the sociological past, religion was a 'repository of fundamental cultural meanings', an essential symbolic resource, 'a kind of copestone which locked all the other components of culture into place'.[8]

As sociology itself has become secularised, this tradition of interest has become obscured in the passage of time, taking on a property of what is culturally normative within the discipline itself. As suggested earlier, sociologists would be the first to use analytical instruments on such a naturalised belief system within culture, to unmask and to reveal the basis of power, disbelief in this case, that effected such arbitrary arrangements. Bourdieu's notion of a motivated cover-up, a concealed truth that relates to a hermeneutic of suspicion, could be applied back against sociology itself in its own dealings with issues of religious belief.[9]

The most important myth to tackle is that early sociologists were disinterested in religion and were unaffected by its ebb and flow. Stuart Hughes noted that in Parisian circles prior to 1900, it was 'bad form to be a practicing Catholic', but by 1912, a third of the student body were so in the Normale, that 'citadel of bantering agnosticism'.[10] In *Jean Barois*, this movement into the new spirit, heavily influenced by Péguy and Claudel, is documented. Barois tries to escape the clutches of a pious childhood into a positivism, a belief in the supremacy of reason, where religion is treated as an illusion. His tragedy is that this secular belief is compromised by a daughter who wishes to become a nun to make expiation for his writings. Reflecting on this, Barois sees his daughter as having a 'complete assurance of the existence of a spiritual world, an assurance no rational arguments could shake'.[11] In an unusual reversal, his tragedy is that the younger generation he encounters have turned to the Catholicism he has rejected. This is illustrated in the dialogue between the two young adversaries he encounters in the office of the journal he edits. Both his adversaries came to a fullness of Catholicism at the Normale, disillusioned with the legacy of the positivists for improving the practicalities of French life.[12] This episode is suggestive rather conclusive. Sociology is seldom mentioned, except by implication as part of positivism in dealing with religion. This small episode does point to the way disbelief can turn to belief on the axis of a cultural context in which sociology flourished. Interest in theology was greater in Durkheim's circle than one might realise. Catholic assumptions rather than those of liberal Protestantism were deemed of greater interest according to Pickering. It is indicative of how much work needs to be done on the intellectual origins of sociology that an essay by Robert Hertz on sin and expiation in primitive society, laden with theology, should occasion surprise.[13]

Since its foundation, sociology has had an equivocal relationship to Christianity. In one sense Christianity is deemed to be part of tradition, is an historical artifact, one peculiarly irrelevant in an age when reason and progress, which sociology embodies, is to triumph. After all, sociology was founded to supplant Catholicism, with a religion of positivism, where reason and progress were to be worshipped. Charlton captures well Comte's effort to found a religion of humanity on the basis of positivism. Elements of Catholicism, such as feast days, priests, liturgies and hymns were all imported into this religion of humanity, the last of whose temples was closed in Liverpool just after the Second World War.[14] Lepenies suggests that Nietzsche saw Comte as trying to outchristianise Christianity and regarded him as 'nothing but a Jesuit "who wanted to lead his Frenchmen to Rome via the *detour* of science"'.[15] Sociology was conceived in a structure of Catholicism denuded of belief in God. Its pedigree was decidedly secular but with an embarrassing amount of Catholic borrowings.

Comte was one disciple of reason and humanity amongst many ranging from Feurbach, Marx, Strauss, to Nietzsche and Freud who, to follow de Lubac, formed their own drama of atheist humanism. In his lengthy treatment of Comte, de Lubac noted that his sociology led to a tyranny and to a blindness which was exalted into a victory of the positive age.[16] That potential for dehumanisation buried in the positivist manifesto has come to haunt sociology. At one level, sociology operated as a science, in the manner of Spencer and Durkheim, employing a strict concern with the explanation of facts, their classification and social functions, but at another level, it encountered a distinctive need to interpret, to understand the meanings that gave humanity to an actor. The scientific ambitions of sociology risked dehumanising the actor but its humanist affiliations left him trapped in his illusions which the discipline was formed to confound.

In dealing with culture, sociology had its own set of antinomies peculiar to its analytical enterprise. There was a worry that reason in ordering social institutions masked theological issues, that ideas of progress were eschatological and that secularisation was an illusion, a point developed later in this study. Milbank has drawn attention to this conservative strand in sociology, exemplified in the writings of de Bonald and de Maistre, the belief that institutions have a revealed quality and that 'every human culture represents a post-Babel fragment of God's original self-presence to humankind'.[17] There is a masking, a property of disguise in the relationship between secularisation and sociology. As Milbank notes, sociology illuminates 'to the extent that it conceals its own theological borrowings and its own quasi-religious status'.[18]

The flirtation of sociology with Catholic theology relates to an intellectual history to be written. Catholic thinkers were only too well aware of the threat sociology posed to its belief. But in France, sociology seemed to have little sense of its limitations in dealing with theology. In its earlier flirtations, its ambitions were largely those of positivism. But the effects were devastating for as Lepenies notes, 'there arose a sociological metaphysics which did more harm to its adherents than any military invasion: the destruction of their inner life'.[19]

German sociology was far more involved in spiritual matters from its inception, although it is difficult to trace a distinctively Catholic influence in its tradition. As a fledgling discipline, sociology was conceived in a climate of political hostility. Its relationship to the aesthetic, the modern and the cultural was at best ambiguous. The scientific pretensions of sociology and the positivist aura attached to it, sat uneasily with the fixation on disenchantment Weber and Simmel noted in a culture of modernity. The spirit of calculation and predictability, the property of power of science, which sociology sought to emulate, became a mechanism for the despiritualisation of culture and also its dehumanisation. In this division, sociology was divided against itself, seeming to be implicated in the advance of what it despised. The more it explained, the less it seemed to understand. Thus, there was something Janus faced about German sociology's approach to modern culture, where it claimed to be its beneficiary but was also fated to be its gravedigger.[20] German sociology recognised that modernity and culture embodied a Faustian paradox which Simmel noted, that 'as man becomes more cultivated, his life becomes more oblique and opaque'.[21] This paradox arises in the context of the reflexivity of the sociologist. As he becomes more aware of the endless social detail he uncovers in culture he seems self-estranged. The typicality he seeks in reflexive terms makes him atypical. In sociological terms, analytical success breeds isolation.

This sense of being trapped, of being a prisoner of advance in knowing, famously arises with Weber's notion of the iron cage. Weber gave sociology its own distinctive antinomy, of the growth of rationality, exemplified in the bureaucratic apparatus, whose inexorable development led to the erosion of non-rational belief and to a condition of disenchantment. Far from providing an escape from religious belief, such as Comte naïvely envisaged, the form of sociology Weber deposited on to posterity, which, in retrospection postmodernity has exposed, is of a discipline riddled with a sense of fate to be suffered with little prospect of escape. Archive work on Weber, his biography and background is now exposing a far more tortured moral critic of culture than sociology has hitherto realised. His Lutheran background, and of course his work on Calvinism and the rise of capitalism gave him a unique interest in the culture of Protestantism that had a profound impact on his sociological vision.[22] Swatos suggests that Weber's concerns with local theological issues justify considering him a Christian sociologist.[23] The secularisation of sociology has effectively masked Weber's theological debts. Speaking of the cold precision of Weber's insights, the famous distinction of types of actions distinguished by the rational from the non-rational, the emotional, Albrow noted that

> several generations of sociology students, both mystified and fascinated by the most tightly framework of concepts in the discipline have in fact unwittingly been confronted with the secularised answers to problems posed by the Protestant reformers: If everything is determined, how are people free? How does reason guide creatures of flesh and blood? In a world of sin and chaos what is the source of certainty?

For Albrow, Weber 'captured in his formulations so much of the routines of a modern life which had been indelibly marked by Protestantism'.[24]

Weber's comments on science and theology are significant. For him, 'all theology represents an intellectual *rationalization* of the possession of sacred values'. But the need to use presuppositions to interpret meanings in the world involved the reaching of limits, where 'knowledge' moved into 'possession'. All theologies presuppose a quest for the meaning of life. Faith lies outside sociological remit (a point Kuhn confounded) because it related to presuppositions that could be affirmed or denied in a way that lies outside the explanatory remit of science. Thus Weber argued that the 'tension between the value-spheres of "science" and the sphere of "the holy" is unbridgeable'. For him, ultimate values had retreated from public life into the realm of the mystical or into 'the brotherliness of direct and personal human relations'. The privatisation of belief is related to the link between reason and conscience that effects a secularisation, a point understood in relation to Puritan interests in science but also their demise. As a discipline, sociology is peculiarly implicated in 'the fate of our times', a world of rationalisation and intellectualisation, but also disenchantment. In this latter gloomy sight, sociology is fated to discern what cannot be transcended.[25]

Weber sees few solutions within academic life, for its prophecy would lead to fanatical sects. Thus, as the academy secularised its interests, disenchantment and bureaucratisation would come to pass. Commenting on both Weber and Simmel, Schaff suggested that their

> language is merciless: possibilities are counterbalanced by trivialization, choices by disenchantment. In the end we are trapped by the culture we have created and of which we are a part, but which we can longer master.[26]

A sense of paralysis, of disenchantment, haunts sociology itself. Its analytical instruments lead to a spiritual malaise, hence Weber's interest in the prospects of re-enchantment. Sociology has a capacity to uncover what it cannot resolve within contemporary culture. Schaff encapsulates well the plight that sociology has exposed, that 'today this world itself, that *we* have created, resists and opposes re-enchantment, while our own "bearing" or human condition has been disenchanted and denuded of its mythical, but inwardly genuine plasticity'.[27] Protecting the freedom of choice of the actor in the face of the hostile claims of an increasingly ordered culture, where little cannot be manufactured, is at the root of sociological obligations to the humanities. These were embodied in the worries of C. Wright Mills over the advent of 'the cheerful robot' whose individuality and human nature was in question. Rationalisation had masked some essential questions on the nature of the human condition. Issues were being disguised that led man to become a stranger to himself. There was something distinctive in the social structure of modern society that generated these questions and this metaphysical disquiet demanded sociological attention. Mills went on to argue that:

> the advent of the alienated man and all the themes which lie behind his advent now affect the whole of our serious intellectual life and cause our immediate intellectual malaise. It is a major theme of the human condition in the contemporary epoch and of all studies worthy of the name. I know of no idea, no theme, no problem, that is so deep in the classic tradition – and so much involved in the possible default of contemporary social science.[28]

Mills did not relate this notion of estrangement, the illusions of the cheerful robot, to theology, but he points to concerns with authenticity and freedom at the root of the sociological imagination, that can be amplified into a theological setting. Estrangement can relate to disbelief that has no limit, but which becomes corrosive of the social bond. It turns aesthetics to issues of deception and enfeebles social transactions. To that degree, it has a central place in sociological interests but in a way that intersects with theological considerations. There has been a theological agenda even to the most secular of sociological interests. Social attributes are read from theological positions, most famously in the discussion of the tightness or weakness of social bonds in effecting suicide rates.[29]

Enchantment stands against secularisation in that it admits the possibility of belief, of what lies beyond reason and transcends its basis. To understand the possibility of enchantment, one needs to speculate on how sociology became subject to a process of secularisation? Clearly, this is a highly complex question. Whereas the emergence of sociology in the United States was closely related to Protestantism, the circumstances of its gestation within the United Kingdom were almost completely secular.

The growth of sociology in the USA was facilitated by its Protestant connections. Reformist links, a conservative belief in science, combined with a Protestant individualism aided its rapid expansion.[30] Protestantism was a resource that legitimised the advance of sociology in the USA. Its advance was assisted by three elements which Beckford highlights: a Puritan concern with stewardship of the collective; the contributions of the Social Gospel to social engineering; and 'positivism's faith in the capacity of scientific knowledge, correctly applied, to solve all of society's major problems'.[31] But the Protestantism that facilitated the rise of American sociology sowed the seeds of its secularisation. Sociology assimilated into its soul instruments of secularisation, an expectation of its legitimacy and an analytical stance that accelerated its basis. Its readings were structured away from recognition that sources of enchantment might lie in theology itself. Its movements were in the opposite direction. Pragmatism and an emphasis on individual self-improvement bestowed a certain optimism on American sociology. As it gained in self-confidence, its Protestant origins became obscured. Science became sacralised as religion became desacralised.

The rise of British sociology was entirely unrelated to religious considerations. Its roots in the early twentieth century were in eugenics, and evolutionary theory, and applied studies of poverty. There was no theoretical background to the discipline, nor the development of middle range speculation that linked theory to research, such as occurred in France and Germany.[32] Prior to 1950, few sociologists engaged in debate with German writings on the autonomy of the cultural sciences, Collingwood being a notable exception. As suggested later, sociological recognition of culture, where issues that relate to theology might have surfaced, has been very recent, and has only emerged in the context of debate on postmodernity. The genesis of recent British sociology was directed away from concerns that might have led it in a theological direction. Whilst British sociology was definitely secular, oddly, the more fashionable social anthropology had some unexpectedly Catholic leanings.[33] If the issue of culture was marginalised in the two disciplines, colonial in the case of anthropology, and patrician and therefore to be despised in sociology, it is scarcely surprising that there has been some uneasiness in handling it in the context of postmodernity. The current issue of the absence of rules in handling culture has to be related to the lack of a English sociological tradition in handling its basis. Sociologists were marginal to British culture and being so de-centred, were estranged also from the Christianity embodied in Anglicanism.

Much of recent British sociology has been associated with the Labour party in the post-war period. In an important exercise in the sociology of sociologists, Halsey has pointed to the provincial origins of many British sociologists. It was a grammar school discipline, conceived in the provinces by those who felt marginal to British culture. This gave a sense of the outsider to British sociology, a left wing quality and a concern with those marginalised, by class, race, or morals. If there was a theological root, it might have been Methodist. Certainly, it was not Catholic. If there was an identifiable religious strand in the rise of British sociology it was Jewish.[34] Lepenies draws attention to a fascinating glimpse into what might have been if the Christian sociology, which interested T. S. Eliot, had blossomed. William Temple and Karl Mannheim were involved in this inchoate link between Anglicanism and sociology before World War II.[35]

The marginality of English sociology was compounded by the circumstances of its late expansion. Uniquely, amongst advanced industrialised societies, such as Japan, Germany France and the USA, England had only a handful of departments up to the 1950s. It was the Robbins report in 1963 that effected its rapid expansion. Some 28 new university departments of sociology were created in the 1960s. Sociology became linked to modernisation and secularisation. But it also came to embody all that many feared would debase and dilute traditional English culture. This has cast English sociology in an equivocal role in relation to English culture. In a perverse way, secularisation joins sociology to religion in affirming the marginality of both within English culture.

This British experience of recent expansion of sociology was less atypical in Europe than its critics realised. Contrary to the reputation of their classical thinkers in forming the traditions of sociology, as a discipline, it only grew in the 1960s also in France and Germany.[36] With student disorders in 1968, sociology was further scapegoated as a dispensable wart on the English cultural landscape. Public schools were remarkably resistant to recognising the subject, despite its expansion in the Tripos at Cambridge. Social anthropology was acceptable in a way sociology was not. Despite these difficulties, sociology consolidated its position in the universities in the 1970s. In the 1980s the combined effect of a deep hostility from Sir Keith Joseph and Thatcherism left sociologists with a siege mentality, always under attack, a perpetual outsider with few friends and many enemies. 'A' level sociology expanded in the 1980s. It also became part of the curricula in professional training for nursing, police, medicine and town planners, to name a few. By the late 1980s it had consolidated its position in higher education. Universities, which had closed their departments in the early 1980s, reopened some of them to meet student demand.

Sociology survived the 1980s, in some cases, through a capacity to change its name and decamp to other disciplines such as social policy, management studies, to name a few. This capacity, to evacuate and to disguise, generated worries about the autonomy of the subject, which were expressed in the subject report on sociology of the University Grants Committee, 1989. Reflecting on this report, Westergaard and Pahl noted the contributions sociology makes across disciplines, in areas such as management, cultural and mass media studies, medicine and race relations.[37] Its use and significance has been grasped in geography, philosophy and history, but imperfectly so in theology for reasons that form a concern of this study.

The current distinctive accomplishments of British sociology, its theoretical richness and its advances in a number of areas provide a setting for sociology of religion, but one of marginality in a discipline that is itself still not quite central within traditional academic culture. Within these marginalities, the number of Catholic sociologists in the United Kingdom is small. Those with a research interests in Catholicism are just sufficient to occupy a section of the back seat of the Clapham omnibus. Again this might seem to make the issue of Catholicism within sociology of slight significance.

In the United Kingdom, sociology of religion is taught in terms of Berger, Freud, Weber and Durkheim. Even though its focus is narrow, the identity of this branch of sociology is unclear. The issue of what appears on an undergraduate curriculum in sociology of religion begs questions as to what is legitimised and how the academic field is identified. Spickard shows that the situation regarding the narrowness of what is taught within sociology of religion also arises in the USA. Typologies of church-sect-cult mixed with current religious trends mark what is presented in the main introductory sociology textbooks. In these, the issue of religion is marginalised from other sections of sociology, effecting a domestic secularisation of its basis. Religion is treated as an institution, amongst others, but not of central sociological concern. In studying texts on sociology of religion, Spickard notes the way non-institutional religions and the position of women are all facets that could contribute to a re-centring of sociology of religion in the mainstream of the discipline. But more importantly, he sees the link between modernity and religion as leading to a fresh rethinking.[38] But in this context no reference is made to Catholicism. Nor is any recognition given to the need for a sociology of religion dealing with modernity to connect to theological discourse to confront issues that threaten to engulf sociological dealings with culture. Failure to link sociology of religion to a theology means that the expected route that might have ameliorated the endemic secularisation of the discipline as a whole has been blocked. This disconnection institutionalises the marginalisation of Catholicism to sociology and naturalises it into a tradition, but one which might have been otherwise.

Dobbelaere indicates that the two major associations in the USA and Europe for the promotion of sociology of religion grew out of Catholic Associations. Reflecting on the genesis of the CISR (International Conference for the Sociology of Religion) formed at Louvain, in 1948, Dobbelaere notes some of the tensions that operated between Catholicism and sociology in Europe. Worries over a crude positivism and a Durkheimian tradition generated caution in Rome towards lending formal recognition to the group in the first two decades of its formation. A sociology of religion emerged that was to be of service to the Church, that was to be confined to the study of facts and was to be pastoral in orientation. Theological reflection was to be done by others.[39] Thus, Baum notes, Catholic sociologists were guided by a theology but 'their studies had no reflex impact on their theological ideas'.[40] Failure at this pre-conciliar period to establish a traditional link between theology and sociology makes the present endeavour seem artificial. Yet, setting a reflexive sociology within Catholicism yields some unexpected insights in its new role as aide-de-camp to theological speculations about how to realise the holy in the circumstances of postmodernity.

Catholicism did try to make some distinctive links with sociology in the United States. An American Catholic Sociological Society (ACSS) was formed in 1938 and seems to have had little difficulty in gaining recognition from the Catholic hierarchy. By 1964, the alienation Catholic sociologists felt from the main body of American sociology seems to have disappeared. There had been worries over a failure to affirm a humanist dimension in sociology and an excess of concern with its scientific status. But ties with Catholicism and sociology led to a divided identity. In 1970, the association lost its distinctive Catholic voice, and became the Association for the Sociology of Religion.[41] Worries were expressed that a Catholic sociology, whatever that might be, was being formulated away from the mainstream of the discipline. Marginality was combined with a sense of low status within the discipline as a whole. Misunderstandings came also from the Catholic hierarchy. Divisions were expressed between the vocation of a sociologist within the Church and the professional calling this entailed, which pointed to other loyalties.[42]

The demise of this group begs questions as to what is the nature of the link between Catholicism and sociology and why is it so different in 1994, as against in 1970? Is affiliation with Catholicism incompatible with the professional calling of the sociologist and if so, in case of dispute which authority is to reign supreme?

In so far as there are sociological dealings with theology, it is clear that it was not orthodox authority that was being questioned but the supposed authority of liberal theologians. On almost every issue possible, sociology has attacked with considerable vigour the readings of liberal theologians of culture that effected the dismantling of elements that gave faith a mysterious property. For liberal theologians, in so far as they cared, these attacks inconveniently came from sociologists prominent within the discipline as a whole. The list reads like a catalogue of fame. For Berger it involved the amplification of a rumour of angels; for Luhmann it related to the unfortunate dismantling of heaven and hell; and for Turner, it was an unexpected anthropological defence of the Tridentine mass, that came to exemplify sociological and anthropological critiques of the unreflexive callow assumptions of liberal theologians between 1963–1993, a date when the absence of their heirs became all too apparent. The arrogance and disdain of liberal theologians enabled them to patronise orthodox Catholic sociologists, but these looked to their Jewish colleagues, such as Sachs, to speak of what they were not allowed to utter. Any fledgling Catholic approach to sociology encounters many intellectual debts to Jewish colleagues who have been first to feel the dangers of modernity – for obvious reasons.

Again, one has to return to Weber to mark that of which sociology cannot speak. This refers to the presuppositions of theology, issues of faith and revelation, marked as being beyond the limits of its scientific and therefore sociological understanding. There is a necessary property of tension to this unbridgeable division between science and the holy.[43] Sociologists understand the nature of this tension which gives curiosity a motive force to theology. They can live with it, because it lends a property of mystery to religion. It marks a limit, a neat division of labour, a self-imposed constraint, that leaves theologians to speculate on what sociologists cannot utter. Unfortunately, some theologians who look at sociology, think differently.

Thus, Baum regards sociology as contributing to the preferential option of the poor, the underclass which liberation theology seeks to represent. For Baum, such a sociology 'enters into the very constitution of theology'.[44] But this assumption regarding sociology goes further. The issue is not one of moral endorsement, but of discernment of impediments to what theology *can* constitute regarding morality and belief in a culture where the power to commodify seems to reign supreme, producing a galaxy of false idols. These corrupt the cultural base upon which theology seeks to constitute its message.

Matters are not helped by the internal fragmentation in sociology between issues that might connect to theology and those appropriated in the sub-division of the discipline, sociology of religion.

Sociology of religion became a specialism amongst others, viewing religious studies as a rival, but sharing a common and well cultivated disinterest if not hostility towards theology. The cult of professionalisation that seemed so attractive to those seeking relief from Catholicism in the USA in 1970 simply transposed one notion of the sacred, that belonged to theology, to another, the mystique, the prophetic mantle of the sociologist. They entered the realm of Andreski's scathing comment that the social scientist is a form of witch-doctor who makes self-justifying incantations without reference to the facts.[45] There is a self-fulfilling prophecy attached to the detachment of sociology of religion from ecclesial links that seemed to legitimise its dominant interests in secularisation. The marginalisation of Catholic sociologists from their own Church seemed to confirm the notion of the decline in influence of the main Churches in the 1970s within sociology as a whole. The prospects of a dialogue broke down. Theologians felt they had their own means of reading culture and sociologists wished to break from ecclesial ties to find refuge in the mainstream of their discipline. Both sides lost in the context of the rise of postmodernity which later came to pass which confounded both in dealings with culture. This disconnection between sociologists and their Church left a gap open for secularisation but more importantly an obsession with New Religious Movements, which came to dominate the interests of British sociology of religion in the 1980s.

Although sociology of religion sought to connect to the mainstream of the discipline in the 1970s and 1980s it became further isolated from its centre. Beckford has indicated that the effect of this isolation from the mainstream of the discipline has been to mask the significance of religion as a social phenomenon. Echoing a point above, Beckford suggests that there was a death wish involved in the concern with secularisation of religion, which seemed to confirm the marginalisation of both within sociology itself, of religious phenomenon but also the specialism that was supposed to characterise its basis.[46] In a later work, Beckford suggests that the success of sociology of religion in handling narrow, but important topics such as church/sect distinctions, conversions, civil religion and of course secularisation led to a 'community closure' most marked in Britain.[47] The placing of sociology of religion in a ghetto both in relation to the main Churches and also the discipline as a whole, points to institutional reasons for a concern with secularisation. It seemed to affirm links with sociology as to what it was expected to say, but it also legitimised its disconnection from theology. Too often, those concerned with secularisation fail to confront the theological issue it implies, that cultural arrangements have to be rearranged because belief in God has died.

Sociology would be an important witness at the inquest on the death of God. But this would flatter its importance. In a rare passage on sociology, Nietzsche viewed it as a willing dupe overly influenced by decadence. Thus, he affirmed that 'from experience it knows only the form of the decay of society, and inevitably it takes its own instincts of decay for the norms of sociological judgement'.[48] This seems to suggest sociology is but a mirror within modernity capable of reflecting decadence but offering no exit point out of its prison. It seems incapable of resisting the forces of secularisation. Being a partner with modernity it also would seem a willing victim. This returns to the link between reflexivity and decadence and to the unexpected theological turn it took for some in their dealings with modernity. Current interest in postmodernity has resurrected a concern with these unpaid theological debts that lurk on the fringes of the discipline. There are darker, deeper issues which secularisation masks which present sociology with unavoidable theological dilemmas. These lurk unseen, unrecognised, suggesting that sociologists might have been dupes in the face of the deeper theological issues which modernity disguises. Few more vexed or inconclusive debates exist in sociology than those arising over secularisation.

Following Wilson, secularisation can be defined as the diminution of the social significance of religion.[49] In this context, his idea of a sociologist is one who describes this social process dispassionately and 'without the intrusion of any religious (or anti-religious) dispositions and extraneous value-commitments which, as private individuals, they might entertain'.[50] In the light of the shift into a reflexive sociology, implicated and confessional in relation to its subject matter, Wilson lends an antique property to debate on secularisation. A death wish to belief is given a professional mask. A willed belief to disbelieve is unreflexively drawn into his sociology, concealing the mechanism of cultural reproduction that structures a supposedly fated outcome, one emerging from the logic of an old fashioned positivism. This masking of dispositions and extraneous values, which Wilson regards as proper to sociology, affirms the privatisation of religious belief and its removal from the public and social arena. A self-fulfilling prophecy is granted to disbelievers, but denied to believers. The sociological instruments of Wilson's approach to secularisation affirm the vaporisation of religious belief.

But Wilson's analysis does seem plausible. There *has* been an ebbing of the significance of the sacred, expressed in the loosening of ties with traditional religions. One departs from Wilson over the neutered response of sociology to this ebbing, arguing that the discipline is implicated in a choice, which *is* theological, whether it likes it or not.

Secularisation seems to embody a tolerance, a polite reasoned attempt to marginalise religious enthusiasts whose zeal could disrupt the fabric of the civic order. Religious belief has become detached from civility by design rather than default. In the USA, the right *not* to be contaminated by the public expression of religion is increasingly regarded as a civil right. Carter, who is a legal scholar, has explored this process, pointing to an ironic turn whereby the civil rights movement, deeply characterised by religious rhetoric and support, in the 1960s, has had this layer secularised if not disavowed by liberals in the 1990s, embarrassed by the notion of God-talk, even amongst Blacks.[51]

The opacity of the term secularisation generates dilemmas for sociologists when liberal theologians uncritically seek to sanctify the secular, to argue that there is an implicit religion abroad. Such attempts to imperialise are misguided and add to confusions over how sociology is to characterise the relationship between theology and culture. Making holy the secular city represents wishful thinking and locks theology into sociology. It also leads to the contradiction which Bryce noted that

> the more the Church identified with the world, the further did it depart from its own best self. The Church expected or professed to Christianize the world, but in effect the world secularized the Church.[52]

This echoes a paradox which Max Horkheimer noted, that a theology with modernising ambitions 'to keep in tune with science and generally with a world dominated by technical rationality is really the instrument whereby God is cancelled from the field of practical human experience'.[53] Secularisation signifies the cultural conditions of the cancellation of God and theologians who read these too innocently become His shroud manufacturers. It points to the erosion of belief from the cultural field, but also an internal ecclesial disbelief in the autonomy of sacred values. This sacralises and validates the process of secularisation by conferring an authority on culture which sociology denies. It is not a question of theological authority but of judgement, and this is founded on a misrecognition of the opacity of culture in the context of postmodernity.

The ebbing of religion away from the public sphere presents sociology with the issue of finding an alternative, a problem that interested Durkheim. But few can be persuaded by his solution that religion is but a reflection of collective effervescence, where, in this surrogate, relief and alternative belief can be found as compensation for a God that dropped dead in modernity. This solution is untenable and is itself founded on an illusion.

Firstly, it argues that beliefs are real, but that there is no God bar what is mirrored in the collective. Durkheim is concerned with the form of faith and what it fulfils and not its substance. He understands the need for faith in social terms, but one where a God is not required. A religion without God now functions to sacralise social bonds and to effect a harmonisation between the actor and the collective. Religious rituals now function to sustain this collective purpose and to affirm social bonds. But in this account *any* ritual is deemed to work. It need not be religious in intention but could be civil or it could be mass forms of entertainment. But by abandoning what is distinctive about religion, its exclusive functions, Durkheim blunts sociological critiques of religious belief whilst at same time awarding them a significance that is inescapable. At one level

Durkheim is useful for affirming the social significance of solemn assemblies to liberal theologians, but at another level there is an illusory basis to his solution. It does not work in its own terms. This leads to the second point.

Durkheim's solution to religion comes unstuck in a climate of a culture of postmodernity. Self-understandings of culture now deal in its fractured condition. These point to cracks in the collective which the social mirrors, and a fall in faith in its capacity to heal and to harmonise. Disbelief in the social now accelerates what Durkheim feared, an asocial rampant individualism, an egoism of right to make any form of culture without reference to the fracturing effects on the social bond. Privatisation of the self, of morality, of social relationships, point to a retreat from the communal, hence the political interest in communitarianism in the Labour Party in March 1995. The need to reinvent community points to a deficiency in collective social relationships, hardly a safe site for belief in a surrogate for religious belief.

Sociological efforts to resist secularisation are likely to elicit hostile responses from theologians who see the necessity for radical accommodation to prevailing culture. They will resist the injunction to keep oneself untarnished by the world (James 1: 27) as being 'unrealistic'. Progressive accommodation rather than retreat seems required in this cultural context. Furthermore they will charge sociology with compounding its own distinctive heresies when it ventures, however piously, into their territory. These emerge over what sociology *might* presuppose in theological terms in characterising assumption and presumption in acting in relation to the Divine in the world, where the issue of secularity emerges. Thus a doceticism can reduce the presence of the Divine to mere appearance, subtracting from the incarnational and mitigating the necessity of acting, whereas an over emphasis on human agency (which might seem most likely to complement sociological readings of theology) can lead to pelagianism, to the notion of a self-starting capacity to act without grace in relationships with God. These are theological notions that can be telescoped in and out of sociological deliberations with impunity. Theologians can run rings around sociological arguments, mocking them for being pious versions of Monsieur Jourdain, speaking neo-Platonism without realising it, in their advocacy of the need to take account of the transcendent, the silent and the antinomial.

But such theological despisers of humble sociological interventions in their realm have to face the issue that paralyses them, that something *has* gone wrong in contemporary culture, which has become despiritualised, that numbers cannot keep ebbing away, and that theologians do not know how to formulate connections to life as lived. Theologians tinker with the scenery. Somehow, their message is not getting below the surface of culture where the issue of God is marginalised. This failure is ironic given the dissatisfaction some feel about the current state of academic culture. A need is emerging to break out from the spiritual apathy which secularisation sustains.

In his splendid polemic, *Real Presences*, Steiner sharply criticises the masking of God in contemporary academic thought. He suggests that to speak of spiritual needs is to risk uncertainties. It is to live with personal thoughts that have no intellectual station and to risk breaking academic conventions about secular thought. Steiner notes that 'structuralist semiotics and deconstruction are expressions of a culture and society which "play it cool"', but he goes on to add 'these are potent rationalizations'. At the close of this argument, he writes

> I want to suggest that they mask a more radical flinching; that the embarrassment we feel in bearing witness to the poetic, to the entrance into our lives of the mystery of otherness in art and in music, is of a metaphysical-religious kind.[54]

Yet behind this reticence is a worry, a sense of unsettlement with the triviality of contemporary culture where there is an incapacity to address matters of serious concern. This state reflects Pascal's comment that

> being unable to cure death, wretchedness and ignorance, men have decided, in order to be happy, not to think about such things.[55]

This movement towards a seeking of comfort based on denial relates to MacIntyre's notion of emotivism. He defines this concept as the position where 'all moral judgements are *nothing but* expressions of preference, expressions of attitude or feeling, insofar as they are moral or evaluative in character'.[56] Thus, a crucial strand of secularity is to imply the irrelevance of religious belief in a self-confirming manner that masks the cracks. The capacity to naturalise, to gloss over, that forms part of the secularisation of culture, makes everything too neat for metaphysical comfort.

It is the indifference that secularisation effects that causes the sociologist to look more closely. Secularisation takes on a timeless ease that enables certain matters to be forgotten. For instance, MacIntyre is not the first to note Weber's debts to Nietzsche.[57] But Nietzsche's hostility to Christianity, however, equivocal, is also forgotten, or rather it is deemed to be of sociological irrelevance so far is the discipline pushed forward into a secularity. Thus, *Ecce Homo* carries no worries for the sociologist, who might settle for issues of the will, and the exposure of priest craft but would miss the Christ that so antagonised and so disturbed Nietzsche.[58] He might well have attached nihilism to modernity, but could scarcely recognise the indifference that has come to pass.

But what sociologist could not be moved by the power of unlimited knowing, of fleeing the crippling antiquarianism of the sacred with its emphasis on sin, mercy and grace for the unclean? There is a seductive quality to removal of those impediments which Nietzsche envisioned that leads to an ideal state. Thus he wrote

> so let us live above them like strong winds, neighbours of the eagles, neighbours of the snow, neighbours of the sun: that is how strong winds live. And like a wind will I one day blow among them and with my spirit take away the breath of their spirit; thus my future will have it.[59]

This lofty ambition, of being above humanity leaves others to judge. Bauman sees a question deposited inconveniently on to a later generation of sociologists, too democratic to be so presumptuous. With God dead, the throne is vacant so who will sit in judgement? The limits which belief in God secured are now limitless and so Bauman concludes by asking

> and yet who more than we, sociologists, are fit to alert our fellow humans to the gap between the necessary and the real, between the survival significance of moral limits and the world determined to live – and to live happily, and perhaps even ever after – without them.[60]

Somehow, living in the limitless makes one wonder if the hand of God is just invisible and whether He is dead.

The theme of MacIntyre's work, *After Virtue*, indicates that the construction of ethics has not escaped its theological debts, and that the Enlightenment has not disposed of these. Issues of will, of aesthetics and culture, all point to a self floundering in a disjunction between private sensibilities and public obligations.

Sociology needs to be reminded that there are other versions of will available from theology and philosophy beside those of Nietzsche, which have so penetrated the culture of postmodernity in the offers it makes of self-actualisation. There is the Thomist version for a start. Aquinas regarded the will as a power superior to understanding. Freewill is about a power to choose that involves the exercise of desire, a capability of the soul that points to issues of grace. Within this power is a property of habit, the means by which choice is realised.[61] For the past two decades, sociology has been undergoing an internal revolution in its approach to issues of ethics, the responsibilities for choice that lead to questions of judgement, which by default turn back into the theological as the purely secular becomes incredible. The present state of affairs is unacceptable.

The endless shifting of culture is increasingly having the property of living in a desert. If as Vattimo suggests, modernity does embody a property of value, a faith in progress which is both 'a secularized faith and a faith in secularization' then the task of finding a safe site has become hopeless in the context of a culture of postmodernity.[62] Abolishing God traps sociology in a collective amnesia and the forgetting of Dostoyevsky's comment that

> the mystery of human life is not only in living, but in knowing why one lives. Without a clear idea of what to live for man will not consent to live and will rather destroy himself than remain on the earth, though he were surrounded by loaves of bread.[63]

This might also seem to return the sociologist back to the window of the bread shop to look again at issues which secularity masks.

The issue of value and choice has been undergoing a quiet revolution in the culture of sociology itself since 1968. Friedrichs captures well this shift in the moral sensibility of American sociology from a cult of clinical disengagement, prior to the 1970s, to an effort to recover a prophetic and priestly mode, of course, different to Comte, that would adjust sociology to the changing cultural sensibilities wrought after 1968.

Morality was expressed in terms of an ethic of responsibility for freedom, liberation and dialogue.[64] Moral engagement aimed to uncover and to root out structures that damaged or hindered forms of self-actualisation. But little attention was given to the *reasons* for being ethical, a neglect signified by the little sociological attention that has been given to MacIntyre's famous work, *After Virtue*. This has now changed. Thus, Connor notes that

> after so long a time in which even to utter the word 'ethics' in mixed critical company was to commit the worst of social gaffes (a worse blunder, even, than blurting out the word 'aesthetic'), the 'ethical turn' which seems currently to be taking place in the various provinces of critical theory, in feminism, Marxism, deconstruction, discourse theory, psycho-analysis and so on, is surprising and also gratifying.[65]

If ethics has made a return to sociological reflexivity, issues of good and bad are permitted to emerge, such as questions of conscience, but also the formation of religious character. A revolution in analytical concerns is signified, that permits sociology to speak of that which it would be too embarrassed to notice: the cultivation of virtue, and the subcultures that embody and realise its basis.

Reconsiderations are abroad, individual, not collective, but present sufficient to require consideration, for postmodernity raises some odd implications. In his effort to engage with the plethora of postmodern culture, Mestrovic conveys an awareness of its endless pastiches, its playfulness where ethics and aesthetics have become subject to anarchism and a feigned optimism that skates along the surface of humanity. The credentials of his reflexivity are well displayed in this study whose theme, of the title, is *The Coming Fin de Siècle*. He is worried by the anomie rampant, the dying of Marxism and that a richness of humanity is being progressively obscured. But, if as he suggests, the West needs a new faith, it cannot come from contemporary sociology which endures its own crisis.[66] Sociologists, themselves, seem to be seeking their own faith for as Mestrovic observes

> contemporary social scientists are trained to be cynics who search for falsehood, not truth. Not surprisingly, and in a typically postmodern fashion, many scientists follow Popper from the hours of nine to five and turn to fundamentalist, religious beliefs after work to satisfy their need for faith. Postmodernism allows one to live in such a contradiction.[67]

There is a growing realisation, possibly not well focused or articulated, that there is a disjunction between public belief in reason and progress that sociology embodies and a doubt, a spiritual angst, amongst sociologists, whose forms of relief are privatised, masked and removed from suspicion and accountability. An unacknowledged insecurity has invaded the sense of self of the sociologist. It is this crisis in reflexivity that has given rise to second thoughts about the link between theology and culture.

In the 1970s, deviance generated a sociological need to represent the underdog. But the focus of representation shifts as culture changes. George Bernard Shaw's comment that minorities are always right, carries a fatal flaw. They become tomorrow's majorities. Yesterday's deviants have become today's conformists. Sexual politics have sought to wipe out a distinctive sociological phenomenon: the study of underground life. Cultural rights dictate that these appear above ground and that sexual deviance is to be normalised. Now, other forms of deviance operate beyond the cultural pale, or lurk below its surface, unsignified, unrepresented in sociology or in the mass media, small in number, but there: those young who seek to construct a life of virtue, as monks and nuns, a fledgling phenomenon, perhaps, but unexpectedly there in the USA, in France and Germany. These new, but tiny minorities seek to cultivate a property in short supply: sanctity.

Amongst the first to signify faith in progress, sociology is also in front affirming its indefiniteness, its inadequacy and the need to look for some other index of cultural quality. Sociology has not sought a theological question: it has simply fallen into one in the context of culture and postmodernity. This fall started before the rise of a culture of postmodernity.

Writing in 1968, at a time of great social unrest, with a decline in institutional religion well under way, occurring at the same time as the ideals of love and peace of the counterculture were being formulated, Huston Smith argued that the sacred was durable and likely to make a return. Reading this essay, one is surprised at how many of its insights, original and critical at the time, have become recycled into a culture of postmodernity increasingly detached from the originals that shaped its basis. Thus, encounter goups dealing with sensitivity to religious experience were being formed. These have now been secularised and incorporated into lifestyle politics, feminism and New Age religions. Smith defines the sacred in a somewhat undifferentiated way suggesting that it deals with what is vital, problematic and exceeds our comprehension and control. It is a property that has come to shape mass culture since 1968. From his experience he suggests that

> the human mind stands ready to believe anything – absolutely anything – as long as it provides an alternative to the totally desacralized mechano-morphic outlook of objective science.[68]

It is this impulsion within sociology that indicates what it is fleeing into, a theology, a basis of belief that will transcend the vacuity of the discipline acting alone. But if it flees into theology, sociology takes flight into orthodoxy, into tradition and revelation. It seeks what it cannot reinvent, what lies at the limits of modernity, the fringes of the wasteland. If sociology does take a pious turn, it is in an ascetic direction, the reckless poacher turned into an inquisitorial gamekeeper. As sociology cannot coin ideals, it can merely confound those who fail, who ought to know better, the discipline takes on some unexpected properties when set in a theological nexus. Whereas the discrepancy between ideal and reality governed a critical sociology dealing with political and social realities, the resetting of such instruments in a theological setting suggests a movement from Marx to John the Baptist, a passage of affiliation as perverse as it is unexpected. To articulate its religious sensibility, its scent of metaphysical dangers within a culture of postmodernity, sociology has to exaggerate its case against a despiritualised culture. This lends an unexpected property of prophecy in the sociological gaze at the link between theology and culture, for sociology feels the icy winds of disbelief stingingly. Being a discipline unendowed with lineages of grace it has to harry theology to rethink its traditions to ameliorate the unbearable vacuity to which it gives unique witness in a culture of postmodernity. In taking a pious turn, sociology is likely to turn its analytical guns on the notion that led it away from religious belief, the enemy it knows best: secularisation.

Secularisation is a myth. The crucial task facing sociology is the persistence of religious belief where it is not supposed to operate. The new religious movements warned of something against the tide; religious fundamentalism signified a revolt against modernity; and the fringe activities of the New Age all pointed to something afoot. Since 1989, and the collapse of Marxism, it is quite clear that tribal divisions, such as in Bosnia have come back with a vengeance. Like Northern Ireland, nationalism is resurrected with religious tags. But as Martin indicates, religion is given an incidental status in these conflicts, which are perversely understood in terms of nationalism. The religious aspect is marginalised and placed under the umbrella term secularisation.[69] Hamnett's telling characteristic of religion as error still rules many sociological imaginations.[70] But there are versions of secularisation that do link into the growth of religious sensibilities that are peculiar to modernity. Hervieu-Léger has done much to think through a new version of secularisation.

She admits a shrinkage of the social, cultural and symbolic space of French Catholicism since 1968 but also notes the persistence of charismatic groups, which point to radical reforms of renewal in the 1980s, which the French Bishops have tried to harness. These signify distinctive phenomena operating that seem peculiar to modernity. This relates to her central point that modernity is now producing its own religious universe. This emerges from the distinctive uncertainties which modernity produces. She conceives these uncertainties in terms of the tension between the rising expectations of modernity '*and* the feeling of helplessness arising from the awareness that it provokes of the world's opaqueness'. Thus, she points to a paradox that a heightened sense of autonomy, of all-powerfulness, arises just as the mechanism which realises this seems to be breaking down.[71] This reflects an important, but unnoticed shift in sociology of religion in France. But it also relates to the issue of monastic foundations, new religious orders that are likely to replace new religious movements as a focus of sociological interest. These relate to a radical revolt against modernity, and point to unexpected processes of re-enchantment within a culture of postmodernity. These religious orders which appeal specifically to the young are not supposed to be present on the sociological landscape.[72]

The issue of secularisation is riddled with contradictions. For instance, the supposed link between industrialisation and urbanisation and religious decline does not operate in the USA.[73] Even more suspect is reference to notions of civil implicit forms of religion which impute a process of sacralisation to the secular as if there had been a melt down of the theological and one was looking for the embers. As Stark and Iannaccone indicate, faith in the secularisation thesis is declining, marking a veritable paradigm shift in sociology of religion, as concern moves from disbelief to that untapped issue – the volume of belief in societies supposed to be highly secularised.[74]

In *The Life of Aelred*, Walter Daniel pointed to the image conveyed of the arrival of monks in England. This clearly fired Aelred to emulate, to go and to do likewise. These

> remarkable men, famed for their religious life, were known as white monks after the colour of their habit, for they were clothed angel-like in undyed sheep's wool, spun and woven from the natural fleece. Thus garbed, when clustered together they look like flocks of gulls and shine as they walk with the very whiteness of snow.[75]

This army of mutual love attracted Aelred, but also others since, to a standardised life that in other circumstances would crush the self, but which paradoxically enables it to flower to the awe of outsiders.

Seeing the bare ruined choirs, it is easy for nostalgia to loom, to believe that secularisation has a case, that modernity represents a fall from grace, from a supposed golden age of practice of the medieval world. But Stark and Iannaccone show this to be false. Superstition and disbelief were rife in the medieval world. What is left to posterity are the golden exceptions.[76] The very richness of medieval life, where Catholicism embraced all aspects, with few profane rivals, perhaps could not last.[77]

The medieval vision still haunts modernity. It casts an impossible injunction of imitation on to contemporary culture. It suggests that in some mysterious manner the soil of this contemporary culture *cannot* be religious. But medieval history increasingly exposes a world of passion and corruption, where life was very nasty, exceedingly brutish and for some, mercifully short. Such revisionism also brings into stark relief the heroic virtues cultivated by some in this period, where charity was organised into hospitals, where learning was gathered into the universities and monasteries and where virtue was achieved in monastic regimes that made real demands on the monks and nuns who lived a life that aroused awe, not only amongst their contemporaries, but which has also fascinated historians since, at its richness, its beauty and its simplicity. Grace can come again.

Part of the myth of secularisation is its cultivation of a supposed indifference to the sacred. The argument being that the sacred has diminished and is in some way irrelevant. It has left a space which secularity now fills. But another part of the myth of secularisation is that this was in some way an accidental happening, without guile or a mechanism of reproduction of disbelief. By the nature of reason, secularisation was fated to happen.

Indifference is not a term one could use in relation to the writings of Franco Ferrarotti, the Italian sociologist of religion. He writes in a language and on topics undreamt of in Anglo-American sociology of religion. Deeply, if not eccentrically engaged in debate on Catholicism, with much sparring with John Paul II, Ferrarotti covers an exceptional range of interests. His main concerns are in the sociology of the sacred and the nature of faith. This covers an attempt to draw together similarities between the main religions.

Ferrarotti's essay on secularisation gives a fresh reading to the term. He traces the term to 1648, as referring to the usurpation of ecclesiastical goods. Ferrarotti suggests that the term had a masking function that concealed an ambiguous terminology, a form of mystification that did not quite conceal the process of confiscation. He goes on to add that it is not 'neutral to have resource to the concept of secularization, which clearly shows its real value as trick and domination'.[78] His essay also draws attention to the process of competition involved in secularisation, a form of displacement, so that processes such as individual autonomy and self-realization are made even more free from the fetters of a religious type. It is the loss of monopoly of functions for dealing with matters of life and death that most signifies the erosion of the Churches.

An aspect of the theft which secularisation signifies is the displacement it effects of objects from the sacred to the profane, with impunity, for the governance of entertainment. Thus, *The Word*, the utterance of the Divine, the designation of revelation, is hijacked from its biblical setting to become the title of a recent, now late, British television programme of irredeemable vulgarity. Blasphemy is now a right, an artistic licence of freedom to invert, to profane the sacred. As Blumenberg notes

> secularization as an intentional style consciously seeks a relation to the sacred as a provocation. A considerable degree of continuing acceptance of the religious sphere in which the language originates has to be present in order to make possible such an effect, just as 'black theology' can only spread its blasphemous terror where the sacral world still persists.[79]

The disappearance of the ideal of imitation and the going from simplicity of mere mimesis to creation has generated an anarchy, one that comes to characterise the condition of postmodernity.[80] Misrecognition of the difference between a black and white mass poses no angst for the unchurched, too ignorant to be frightened. But behind this studied indifference lies an easy dalliance with blasphemy in aspects of popular culture. This reflects a nagging wish that some frontiers of shock can be uncovered in an age when the tide of religious sensibility is running out and indifference and boredom are all too threatening. Unfortunately, the power to shock has also diminished.

The playing profanely with impunity with sacred images in a careless blasphemy is a licence which a secular culture grants to itself. But the play stops when deep seated taboos are violated in a manner that is a public affront. The privatised rhetoric of moral indifference is found wanting and unfamiliar metaphors are resurrected. Thus, the shocked response to the Bulger case and the relentless murder in Rwanda pointed to a sensibility that divisions of human nature still persist in a culture characterised by postmodernity. Few wish to speak of evil or the Satanic. Despite dismissal by psychiatrists as scare stories, as rhetoric of the dark ages, reference to evil forces afoot in the Bulger case became part of public response.

But the wish to explain away evil in terms of reason could itself be a deception as Ferrarotti notes in a splendidly entitled essay, 'The Satanic Ambiguity of the Sacred'. Images of evil are no longer the property of organised religion but of the leisure industry. Films and videos play on the fascination with evil in horror films, where metaphysical dangers are masked and deeper theological issues are seldom confronted. The neo-Gothic legacy of the Romantic era, when monks were cast as mad and bad and when vampires were abroad, has left a legacy which Hollywood spends with impunity. These dark tales are cast as harmless fantasies that veil deeper issues through the technological miracle of film and video. The evil so presented is rendered innocuous. The aim is get viewers to return for more entertainment.

Ferrarotti is interested in this blindness to evil within industrialised societies. He argues that a society that wishes to disengage from tradition, that does not wish to hear of evil, or the Fall, reaches a limit. He suggests that 'its limit lies in not knowing the meaning of limit. It reduces evil to an organisational dysfunction'. Again, echoing a point of Smith, mentioned above, Ferrarotti indicates that

> the 'paradox of the sacred' seems indeed to lie in the empirically ascertainable fact that the more a society is rationalized, the more the hunger for the supramundane and the invisible grows.

Ferrarotti goes on to argue that hell is increasingly seen by some theologians, such as von Balthasar, as a void, one dealing less with punishment than with privation and distancing.[81] The characteristics of hell, which Ferrarotti touches on, seem also to denote the condition of postmodernity.

But they also relate to conditions of disguise and misrecognition. As John Paul II stated 'the skill of Satan in the world is that of inducing men to deny his existence in the name of rationalism and every other system of thought that seeks every pretext so as not to admit his works'.[82]

These comments raise some awkward questions for sociology. They suggest a failure of reflexivity that is theological in implication. They also point to a divergence in characterising moral pathologies in society, from a fallen condition, a disarrangement resulting from the sin of Adam, to a grounded Durkheimian notion of anomie that relates to the division of labour whose structure embodies an issue of organic solidarity. The levels could be complementary but they are unlikely to be, because the terms of reference diverge in their limits. The former admits a theological issue which the latter assumes to be missing. But if a sociology of evil is accepted, this relates to issues of judgement that reach back to Genesis. The narrative of the first temptation of man might seem even further outside sociological remit, but it was an issue that fascinated Blumenberg and Benjamin. Even if they were so haunted, this relates to theological and ethical issues on the fringe of sociology, or so it might be argued. Sociology has no arena where it is called to account to consider a question of evil. But if such sites exist, these graft theological issues on to sociology, whether it wishes it or not. They implicate a sociological reflexivity into theological issues.

Placing the issue of evil in the context of sociology might arise in the case of the relationship perceived between pornography and women. This is a new, important, site where gratification and evil are interlinked. But the immediate response to the question of evil is to dispatch the problem to anthropology, to issues of witchcraft, spells and oracles where such questions are believed to belong. Such marginalisation, however natural, obscures the way the issue does continue to lurk in sociology. An obvious site for the issue of evil arises in the context of sociology of medicine. Pain relates to suffering which always begs a question as to why? Anxiety and pain thresholds relate to cultural dispositions but also to forms of meaning which they generate. Apart from sadists, few people now bear pain for the strengthening of character. It is an embarrassing disvalue in society, a condition to be eradicated, but at a price, for as Illich notes, the eradication of pain enhances dependence on the miraculous powers of the medical profession. But it also has meant that 'pain has ceased to be conceived as a "natural" or "metaphysical" evil'.[83] The reduction of pain to a technical issue of disposal removes a crucial ingredient for compassion, but also a facet of reflexivity that points in a theological direction. Illich betrays a Catholic background, when he suggests that 'pain-killing

turns people into unfeeling spectators of their own decaying selves'.[84] The
insensibility is not only physical, but is also moral and social. Uniquely,
the self in a culture of postmodernity is highly likely to come to theological issues without going through a passage of suffering. This technical
management of the body means a dullness towards issues of sin and the
need for penance, an imperative that seems to have almost vanished even
from Catholic culture.

The suffering of innocent children always raises difficult questions, that
relate to a wager as whether to believe in God or not.[85] It might be said
that these issues are to the side of sociology, somewhere in a nether region
between psychology and theology. Certainly, issues of the bearing of pain
might relate to cultural styles of suffering, but again these relate to anthropology rather than to sociology.

But any sociologist reading Bauman's *Modernity and Holocaust* is likely
to have a disembodied reflexivity sharply shaken by a disquieting study
that asks some very awkward questions. Idle secularity might conjure with
the issue of whether God is dead or not, but those who suffered in the
concentration camps faced a different issue of an absent God. The issue
was not so much about God being hidden or concealed, that was important,
but about what civilisation itself had masked, and hidden from judgement,
a capacity for evil that was interwoven in a culture whose style had dis-
pelled such a medieval notion. The industrialisation of death, that became
an excellence in dispatch, occurred in a veneer of normality that disguised
an evil, the grossness of which still cannot grasped in words that do not
debase the tragedy of the event. How could sociology be involved in this
issue? Has it anything to say, given that it is implicated in a secular
rhetoric where evil is treated as a medieval nonsense?

The issue of this disguise of evil relates directly to a distinctive concern
of sociology: the question of a disinterested bureaucracy. The bureaucratic
disinterested values of calculation that facilitated the growth of capitalism
were turned to coordinate efficiently the production of mass murder. Im-
personality in operation aided an increase in production and at the same
time diminished the intervention of unproductive feelings of compassion
for the victims. It is somehow insufficient to use a Weberian characterisation of these organisations in terms of an indifference to goals, or values,
when they were geared for the production of death. Absence of comment,
of judgement, would leave sociology open to charges of analytical collusion.
But forcing sociology to comment reveals the inadequacy of its moral
rhetoric for characterising such transactions. This places sociology in a
moral dilemma, but one that reaches into theological issues it long thought
it had discarded: the issue of good and evil. Sociological conventions of

reflexivity become grotesquely inadequate when faced with such collective evil. Bauman is right to ask why in the light of the Jewish contribution to the formation of the discipline, and its characterisation of modernity, did the sociological dog did not bark in this night of murder?[86] The weakness of German sociology could be one reason for the silence.[87] Another could be the link between sociology, Social Darwinism and eugenics.

The limitless right to know by scientists, whose use of data without qualms over the immoral circumstances of their construction, forms another strand of disquiet in Bauman's book. This freedom from moral accountability for limitless curiosity arises in the Faustian tragedy that also afflicts sociology. But it could be just reflecting the limitless quality to knowing that characterises a secularised modernity. The combination of masking and the limitless right to know seem to point to traits of modernity that belong to secularisation, but also account for the failure of this particular culture to confront theological questions. Beneath its predictability and the safeness of its promised pleasures there is something unsafe about modernity that leads to theological reflection. The cultural ground has made theology somehow unsafe.

Issues of choice, pluralism and secularisation have been linked to Berger's critiques of modernity. Secularisation fragments religions so that they operate in a marketplace, one characterised by a growing indifference. Shopping around for beliefs puts a premium on subjectivity. A crucial aspect of his refinement of the term is the way secularisation is associated with a 'crisis of credibility', of plausibility structures, which come to compete with each other in a market characterised by pluralism. In his analysis, pluralism poses a crisis of legitimation in theology which secularisation signifies.[88]

Cultural circumstances of religious belief have changed, as '*modern consciousness entails a movement from fate to choice*'. Thus, modernity is 'a great relativising caldron'.[89] Choice relates to a right in modernity, but one that embodies a property of heresy, a capacity to transgress boundaries with impunity. But following Weber, one can suggest that this capacity to transgress seems itself fated, as is the disenchantment that follows whose effects preclude choice. This self-defeating aspect of modernity, of grasping but not possessing, impales the self on its own particular antinomy peculiar to this culture. Relativism is another form of pluralism, but a more pernicious one, because it does not so much characterise favourable conditions of a market, but a property that corrodes sociology itself, a condition without apparent prospect of philosophical relief. Echoing others, Berger criticises as sterile, efforts to make religion palatable to contemporary sensibilities, on the grounds that modern secularity itself is in crisis.[90] But he needs to be more specific, for as Wuthnow notes, specification of context forms an undertheorised dimension to Berger's approach to plausibility structures.[91] Habitus and the notion of the field, discussed later, illuminate the contextuality of plausibility structures and the beliefs they realise. These form an antidote to secularisation and the vacuity of modernity.

The question theology needs to ask from sociology is: if ecclesial plausibility structures reproduce themselves into conditions of implausibility, how is a sociological argument to be constructed to reverse this apparently fated process of secularisation? The problem arises from within sociological reflexivity and it is from here that the genesis of reversal needs to be found.

The present crisis of sociology is not about the need to uncover further permutations on culture. The crisis is not about quantity (although for those in poverty this is a prime point) but about the quality of culture. This concern elicits a question of judgement which relates to theological questions on the nature of culture. There has been a change in sociological concerns in this direction very recently. For example, the ESRC has opened up a section for grants and fellowships dealing with the quality of life. This switch in interests adds another dimension to modernity and reflexivity. It generates a language of choice but one with theological implications. It is difficult to understand how the question of the quality of life can be separated from the issue of its meaning and the need to reflect on what is understood. Thus, Giddens sees modernity as a term that relates to an understanding of itself, where sociology has a pivotal influence. He suggests '*modernity is itself deeply and intrinsically sociological*'. But what is problematic for the professional sociologist

> as the purveyor of expert knowledge about social life, derives from the fact that she or he is at most one step ahead of enlightened lay practitioners of the discipline.

He argues that sensibility of doubt is not confined to sociologists, but forms an anxiety which increasingly affects everybody and the culture they inhabit. This relates to a problem he raises of ontological security, the confidence actors have over their self-identity in relation to social sites for action. This confidence is insecure, hence the dependence on experts to ameliorate a sense of risk and anxiety.[92]

Globalisation effects a radical recontextualisation through technology in a way that compromises the local. The implication of this insight of Giddens is that what was a problem of the rationality debate, the incommensurability of local forms of belief to the rational scientific expectations of the inquirer, is now a dilemma that has invaded culture, a point signified in the term late modernity. Giddens tries to find a solution to globalisation in the notion of re-embedding, pinning down social relationships to local conditions of time and space.[93] This notion of re-embedding contains a property of resistance. It injects into sociology a notion of judgement as to what is worth re-embedding. This leads back to an issue of enchantment, but more especially to sociological imperatives that derive from a reading of culture that seek this process of re-embedding and which generate a witness to the need to conserve its basis of reproduction. Rituals are an example of this process.

For Giddens, ritual forms touch on the most basic aspects of ontological security. Affirming the importance of rituals, the losses that emerge from the passing of traditional and communal forms are noted. Thus, he observes

> *rites de passage* place those concerned in touch with wider cosmic forces, relating individual life to more encompassing existential issues. Traditional ritual, as well as religious belief, connected individual action to moral frameworks and to elemental questions about human existence. The loss of ritual is also a loss of involvement with such frameworks, however ambiguously they might have been experienced and however much they were bound up with traditional religious discourse.[94]

The project of the self in the context of a search for reflexivity in late modernity plays on the distinctive discernments of the sociologist. It is the peculiarity of the sociological vision that it feels the need for re-embedding more poignantly than those who gaze innocently at the endless transformation of cultural forms. In this context, a religious imperative still persists, a point even Giddens recognises when he notes that

> new forms of religion and spirituality represent in a most basic sense a return of the repressed, since they directly address issues of the moral meaning of existence which modern institutions so thoroughly tend to dissolve.[95]

Part of the revolt which late modernity or postmodernity signifies is its rebellion against the myth of secularity and its seeking of sources of enchantment. But a crucial issue emerges: has modernity escaped theology and is postmodernity simply a cultural recognition of the point that it has not?

Through a reflexive form of self-accounting, sociology is implicated in seeking understanding of these endless cultural forms, but at the same time it feels an increasing disenchantment with their basis. It finds itself knowing too much. This relates to Giddens' notion of a double hermeneutic that characterises the way '*sociological knowledge spirals in and out of the universe of social life, reconstructing both itself and that universe as an integral part of that process*'.[96]

Something has been subtracted from culture, a property of enchantment, and this has become a focal point of public debate on the limitations of secularisation in education. Any sociology with reflexive ambitions has to be aware of this consideration. Increasingly a reflexive sociology finds itself outpaced by debate in secular society, where issues of pluralism, multicultural rights and the problem of religious belief in a post-Christian society have become matters of practical concern. The masking capacity of a secularised culture increasingly confirms a population in their plight where the grammar for securing religious affiliation has been lost. It is as if modernity is incompatible with theological thought and for that reason is distinctive as a cultural epoch and style. Yet, has modernity escaped theology?

The issue of how far the secularisation embodied in modernity has escaped preceding theological moral, social, political and epistemological dilemmas raises remarkably contentious issues, some of which are confronted in Blumenberg's major work, *The Legitimacy of the Modern Age*. He argues that modernity is a product of a crisis in the medieval world and has simply carried forward or rather unwittingly reoccupied some of the dilemmas it could not resolve. He suggests that modernity is based on an illusion that it has escaped theology, when in fact it is transfixed by it. Blumenberg writes with ease and deep knowledge on theological matters in a way few Anglo-American writers can. He joins with Gadamer and Benjamin in having an intimacy and depth of concern with aspects of theology. Like Benjamin, he is much worried about the implications of Genesis, the problem of knowing and naming. Blumenberg is concerned with the particular dilemmas of knowing within modernity that lead to a theological blindness.

Koerner notes that his concerns are about man's finitude, about myth and metaphor within culture that survive even in an area of secularisation.[97] Krajewski points to his definite theological interests in his response to Bach's *Matthew Passion* in a book published in 1989 (untranslated). It is a work of apologetics, using reason but not to the point of doubt. It is a critique of doceticism, arguing that Jesus was fully human and was not mere appearance. Krajewski suggests Blumenberg wants to explore self-assertion in relation to the issue of Christ. But this knowing relates to Genesis, to the Garden of Eden and to the antinomial dilemma Adam and Eve seek to resolve through eating from the Tree of Knowledge. This causes God to fear the human capacity to want to know too much, to exercise a limitless curiosity, hence the dispatch of Adam and Eve from the Garden into confusion for their ambition.[98] Prometheus and Faust are two heroes who sought to pass the limits of knowing who fascinate Blumenberg.[99] But to go too far is to be destructive, for as Irenaeus wrote 'whoever flees the double knowledge and the double spiritual sensation is secretly destroying himself as a human being'.[100] It is scarcely surprising that the public reading of Genesis, in the Festival of Lesson and Carols, is entrusted to an individual innocent of ambition, the choirboy in his ruff, cassock and long white surplice, who signals a disavowal of design in his utterance sufficient to absolve him from risk of metaphysical injury.[101]

The issue of the angelic and Genesis also arises in Benjamin, though being Jewish, not in the above mode of presentation or theological setting. Genesis relates to the price of choice, between past, present and future. Expulsion admits no return, save going forward to retrieve what had been lost in the past. The plight of time between young and old is represented in a verse on an 18th century memorial for a 14 year old boy who died, that is in St Patrick's Cathedral Dublin, where it is written

> As you are, so were we
> And as we are, so shall you be

This dilemma of knowing and not knowing is embedded in the issue of postmodernity, as it oscillates between a future it disbelieves in and a past to which it cannot return that is equally incredible because it betrays an escape into nostalgia. The dilemmas sociology faces within postmodernity relate to issues of choice and self-identity. Postmodernity signifies an awareness of modernity coming to doubtful maturity. In this context, Bauman suggests that sociology itself is a cultural activity, an exercise of human spirituality where self-allegiances are to be expressed. For sociology to be effective in this context, Bauman asserts that it

> must conceive of itself as a participant (perhaps better informed, more systematic, more rule-conscious, yet nevertheless a participant) of this never ending, self-reflexive process of reinterpretation and devise its strategy accordingly.[102]

In seeking a site for this strategy, the sociological act carries a quality of presumption of making an image, an icon for analytical reflection, but one that generates its own ambiguities over what to assume and what to discard. Again, this relates to theological considerations which can be underestimated in terms of their cultural significance. Thus, in a secularised society, such as Britain, greatly difficulty is experienced in understanding the forces of nationalism that embody the divisions of the human condition between reason and sentiment. Nationalism evokes dangerous theological metaphors which the notion of a state founded on reason and assent had supposedly expelled. It is interesting that two of the most insightful British accounts of nationalism, written from a Marxist persective, both ended with reference to Benjamin's angel.[103]

Walter Benjamin left a mark of melancholy on notions of modernity. A tragic traveller, he crossed terrains of mysticism, Marxism, literary and artistic studies with an awesome versatility. This enormously complex thinker, fragments of whose writings have been translated, defies categorisation. Working with Adorno, Benjamin was an important critic of the culture of modernity. The multifaceted interests of this highly important Jewish thinker are hard to summarise. His theological writings, as unexpected as they are fascinating, related to mysticism and carried elements of a negative theology. Kabbalahism had an important influence on his thought. His interests in the philosophy of language related to an interest in the philosophical and theological implications of the Fall. His concern with modernity was closely linked to his unfinished Arcades project on nineteenth century Paris, a pursuit that reflected his deep interest in Baudelaire, whose biography he wrote.[104] Benjamin never quite escaped his Judaism nor did he break free of his Marxism. Fleeing the Nazis in 1940, he committed suicide in mysterious circumstances at the Spanish border.[105] Like Simone Weil, Benjamin was a refugee escaping the fragments of modernity and fell through its cracks.[106]

In a brief passage in *Illuminations*, Benjamin refers to the angel of history. He is about flee from what he sees in the past, a single catastrophe to him, a chain of events to us, which keeps piling wreckage at his feet. Wishing to warn and to make whole what has been smashed, his wings become paralysed by a storm blowing from Paradise that irresistibly propels him into a future to which his back is turned. For Benjamin, 'this storm is what we call progress'.[107]

Revival of interest in Benjamin has carried with it a certain embarrassment at the significance of his early theological writings and their relationship to his later work and concern with historical materialism. His friend and Jewish mentor, Gershom Scholem makes a defence of the importance of the angelic in Benjamin's work. Like Berger, though in a different way, Benjamin was concerned with the new angels, those of the kabbalah. His own image of the angel was derived from Klee's painting, 'Angelus Novus' which Scholem claims was his most important possession. Benjamin affirmed the Jewish tradition of the personal angel of each human being who represents the latter's secret self and whose name nevertheless remains hidden from him. In angelic shape, but in part also in the form of his secret name, the heavenly self of a human being (like everything else created) is woven in a curtain hanging before the throne of God.[108]

Scholem argues that the image of Klee's angel, for Benjamin, became 'the occult reality of his self' being pulled forward, irresistibly to an indefinite future. Benjamin's interest in virtue needs to be offset by a similar concern with the problem of evil. Scholem claims that an interest in evil, in Satanism, came from his study of Baudelaire.[109] This issue of evil relates back to the pile of debris, which had come from the past, which was smashed, but needed to be re-constructed. But this was a task, not for an angel, but for a Messiah.[110] Divided against himself, Benjamin failed. As Habermas indicates, he could not make his 'messianic experience serviceable for historical materialism'.[111]

Alter sees in Benjamin a terrible tension between past and future, where the angel 'is a kind of dumbfounded refugee from the world of religious symbolism' lodged between 'the dream of paradisiacal origins and the unimaginable vista . . . of whatever lies at the end of history's long catastrophe'.[112] Alter goes on to suggest that all three Jewish figures concerned with modernity, Kafka, Benjamin and Scholem, could not find any way of return to origins, to where God had been. With this absence of God in modernity, melancholy reigned. Nor could they find an adequate substitute in modern thought for 'the richly layered spiritual vocabulary that the bearers of tradition had developed in their quest for the truth'.[113] The figure of the angel represents what glimmers from transcendence which tradition could address, but which, somehow, modernity cannot.

The issue of the angel in Benjamin relates to a problem of choice which goes back to a root Christianity and Judaism share, a concern with the effects of the Fall. The enigmatic nature of the angel is related to the issue of naming and the problem of presumption it embodies. Benjamin's life seemed to embody what he discovered in the issue of modernity – despair, melancholy, allegory and the ruins of a life affected by circumstances he could prophecy but could neither transcend nor control.

A glimmer of some of these unexpected theological possibilities, described as Jewish motifs, appears in Wohlfarth's account of his writings. These bring us to the issue of the field, the original one in the Garden of Eden. Between Bauman, Bourdieu and Benjamin a decided horticultural turn can be discerned in the debate on the culture of postmodernity. Benjamin was much concerned with the relationship between the Fall and language, a problem which Steiner has pursued in *After Babel*.[114] In Wohlfarth's subtle reading, a loss of aura and a loss of capacity to name relate to a chaos, where marking difference is possible but in some way is impossible. Benjamin comes to his difficulties through German Romanticism and Baudelaire. He links the effects of the Fall to the growth of subjectivism, the wish to possess, which is combined with a failure to grasp. Wohlfarth suggests that for Benjamin 'the Fall is already, in some sense, the infernal machine of modernity; and modernity, the free fall of history'. But it is more than this, for the Fall effects a forgetting of the way back, thus to come back on a metaphor used before 'the Garden of Eden turns into a labyrinth'.[115] The chaos of modernity piling up, which transfixes the angel, points to another form of paralysis, the incapacity to return, which is matched also by a failure to perceive the need to go back, to recognise the basis of the Fall.

Following Wohlfarth's account, Benjamin argues that the demand for knowing both good and evil, that constitutes 'perfect' knowledge found in the tree, becomes dangerous in human hands for it makes choice seem free but unfree. Unresolvable antinomies lie in the way forward. Somehow, there is no escape from doubt, from interrogation, but nevertheless there is a need to ask. For Benjamin, this rendering of language and its imperfect categorisation points to a notion of trial. It also involves a protest at the chaos, at being judged for that for which there is no redress, hence the complaint lodged against the judge in his writings. This points to a dramatic quality in relations between man and God which von Balthasar would have understood. For him, the verdict would point to a matter of free will, where options for salvation are open, whereas for Benjamin the judgment is in someway rigged. The trial turns into a waiting for the Messiah to come to overturn the chaos. Melancholy, silence and siding with the weakest of the weak are some other themes Wohlfarth uncovers in Benjamin, all adding to a sense of waiting for redemption.

In his reading of Benjamin, Wohlfarth points to God's judgement that retains the immediacy, the purity and magic of unfallen language. For Wohlfarth, 'what distinguishes the two is the vigilance with which one guards over the other'. He notes in Benjamin a concern with the 'magic of signs', but notes that 'magic survives the Fall, however, only by forfeiting its innocence'.[116] Benjamin's reference to the Garden also involves a problem of taking a chance, of making a wager, where the Fall is the price of getting it wrong.

Blumenberg's study of the legitimacy of the modern age is a remarkably complex defence of the distinctive nature of modernity in relation to its theological debts. The issue of when sensibility of modernity began is complex as Dupré has shown recently. It is buried in humanism, theology and philosophy, in a history predating the formation of sociology. Thus, Dupré dates the genesis of modernity from the late fourteenth century, whereas most sociologists conceive of the term as being born in the middle of the nineteenth century.[117] Although they differ greatly in their favour or disfavour of modernity, and over its uniqueness, both Blumenberg and Dupré seek to rectify an amnesia over the theological forms of thought that have been unwittingly carried forward into the secularity that characterises the modern era. It is the subterranean nature of theological wisdom, metaphor, antinomy and the consequences of the naming of moral categories that lies as a hidden agenda to modernity, but which secularisation has kept below its cultural ground.

Blumenberg's concern is with the issues of detachment, of occupation and appropriation involved in the movement from religious belief to ideology, which the term secularisation signifies. The debate on progress, as the secularisation of the eschatological points to a transference of faith in God, a dependence, which evolves into an independence embodied in the development of the notion of self-assertion which has come to signify the modern age. The issue of self-assertion moves from a dilemma posed by Gnosticism to one arising in a world detached from belief in God. This movement from providence to praxis denotes distinctive properties of modernity, but it is a site where medieval problems return in disguised form. Secularisation embodies a 'spiritual anathema' over history since the Middle Ages. Its assumptions are not available to theory, nor to an understanding of reality that is worldly.[118] Thus, Blumenberg suggests that 'the philosophical program for the beginning of the modern age "failed" because it was unable to analyze away its own preconditions'.[119]

Lying behind his approach to secularisation and modernity is a hermeneutic issue. He is looking at the migration of attributes that have become secularised as a result of the disappearance of their original bearers, their masking and their marginalisation. This migration can be understood in terms of the secularisation of theology into metaphors as a means of enlightened understanding of the world. Theological metaphors haunt a secularised approach to culture. They signify deference to a rhetoric to constitute that which lies outside its self-generating means of understanding. They articulate and redeem shortcomings in accounts, and by filling in the gaps, disguise their borrowings. For instance, there is Marx's extended use of the Jesuits as a metaphor to characterise bureaucrats as the inner theologians of the state, who mask and at the same defend its interests in a way in which the private and the public become confused.[120] Metaphors signify deficiencies in account. They relate to recourse to forms or accounts that lie elsewhere, to account for circumstances that cannot be fully understood. Their use signifies changes in the way culture is read. In recent years, one of the most interesting and unexpected movements has been the recourse to medieval thought and practice that appears in a culture of postmodernity, a link Eco has recently noted and which has entered sociological literature.[121] This borrowing from the medieval has obvious implications for the link between theology, sociology and culture, for it signifies what can be read and understood when all three are combined.

Blumenberg's study of secularisation opens up a can of philosophical worms. Debates with Gnosticism and neo-Platonic positions are likely to afflict the sociological imagination with acute paralysis. The notion of reoccupation of a site of medieval problems by a modern age drags sociology into a history of ideas outside its remit. But it does point to a theological continuity between the medieval world and the site of postmodernity that is expressed in terms of philosophy. As argued later, this continuity also marks Bourdieu's approach to sociology of culture, not least in the genesis of his term habitus. If modernity embodies forms of knowing that relate to medieval arguments, how are they to be used to understand sociological dilemmas? Clearly, this is an enormous question and one can just pick at its surface.

It is in Part III, of Blumenberg's concern with secularity and modernity, the trial of 'theoretical curiosity' that matters of relevance to sociological issues of reflexivity and secularity emerge. For Blumenberg, the issue of self-assertion emerges in the collapse of order within the medieval world. Self-assertion embodies a capacity, a need to know, one that the Enlightenment makes a responsibility. Science signifies this right, this need to uncover, to experiment, to reveal, to explain and to establish the cause of order in nature and by implication the structure of society. Its mandate is to encounter puzzles and to reconcile these with its paradigms, its conventions for overcoming curiosity. Dissatisfaction with procedures for handling matters of the curious relate to paradigm shifts. But curiosity is not a limitless right, as recent concerns with scientific debate on ethics show and as Bauman's strictures on the behaviour of scientists after the Holocaust indicate.

The thrust of Blumenberg's interest in curiosity is to give it a wider theological implication, one that echoes earlier concerns about choice between good and evil. How much is it prudent to unfold of matters that belong to the mysterious and to the Divine? These insights have particular implications for sociology and its confrontation with secularisation.

The legitimacy of sociology derives from the endless curiosity it displays about social arrangements and their apparent basis. In its endless interest in curiosity, sociology exemplifies a right to know, to uncover, to reveal that borders on the presumptuous, that admits no limit, no world to remain unhidden and no tribe to be unstudied. Thus, as Blumenberg notes it is not accidental that Nietzsche regarded '"ruthless curiosity" as one of the epochal characteristics of the modern age'.[122]

If secularisation releases an unfettered curiosity, it would be a curious argument that qualified this freedom. After all curiosity is an impulse to know, an assertion of a right relating to disclosure of information, such as in the realm of parliamentary responsibility. Likewise, curiosity forms a crucial ingredient of sociological reflexivity. Questions about the persistence of social patterns or arrangements, that become naturalised, generate sociological queries as to the means of their reproduction and the forms of redress that might be required. Descrepancies excite curiosity and the need to reconcile social arrangements with the beliefs they are supposed to embody. The exposure of hypocrisy is a fundamental ingredient for the press, which feeds on the curiosity of the public, for example over the state of marriage in the Royal Family. If there is something natural about the issue of curiosity, why qualify it?

This impulse to have all matters private exposed, expressed as the 'ruthless curiosity' of modernity, generates an instability, a continual and unresolved quest for the sociologist that seems to end with uncuriosity. Resolution leads to the seeking of another tribe, another issue, for answers to curiosity can relate to disenchantment and to further quests for enchantment. The issue of curiosity relates to the antinomy of innocence and experience, and the puzzle it represents.[123] A curiosity that seeks the 'real' basis of a tale, its original setting, often leads to disillusion. A confusion is made between the indefinite nature of the imaginative urge that gives rise to curiosity and the more definite and mundane original that formed the basis of the author's creative fantasy. A poignant example of this is in the film *Shadowlands*, where C. S. Lewis takes the rather sad boy to the attic to see the wardrobe which in one of his tales was the means of entry to a world of dreams and imagination. Left in the attic, the boy, unable to resist curiosity, goes to the wardrobe, with evident trepidation and expectation of disillusion. Half-believing, he opens its door only to find it empty, as he expected. The imaginative act cannot be repeated in reality, and with sadness, the boy moves from an uncertain innocence to a rather definite experience.

Somehow, the seeking destroys the focal point of the question and illusion is destroyed by disillusion when curiosity is resolved. This relates to issues of the moral accountability of curiosity, a limit on how much is to be known, if tactlessness is not to arise. The counterproductive nature of answers to curiosity are endemic in sociology. For instance, its seeking of the mechanism of reproduction of a ritual can have unintended reductionist implications of forcing attention away from the intangible, the aesthetic and the spiritual to the literal, the ceremonial and the social form, which is what the rite is literally *not* about.[124]

Theoretical curiosity characterises the modern age, and represents a self-conscious development that arises at the end of the medieval period. Blumenberg sets the issue of the limits of curiosity in the context of the debate between Nicholas of Cusa and Nolan and the threat this posed to a world poised between the medieval and modern. In its modern format, curiosity can be linked to self-consciousness, the pursuit of an elective affinity with what attracts. It is also about a seeking to know about boundaries and what lies beyond in the field that can be discerned.[125]

Blumenberg is concerned with the notion of trust in terms of what is beyond sight, an anticipation possible only through transcendence.[126] This visionary quality to self-knowledge combines curiosity with memory. Curiosity becomes related to recognition, a grace of insight, a gift of God, that also embodies a capacity for relationship. Although there are limitations to this curiosity, which Blumenberg pursues, there is also a quality of freedom of release. This returns us to the issue of free will, to what is found in the answer to curiosity achieved at the level of the transcendent. It relates to a point of Pico, which von Balthasar notes, that the freedom given to the actor by God is

> 'the greatest marvel in nature', enabling him to go beyond his pristine indifference and determine his own nature: he can become mortal or immortal, angelic or bestial. 'We have been placed in a situation in which we are what we want to be'.[127]

Unfettered freedom to ask relates to limitless curiosity, but also the illusion that the questions raised are self-generated. Blumenberg's concerns are epistemological, and point to the dependability of forms of knowing attached to theology or detached from it. Mere curiosity, that can become an obsession, a vice, a 'superficial dwelling on the object' forms the basis of Thomist and Augustinian concerns. It informs a seeking of knowing detached from prudence. Qualifications to the issue of curiosity relate to the purpose of knowing, its theological and moral basis. Idle curiosity, or a form that enlarges vanity relates to a self-accountability, a sense of narcissism that makes the actor independent of God rather than dependent and part of a plan of grace. There is therefore an appetite in unrestrained curiosity that settles for worldly forms of knowing, which become substitutes for those that lie in the transcendent. It is this confusion that has been carried forward from the Middle Ages into modernity. The exercise of unrestrained curiosity has been rewarded by a God that has become unmanifest and unapparent in a culture of postmodernity. Thus Blumenberg suggests that

> the modern age began, not indeed as the epoch of the death of God, but as the epoch of the hidden God, the *deus absconditus* – and a hidden God is *pragmatically* as good as dead.

He goes on to add that the need to behave as if God were dead 'induces a restless taking stock of the world which can be designated as the motive power of the age of science'.[128] It leads to a state which Blumenberg characterises, as one where 'curiosity is the mark of a finite being with infinite pretensions'.[129] But it also relates to a self-fulfilling prophetic aspect to secularisation that deludes. By marking God as vanished, secularisation believes it has deposited a freedom on to modernity. It is scarcely surprising that the condition of postmodernity suggests its own distinctive theological style, that of the apophatic.

Blumenberg points to the emergence of a more humbled, but theologically adequate form of knowing formulated by Nicholas of Cusa that responds to the threat medieval knowledge faced which modernity has no longer been able to surmount or indeed to recognise. The solution to the expansion of knowing of Nicholas of Cusa is presented in the manner of a paradox, of a method of restricting curiosity, channelling it away from the superficial, and in a direction where providence, transcendence and immanence are neither marginalised nor destroyed. There is an antinomial quality within the concept or method of accepting a limit, an inhibition, but one that facilitates access to something greater. 'Ontological imprecision' is presented as the essence of 'knowing ignorance'.[130] One might think that Nicholas of Cusa is presenting a warning to the curious,[131] a salutary lesson that also relates to Marlowe's Faustus.

The learned ignorance which Cusa wrote of in the *Docta ignorantia* 'unites an element of sceptical resignation vis-a-vis the metaphysical pretensions of the age with an element of indefinite expectation of a knowledge that could no longer have the form it had had hitherto'.[132] This resignation does not to lead to passivity, but to an activity of finding in recognised circumstance of limit in dealing with the limitless. It presents a paradox of knowing with a possibility of theological resolution. Cusa is nearer the dilemmas of postmodernity than one might expect. This is exemplified in his cherished idea that God 'is inconceivably conceived in the coincidence of opposites'.[133] The notion of a *Docta ignorantia* needs to be allied to his belief in a coincidence of opposites within God. Attempts at breakage of this barrier represent acts of pride such as those heralding the fall of Satan, which are carried forward into the Faust legend. This theological insight of Cusa can be grounded in the ambiguities, pastiches and emptiness of a culture of postmodernity, suggesting that even in its unprofitable circumstances, sealed in a secularisation, that the distinctive nature of God so characterised *can* be found, that, within limits of revelation, can be articulated.

It is important to note that the *Docta ignorantia* represents less a state of knowledge, but as Blumenberg indicates, a praxis, a method, that involves the need to go beyond the purely visual. This pursuit creates a consciousness of the path that can be followed.[134] The connection between knowing and knowing too much, of not being able to find a limit to curiosity, marks a problem that connects the end of the Middle Ages to modernity, and more particularly postmodernity. This worry about knowing, about how to discriminate between the limits of knowledge and the realisation that it is limitless, hence playful in terms of postmodernity, also represents a theological question that has become obscured. The demand to know too much de-humanises. In exercising unlimited curiosity, man has become a stranger to himself. Thus, Blumenberg suggests that in civilised European form of culture there is 'a marginal phenomenon of the total reality called man'.[135] This is also a theme in Simmel's tragedy of culture.

The paradoxical notion of learned ignorance relates to properties of discernment, of risking confusing the visual with the unseen. The knowing of God in Paul, which Blumenberg cites, relates to seeing in a glass darkly. Cusa is trying to point to the need to realise that going beyond visual clarity prevents the mind being lulled by mere sight. Seeing is a basis of believing, but it can also be misleading. Sight to the blind generates numerous paradoxes which have been explored in drama and literature. Hazel Moses in Flannery O'Connor's *Wise Blood*, only sees when he blinds himself; *Molly Sweeney* of Brian Friel's play faces tragedy when sight is restored and longs for the discernment of blindness; and J. B. Synge's *The Well of the Saints* points to the confusion of sight restored to the elderly who see without illusion, much to their disenchantment. In Cusa's case, Blumenberg is pointing to a path, a trace, the beginning of the chase, a hunt for wisdom, which might be impeded by excessive attention which knowledge rather than wisdom gives to what can be seen.

This might seem miles removed from sociological speculation. Yet, in this study, the mapping of fields, the pursuit along paths of culture all link into the issue of a trace of God, to be discerned in the hidden contours of the site, in realms of disguise within culture which can be deciphered by means of symbols.

The issue now faced is what makes the trace of God so unfruitfully disguised within the culture of postmodernity? Such a question moves the issue of sociological intervention into the theological link with the cultural, from the passive into the active. It points to some strands of Shiner's approach to the practical implications of secularisation, the issue of plunder and to the transposition of religious beliefs and institutions into the secular. Shiner disavows these terms for their methodological vagueness. Yet they do have significance for they point not only to circumstances of curiosity about the contours of the field, but a wonder as to how it is so constituted as to keep rubbing out marks of the Divine.

The field is but a site, a ground of culture, that contains something to be deciphered, otherwise it does not belong to the cultural. Something is signified in what is missing, in what is hidden, hence the curiosity its contours elicit. Curiosity might generate a hermeneutic of suspicion, of an interest concealed that magnifies a power to define. But it can also point to a hermeneutic of appropriation, of a discerning of traces that betokens something that exceeds the idle demands of mere curiosity. In this sense, sociological forms of reflexivity move into theological contemplation in a mutuality of implication that changes the nature of what was sought in mere curiosity. The hermeneutic act of understanding can shift the sociologist from a reading of the surface of culture to a decipherment that embodies an issue of theology, But if the reading points towards seeking a trace of God, then assumptions about what is concealed turn to issues of what has been misappropriated, what is missing from the site that has been stolen, that might signify other states of affairs, those relating to God. This relates back to an issue of cultural reproduction. The form that effects disbelief can also actuate belief. The secularisation of religion is not fated. It is partly the outcome of a mechanism of reproduction, which can be turned in a contrary direction, to sacralise. This relates to Shiner's notion of secularisation as effecting a de-sacralisation which links to Weber's fears regarding disenchantment. The difficulty with this approach, as Shiner notes, is that certain forms of theology de-sacralise themselves in their formulations about the world.[136] Apart from theological formulations that would qualify sociology opting for de-sacralisation as the term to characterise secularisation, because it links with Weber's notion of disenchantment, which occupies the heartland of sociological approaches to modernity and culture, there is the issue of whether such an outcome is intended by theologians, or is a dysfunction of their pronouncements, their misreading of the cultural.

But if secularisation is seen in terms of fragmentation of belief, and as an effect of de-sacralisation, the melting of the glue that bonds communities, then the term takes on a persuasive characteristic. It points to what

Catholicism and sociology both fear and that from which they both wish
to escape. This mutuality of interest presents both with issues of choice.
The more Catholicism seeks to resite itself into the culture of postmodernity,
the more it risks refracting the properties of fracture it is there to transcend. The more sociology confronts the implications of its reflexivity, the
more it realises the illusion of finding solutions within its argot. It has to
recast its analytical moorings. It has to give witness to what theologians
fail to recognise, the dangers that lurk within a culture. Somehow, theologians seem to fail to see their own fate in what has come to pass.

Lambert has provided an excellent ethnographic account of this movement in his study of a rural French parish. There is an uncoupling of
obligation over the past fifty years. In reading this study of the disconnection of a Catholicism from an almost complete regulation of the culture of
the village, one is conscious of the way rituals, obligations and associations
have been loosened and let lapse with theological sanction and popular
connivance. Faith and culture were intermingled into the cycle of life, in
the seasons, in the recent past, in a way current Vatican thought is seeking
to restore as the issue of rebuilding communities of faith returns to the
theological agenda. Lambert sees a condition of dispersal and indifference
as affecting the strength of religion but also definitions of its significance
and use.[137] This process of disengagement is not wholly due to changing
cultural and social circumstances. It also reflects a misguided theological
strategy since Vatican II that bears on a comment of Neuhaus that Catholic
theologians nowadays 'sometimes give the impression of having spent the
last twenty-five years working out how little, as a Catholic, one need
believe and how little do'.[138]

The denial of the theological roots of sociology, combined with the
dispatch of religion to a sub-branch, signified the secularisation of the
discipline itself. Yet, the issue of religion as a social phenomenon keeps
returning to the sociological agenda. The rise of new religious movements
and New Age religions, were exceptions to secularisation that sociology
recognised. But these were exotic activities belonging to the periphery of
the discipline. They belonged to an analytical limbo between sect and
social movement, harmless but interesting exceptions to secularisation,
insufficient to set off theological alarm bells. It is in the change of the
agenda of sociology itself in relation to a culture of postmodernity that
glimmers of theological issues can be discerned.

The intensification of a reflexivity within sociology recognises an unsettled despiritualised culture increasingly engaged with matters such as
the body, the self and ethics of appearance, that relate to issues of authenticity, of meaning and understanding. These elements are proximate to a

theological agenda but are in someway disembodied from them. They are, however, sufficiently near, that a recontextualisation might seem possible rather than arbitrary. The recentring of culture into sociology, as a result of its engagement with postmodernity, draws it back to issues of aesthetics and ethics, meaning and purpose. But as culture is so recentred, issues of concern of Simmel and Benjamin are also recovered, and these have definite theological agendas. Equally, if Weber and Simmel share a concern with the disenchanting effects of calculation within culture, they also have a concern with its antidote. For Weber, this related to the issue of enchantment. If modernity was about disenchantment, postmodernity is about enchantment, perhaps its trivial pursuit, but one that risks taking a theological turn. Part of Weber's interest in the term relates to the reproduction of grace. It was his form of argument that so influenced Bourdieu's approach to sociology of culture. It is hardly a radical deconstruction of their argument, to turn its form back to its sacramental origins and to reset that within a sociological framework that can characterise the links between theology and culture. It is to examine what sociology has forgotten, that relates to an observation of Simmel. He noted in the context of the issue of trust, that while 'the social role of the faith has never been investigated; ... this much is certain, that without it society would disintegrate'.[139]

There is a sense of disintegration abroad, a public fear, a climate of distrust and reconsideration. Postmodernity embodies this sensibility, that of tiredness, of a modernity that formed the focal point for escape from religion, that has itself become a trap, one that obscures a means of exit. As Heller and Fehér note, there is 'the spreading feeling that we are permanently going to be in the present, and, at the same time, after it'.[140]

In one sense, secularisation manages to mask the prospect of belief, to make doubtful whether it was ever possible. As Robinson indicates 'habituated to an easy satisfaction, after a time we cease to realize what it is we are missing out on'.[141] Yet the issue of secularisation has taken an ironic turn in relation to postmodernity, in a manner sociology cannot ignore. Postmodernity signifies a disbelief in the properties of modernity where the tale of reason in a grand narrative has collapsed into fragmentation, ambiguity and disconnection. Heller and Fehér suggest that secularisation is 'the civil religion of the atheist', for whom it held out 'such redemptive promises as making society fully transparent, creating a paradise on earth, compensating for the limited duration of human life and the like'. This belief is falling into disrepair as a religious fundamentalism emerges, which they describe elegantly as 'the voice of the bad conscience of the postmodern condition flagellating itself for its excessive indulgence in relativism'.[142] For them, postmodernity represents the intensification of the dilemmas of modernity and is parasitic on it. This also means that theological issues buried in modernity are intensified in the context of the postmodern. The game is played for higher stakes. It is clear that secularisation is less about the marginalisation of religion, than about a mode of thought that has come to ambiguous fruition in the context of postmodernity. But the ambiguity of choice it effects generates its own ambiguities, which the condition of postmodernity exemplifies, so that the certainty that marginalises religion has itself become uncertain. Postmodernity permits no binding choice, and faith is beneficiary of this freedom. Modernity signified rules that marginalised issues of faith. As modernity itself has been marginalised, there is a whole new ball game emerging that changes the relationships between sociology, theology and culture.

A sociology dealing with culture in postmodernity with theological intentions can exaggerate the chaos into a doom ridden account to scare disbelievers back into need to use religious faith to seek some understanding better than the anarchy on offer. Relativism has forced sociology to throw away the key, so that its comparative strengths become instruments for exaggerating the chaos, the disconnectedness of the detail it uncovers in the cultural and the arbitrary, but incomplete links, it maps. But the visitation of such chaos bears a conceit, which plays on the human condition of the sociologist, tempting him in a Faustian manner to exasperate the discord, thus confirming the vice of his trade, pessimism and melancholy, but spread liberally on to others. A more fruitful via media for sociological interventions into the relationship between theology and culture needs to be found.

How could one turn the argument around and build up an argument *for* religious belief, one based on an idea of sacralisation and enchantment? If one assumes an issue of faith and sacralisation, the sociological question is concerned with the cultural impediments to their manifestation and reproduction. It is to turn issues of culture back to theology in a form it can recognise and can appropriate. This is to give a prescriptive property to sociology that has no theological warrant. But given the misunderstandings that have characterised theology's dealings with culture, this is a risk worth taking.

5 Concealing and Revealing: The Cultural Prospects of Belief

Surrounded by its close to the north and by meadows to the south, Salisbury Cathedral represents a completeness of early English Gothic at its most edifying, a structure of awesome beauty that signifies a completeness of culture. Painted by Constable, this building betokens Barchester. The spire inspired a book of the same title by William Golding. This Cathedral might seem to represent a notion of culture impervious to sociological interventions. Aesthetics, tradition, the glory of its architecture might make it safe from sociological attention. Yet, it is not sociology that poses dangers to the building in its relation to its surrounding culture. These emerge from the misperceptions of the Dean and chapter over what to appropriate to make the mission of the building more open, more relevant to what they perceive to be the surrounding culture. A strange number of sociological issues collide in their efforts.

The Dean and chapter permitted McDonald's to have medieval pastiches given out to the flocks of tourists charged entry to the building. This idea was dropped, not because of its tastelessness, but because of an invasion by animal rights activists protesting at this sponsorship. To make the Cathedral even more relevant, a girls' choir was recruited, overturning a tradition of 700 years at a stroke, in the interests of equality of opportunity. The form of worship thus becomes a witness to political correctness, rather than to the hallowed tradition choral singing embodies, which is inconveniently male.[1] This drift into a postmodernist culture even worried the Bishop of Salisbury. He wrote a damning report on the achievements of the Dean and chapter that expressed fears at the commercialisation of the Cathedral. Among his concerns were the proposed development of a separate visitor centre and restaurant (possibly moving the building from a site of the sacred to a museum that forms part of the heritage industry). He was also worried about the Cathedral becoming a place of entertainment. The Bishop had in mind the hiring out of the nave to the BBC *Antiques Roadshow*, thus 'crossing the wrong side of even a necessarily broad and hazy line'.[2] It is difficult to rank which of the above innovations is more unfortunate. Certainly, they are less offensive and ill-considered than the 'rave in the nave' for youth organised by the Dean and chapter

147

of the neighbouring Cathedral at Winchester, which even aroused a secular press to anxiety at the broadness and haziness of the line between the
sacred and the profane which the Cathedral authorities seemed unable to
discern.

In this failure, they are in good company, for there is puzzlement in
the world of the profane as to how far one can go in misappropriating the
sacred to the cash nexus. Secularity ignores the boundaries between the
sacred and the profane by intermingling them, a process that reaches an
advanced state in postmodernity. If ecclesial authorities cannot act as
guardians of their tradition, by conserving a sensibility of the sacred, then
others can see the value of what they neglect. Profanation can be linked
to profit to make other idols and icons. This presumption of the marketplace worries even those unaffiliated to ecclesial tradition. In his discussion of commodity aesthetics and values in relation to the 'jeans culture'
Haug bemoans the way religious subjection becomes trivialised and
subject to marketing demands. Thus, 'Jesus Jeans' are packaged so that
the primary effect is 'the sustenance of commodity aesthetics in the mode
of calumny of God. The jeans – certainly ironically – become deified'.[3]
There is an irresistible tide in the marketing, the repackaging of culture
that makes it own rules of enchantment, but which conceals a spirit of
calculation.

The Dean and chapter, if they were so disposed, might wonder at the
credibility of sociology's own understanding of culture. They might well
catch sociology in a moment of analytical embarrassment.

The growth of sociological interest in culture is recent, rapid and difficult to track. As Peterson has indicated, the growth has been enormous
since 1989, and although one of the largest divisions of the American
Sociological Association, this interest has not yet been fully manifested in
its journals.[4] But why has sociology only so recently recentred culture into
its theoretical interests, and more importantly, how could an issue of such
central importance have been so conspicuously neglected? The issue is
ironic, in view of the earlier strictures in this study against theologians for
failing to grasp the significance of culture, either in *Gaudium et Spes* or
in theories of inculturation, given sociology, with some exceptions, seemed
oblivious to the issue.

Culture has been recentred into sociology out of necessity to cope with
postmodernism and postmodernity. These movements relate to changes in
the social structure, such as the growth of service industries and the
commodification of culture, which sociology increasingly has to recognise
as lifestyles and politics take on crucial importances for the construction
of the self. Secondly, the translations of Bourdieu, the sociologist of culture,

point to the way power and issues of definition are intermingled in characterising the structure of society. Thirdly, the need to respond to a public mood of postmodernity suggested the need for sociology to rehabilitate Simmel and to examine his theories of culture. Simmel developed a sociology of culture a century earlier that related to the cosmopolitan, to money and to configurations that suggest postmodernity is an heir to what he understood.

For sociology, the broad issue of culture was marginalised to anthropology and to ethnography, where it formed part of the need to make comparisons that loosely embodied ideas of progress. In so far as culture had a domestic place in sociology, it was regarded as a matter of ideology, or was fragmented in the treatment of subcultures. In both settings, culture was treated as elusive and beyond the fringe, either because it misrepresented notions of reason in the exotic belief systems anthropology presented to sociology, or because it pointed to a problem of false consciousness that was a function of economic formations. Somehow, issues of modernisation disguised the need for sociology to confront domestic understandings of culture. But a fracturing of culture within sociology has become accentuated in the climate of postmodernity. As sociology becomes implicated in this fracture and the supposed demise of modernity, the attractions of understanding a holistic theory of culture become more apparent, however elusive.

Up to recently, Tylor's definition of culture, established in 1871, was the standard citation in sociology. Culture or civilisation was defined as that

> complex whole which includes knowledge, belief, art, morals, law, custom, and any other capabilities and habits acquired by man as a member of society.[5]

Many would now follow Kroeber in regarding culture as 'the totality of products of social men, and a tremendous force affecting all human beings, socially and individually'.[6] This universalisation of the notion of culture emphasised its human dimension, its quality of potentiality, but it also bore problems that would emerge later. If culture was related to civilisation then an invidious comparison was built into the definition. Cultures had to be evaluated, for they could not be endlessly described in ethnographic terms. Issues of universalisation had to be related to the particular if for no other reason than the demands of fieldwork to select out types of practices. Unselective pure description simply postpones the issue of classification and the assumptions that govern its basis. But disembodied description could be contextualised into the anthropologist's

own cultural assumptions, a point that reflects earlier discussions of reflexivity. There was an implied judgement in earlier anthropological accounts
of culture that few wished to confront.[7]

Early anthropological notions of culture associated the term 'primitive'
with notions of the uncivilised. This partly reflected the missionary assumptions and the colonial context within which much of this thinking
evolved. Under the influence of Durkheim, the term 'primitive' was equated
with the elementary nature of a social system, the simplicity of the functional relationship of its parts in a division of labour that evolved from the
mechanical to the organic. The notion of function related to ideas of evolution, of progress, but in a nonjudgemental manner that avoided questions
of evaluation of the meaningful basis of the cultural arrangements so classified. The organic metaphor used seemed to exempt anthropologists from
worries of judgement, for worth was self-evidently a matter of function,
or persistence and contribution to the whole. The notion of culture that
emerged in this context settled on issues of procedure and consequence,
with little direct relation to the principles of evaluation of the actors who
produced what was to be explained.

Alien cultures offered an image of alternatives that did elicit judgement
about the debased nature of Western civilisation. Thus, the American Indian
seemed to embody principles of nobility and appeared to have an integrity
free of the artifices of civility. This image of the Noble Savage oscillated
between patronisation and admiration. The Noble Savage could be deemed
to be an uncivilised Barbarian, but he also could be discerned as embody-
ing a pastoral innocence, living in Arcadian contact with nature with a
nobility of self-sufficiency that expressed what civilisation had lost.[8] Issues of innocence and experience lurked in notions of primitive culture
and its relationship to civilisation. Early anthropological treatments of
culture were riddled with ambiguities that lent a circular quality to their
efforts to find a satisfactory definition. The image of the uncivilised related
to a failure of regulation of desire, but also a pre-lapsarian notion where
social regulation was unnecessary.[9]

A number of tributaries feed into answering the question of why culture
has been recentred into sociology. The first relates to the way handling
culture has recently become a philosophical matter with unavoidable sociological implications. This arose from E. Evans-Pritchard's studies of
the Azande and the Neur. By tracing their forms of accountability for their
practices, however nonrational, such as the use of poison oracles, or an
excessive concern with a bovine idiom, anthropology came to postmodern
dilemmas through the study of pre-modern cultures, earlier than sociology
or philosophy. The relativism these studies introduced regarding the context

of the subject and that of the inquirer gave added force to the realisation that hermeneutics provided the means par excellence for reading all cultures.[10] Suspicion characterises hermeneutics, but also decipherment and appropriation, which have theological implications in the context of culture. A softer version of interpretation and understanding has emerged.

Secondly, anthropological definitions of culture did appear in sociology textbooks, but purely for ethnographic and comparative purposes as they related to the classical tradition. For instance, it is hard to handle Durkheim without reference to the anthropological debts embodied in his approach to religion. Sociology was divided against itself in dealings with culture. In its domestic concerns with culture, sociology concentrated either on amplifying the voice of the marginal, or on dealing with the concept as part of the notion of hegemony, the domination of a ruling class through representations that enhanced its power to exploit and to govern. These two strands were characterised by a moral concern with re-centring, and redefining prevailing notions of culture. This effort to redress conditions of marginality forms a radical strand of sociology, but one that signalled its own marginalisation from culture as conventionally understood.

The notion of subcultures became popular in sociology in the 1950s, and of central importance in studies of deviance in the 1960s and 1970s.[11] The study of the underlife of society gave sociology its own tribes to discuss, that were exotic, alien and marginal. In so far as there was a notion of culture, it formed part of the counterculture promulgated and romanticised in the late 1960s. Ethnicity in terms of assimilation of ways of life that appeared alien, formed another strand that drew from notions of culture. Sociology of education also had its own interests in the 1970s in examining the cultural patterns that underlay the reproduction of inequality. This distribution of the notion of culture within the tramlines of sociology, so that it is slotted into issues of class, gender, race, imperialism and education still persists.[12]

A more central and direct interest in culture emerged in the context of the study of the mass media. This centred on issues of the reproduction of culture, on the control of images in an analytical context where symbols were manipulated and where cultural understandings were enhanced. All dealings of sociology with culture, however fragmented and marginal, embodied issues of definition and judgement that were never adequately confronted.

A third source for the recognition of culture within sociology relates to the rehabilitation of a literary and socialist tradition pioneered by Raymond Williams but also by E. P. Thompson. Williams was primarily concerned with the products of culture in the mass media, their distribution, regulation and control.[13] The imperative to remake culture, to use it to recast an image, spoke to the marginality felt by many sociologists in the 1970s and 1980s. It gave them a romantic cause that redressed their sense of alienation from English academic culture.[14]

With the ebbing of socialism in the 1980s, a pluralism of opinion entered the agenda of culture in its relationship to sociology as a variety of lifestyles sought redress for their felt marginality and sense of indignity within existing traditional cultural definitions. As Peterson has suggested

> the focus on drama, myth, code and people's plans indicates a shift in the image of culture. While it was once seen as a map *of* behaviour it is now seen as a map *for* behaviour. In this view, people use culture the way scientists use paradigms ... to organise and normalise their activities.[15]

The theological implications of this shift in sociological understanding of culture represent a paradigm shift of considerable importance. It means that in other aspects of culture, as well as in the religious field, sociology has moved from seeking understanding predicated on disbelief and suspicion to an interest in the arrangements used to realise belief and the means through which it is reproduced and normalised.

Advocacy has become linked to culture over the issue of who has the right to define it. The marginal and dispossessed demand the right to define, so African Americans, feminists and homosexual groups in the USA have formed a rainbow coalition to repossess the centre of culture and to establish their own autonomous forms that would secure recognition without patronisation. The galaxy of special pleading by these various groups engaged in life politics presents sociology with issues of arbitration that beg questions about how culture is to be defined.

The dismantlement of barriers between forms of culture, so that the patrician is mixed with mass versions, adds to a sense of perplexity and ambiguity that threatens to engulf fragile sociological sensibilities about speaking on cultural matters. Postmodernity mixes high and low forms of culture, so that Bach and the Police are deemed to occupy the same cultural band, judgement between the two being abdicated, or regarded as in some way politically incorrect. Judgements on culture reflect the right to exclude, a prospect that goes against the inclusive imperatives of sociology. This accentuates the sense of paralysis it faces in dealing with culture, making postmodernity an alibi for what it cannot differentiate between.

This notion of choice, of using culture with a view to finding a place on the marketplace, coincides with a recognition of reflexivity in fieldwork. Returning the sociologist to a sense of the society he inhabits generates a question as to the beliefs that characterise his dealings with culture. Some affirm particular lifestyles. Advocacy of their basis has become part of the sociological vocation. This shift has had a profound impact on teaching and research, the effects of which can be noted in burgeoning publisher's lists in areas such as feminism and sexuality. As indicated earlier, reflexivity increasingly presupposes engagement and representation of the sociologist's tribe, the one of his choice of affiliation.

These issues of culture, choice and judgement have only recently been recognised. Yet, they incorporate questions that have long existed in the history of culture, in politics and in sociology itself. Issues of culture, of its boundaries and definition are lodged in any treatment of ethnicity and nationalism. Colonisation related to ambitions to dominate the alien but indigenous culture of the colonised, to remap their social relationships. The need to control culture related to issues of trust and distrust, but also to problems of quality conservation for the colonisers. Barriers were erected to regulate the traffic between the two cultures, so that assimilation for both was regulated. These efforts had physical manifestations such as the pale, the ditch around Dublin, to keep the natives out. The Great Wall of China and Hadrian's wall are other examples, where the securing of definitions of culture was deemed risky and where defence was required.

Ireland, the site of English discovery of how to colonise, had laws enacted in 1364, the Statutes of Kilkenny, to regulate what could be appropriated from the indigenous culture to prevent the colonisers going native. As Lydon indicates, worries over cultural degeneracy lay behind these prohibitions.[16] Economic and cultural relationships were strictly monitored to maintain boundaries, thus 'no contact was to be made with Irish musicians, poets and singers in view of the danger of espionage'.[17] In *Making History*, Brian Friel, the Irish playwright, beautifully expresses the choice facing his hero Hugh O'Neill, the Ulster Prince, between 'the cold pragmatism of the Renaissance mind' and the capricious genius of the Gaelic intellect, lying beyond the pale. Savagism and civilisation formed familiar issues of choice.[18]

As sociology permits the issue of culture to become its central theoretical focus, questions of civility and refinement will emerge. Being a marginal, provincial discipline, sociology will affiliate with the margins, the underrepresented. But this is an equivocal affiliation. In one setting it might well be the working class and ethnic group which it seeks to represent, but on another reading it could be Catholicism, marginalised in the mass media, where secular values keep this belief beyond the pale of public cultural inspection. The difficulty with efforts to link culture to theology is that they relate to patrician values which sociology instinctively despises. Thus, the established link between Church and State, and the hierarchical divisions these represent, can give a misleading impression to the debate on the theological nature of culture.

These issues become apparent in the unfashionable classical English approaches to culture, which have distinctive theological overtones. Matthew Arnold and T. S. Eliot hover on the fringes of contemporary sociological approaches to culture. The values they sought to preserve might seem irrelevant. Yet a writer such as Eliot did try to link the issue of the vitality of culture to Christianity, which he regarded as representing its highest form of expression. Eliot argued that

> a 'mass culture' will always be a substitute-culture; and sooner or later the deception will become apparent to the more intelligent of those upon whom this culture has been palmed off.[19]

The definition of culture Eliot uses seems a thinly veiled version of Tylor, again showing the unexpected influences of anthropology and sociology of knowledge on his thought. Although they differ in terms of consequences of the deception, the left and right, as in the case of Adorno and Eliot, come to despise the degeneracy of mass culture.

A similar connection with anthropological notions of culture can be found in Matthew Arnold's *Culture and Anarchy*. Published in 1869, it would be odd to expect Arnold to connect his notion of culture to sociology, yet again, in the context of debates on postmodernity, there are some unexpected resonances. Arnold was writing in a climate of political instability, where anarchy seemed at the door and culture was breaking down. This potential threat to culture came less from revolution than from the combined effects of utilitarianism and an unimaginative middle class, who confined their vision of life to technology and industrialisation. His worry was about the despiritualisation of culture, the loss of spiritual sight. There is a bookish religious cast in his approach to culture which he defined as the 'disinterested endeavour after man's perfection'.[20] Stocking is correct to argue that Arnold's approach to culture was nearer than Tylor's to modern anthropological formulations.[21]

In his introduction to *Culture and Anarchy*, Dover Wilson notes the Tractarian background to Arnold's writings and the degree to which Newman's idea of a liberal education had a crucial influence on his view of culture.[22] Arnold conceived of culture in terms of inward operations. This involved the cultivation of a superior sight that enabled man to see past the purely material to find sweetness and light. Arnold was worried about the vitality of a spiritual eye being corrupted by the glare of technology. He felt that 'faith in machinery' was 'our besetting danger'. Furthermore, he argued that culture did not have its origin in the cultivation of man's curiosity. Rather it is concerned with the pursuit of perfection. This was based on a capacity to discern in a notion of culture, covering all forms of life, that works 'through *all* the voices of human experience which have been heard upon it, of art, science, poetry, philosophy, history, as well as of religion'.[23] In Arnold, one finds traces of Weber's concerns with the imbalance between disenchantment and enchantment in culture.

Shifts in anthropological understandings of culture in the late 1960s changed the agenda of its concerns from those of classification and explanation to issues of understanding and interpretation. These changes were especially marked in the writings of the American anthropologist Clifford Geertz. As suggested earlier, deciphering ritual, symbols and actions increasingly came to mark anthropological interests in culture. The theological implications of this shift are profound as they percolate into sociology, subtly changing its expectations of understanding in relation to culture in the context of postmodernity.

Geertz is concerned with the systems of meanings embodied in symbols, which require a 'thick description'. His notion of culture as text, points to more indeterminate readings, a more opaque approach, that recognises the situation of the agent, but also the autonomy of his practices. This shift in approaches to culture makes way for an analysis of any religious ritual.[24] A ceremony involving the baptism of a baby is no more inexplicable in anthropology than a consideration of 'the Balinese cockfight as play'. Both are concerned with strategies to effect the manifestations of particular properties through similar means of ritual and symbol. Wider themes are bound up in these rituals. Thus Geertz argues that

> an image, fiction, a model, a metaphor, the cockfight is a means of expression; its function is neither to assuage social passions nor to heighten them (though, in its playing-with-fire way it does a bit of both), but, in a medium of feathers, blood, crowds, and money, to display them.[25]

The notion of culture as text, which Geertz has done so much to advance within anthropology, involves a recognition of the ambiguity of an event, such as a religious ritual, between its enigmatic surface and the deeper meanings that can be appropriate or discarded.[26] The effect of these interpretative movements is to enhance the more indeterminate properties of meanings of culture and to admit the central significance of symbols, whose decipherment presupposes an understanding of the context of enactment and the intentions of the actors realising the event. Assessing these changes, Swidler argues that culture has now become a 'tool kit' of symbols, rituals and perspectives, whose causal effects involve strategies of action. Culture supplies the components used to construct, effect and to manifest these strategies. Her anthropological concern is with how culture is mobilised and used by actors to shape their rituals, symbols and concerns.[27] These issues of symbol, ritual and deciphering of meanings seem to bracket the issue of suspicion so as to concentrate on the actor's self-understanding of acts.

Postmodernity is another means of encapsulating the present sociological mood about culture. It admits issues of aesthetics, but in a way that gives rise to questions about ethics.[28] Within postmodernity, a tension operates between aesthetics and ethics that calls for judgement which its relativism denies, hence the paralysis the term embodies. The issue of postmodernity is discussed later.

Anthropological accounts of culture qualify this paralysis. They draw attention to a detail theologians forget, that any fruitful understanding of culture has to attend to the site, the field, the context of cultural reproduction. This places theologians in unfamiliar territory, for it asks how religious events are constructed, such as liturgies, how they are manufactured and what forms of reflexivity the actors employ that sociology must understand to have understood the event?

Contextualisation of forms of culture to their site of manufacture also draws attention to rival transactions with which those who manifest the holy have to compete. Thus, a crucial ingredient in postmodernity is the attention it gives to the power of specialists in symbolic production. Featherstone goes on to add that a sociology of postmodernism rather than a postmodern sociology is what is required.[29] Issues now turn to how sociology appreciates the cultural significance of postmodernity as a cultural phenomenon. The shared interest between anthropology and postmodernity in symbols, their power, production and allocation introduces a range of topics that might link sociology with theology. These items, of ritual, symbol and the aesthetization of culture, point to a re-centring that overturns the reason which secularity deployed to misread their basis and presents a field for sociological inspection marked with lots of theological clues less to be deciphered in terms of suspicion than in terms of prospects for use for belief. Between anthropology and postmodernity, the place of culture in sociological reflexivity has changed, with obvious theological implications. But there are other reasons for changes in sociological sensibilities of culture.

The sociologist who has emerged as one of the key figures in understanding contemporary culture and postmodernity is Georg Simmel (1858–1918). Many of his major writings are still untranslated, yet his influence is pivotal. The writings of Simmel cover a vast range, from philosophy, culture to sociology, aesthetics, ethics, and a litter of other topics ranging from the city to tourism. Embodied in his notion of culture is the stranger, the person seeking to connect in an impersonal cosmopolitan society. Bauman sees Simmel as the most powerful and perceptive analyst of modernity. His fragmented sociology and its concern with the mystery of sociability seemed to exemplify all too accurately the properties of modernity, its limits and its illusory basis. Dubbed the flâneur by Benjamin, Simmel represented the Jew, the witness but not the participant, in, but not of the place, who walked the city as a spectator in search of never ending spectacle of 'splits into episodes without cause and consequence'.[30]

With the rediscovery of the vast legacy Georg Simmel left sociology, the increased emphasis on understanding the effects of modernity, the recognition of the place of Walter Benjamin in critical theory and the culture industry, and the realisation of the importance of Bourdieu's writing on cultural reproduction, one gets a sense of the discipline being reconnected to the humanities and back to questions of the human condition. As suggested earlier, those most sensitive to the corrupting effects of modernity have been Jewish writers. Bauman, Benjamin, Goffman and Simmel have all pointed to theological and unresolved spiritual dimensions to the issue of culture and its forms of self-realisation in modernity, now accentuated in postmodernity. Issues of trust, judgement and deception increasingly emerge in a culture characterised by an aesthetic reflexivity. This relates to awareness of the background features of communitites, imagined or invented.[31] Sociology tries to grapple with the implications of this shift in the reflexive basis of culture.

The tension Weber saw, between disenchantment derived from calculation and prospects of enchantment of liberation from its basis, is embodied in cultural forms of is marketing. Enchantment is given a predictable property in the miracle of manufacture where image transcends the mundane. Thus, corporate packaging permits the mundane hamburger in McDonald's to be transformed into the acme of a globalised universal culture where wants are gratified predictably and instantly. The product becomes endowed with an allure, a degree of aura, that disguises the mechanism of reproduction. As aspects of culture become commodified, they are subject to forces of calculation, where artifice is disguised in advertising and where dependence is cultivated. Risks of disenchantment are masked in an illusory principle of freedom and convenience of choice. Thus, for Ritzer, the iron cage of Weber takes on plastic properties in a culture that involves the McDonaldisation of society, where the artificial is easily confused with the authentic.[32]

Availability carries a price in a culture where few of its icons and artifacts can resist commodification. If the sacred has become subsumed to the secular in acts of plunder, this reflects a process of appropriation in a fiercely contested marketplace of symbols and signs that circulate in a remarkably complex manner. But as Lash and Urry suggest, through technology, globalisation and advanced producer services, a form of symbolic violence is exercised in this cultural marketplace that subsumes everything in a final nihilism, to fit with a 'three-minute culture' – the attention span of gazes at image.[33] Technology has made images even more fleeting and ephemeral, intensifying the dilemmas of modernity into those of postmodernity where originals are not necessary and where any pastiche is possible. Yet even in this cultural anarchy some form of regulation is required.

Whereas the problem of naming might be traced back to Genesis, it forms a crucial facet of the cultural marketplace, a point Benjamin understood. The power to re-name relates to the packaging of style, as images and icons become reclassified and objectified to secure demand for the products of the service industries and the social relationship these offer. Naming and protecting a brandname, or trademark is a fundamental characteristic of commodity aesthetics. Without this power to exclusively name, service industries cannot secure a distinctive advantage over their rivals on the marketplace. The commodification of image is central to the basis of the operations of the service industries. As Haug argues, it effects a contraction of all messages, a monopolisation that gives an exclusive attracting property to an image.[34] He goes to suggest that the appearance of a commodity promises more than it can deliver. Images manufactured exploit dissatisfactions in endless alluring mirrors that seem to provide what consumers *think* they want. In such cultural circumstances, 'greed is served with just as much anticipation as idleness'.[35] This regulation of culture, where names, images and icons are controlled, breeds a dependence on the facile and the instant. In this commodification of the aesthetic, the instant becomes confused with the ideal and issues of beauty relate more to surfaces than to hidden aspects to be discerned with endeavour that draws on character. The problem theology faces is not of competing with the facile, but of securing fields of autonomy for the sacred, where expectations of discernment can be cultivated. These require the nurture of spiritual eyes to see and the cultivation of a disposition that wishes to notice the sacred.

It would be occupational suicide for taste and symbol makers *not* to make judgements. But worries arise over what these judgements disguise. There is a mechanism of reproduction and control regulating the marketplace which its producers keep well hidden to maintain the illusion of the escapism they seek to cultivate. Worries over the unaccountability of ecclesial producers have been transferred to the commodity brokers of culture who follow profit rather than prophecy. A hermeneutics of suspicion that hitherto applied to cultural aspects of theology has now been passed over to the process of reproduction through which the commodification of aesthetics secures its credibility. An accomplishment of the commodifiers of culture, of icons and lifestyles, artifacts and service products, has been the exercise of a symbolic violence that wrests the capacity to sacralise from their traditional users, the priests, so that these secularised products are endowed with similar sacramental qualities, of aura and mystery, where grace is deemed unnecessary. The most important causality of this process has been the abdication of the need for moral judgement from the pursuit of gratification. The decadence that gave birth to modernity has been universalised into the culture of postmodernity. Whereas, earlier pioneers of decadence achieved spasms of delightful guilt in plundering moral and religious sensibilities in the pursuit of pleasure, the democratisation of this chase into an infinity of delights in postmodernity, wrought through the miracle of technology, operates in an ethical vacuum. In this context, the pursuit of pleasure takes on a destabilising property as its stakes and demands rise, taking the self far away from any worries about moral constraint. Thus, continued representation in the quality English press of hard pornography as just another lifestyle that gives pleasure between consenting adults, moves evil into the banality of a culture of postmodernity. Privacy and consent, tokens of public indifference, are the only values that matter, because judgement is abdicated and moral principles are deemed irrelevant.

For sociology not to judge the contours of the cultural marketplace would be to abdicate its analytical responsibilities. Simply mirroring the range of commodities, the forms of life in the marketplace – attending raves and buying second hand clothes for fieldwork – as in cultural studies, hardly gives sociology a distinctive voice in the present cultural hubris.[36]

In his splenetic attack on cultural studies, for its part in legitimising a vacuous immoral mass media, Tester looks to what he terms the fetishisation of everyday life. This relates to Marx's notion of commodity fetishism, where capitalism disguises the social relationships embodied in production. Tester uses the term to show the way the mass media renders events independent of social and cultural position and conditions of existence.[37] This escapism from confronting the implications of the human condition lay at the root of critiques of the culture industry by Adorno. The sense of moral indifference which the culture industry generates points to a process that facilitates the abdication of moral responsibility. The sense of morality being spectacle for the uninvolved has always worried sociology. The worry that haunts Tester is the indifference images of starving children evoke on television. Something in contemporary culture facilitates this seeing, but uncaring, a sense that leads him to call for something deeper from sociology. Thus he argues that

> sociology ought to be driven by a sense of moral commitment and by a moral outrage at what presently passes for the good life; an outrage that cultural studies with its increasing emphasis on things like clothes and shopping can say absolutely nothing about.[38]

In dealing with the sacred, Durkheim underestimated the cultural properties that would diminish its capacity to effect a distance from the profane. More importantly, he did not realise the degree to which the profane could imperialise the sacred. This capacity has become apparent in the context of postmodernism.

To sociology, postmodernism is less an analytical solution for dealing with modern culture than a trivialising irritant, one whose intellectual sell by date has passed. In one reading, postmodernism points to a crisis of cognitive mapping within the cultural logic of late capitalism. This crisis is played on an urban field. Covering aesthetics, pop art, films and other forms of culture, postmodernism captures critical movements of reflexivity that have an unworried doubt about making categorical judgements. Largely a movement of critics operating outside sociology, the term has captured an unease, a disquiet. Irony, indeterminacy, anti-narrative, fracture, surface readings and images in bizarre combinations characterise the interests of postmodernism.[39] Changes in recent architectural styles, with playful brick patterns, metal embellishments and sloping roofs, mark a revolt against the brutal concrete style that marked modernism. This endless property of pastiche in style also relates to commodities, to images and icons in a way that amplifies choice but delimits possibilities of discernment of the authentic and the inauthentic basis of its outcome. Increasingly, ambiguity rules the litter of detail of the mosaic, but in a way that blinds the need to judge to see the pattern.

Postmodernism also relates to an intensification of symbols, their availability and expectations of consumption. It affirms a capacity to reorder endlessly through technology in a way that marks an incapacity of the individual to assimilate its endless products. In postmodernism, icons and images have their own playful logic, offering endless prospect of re-arrangement but with a moral impunity for there are no values embodied within this endless plethora of cultural products. As Jameson argues, attempts to conceptualise postmodernism 'in terms of moral or moralizing judgements must finally be identified as a category-mistake'.[40] But as Heller and Fehér note 'if total moral relativism, which is undeniably one of the options of postmodernity, gains the upper hand, even the assessment of mass deportation and genocide becomes a matter of taste'.[41]

Postmodernism signifies the blurring of this sensibility in a certain blinding and dehumanising. In mass communication in the global village, the medium is the message, governing a precarious line between fact and fiction, one that entangles especially followers of soap operas. Unreality has become more 'real' than reality and in this confusion, the issue of the accountability of their cultural producers generates vast sociological questions. Escapism and paralysis have become interlinked as the spectator of television becomes an object rather than a subject. Postmodernism is not so much an instrument of analysis as a characterisation of this state of cultural and moral chaos. But it also has its own problems of self-definition. As Hassan has noted, 'postmodernism suffers from a certain *semantic* instability'.[42] A sociological attempt to think about a culture of postmodernism manifests the plight of Pascal's aphorism, 'a thought has escaped: I was trying to write it down: instead I write that it has escaped me'.[43]

Postmodernism relates to a right to choose, in a way that leads to a hybrid of cultural products, ambiguous and playful in intent. It operates through improbable juxtapositions in an unsettling, slightly subversive manner. As Jencks suggests the postmodern world brought a 'new taste for variety, even incongruity and paradox'.[44] This concern with the elusive points to an odd facet of postmodernism, which Connor highlights as the 'desire to project and to produce that which cannot be pinned down or mastered by representation or conceptual thought'. This has been identified by Lyotard as 'the pull towards the sublime'.[45]

This seeking of the intangible, without religious belief, points to an enduring paradox of recent decades: the capacity of theologians to sanctify that which cultural theorists discard. This facet of cultural lag amongst theologians effects an undermining of structures of religious plausibility for no sooner do they show signs of sedimenting, than they are uprooted as a new reading of culture is issued. This incapacity to read culture contributes to a continued destabilisation of the religious field. It accentuates the process of secularisation, for it conveys the notion that theologians have no enduring belief in the cultural forms that are supposed to signify the holy and timeless. The implication is that the truth lies in the form, hence the endless adjustments, and not the content they are to signify which is above time. The issue about cultural forms in a post-Christian culture is not one of their adjustment but of their decipherment.

There is a restlessness in the term postmodernism that plays on the ruins of theology yet harks back to its agenda. This relates to an intriguing comment of Jencks, that modernism, with its spare functional architecture, almost puritanical, expresses a Calvinism, but that in postmodernism, one can find a quality of the Counter-Reformation, a new Baroque, but one without faith or belief to give it substance. Jencks seeks in his vision of postmodernism a shared symbolic order that religion provides, but without the need for a religious substance that is theological.[46] The trouble with postmodernism is that it either witnesses to the maturation of culture into a moral vacuum or it points to an unstoppable process of globalisation that reflects the same vacuity. One way or another it forces out an issue of choice in dealing with culture, a wager which cannot be postponed.

Most approaches to postmodernism centre on the issue of disbelief. This has been apparent since the translation of Lyotard's *The Postmodern Condition: a Report on Knowledge* in 1984. This work did more than any other to make the term postmodern significant in academic circles. Yet, from a sociological perspective, it is a deeply flawed book that has been read with expectations it was never geared to deliver.

Lyotard was concerned with the collapse of a totalising metaphysic, the fragmentation of a consensus which the Enlightenment had seized from religion in the name of reason, but which it now has lost. Relativism, Kuhn's paradigms, the contextualisation of language in Wittgenstein and performative utterances of Austin, dominate the concerns of this work. In his forward, Jameson makes a crucial point that Lyotard is dealing with knowledge *not* culture, a point its critics seem to have forgotten.[47] This point is acknowledged in the appendix, where Lyotard provides a highly sketchy idea of postmodern culture. In his report, an exercise in epistemology rather than sociology, postmodernism is defined as 'not modernism at its end but in the nascent state, and this state is constant'.[48] It involves living experimentally without consensus, but in a way that denies the solace of good forms, the consensus of taste, which would make it possible to share collectively the nostalgia for the unattainable.

Postmodernism points to the collapse of narrative, that which can be unified and legitimised in a coherent and authoritative fashion. The report is on the need to live with this condition of scientific incoherence. This fragmentation, an incapacity to articulate a consensus on truth, reflects a disbelief in meta-narratives. These are the unifying sense of spirit of life that legitimise scientific endeavour. In short, metaphysics has collapsed, and with it the narratives that tyrannise. Thus Lyotard argues that 'lamenting the "loss of meaning" in postmodernity boils down to mourning the fact that knowledge is no longer principally narrative'.[49]

This crucial work of Lyotard can be understood as an analysis of the rules of the game, of producing knowledge by reference to notions of performance and context. These affect scientific narratives and undermine claims of meta-narratives to provide consensual foundational transcending devices that harmonise seemingly indefinite difference. But these issues were confronted by anthropology and sociology in the 1970s, in Winch and in debates on rationality and relativity. Lyotard writes as if these debates never occurred. Performance implies social enactment, ritual displays of images that persuade according to context. Narratives have ambitions for dialogue, hence the possibility of negotiation which draws in hermeneutic considerations. It is noteworthy that Lyotard places his comments on postmodernism and sociology on the site of functionalism and Marxist theories and not in the field of culture where the need to refer to hermeneutics has emerged. Reference to hermeneutics would have resolved some of the problems that emerge in the context of the social bond and language games in culture. On the wilder shores of postmodernism, the social itself becomes at risk, a point Smart considers in relation to Baudrillard. Naturally, if the social vanishes in the intersections between media and the masses, sociology will receive its dismissal notice.[50] It is scarcely surprising that Featherstone should utilise sociology of knowledge to seek the producers and carriers of postmodern symbolic goods and their location in a new middle class dealing in the service industries.[51]

Part of the difficulty of reading Lyotard's report is that it is a tilt against Habermas' attempt to resolve the legitimation crisis over Enlightenment truths of reason. There is a corrosive characteristic to the commensurability of scientific games where humanistic knowledge expands into compartments, all with uncommon keys. The demise of consensus generates a mourning process for what cannot be achieved. Echoing Benjamin's comment on the Fall, but applied to the consensual dreams of the Enlightenment, Lyotard suggests that 'most people have lost the nostalgia for the lost narrative' and this has come to characterise what 'the postmodern world is all about'.[52]

But democratisation of mass culture has become associated with nostalgia, the feeling that the past was better, not to be lived in, but to be viewed as spectacle, hence the rise of the heritage industry which coincides with increased deference to postmodernism. Stauth and Turner, who noted this paradoxical trend, also point to the effects of a pessimism in approaches to culture that has left academics afflicted with an ontological nostalgia.[53] Thus, for Callinicos, postmodernism is a symptom of an historical epoch.[54]

He goes on to argue that the drift towards postmodernism was a rallying point for those disaffected and disillusioned by the events that came after 1968. The socially-mobile intelligentsia, who affirm the significance of the term postmodernism, have an apocalyptic cast to their rhetoric, a pessimism that signifies an emptying of ideals.[55]

In this context, postmodernism can be regarded as reflecting the maturation of secularisation, where an ironic effect is that intellectuals are themselves marginalised. God has died and there is no consensus as to who takes over. Forms of religion are emptied of belief and are transposed as metaphors in a commodification of culture that exercises its own tyranny. Thus, postmodernity, in differing from postmodernism, reflects the price of secularisation, hence the interest in a culture that seeks both nostalgia and enchantment, options of past and future that seem superior to the tyranny of an eternal present.

Part of the pessimism that governs academic approaches to culture, that is embodied in ambiguous attitudes to postmodernism, is the dehumanisation it mirrors in culture. Apart from rendering invisible those of the working class with limited access to the endless pastiches and images endorsed by postmodernists, issues of theodicy that relate to the human condition are equally and arbitrarily absent. Nobody seems to get ill, to suffer or to die in these postmodern worlds. Postmodernism deals in sites where human experience is scarcely mentioned.[56] Thus, the Bonaventura Hotel, the exemplary site for Jameson's postmodernist considerations, representing

> this latest mutation in space – postmodern hyperspace – has finally succeeded in transcending the capacities of the individual body to locate itself, to organize its immediate surroundings perceptually, and cognitively to map its position in a mappable external world.[57]

But this sense of engulfment, of being lost on the map, where past directions have been wiped out has been characterised earlier in other terms, from a theological perspective, by Guardini. He suggests

> the limited world picture of the Middle Ages was cancelled out by the modern picture of a limitless world. To speak precisely, God lost His dwelling place; thereby man lost his proper position in existence.[58]

This relates to another difficulty that Jameson sees, of an incapacity to fashion representation of current experience. The past is plundered for former images, when invention becomes impossible. Jameson refers to Plato's notion of simulacrum as identical copy for which no original exists. The culture of the simulacrum comes to life, for Jameson, in a society where the past becomes erased and nostalgia becomes an outlet for pastiche and play.[59]

This sense of loss of place, but also of being unable to reinvent solutions, points to a malaise in contemporary culture. Its images have become counterfeit and few have illusions otherwise. Furthermore, these images relate to narrow concerns. As Harvey observes, 'if we stripped modern advertising of direct reference to the three themes of money, sex and power, there would be very little left'.[60] But Harvey goes on to note a paradox that

> the greater the ephemerality, the more pressing the need to discover or manufacture some kind of eternal truth that might lie therein. The religious revival that has become much stronger since the late sixties and the search for authenticity and authority in politics . . . are cases in point.[61]

Theologians cannot just ignore these movements in postmodernity and culture. As Blanquart rightly suggests 'a serious risk occurs: that of not so much playing with the flux as being played with by it'.[62] The problem with theologians, Van der Vloet notes, is that they think in terms of modernity, whereas most people act in a postmodern fashion. He calls unabashedly for the development of 'asceticism as decisive action'. He also demands a witness to revelation, whatever its scandal, rather than an unwitting adoption to the restrictive demands of modernity. This is in a world where the 'void' of nothing is the sole 'certainty' of man.[63] In commodity aesthetics, as Haug indicates, the self becomes trapped in disillusion. It is believed that the source of failure must lie in the product, not in the actor who makes the purchase, who will be induced to buy again.[64] This capacity to commodify images, to detach the ascetic from the aesthetic, forms part of a tyranny, an illusion that deceives the self. The freedom to endlessly appropriate eventually commodifies and entraps the self as well. It has no illusions left bar the realisation that the capacity to endlessly commodify images without accountability to a superior and external belief system is itself an illusion.

Unfettered access to images and likenesses characterises postmodernity as it makes it own images for play. Through technology, appearance is feigned in a manner that confuses the real with the unreal. This property invades contemporary culture, and suggests that the sociologist is not alone in finding uncomfortable resonances in the tragedy of Faustus.

His fate is that of a scholar unsatisfied with the limits of what he knows. Seeking to resolve his curiosity, and being absolved from all ambiguities after his wager with the devil, Faustus has a particular magical gift which the Emperor at the court seeks to test to find the basis of power of others who have ruled in history. Through the cunning of his art, Faustus is asked to conjure up a sight of Alexander the Great and his 'beauteous paramour', but to satisfy his desire, both are to be 'in their right shapes, gesture and attire they used to wear during their time of life'. Faustus indicates he cannot present their 'true substantial bodies', but he can offer the sight of such spirits as can resemble both figures. These bear inspection as if they were the real objects.[65] In the B-text of the play, the Emperor is told to employ a 'dumb silence' as these spirits come and go. Faustus prevents the Emperor from embracing them, warning that 'these are but shadows, not substantial'.[66]

These matters are part of a wider illusion, one as to where hell is, for as Mephistopheles noted earlier

> hell hath no limits, nor is circumscribed
> In one self place, for where we are is hell,
> and where hell is must we ever be.[67]

Having wagered to seek everything, Faustus finds his knowing is still insubstantial but also elusive. Just before he goes off with the devils at the end he calls, 'I'll burn my books'.[68]

Marlowe's play has shown a remarkable capacity to present indefinite readings that vary according to the cultural circumstances of its reception. In its Elizabethan era, it emerged as a morality play, to Enlightenment sensibilities it embodied archaic superstitions, but in the modern age the character of Faustus takes on a more substantial philosophical and theological interest.[69] He seems to warn of the deceits of postmodernity. The sins of Faustus are of pride and vanity in knowing. His tragedy relates to the gamble he makes with his will to transcend the antinomies of knowledge and also to possess its fullness. But his tragedy seems a parable that characterises the operations of the culture industry where the real has been confused with the unreal.

The culture of postmodernity embodies unrecognised the wagers of Faustus. The illusion of God being dead frees the consumer to conjure up any image through technological miracle without resort to Mephistopheles. All images so wrought are not evil, but the luxury of instant incantation denies the need to cultivate a spiritual gaze. The focus of adoration becomes fragmented into the worship of a plenitude of icons, none of which admit grace. In asking the question 'What is Postmodernism?', Lyotard states:

> modernity in whatever age it appears, cannot exist without a shattering of belief and without the discovery of the 'lack of reality' of reality, together with the invention of other realities.[70]

Lyotard suggests that for Kant, the most sublime passage in the Bible, is in Exodus, in the commandment 'thou shall not make graven images', one that prohibits all presentations in visual forms of the Absolute. This could refer to the notion of presumption of making definite in image that which of its theological nature is indefinite. But Lyotard is ending on the notion that the postmodern is that which in the modern 'puts forward the unpresentable in presentation itself'.[71]

It is the ambitions that postmodernity feeds, where the icon is removed from grace to pleasurable manufacture, to fulfil desire without moral qualification and to be available to all, that generates the risk of pride in the making of any image, but without realisation of the danger of fall. Technology can make any image, however insubstantial and unreal, sufficiently real for the consumer to desperately seek to appropriate. The issue of tact, of distance before the hallowed has vanished from a culture of postmodernity. To preserve its images with the illusion of endless availability in the each nexus, service industries mask the need for discipline in the gaze, the necessity of linking distance to worthiness and proximity to virtue. Such properties that relate to appreciation of the sacred are disregarded in a culture that promises the commodification of anything. The inward eye that illuminates the inner culture of the self is left sightless, so that the spiritual blindness, which Arnold so feared, is left unsignified and unrecognised as a malaise.

As sociology takes a reflexive turn into the culture of postmodernity to decipher the spells of symbol brokers in advertising and the marketing of lifestyles, where all is commodified, the issue switches from the wagers of the sociologist to those of his tribe operating in climes of postmodernity. Both Simmel and Weber foresaw the tragedy of culture as it has moved into a fullness in postmodernity. But culture's own tragedy is the deceiving way it has been anaesthetised and is so prevented from revealing these tragic elements. The sociologist bears an estranging self-defeating property that compromises his reflexivity and makes his plight tragic. Analytically he can discern, but spiritually he lacks a means of containing what he unfolds, an unrecognised tragedy of culture.

Sociology sees too much in culture, but the price of its analysis is an incapacity to resist what it discloses. This power resides in the understandings of the theologian with the grace to link insight to prayer for redemption. But theologians seldom see through sociological lens cast so darkly. For the pious theologian, hope springs eternal over the gloomiest of analyses; but that which sinks into piteous detail in the sociological sight, offers little redemptive prospect. Witness to this without prospect of amelioration formed the tragedy of Weber's own sociological career.

Weber's life was dedicated to an enormous effort to see how much knowing he could bear. He saw without prospect of theological relief, being deaf to its sensibilities. This enormously complex figure has left a terrible legacy to later sociologists, of a capacity to discern combined with an incapacity to resist that which was envisaged. In his appreciation of Weber, Jasper regarded him as the greatest German of the present age.[72] In his concluding section on Weber as a man, Jasper draws out his struggle for the truth, that underlay his sense of faith. Part of the discomfort of his legacy relates to the sense of pessimism and failure that surrounded his life. In his concern with disenchantment, he saw the price of endless calculation. A crucial difference between Faustus and Weber is that the former willed his fate, whereas the latter was fated to be a victim of what he could not resist.[73]

Weber's approach to the issue of enchantment and disenchantment can be understood in many terms, all opaque. Disenchantment arises from the growth of rational forms of authority based on legal codes, subject to calculation, exemplified in the notion of bureaucracy, whose growth is irresistible in the context of modernisation. The less well defined term, enchantment, relates to non-rational forms of authority, whose legitimacy, as in the case of charisma, is derived from incalculable powers of grace believed by followers to galvanise credibility. The power of enchantment lies in the recognition it can effect. In crude terms, disenchantment and enchantment embody analytical dilemmas that can be rooted in the divisions of the human condition between reason and passion and 'reality' and aspiration. Although the terms relate to politics they also have important theological implications. They also bear on Catholic considerations more than Weber's Lutheran disposition might seem to indicate.

In this context, we are more concerned with Weber's approach to enchantment. As it is considered an antidote to disenchantment, enchantment transcends and contains the endless effects of an unstoppable capacity to calculate. The issue of enchantment can be likewise understood in relation to secularisation. While enchantment is related to the wild card of sociology, charisma, to exotic prophets, wider issues of reproduction and routinisation of channels of grace in terms of ritual can be found in Weber's writings on the term that relate to the tenets of Catholic theology. It is this latter facet that underlies Bourdieu's approach to a sociology of culture. Combining Weber and Bourdieu enables us to glimpse a means of constructing an argument for re-sacralisation, that is peculiarly sociological, but one which complements theological arguments. It is important for theologians not to underestimate the significance of Bourdieu's contribution to sociology of culture.

Bourdieu has had a long-standing interest in sociology of religion and has published three significant articles, on the genesis and structure of the religious field,[74] on legitimation and structured interests in Weber's sociology of religion[75] and on authorised language, which is a study of power and authority in liturgy.[76] These have had a formative effect on shaping his approach to the reproduction of culture.

Bourdieu derives his notion of struggle, of routinisation and deroutinisation, of heresy and orthodoxy from Weber's sociology of religion. Autonomy and power relate to prophecy and orthodoxy, to the need to routinise, to incorporate and to recognise these properties. Power relates to position on the field and to the masked basis of structure and definition. Robbins admirably captures the functions of Bourdieu's analyses to expose the powerlessness of those excluded from these fields of culture, symbol and power to classify, such as in the university or those who deal in a marketplace of aesthetics. He seeks to produce a reflexive sociology that would effect the modification of these structures of domination by the analytical revelation of their basis. These would reveal the mechanisms of diminution of social space and the unequal exploitation of cultural capital to secure advantage.[77]

The field is a site for securing credibility of belief. Although issues of power and domination govern his interests in liturgy and his approach to symbols, nevertheless the medieval roots of Bourdieu's approach to sociology, exemplified in his notion of habitus, give his placement of culture in sociology some particular theological resonances that relate to debate on re-sacralisation. Furthermore, the notion of habitus, relating to dispositions, can be extended into issues of faith that link theology with culture. It permits the notion of edification to be attached to the idea of enchantment to service a link between theology and culture that could only emerge from within sociology. A theologically inclined reading of Bourdieu's approach to habitus, the field and his definition of culture permits a resistance to secularisation to emerge that is distinctly sociological.

The issue of the field, the site and the question of the map seems a matter distant from the artificial dilemmas of the lobby of the Bonaventura Hotel. But on other sites, definitions of the field, and the entitlement to occupy, can take on tragic proportions for those threatened with dispossession. They might have their fields of traditional occupancy re-named in a process of conquest that marginalises them out of existence. With differing tragic outcomes, the field represents a dangerous site for the Irish and Jews.

As indicated earlier, contemporary culture embodies the notion of a moral maze, a labyrinth, but one that eludes a consensus as to what to map. As the draughtsman of modernity, sociology seems implicated in the shambles that has emerged. The field carries the notion of a place of play, a site for the enactment of language games that seems to fulfil sociological expectations of being engaged in fieldwork, but to what end and for what judgement?

Bourdieu's notion of the field grants autonomy to a number of games, or forms of transaction, including those of theology and liturgy. It is an extremely good metaphor for dealing with contemporary culture. The problem is that interconnecting fields present themselves as a patchwork whose boundaries are difficult to map. This pluralism of sites for social and moral struggle exhibits a diversity that disguises a problem of consensus over the definition of what is authentic and proper to play in particular fields. The bias of sociology is towards neatly defined fields that are discrete and autonomous, where play occurs in a clear cut manner, and where the habitus of the actor can be linked to its structure in an uncontested manner. Unfortunately, some fields are marked by an ambiguity embodied in their terms of praxis, such being the case in liturgical engagements where civic and sacerdotal meanings can be produced simultaneously. Securing authenticity is often an accomplishment of habitus.

In Bourdieu's approach to culture, the field serves as a site to resolve the antinomy between the subjective and the objective and between agency and structure. But the field is also the site for struggle, for strategies played in a game, whose autonomy is not in question. It is the setting in which habitus operates, where a sensibility of the game is cultivated and strategies, semiconscious socialised forms of knowledge, are used to maximise position to find an advantageous social space. The struggle for scarce resources of critical recognition operates through winning this social space to maximise autonomy of effort and opportunity. The game is played out of self-interest to win where stakes are high. These stakes can be related to economic or cultural goals, prizes that involve recognition. Limiting and delimiting opportunity forms a moral concern of Bourdieu, where the marginal have to cope with apparently endless advantage, which a democracy permits, but which disguises equally endless disadvantage. Services seem open, but in some puzzling manner are closed off, save to the cognoscenti. They define the cultural terms of what is to count. Thus, habitus structures and is structured in judgements of orthodoxy and heresy about the field of cultural production. The field can be a site for struggle to preserve boundaries, a lineage with tradition and what is believed to be an authentic definition of the situation.

The metaphor of the field in sociology carries a notion of territory, of possession of a culture, where boundaries are to be defended against rivals, who will knock down fences and who will seek to trespass with impunity. This right to exclude, to defend a tenancy, is exemplified in the film, *The Field*, based on the play by John B. Keane of the same title.[78] The notion of a field in sociology presupposes use but also recognition that its boundaries can be contested. It is what is embodied in the field as a site for struggle that matters.

The issue of the definition of the field mirrors problems of contested identity as in the case of Ireland. Boundaries and territories have profound political and cultural consequences for the Planter and the Gael over who is to occupy the field of Irish identity, and who is to be excluded. A search has become obsessional for images and symbols to reconcile these divisions, to overcome the endless making of an unprofitable history. The Field Day Company, founded by Stephen Rea, Seamus Heaney and Brian Friel in Derry, has sought to deal with this fractured sense of being Irish. Their notion of a field has a number of purposes. It conveys the idea of a break from normal activities, summarised in the phrase 'the critics had a field day',[79] but it also relates to the conscious seeking of a fifth province for Ireland, a place for dissenters and traitors to meet.[80] Thus the field is deemed to be a site of reconciliation. But it also has the notion of contest, a site for military manoeuvres, where battle plans need to be drawn and mapped. To win, the field has to be known in all its contours, its strengths and weaknesses. Marking out the tactics for engagements assumes an understanding of positions where the least damage will be done by the enemy. The task, as Seamus Heaney aptly observes, involves 'a search for images and symbols adequate to our predicament'.[81]

Brian Friel, sometimes described as the Irish Chekhov, is a playwright who has tried to redeem the divisions of Irish culture, especially in Ulster. Pine describes Friel as a landscape painter of small worlds. In his account, Pine makes extensive use of Victor Turner's notion of the liminal to characterise the interlinking between ritual and drama and between an identity secured in childhood but unsecured in adulthood. He argues that there is a continual tension in Friel's drama between the known, the secure past, receding and fading and the unknown beckoning future which 'baits and challenges'.[82] The divisions between past and present, innocence and experience, modernity and nostalgia are all exemplified as themes in his plays.

The problems of defining a field and drawing boundaries on the basis of reason rather than on communal sentiment and by appeal to tradition, is given dramatic form in one of his best plays, *Translations*. It is an unexpected drama about mapping, about language and sense of place, its rupture and the tragedy that befalls those involved in the effort of some

English Ordnance Survey Engineers to map and to rename a country district in the North West of Ireland in 1833. Making maps might seem a harmless civic exercise to make travel and exploration for the stranger possible. It is a facility associated with civilisation, where one can accurately read the contours of a district. Maps require a reading, so that the unfamiliar is translated into the familiar in an identifiable manner. Map makers construct what Andrews has termed a 'paper landscape'.[83] But there is a political and social dimension to cartography which is easily neglected by a colonial culture. The marking of a territory is a means of rendering it to disinterested account, but it also facilitates an interested appropriation by agents of colonial oppression. As Pine suggests

> a map, like an icon, puts before us a paradigm, something which mediates between an *absolute* and that which we can comprehend. Through maps, icons and myths, the unrealistic concepts of controlled space, being and time are made real.[84]

Mapping involves a process of marking a territory in a way that renders the natives strangers in their own communities and that is the tragedy Friel traces in *Translations*.

Of all the contemporary major English speaking playwrights, Friel is perhaps the most sociologically resonant.[85] There are two acknowledged debts in *Translations* that bear on sociology. The first is to Steiner's *After Babel*[86] and the second, as indicated above, is to Turner's approach to the liminal.[87] But other themes emerge.

The play relates to a problem of hermeneutics, but also echoes some of the themes embodied in Benjamin's angel. The map is a text that breeds misunderstandings. It comes to represent an attempt to translate subjective sensibilities of place into an alternative objective form, an unintended consequence of which is the advancement of cultural imperialism. Ironically, the natives subject to the civilising intentions of cartography find their definitions of place and social space redrawn under alien terms. A disjunction occurs between an inner culture of location and the redefined external culture that now breeds a sense of dislocation amongst the natives. There is a price to this pursuit of colonial exactitude, one which echoes themes drawn by Bauman in relation to modernity and the issue of ambivalence. It is not so much that the Irish are expelled from a redrawn territory as that cartography is an instrument of estrangement making them feel they no longer belong. It is no longer their site but has been re-named for other purposes.

In his writings on postmodernity, Bauman has raised some inconvenient sociological questions. Bauman's work is concerned with the issue of classification and the intolerance of indeterminacies within modernity. Jews exemplify qualities which modernity requires, but distrusts, of being the rootless, restless strangers in cosmopolitan life. But the property of being strangers resistant to classification generates an insecurity in a modernity which denies differences matter, but they do. Jews were the early victims, pioneers, of a weakness in modernity that it sought to disguise. The weakness was the question of ambiguity. Bauman argues that 'ambivalence is *the waste of modernity*'[88] a comment that occurs in the context of worries about the illusory ambitions of the Enlightenment.

In an observation that could also apply to Catholicism, but draws from Jewish reverence of the Word, Bauman notes that 'the gift of God was, so to speak, the knowledge of *ambivalence* and the skill of living with this knowledge'.[89] A secularised world intolerant of ambiguity, which it feels it has a right to resolve, becomes unsettled. In so becoming, it seeks scapegoats for that which it cannot resolve. Thus, an imperative to order, that lies behind politics and a sense of nation, can become a distinctive self-destructive urge of the Enlightenment.

Citizenship is about a right to define a sense of place for duties which are granted to the state to administer. The right to mark boundaries on the basis of reason, embodied in the notion of state, can be contrasted to the appeal to emotion, to the sense of attachment to an ideal signified in the nebulous term nation. Nationalism is about a right to include and to exclude, to set a boundary on a field. When nation and state combine to exclude, the effects can be devastating for minority ethnic groups.

Giving a brilliant and extended account of 'the practice of the gardening state', which cultivates order on the field, Bauman links breeding, pruning and fertilisation to eugenics. The pursuit of order, the taming of weeds, the rooting out of the untidy seem all part of a scientific dream, where reason overturns nature.[90] This horticultural turn in sociology points to unsavoury practices of ethnic cleansing to purify cultures of the unfit. The effect is to dehumanise and to release a ruthless endeavour, where, without a shred of humanity, the imperfect are sacrificed in the interests of scientific perfection.

The tragedy of the Jewish relationship to modernity was the belief that it would give them a place where difference did not matter, where the blind force of their history could be overturned in a civilised society, such as in Germany. Bauman suggests that Jewish intellectuals found in modernity a notion that would resolve their marginality and would effect their assimilation into the city, less as strangers and more as sophisticates who would change German culture. But their tragedy was that this culture they so admired, which seemed so civilised and enlightened, concealed a trap.

Modernity represented their disconnection from ethnic roots of tradition, but in becoming the pioneers of the homeless mind, they posed a threat to the German mind. So entrapped, so assimilated, the civilisation turned on them for what Bauman sees them as being still – Jews.[91]

The field resonates with theological images and metaphors. It is a dangerous site, containing hidden perils and treasures. Certainly, it cannot be crossed lightly in a mere mapping exercise. The field, the garden, the site, all point to circumstances of playing where leading and misleading transactions occur, where some are morally duped, and others know insufficient to be aware of this risk, yet feel emptied of some ill-defined promise. The emptiness of the field in a culture of postmodernity generates worry not so much about the games being played as the absence of play. So much confusion makes games pointless. There seem no rules and therefore there is no incentive to engagement.

The moral confusion that lies behind a sense of a social chaos is not a figment of a sociological imagination. A half page in *The Observer*, October 1994 headlined 'young adrift in the moral maze' was devoted to the findings of a MORI survey involving face to face interviews with people aged between 15–35 on their attitudes to religion, morality and trust. Relativism, individualism, a privatised morality in a post-Christian society that emerged in the survey showed a similarity between the agenda of public debate and that of sociology.[92] But it also points to a worry that arises in another setting, the rapid increase in suicide rates of young males, for whom crises of identity, insecurity of life and no resources to cope, kill. Issues that relate to theology and culture do matter. A radical rethinking is increasingly a sociological necessity. If sociology is to contribute to this debate, it has to offer some radical reflections, even if these risk seeming perverse. One has to ask how do false Gods come to be trusted, so that faith in the counterfeit exceeds that of the authentic? It is not a matter of looking passively at secularisation as an ebbing away of belief, as some unmendable leak of religion. There is a property, also a process, that has come to fruition in postmodernity, that sociology can discern, that inverts religious belief, that conspires against commitment, which needs to be understood. What false gods militate against the divine in a culture of modernity? What in this culture so cripples religious commitment?

The freeing from tradition, which no longer binds, the intensified processes of aesthetic reflexivity, which Lash and Urry mention, combined with the endless commodification of icons, images and symbols, all point to a standardisation and globalisation within culture. Like Bourdieu, they also look at cultural objects in terms of an economy of exchange operating ever increasingly in a marketplace, which is regulated by symbol brokers and those who control and commodify images, their packaging and allure. For these sociologists, the cultural has become a form of capital. The intensified accumulation of these symbols begets an economy where the basis of exchange makes reflexive response problematic. It gives a sense of being overwhelmed by the new gods of commodities, their symbols, images and icons. They become illusory projections that do not illuminate social reality, but rather mask its basis. Culture, itself, is taking on the deceptive properties associated with religion. Indeed, culture itself has become a religion. Thus, Lash and Urry argue that

> globalized popular culture, functioning as poetic discourse, thus becomes everybody's 'elementary forms of religious life'. It imparts form to an unreflected, relatively immediate and internationalized habitus.[93]

The issue of fetishism 'and the secret thereof' within commodities has always had a teasing religious property, even for Marx. For him, its analysis is a 'very queer thing, abounding in metaphysical subtleties and theological niceties'.[94] Commodity fetishism is the illusory transcendent property of objectivism that disguises a cash nexus and the social relationships affecting and effecting its production. To understand this process of mystification Marx felt an analogy had to made with the 'mist-enveloped regions of the religious world'.[95] But echoing Feurbach, Marx asserted that the 'religious reflex of the real world' would vanish when production by freely associated men was revealed.[96] Far from the 'religious reflex of the real world' vanishing, commodity fetishism has become attached to money and in consequence shapes culture. Secularisation is a symptom of this commodity fetishism, not a cause of it. It is what has dethroned God. Commenting on Simmel's sociology, Hans Sachs observed that 'money is the secular God of the World'.[97]

Warnings on the dangerous attractions of money litter theological texts. It is an issue riddled with ethical worries about lending, borrowing, covetousness, possessiveness, but most importantly, its idolatrous properties. As Paul wrote 'the love of money is the root of all evil' and enjoined his followers to flee such things, to seek virtue and to 'fight the good fight of faith' (1 Timothy 6: 10–12). For the spiritually ambitious, such as monks and nuns, vows of poverty signify a freeing from its possessive claims and the disproportions it effects in the relationship between theology and culture. Yet, even the most religious of houses encounter the dubious powers of money. In *An Apologia for Abbot William*, that related to disputes over monastic styles, whether they should be severe or comfortable, Bernard of Clairvaux, writing on embellishments of wealth in monastic settings, noted (in a manner Simmel might have understood) the way 'the money for feeding the destitute goes to feast the eyes of the rich'. Earlier in the text, he observed that 'riches elicit riches and money brings money in its train, because for some unknown reason the richer a place is seen to be the more freely the offerings pour in'.[98]

In the *Early Texts*, Marx wrote a critique of the false claims of money, and the idolatrous dangers it posed. Writing in terms a theologian could endorse, Marx eloquently criticised the false claims of money, that it could buy anything, even love. For Marx, virtue could only be exchanged for the same, not for money. It was this disinterested property of exchanging virtue for virtue that was all that was noble in man. In terms that relate to the issues of revealing and concealing, Marx noted the way money inverts virtues, turning fidelity into infidelity. As it invades culture, its power to change representations into reality is expanded. Again, theologians who read culture on the surface, are seeking a relationship with a mirage. Thus, for Marx

> the power to confuse and invert all human and natural qualities, to bring about fraternization of incompatibles, the *divine* power of money, re-sides in its *character* as the alienated and self-alienating species-life of man. It is the alienated *power* of *humanity*.[99]

Money signifies an estranging power for critical philosophy and theology in its false capacity to actualise almost anything. It is the instrument of social magic that seems to have invaded all aspects of culture. Its very uselessness for any other purpose than to signify an index of exchange makes money a brilliantly disinterested instrument for concealing the inversion of values of calculation in all aspects of culture, thus making all its products subject to these values. Money *is* the crucial instrument of commodity fetishism, the instrument of confusing processes of revealing and concealing within culture. It hijacks issues of wagers with the Divine into principles of accumulation in accord with the values of this world.

First published in Germany in 1900, and only translated into English in 1978, Simmel's *Philosophy of Money* underwrites much of the debate on the culture of postmodernity. It is the pliability of money, its capacity to transcend social relationships that gives it a unique cultural power, making it both ubiquitous and indispensable, a mysterious but necessary resource that governs social exchange. Before other writers, such as Blumenberg, Simmel referred to Nicholas of Cusa to show the way money secularised the power of the Divine. For Nicholas of Cusa, all antinomies, estrangements and irreconcilables achieve a unity within the Divine. Simmel suggests, however, that money is a blasphemous upstart in this process, for it seems to possess a psychological power that rivals, if not overtakes, this capacity of the Divine in a similarly mysterious manner. Money is the common denominator that transcends all differences, but also it arbitrates on these in a way available to all and excluding none by nature of their class, religious or cultural origins. It forgives all their delinquencies, absolves issues of differences in a way that matters ultimately. Money embodies the power, the capacity to reconcile all contradictions, displacing God in this task.[100] It has a Faustian characteristic of making the ambiguous unambiguous for the purposes of exchange and of being able to enter anywhere without hindrance.

The elusive nature of the power of money gives it a fascination. It is the ultimate antinomy in a culture of postmodernity. It has a sacramental power of being able to convert properties of the incalculable into the calculable and to effect the placement of any aesthetic entity into its cash nexus. It seems to have an infinite ability to arbitrate on the relationships between the particular and the general. As a symbol, money possesses a fundamental capacity to govern exchange relationships; it is the universal gauge of value, offering endless capacities to enchant, but it has an equally impressive power to disguise the seeds of disenchantment which reliance on its use brings; and above all, it embodies an ultimate ability to elicit deference and worship for its possessor even if this is precarious, insincere, and in the end, vacuous.

As Frisby observes, a contemporary of Simmel had noted that he seems to 'have extracted the totality of the spirit of the age from his analysis of money'.[101] By appropriating the principles of cultural value into its ability to calculate, money has taken on a capacity to kill the spirit. It is the force that secularisation masks, but never confronts, such is its power to conceal that which might be dangerous to reveal. As Bourdieu has indicated the nakedness of the cash nexus brings a glare of calculation to aesthetic entities that survive on the basis of their incalculable properties which form the basis of their mysterious power to attract. But the power of money lies in its indifference to the aesthetic object it gauges, yet it regulates its subjective basis of appreciation, thus confusing a fundamental point of Simmel that 'just as the world of being is my representation, so the world of value is my demand'.[102] By regulating forms of representations, money as an 'abstract value' seems to have the capacity, or rather allows it to be inferred, that it governs truth by the infinite constructions of culture it permits.[103] Money also takes from God the ultimate power to construct symbolic objects, and in this context it becomes a sacramental surrogate. It makes what is singular universal. It can endow the mundane with values that pertain to the incalculable.[104] Unfortunately, there is a price in this power, that 'one of the major tendencies of life – the reduction of quality to quantity – achieves its highest and uniquely perfect representation in money'.[105]

The antinomy of money, of mysteriously effecting the prospect of enchantment and at the same time inserting into culture debilitating effects of disenchantment, points to a division between life and form that haunts Simmel's writings and lies at the root of his notion of the tragedy of culture. It widens its remit from the bureaucratic site of Weber into the marketplace of everyday life. The depersonalising power of money sustains its pliability as a means of exchange free of social obligations. Unfortunately this property invades social relationships and poses a continual threat to their basis. From a theological perspective, its most dangerous power is to facilitate enjoyment without commitment. The capacity of money to despiritualise represents another force that permeates culture, adding another dimension to the secularising process. As Simmel notes

the more the unifying bond of social life takes on the character of an association for specific purposes, the more soulless it becomes. The complete heartlessness of money is reflected in our social culture, which is itself determined by money.[106]

Equally damaging to theology, is the capacity money has for depriving modern man of a sense of ultimate value, one which Christianity affirms. Furthermore, there is an ambiguity in the freedom money grants to the individual. It frees him from obligations, but at the same time generates a capacity to uproot and to sell personal values which become subject to commodification.[107] It is the structured disjunctions Simmel reveals in his account of money that are of theological interest. These can be found in his analysis of the notion that relationships and obligations are not directly reciprocal in the context of money and subjectivity is destroyed in the objectification of relations of exchange;[108] the discrepancy between material and individual culture, defined in terms of refinement;[109] and the indifference the tyranny of possessions effects.[110] Cultural growth of the intangible lags behind the expansion of the tangible, a disjunction that echoes concerns of Arnold, but which can also be found in Simmel and Weber. The intangible in culture requires social procedures of rescue for it continually risks evaporation by cultural artifacts that betoken the tangible. There can be no neutralities in dealing with the secular.

Perhaps Simmel's most unexpected worry over the cultural effects of money lies in his concern with spiritual matters. For him, there is a distancing embodied in a culture dominated by money that can be represented as a paradox of progress. He suggests that 'the more the distance in the external world is conquered, the more it increases the distance in the spiritual world'.[111] In the end, money accelerates a self-estranging property in modern culture. The potential of modern life has not been transferred from the individual to mass culture, but rather to objects. Simmel suggests that individuals have become slaves of the production process but also its products. What nature offers 'by means of technology is now a mastery over the self-reliance and the spiritual centre of life through endless habits, endless distractions and endless superficial needs'. Thus, Simmel argues that

> man has thereby become estranged from himself; an insuperable barrier of media, technical inventions, abilities and enjoyments has been erected between him and his most distinctive and essential being.[112]

It is not difficult to understand why von Balthasar found so much to admire in Simmel's sociology. For Simmel, the continual indefiniteness of the soul accounts for its endless searching, a seeking that seems to have come to maturity in a culture of postmodernity. The endless process of restructuring that characterises culture, of distancing and separating effects in a continual task of reassembly of ambiguous and antinomial elements, underwrites the issue of despiritualisation, one concealed, but seemingly never revealed.

Despite the belief that secularisation is the dominant regulator of contemporary culture, there is little evidence that Marx's 'religious reflex' has disappeared. But its form emerges in parts theologies cannot apparently penetrate. Mystification has passed from traditional religions to the cultural producers who regulate the marketplace. Intangibilities, hitherto attached to religious discourse, are now woven into the representation of cultural products. Misdescriptions and deceptions abound as a surplus value is added to commodities beyond those embodied in capitalist production. Commodities have to be fetishised to secure that intangible desire to possess, that allure that is a fatal attraction to the purse. Such moulding of an image involves a delicate social construction whereby a prosaic commodity is converted into a work of art, one that can be purchased.[113] A language of inference, that forms a basis of recognition, has to be given a social construction that is selectively available for the desired purchasers in the market. Enchantment is the process of the marketplace, of advertising, marketing and packaging, all of which thrive on an image of suggestibility, allure, and proximity to escapist values that are irresponsible and relentlessly pleasurable. But for Haug this process of commodity aesthetics has corrupting consequences. He suggests that

> it is as if people's consciousness is bought off. They are trained daily in the enjoyment of that which betrays them, in the enjoyment of their own defeat, in the enjoyment of identification with the superior powers.[114]

It would not be too strong to say that for critical theorists, such as Haug, Adorno and Benjamin there is a dangerous, deceiving property to the commodification of culture, and the technology that realises this process, that makes such extensive use of symbol and images. The divisions of the human condition, mirrored in the Divine, now reflect unregulated desires and opportunities that give rise to pessimism, to disenchantment with these secular opportunities for self-realisation within the cultural marketplace.

Adorno was particularly scornful of the counterfeit beliefs that seemed to replace traditional theologies. In his theses against occultism, which he described as 'the metaphysics of the dopes', Adorno asserted that occultists push 'speculation to fraudulent bankruptcy' and by submitting 'objectified spirit to the test for survival . . . the outcome must be negative. There is no Spirit'.[115] Adorno had deeper worries about the dependence, the illusions and surrogates for religious belief which a mass culture permitted. These represent the price of secularisation. In his critique of popular astrology in his famous essay 'The Stars Down to Earth', Adorno suggested that such illusory superstitions bought off the public from thinking deeper, from confronting their own limitations. Far from freeing the public, from the tyranny of religious belief, they facilitated a form of social control by presenting a illusory notion of rationality about human affairs. For Adorno, these 'prophets of deceit' generated their own '*ideology for dependence*'. Far from escaping religion, the public have now become victims of a cult of facts, of a reverence for science, all expressive of a 'disoriented agnosticism'.[116] Even this has changed, for all that is left in postmodernity is a disbelief in science and a belief in anything ranging from astrology to other fringe arts.

But the most devastating critique of the illusory basis of the culture industry, of 'enlightenment as mass deception' appeared in the context of a concern with the way commodification and advertising could be combined to deadly effect. The essay was written in 1944. It drew very much from Adorno's experience of Hollywood, the cinema and radio, where he worked. The essay also embodied worries about fascism and Anti-Semitism. The question of the cultural industry raised issues of how a control of the means of production of images, and to what end, affected mass cultural sensibilities. The essay contains an ambiguity, that the masses ought to be liberated from the illusions the cultural industry generates, but also a worry about their capacity to be deceived, given the price such deceptions generated. A crucial effect of the culture industry was its capacity to trivialise but also to assassinate tragedy. An image of life was presented as authentic, but one that could never lead to any metaphysical depth.[117] The capacity the culture industry signified, of dispatching both metaphysics and tragedy to the margins, punishing both for their capacity to ruffle illusory layers of pleasure, complements the process of secularisation and its apparent ability to dismiss God to margins. Being creatures of modernity, the culture industry and secularisation despise and fear that which untidies their fields and which might unsettle the illusions they seek to project. Unfortunately, for a fledgling sociological reflexivity with theological ambitions, interest in a sociology of culture has occurred at the same time as the marginalisation of interest in religion.[118]

Critical theorists and theologians in their dealings with a culture of postmodernity have more in common than each realise. The fetishisation of culture is a process that accomplishes an endemic trivialisation of life and the denial or postponement of a need to interrogate cultural formations in depth to detect their artificial basis. Illusions apply to religion not to the products of the culture industry. But in criticising the illusions which the culture industry sustains, Adorno and Horkheimer asserted that it 'perpetually cheats its consumers of what it perpetually promises'.[119] The capacity of the culture industry to arbitrarily appropriate images, where the counterfeit and the authentic becomes intermingled and disguised through the miracle of technology, requires a rationalisation of style, a process that robs artists of their more classical function 'of hardening themselves against the chaotic expression of suffering, as a negative truth'.[120]

The cultural landscape has often been redefined in ways where secular constructions were to be understood by reference to ecclesial metaphors. Thus, Scaff points to the writings of Gohre in 1907, 'the first sociologist of the department store'. Unexpectedly, the Wertheim shopping mall in Berlin was an abstraction from the Gothic Cathedral, combined with Roman arches, thus 'what one saw was classical balance and medieval harmony, public and religious idioms, but now re-presented as a temple of commerce'.[121] But this mixing of form within architecture is different to the advance of the process of appropriation of the sacred into the secular in a culture that supposedly despises or is indifferent to religion. Yet, despite the indifference or hostility to religion, it still leaves a legacy as *the* paradigm for reading culture and all its works. Thus, Featherstone makes a Durkheimian point regarding discerning the basis of consumer culture and the aura it simulates, that the property of the sacred has become detached from religion and is universalised within consumer culture, its rituals, symbols and commodities.[122]

This transference of the sacred into the profane operates in a context where there is a Ghost of God operating on the agenda of postmodernity, that does not seem to have vanished entirely. As Bell wrote prophetically, in 1977, with

the exhaustion of Modernism, the aridity of Communist life, the tedium
of the unrestrained self and the meaningless of the monolithic political
chants all indicate that a long era is coming to the close.[123]

O'Neill has noted in Bell and Jameson a Durkheimian interest and suggests that both are calling 'for a renewal of religious symbolism to restore
the social bond against postmodern values which undermine equally the
conservative and Marxist tradition'.[124]

Worries about the viability of the social bond have involved a recognition of the strengths of Catholicism in sustaining it. For Durkheim, Catholic communal ties ameliorated egoism and effected the lowering of their
suicide rates, whereas Weber saw the sacramental comforts of Catholicism
as mitigating salvation anxiety. This offered a relief denied to Calvinists,
who had to seek the means of after-life in the world.

Protestantism bears a property of individualism, of liberty of conscience,
of reason and interpretation at odds with the communal and ritual comforts
of Catholicism. This presents Protestantism as a problem to sociology in
a way Catholicism does not, for the latter is more capable of providing
those social bonds which accord with sociological notions of societal health.
If Protestantism inclines to secularisation and disenchantment, then Catholicism points to the means of resistance to these fragmenting and indi-
vidualising properties. It supplies the means of enchantment which fits
with the domestic cultural expectations of sociology itself. As indicated
above, anthropological accounts of primitive society bore Catholic forms
of appreciation of symbol and ritual that left a hidden mark in debates on
culture. These were derived also from dealings with missionaries who had
pioneered a field work in understandings of alien cultures.

Lurking within anthropology and sociology in dealings with the social
bond and the health of culture is an expectation of theological relief, but
this requires battle few theologians understand the need to wage. Since
Vatican II, they have been paralysed by a benign attitude to the world that
has permitted initiative to pass to the cultural marketplace. As they have
masked properties of metaphysical comfort and discomfort, such as heaven
and hell, and as they collapsed inconveniently traditional forms of belief
and practice, as not being in accord with modern reason in the 1970s and
the 1980s, the tragedy theologians effected was their own irrelevance in
the cultural marketplace in the 1990s and also for the religious beliefs they
supposedly represented.

Secularisation contains a duality within theology, a recognition of the
supremacy of the secular, but also a self-fulfilling disbelief in the sacred
that marked its irrelevance in the 1970s and the 1980s. Theologians

capitulated to the supposedly superior faith of the cultural market-place, but face their own crisis as disbelief comes to mark its basis in the context of postmodernity. Theologians now only realise their own crisis, when a culture of postmodernity indicates that it has lost faith in itself.

The limitless capacity to commodify breeds a restless sense of searching, a realisation that it is difficult to arbitrate between the authentic and inauthentic as postmodernity stipulates that there are no transcendent rules of distinction – belief in meta-narratives signifies the collapse of such a comforting consensus. Thus, the field of culture cannot be treated in a neutral manner. The theologian is forced to fight for a place for the holy, between those indifferent to the sacred and those who would plunder it for their vacuous notions of fashion. It is clear that a property of judgement in dealing with culture is required, otherwise the distinctive gifts which the holy signifies are just mocked and treated as irrelevant or are rendered invisible. The tragedy of theology in relation to culture between 1963–94 has arisen from its own self-inflicted wounds. The most serious charge sociology can make against theologians is that they have failed to provide the cultural means of generating religious commitment. Sometimes, this is not their fault, but they do need to understand what they have to work against.

One of the cultural phenomena of the 1994 was the hit record of Gregorian chant from the Benedictine monks of Santo Domingo de Silos in Spain. This unexpected hit was a reminder of the issue of nostalgia, of the pre-modern invading the postmodern. The music might well have therapeutic effects[125] for those listening in the bath after a long day. But for those who live by it, who sing it in a context of witness, what is therapeutic to the leisured class, is part of the daily grind of office of the monastic hours. Perhaps sung before dusk, this chant reflects the seeking of inner beauty in an ascetic life where the aesthetic is a by-product of the seeking of God. A young monk singing in his stall might get profane thoughts of a beer, but by attending to what he is consecrated to seek, he fights against such longings of the body, as the beauty of his chant enters parts of the self no draught can reach. The technical means of appropriation, through a CD player beside the bath of the flâneur desperately seeking leisure, mask this journey, this biography of seeking of his monastic counterpart. Sometimes the worlds collide, when the desperate are transmogrified from tourists into pilgrims.

The Anglican report on Cathedrals, *Heritage and Renewal*, noted a paradox that 'when public observance of religious belief is not as widespread as it once was, the cathedrals are, paradoxically, popular as never before'.[126] Drawing on a significant amount of research, they noted that

14.6 million visited English Cathedrals. St Paul's Cathedral was the fifth most popular tourist attraction in the United Kingdom.[127] Most visitors were from social groupings C to A, which is reflected in the data on visitors to art galleries and museums in France, in the study by Bourdieu and Darbel, *The Love of Art*.

Clearly, Cathedrals suffer from a variety of use and expectations, from those coming to pray, as pilgrims, or to attend service, to the greater majority, tourists, who stroll and gaze at the building, secular sightseers who treat it as a museum with sacerdotal interruptions that witness to its living tradition. In a sense the English Anglican Cathedral is a victim of its success. But this reflects its ethos. Apart from matins and choral even-song, one is most unlikely to encounter somebody praying in the nave. This absence of a culture of prayer between services accentuates the ar-cheological and civic tradition embodied in the building. It renders them accessible to tourists without the embarrassment of estranging activities, such as private prayer, which might discourage, although they signify the purpose of the building. It is not that prayer is discouraged; somehow it just does not manifest itself. Thus, in London one can contrast the spiritual atmosphere of St Paul's Cathedral with that of Westminster Cathedral. Cathedral guides seldom show illustrations of services in progress, but rather accentuate the place of these buildings in the heritage industry by concentrating on the history of their architecture, their treasures and their place in the civic past. Little attention in these guides is given to spiritual matters or the theology these Cathedrals embody, which might raise em-barrassing issues.

Increased leisure, accessibility through enhanced transport links, all make the Cathedral accessible, but in someways inaccessible. The cultural sig-nificance of the Cathedral has shifted from its original medieval purpose of giving visible witness to the Glory of God, in its architecture and its liturgical round of prayer, to being an archetypical site for the tourist. Imperceptibly, the Cathedral has moved from being a site of pilgrimage for the private individual seeking a reassurance of the Divine in a building hallowed by the journeys of others so seeking, to one unwillingly recast into the cultural marketplace of mass tourism. The issue of admission charges expresses this dilemma well, though no Catholic Cathedral would consider so charging. Accessibility for prayer is still their primary pur-pose. Drawing the line between making the buildings more accessible for tourists and at the same time avoiding making them inaccessible to pil-grims is fraught with perils and pitfalls.

This conundrum becomes apparent in Lowenthal's account of the cul-tural significance of the past, where nostalgia becomes ordered and commodified. Lowenthal tries to deal with an extraordinary range of cultural artifacts that are commodified in a telescopic manner. Thus, artifacts surrounding the American civil war, become recommodified and repackaged to reflect the culture of 'Gone with the Wind', but these are in turn open to recasting in the context of theme parks, such as desired by Walt Disney for a battlefield in Virginia, where history is to be neutered of passion, blood and fire and to be reordered for spectacle for the tourist eye. In this circumstance, the past is sanitised and packaged as an undemanding form of escapism. The quest for authenticity, of photographs and artifacts of the time, for display renders the past inauthentic, and in a counterfactual manner, unrecognisable to the participants. The effect is to make the past unambiguous.[128] The wager of Faustus seems to be realised in the imaginative adventures which the industrialisation of nostalgia promises, of being able to see everything unambiguously in a way that disguises the need for commitments. But the effect is also Faustian in that the objects sought, when found, quickly lose the desirability that generated their initial attraction. Proximity dissolves curiosity and there is no grace to permit a review.

The archaeological quest for the past, the insatiable desire for total knowing and an exactness in image is ultimately estranging. Thus 'a past remoulded in the image of the ever-changing present may enable a whole age group to share perspectives, but cuts them off from those historical perspectives that preceded and will follow them'.[129] Postmodernism represents an attempt to transcend the imperfections of the past by rearranging its basis in contemporary culture. But in so doing, it manages to disguise the issue as to whether the past existed at all. The capacity of postmodernism to harness the past to present cultural needs gives a more credible and satisfactory account of what it *should* have been like, but in so rendering credible, these re-orderings become incredible to their original location in time. Not to act on the past is to allow it to be destroyed but with this comes 'the stronger urge to preserve and restore'.[130] The cultural responses of a postmodernity to the past reveal another antinomy that places another coin on the table for tossing.

As the past is moved into the processes of commodity fetishism, to be repackaged in theme parks, in ordered display in museums, where sites of toil become objects for spectacle for the leisured, the forces leading to such a reconstitution of heritage to meet the needs of tourism generate their own distinctive illusions. Worries over these endless prospects of escapism, an infinite capacity for spectacle without moral involvement, underwrite Walsh's study of representations of the past. His concern is with the distancing from obligation, from the processes that affect life as

lived, by allowing the actor to live as a spectator on its surface. But this
capacity is also an ability to delude. Thus, Walsh suggests that

> the dialectic between reality and fantasy is threatened by the postmodern
> representation; the post-modern past is one where anything is possible,
> where fantasy is potentially as real as history because history as heritage
> dulls our ability to appreciate the development of people and places
> through time.[131]

In this context, there is a self-confirming property to tourism that involves what Urry has termed the tourist gaze. For the sophisticated tourist,
gazing is a form of seeing, of disbelieving in the reorganised landscape
that validates the basis of his visit that gives it an expected gratifying
quality. All the time, the tourist is gazing in a postmodern context where
forms of representation are rendered more 'real' than the past reality they
proclaim.[132] In his study, Urry is trying to find what is extraordinary in the
tourist gaze, for it seeks objects that are deemed to be so characterised,
that have an aura, that makes the metaphor of the pilgrim a little less
metaphorical. He points to a ceremonial quality in the seeing that comes
to believing when faced with what is deemed an authentic work of art.[133]
There is an anticipation, an expectation in the tourist gaze, that wishes for
self-confirmation. If the gaze is to be more than something initial, something fresh, but which might quickly become stale, then seeing has to be
related to a seeking of something deeper, an attachment to what might
offer a relationship.

The making of spiritual surrogates in the civic realm that draws from
traditional theologies becomes problematic when the theological basis of
the borrowings are masked and are deemed so enfeebled as to be irrelevant
to cultural sensibility. Unfortunately, this detachment carries a price of
modernity being stuck in a spiritual crisis that it has no ability to recognise
or to resolve. The dilemmas it embodies that have come to fruition in the
condition of postmodernity have changed the direction of sociological
attention. There is a nascent theological ambition in what it tries to discern
in culture. As Scaff notes

> cultural critique in its various modes represents an attempt to breathe
> life and soul back into the human sciences in an environment where the
> external forms and structures of social life, from the state to the lan-
> guage of science, threaten to become oppressive, reified and empty.[134]

Sociological reflexivity involves the need to reflect on the activity of
being a sociologist. It is a methodological version of a theological injunction
'know thyself', the introspective application to biography of the tenets of

sociology of knowledge. But this enhanced knowing generates an awareness of the degree to which sociological insights are reproduced in culture
and mirrored back in the reflexivity of the sociologist. It is as if postmodernity is the 'success, of modernity, but for the sociologist a pyrrhic
victory. In facing culture, the sociological soul sees an emptiness that
haunts as a dream succeeds. Explanation becomes disenchantment, and
attention to detail forms the tyrannous agenda of postmodernity. Sociology
has moved from a state of poverty of knowing to one of excess. The more
it authentically mirrors culture, the more it refracts its tragedy, which for
Simmel, was the disjunction between forms endlessly available, but never
sufficient to enclose, and the content they are stipulated to capture. If it
does not cultivate an awareness of the cultural, however trivial, it is nothing as a discipline. But if it seeks knowing, then something more than
refraction is required. Some analytical distance is required, some alternative vision is needed. Being engulfed with what one can analyse leaves
some sociologists impotent. Being there in sociology generates a particular
form of knowing to mark the self of the sociologist, to give it a sense of
estrangement, peculiarly that of the discipline. Thus, a candour has crept
into recent sociology, as the persona of the sociologist is fleshed out in
response to what is discerned as a result of the ethic of self-implication in
culture. This recentering, both of culture itself and the sociologist himself,
in sociological deliberations marks a paradigm shift. Embedded in culture,
the sociologist comes to represent to his self what is noticed in the cultural
marketplace, what is valued and what is feared. But there are others engaged in discerning: the symbol brokers selling images for cash; cultural
trend spotters; and journalists, working uncommonly close to an interface
with cultural studies. All these have their argot of reflexivity which com-
petes with the grammar of the sociologist also seeking understanding.

Such movements generate a disquiet, a worry about the quality of culture that a reflexive sociologist cannot but note. These worries also emerge
from the writings of journalists, reflecting a bit more deeply on their craft
and the ethical implications of what they notice. If good, they capture a
public worry, a sensibility that something is corrupting in received notions
of culture.

A case in point is Simon Winchester who chronicles the potential for
depravity in the use of Internet computer networks, to spread forms of
pornography.[135] This capacity to adjust story lines, to transmit images in
the ether for sordid gratification gives a power through technology that
even Faustus could not imagine the devil might supply. These images can
be wiped out making receipt anonymous and unaccountable. There is public
unease over these forms of technology, 'video-nasties', war games, that

breach a fine line between simulation and imitation. With impunity, they create a virtual reality, making their operators like gods, spectators on endless permutations of corruption, where any narrative, any ending can be written, no matter how evil, as long as pleasure is given to the imagination. This technological voyeurism permits the making of any death, any pain, any mutilation, with impunity, because there is no victim bar the self, the operator of the Internet. There is no morality, because the pornographer operates in a realm of fantasy. The culture of postmodernity has given this 'gift' to the self of the Internet operator, to the disquiet of the sociologist, who discerns a numbing to social reality, a disengagement from reality to the point of wilful confusion. The Internet operator has found a means of bypassing the untidy field of the social, the humanity embodied in its basis, to create a virtual reality, more real than reality for the detail it permits. There is no need for compassion in the pleasurable sufferings of the innocent, for conscience has also been snuffed.

This moral lobotomy, effected by this technological miracle of a computer linked to Internet, signifies the potential of the cultural condition of postmodernity to commodify in a limitless manner that disguises the growth of a culture of moral indifference. Dehumanisation and the evaporation of the spirit facilitate this commodification of evil. But if sociology *does* judge in this descent into evil, it has to consider ascent into good. It has to think in terms of an opposite, of good, of innocence and the practice of virtue, images that supply correction to evil.

Reflection on the sociological condition points to a catalogue of most curious transmogrifications in its disciplinary history from the sociologist as superhero of positivist science, into chronicler of progress, into angst ridden advocate of the underclass, into concerned agent for social improvement, into prophet of the counterculture reading the spirit of the times, then flitting off into engaged but confused commentary on the mass explosion of cultural studies, then turning into flâneur to see cosmopolitan culture, then ending up as a pilgrim. If so, whence the direction of this unexpected pilgrim's progress abroad in this culture of postmodernity, where disenchantment is all too possible and enchantment near but impossible?

6 To Canaan's Side: Crossing Culture in Theological and Sociological Safety

Postmodernity caught a sociological mood a decade ago. It seemed to represent a disciplinary consensus, an umbrella term that unified sociologists around a question of disunity. But that consensus has now become fragmented. Now in sociology everybody seems to have split off into different analytical groups dealing with the city, with gender, ethics, all with crossing references to culture, space, time and risk, but with no transcending affinities. The cultural landscape looks bleak and desolate. There is a property of a slough of despond creeping into the sociological imagination. Bets are on as to what comes next and wagers are increasingly made on self and ethics as the new foci for sociological debate. Again, these issues betray a proximity to theological discourse and a grammar that lies at the fringe of sociology. Likewise, disenchantment penetrates further into culture, witnessing to Weber's penetrating analysis. But then, some have been here before.

In facing a culture of postmodernity, English Catholics might forget their own history. Hearing William Byrd's anthem *Bow thine ear, O Lord*, a meditation on the fall of Jerusalem, there is an ethereal beauty in the poignant phrase 'desolate and void'. This anthem, written during the Reformation, speaks from the tragedy of desolation at the destruction of a Catholic culture exiled in its own nation, deeply reluctant to let go the vestiges of faith.[1]

But for present believers, however small the huddle, times are different, if not equally grey and bleak. Instead of persecution and plunder, there is indifference and decay, a withering of grace, as church numbers fall. There is a sense of collapse within and without the church. Failures in theology in dealing with culture are not solely due to programmes of engagement, managerial plans for use of church plant and the repackaging of liturgies into supposedly relevant culture forms – all these have been tried but do not work. Reasons for present difficulties lie deeper. They lie in the breakdown between faith and culture and the impoverishment of the concepts used by theology to heal this fracture. Davie rightly suggests that 'in many ways the conceptual framework within which to describe the nature of belief in contemporary Britain still seems lacking'.[2] It is not clear that sociologists writing on culture will supply these concepts. For some, the turn into culture precludes the need to mention any religious claims to what is represented and reproduced in the cultural field.[3]

The omens might seem dim. In this post-secularisation argument, religious symbols have lost the power to grip, to express an aura. No longer mysterious, now unhallowed, more plastic versions wend their way into the flea market for sale as tokens that witness to disbelief, to the insurrection of the godless over the pious and the blessings of powers of commodification. Religious objects are resited on a field of religious indifference, unsignified except in their relationship to the cash nexus. Present culture seems to lack the capacity to discriminate between functions of ornamentation and edification.

Sociology is an ambiguous instrument for understanding culture. It can merely point to enabling processes but also to disabling ones, depending on the subjective pre-suppositions one wishes to use. But sociology's most important and obvious insight is that the cultural field does not 'naturally' organise itself in a disinterested manner, but that in the detail of its configurations it represents an unsafe partner for a passive dialogue, as suggested in *Gaudium et Spes*. On the field of culture, wars are fought over position, over the siting of forms of representation and their reproduction. Culture has always been a battleground, but in the past the rules of engagement were apparent. Now, they are less so, for the means of reproduction contain hidden properties that need to be deciphered. The conventional masks the exercise of power to name, to disguise and to secure advantage thus making the present cultural field unsafe territory for hallowing that which belongs to the theological. There are definite agendas for securing territories that presuppose the endless exercise of symbolic violence between the tastemakers, the symbol brokers, and those who manufacture images of virtual reality.

On this site, Catholics are lambs awaiting slaughter, for their instruments of defence have been abdicated unwittingly by theologians who know not the argot of the field. They lack the sociological means of reading the marketplace of the reproduction of culture. Within Catholicism there is a realisation that something seriously has gone wrong since Vatican II. For instance, one can note the unexpected comment of Richards, on the unprecedented numbers leaving the priesthood in the 1960s and 1970s, that what the Reformation and the French Revolution had not done 'the Church now seemed to have brought upon herself'.[4]

The expansion of the cultural marketplace relates to people exercising consumer choice and shopping around for beliefs, a process of selection that particularly applies to sects.[5] This notion of a marketplace applies generally to all cultural artifacts and commodities. It is the site where traditional religions have to compete. Effective competition with those who would plunder their holy instruments, to commodify them in the cash nexus, presumes a theological understanding of how the market operates. From the Acts of the Apostles, to the order of preachers, to missionaries, Catholicism has always understood itself to operate in a marketplace where it has to compete with rival belief systems. Understanding the rules of engagement is necessary and this is a contribution sociology can make to theology in its dealings with culture. Retreatism into nostalgia is neither possible nor desirable in theology. It has to affirm the public sphere, the communal as lived now, by the nature of its calling.

Dupré examines the way those seeking belief often find personal refuge in the spiritual masters, where the issue of belief finds its ultimate source. This leads to a necessary, but self-limiting introspection, the cultivation of the eyes of faith within. But Dupré argues, belief involves a social dimension, the finding of a site for edification. There has to be a connection between a highly personalised spiritual religion and the notion of community, for in this link,

> however, loose, with a mystical body, the believer becomes united with his model, which ceases to be a mere ideal, because the community makes it into a *present* reality. By providing him with sacraments, scriptures, and a whole system of representations, the religious community enables the individual to incorporate his attitude into a living union with his model.[6]

Faith requires a cultural site of manifestation, edification and realisation to reflect the Gospel imperative to act, to do, to find and to give communal witness. Sites of witness are never ideal. The scandal of particularity is scandalous in any culture, even one dominated by the chaos of postmodernity. Sociology can assist in this task of doing and witnessing by precluding false readings, unsafe assumptions of what will pass in present culture, and above all the context of authenticity. By supplying other readings, sociology enhances the reflexivity of theology itself in its dealings with culture.

Sociology has to find a theology and a theologian to match its distinctive needs in dealing with a culture of postmodernity. One of the advantages of dealing with an apophatic theology is that it relates back to a tradition rich in symbolism, icons and images that firmly belong to the heavenly and the holy. It supplies an antidote to the misuse of symbols by placing them in the context of revelation, one that transcends present chaos. It takes these out of sociological reach, but places them in it. Furthermore, an apophatic theology compliments the nihilism of contemporary culture and gives a distinctive spin to the coin in Pascal's wager.[7] The incompleteness of form to which sociology gives witness leads to a stress on the transcendent, to irreducible phenomena such as silence to gauge relationships with the holy.[8]

The present concern of sociology with aesthetics and culture finds a complementarity in the theology of Hans Urs von Balthasar.[9] Sociology forms a very small but significant part of his writings. It is part of a mosaic of a greater concern, a vision of the form of revelation of the Glory of God, the essence of Beauty, in an understanding which runs from the self, through literature, culture to metaphysics, but also to sociology. Von Balthasar's attention to sociology is significant given his incredible productivity. Henrici noted that von Balthasar 'wrote more books than a normal person can be expected to read in his lifetime'. He produced 85 books, 500 articles, over 100 translations and, in addition, edited and published 60 volumes including the works of his spiritual mentor, Adrienne von Speyr.[10] He also found time to found and to run his own publishing house for his own works and those of others, and also a secular institute, the Community of St John. It would be better to describe von Balthasar as a faculty of arts embodied in one man. He had an intimate acquaintance with patristics, classical and modern philosophy, French and German literature and wrote with an ease and familiarity through a bewildering range of sources. His major works, the seven volumes of *The Glory of the Lord*, and the five volumes of *Theo-Drama*, display a depth and breath of erudition difficult to find elsewhere. They encompass primary research spanning almost all of the humanities with an intimacy that is difficult to comprehend as the product of one man. More impressively, von Balthasar writes about sociology with an insider's understanding that marks him as unique among the major theologians.

Any comment on the relationship between von Balthasar and sociology must be highly tentative. Many of his writings have not been fully translated. Considerable work needs to be undertaken on refining the place of sociology within his wider philosophical and literary approach to theology. Other major theologians, such as Barth, Bultmann and Rahner handled an anthropology cast at a philosophical and systematic level that was inaccessible to sociological intervention. One admires their writings as much as one cannot discern their sociological significance.

Von Balthasar was interested in sociology in terms of role theory and the construction of identity of the actor. It is in this context that his interest and appreciation of Goffman emerges. Von Balthasar's theology was formed against a deep awareness of the crisis of modernity, aspects of which he understood from Guardini. Von Balthasar's deep appreciation and an extensive knowledge of the German sociologist Georg Simmel occurs well

before his recent re-appraisal as a crucial figure in the shaping of sociology's understandings of modernity and culture. Re-evaluation of the central
significance of Simmel in Anglo-American sociology is largely due to
efforts to trace the intellectual influences on Erving Goffman.[11]

As in many aspects of his writings, von Balthasar showed a prescience
in grasping trends before they later emerged in Western thought. For instance, his dissertation traced philosophical developments from the Middle
Ages to the modern age and was later published between 1937–9 in a three
volume work entitled the *Apocalypse of the German Soul*. These volumes
provided a detailed handling of Herder, Kant, Ficthe, Hegel and more
significantly Kierkegaard and Nietzsche. Like his former teacher, Romano
Guardini, von Balthasar was only too well aware of the crisis facing theology in the context of modernity. Instead of capitulating passively to its
nihilistic aspects, he tried to formulate a theology that would provide a
counter image to it, one that dealt with a theology of aesthetics that would
enchant and enhance a culture seeking belief, for whom no relief seemed
at hand. His ambition in his major writings was to wrest a vision of
revelation of the glory of God from the corpus of the humanities that have
so shaped European culture. His efforts to deal with modernity owed much
to his admiration of the French literary tradition, and especially Claudel
and Péguy, whose writings he translated into German. Von Balthasar provides sociology with a passage into the deepest parts of the theological
tradition, reaching back through some of the major medieval thinkers to
the Fathers of the Church.

Von Balthasar's exploration of a theological aesthetics drew him into
the issue of understanding the significance of the theatre and the question
of performance, a theme he developed in the five volumes of *Theo-Drama*.
He pursues his theme with enormous skill, the sociological resonances of
which are obvious, not least in his use of Goffman's *The Presentation of
Self in Everyday Life*. Both use a theatrical metaphor in a way that can
unite theology with sociology. Von Balthasar's concern with the viability
of tragedy, combined with properties of risk and anxiety of the self, link
him to present sociological themes.[12]

In dealing with culture, sociology fulfils an uncomfortable role as an
antinomial discipline refracting antinomies. A litany of antinomies litter its
analytical tradition. Thus, form is split against content in Simmel, where
what enables also disables. For Weber, disenchantment has an antinomial
relationship with enchantment and his sociology is caught between the
temptation of value free explanation and the need for verstehen. Likewise,
Durkheim sets up his own antinomy between the sacred and the profane
in his religion without belief. The link between action and structure, the

primary focus of sociology, has its own antinomial dimension. Finally, sociology suffers its own antinomy in the abiding division of loyalties between the cultural and the natural sciences. All these have become exasperated in the context of postmodernity and it endless capacity to commodify. The issue is less one of description than of discernment in reading and judging. Getting below the surface of culture forms a contrasting task for theology and sociology, for the issue of what is unseen poses a choice for both, between what is revealed and what is concealed in the hidden. In the end it depends on the values, the expectations brought to the readings.

In his funeral oration on the death of von Balthasar, given at Lucerne in 1988, Ratzinger commented on the vast range of his erudition. Unlike Weber, who felt called to find out how much he could bear in his studies, Ratzinger indicated that von Balthasar was not concerned with the accumulation of knowledge as end in itself, rather in the manner of Thomas À. Kempis, but with his vocation as a theologian, whose calling could be summarised in the single phrase of Augustine, that 'our entire task in this life, dear brothers, consists in healing the eyes of the heart so they may be able to see God'.[13] Two years before he died, von Balthasar was asked in an interview if there was any distrust of modern culture in the Church. He felt that if 'adequate spiritual discernment is exercised' there was not, but added that certain features of modern culture could be considered dangerous, even 'demonic'. He had in mind the mass media and the seductive influence it exerted on young people 'who, assaulted by a multitude of chaotic images flitting across the screen, are no longer capable of asking questions about the meaning of life'.[14]

For different reasons Bourdieu, is concerned with the issue of the hidden, what is masked in culture that effects an estrangement. His concern is with the cultural resources to see and to judge matters of taste, issues that belong to aesthetics. Whereas, Catholicism might be worried about what estranges from ecclesial culture, Bourdieu is concerned with the barriers that appear to exclude from culture in general. There is a masking property in the practice of cultural reproduction that includes some in the same process that effects the exclusion of others.

In their account of French art galleries and museums, Bourdieu and Darbel were concerned with differences in accessibility by class. Although free and endlessly accessible, somehow these institutions are inaccessible to those whose cultural capital was low. Thus, they share with the Churches a notional availability to all that makes them at the same time somehow unavailable to some. Like the Churches, these institutions are accessible but at the same time are mysteriously inaccessible.

In considering the issue of differential aesthetic appreciation, Bourdieu's language is characteristically rich in theological metaphor. Thus he argues that

> religion of art also has its fundamentalists and its modernists, yet these factions unite in raising the question of cultural salvation in the language of grace.[15]

If 'cultural salvation' is available to all, why do some avail and others do not? Having the cultural dispositions to see past appearances of images and symbols is crucial and this is differentially cultivated in society in an allocation of cultural skills that are socially constructed and are unevenly distributed. In short, some are afflicted with a 'cultural blindness', an incapacity to appreciate.[16] Bourdieu is interested in the sense of unworthiness, of profaneness, which the culturally blind feel entering a cave of aesthetic delights, such as an art gallery.

Von Balthasar and Bourdieu differ in terms of their reference to the illumination they seek from their differing disciplines. For Bourdieu, disclosure effects a demystification of the arrangements of the cultural field and the hidden agenda of power that regulates inequality of positions of appreciation, of access to what he terms cultural capital. But for von Balthasar, illumination relates to hidden properties of grace, a clarification of mystery that leads to a revelation of the Glory of God. It affirms a belonging in God, and so 'faith is the light of God becoming luminous in man'. This is where the heart of his theological aesthetics lies.[17]

Efforts to relate to the power of images have been littered with ambiguities. Disputes are familiar between iconoclasts and those who believed in the efficacy of icons. The use of religious images points to risks of superstition, idolatry and possessiveness, to name a few misuses. Because they betoken the invisible and the uncheckable, symbols bear endless potential for misunderstandings. For instance, the symbolism produced by the medieval mind was gloriously overelaborate in terms of allegories, images and icons, relics of which can be found in medieval Cathedrals. This advance into symbols generated its own risk society in the medieval world, though the damages were theological rather than ecological. The potential for abuse was enormous as Huizinga has indicated. These risks arose from literal interpretations of symbols, overfamiliarity, overelaboration, obsessions with detail and a galaxy of images that got out of control. The divide between nature and the sacred was fractured frequently.[18] This technology of enchantment wrought its own risks of disenchantment, even to the holiest of minds. Values of perfection, proportion and splendour were given a context of realisation that was as open to use and abuse as any contemporary generation of symbols. All capacities to overelaborate are relative. Thus the medieval mind could be as overcome by the wonder of endless symbols that mystified in their elaboration as the actor in postmodernity is baffled by the issue of endless choice and reproduction.[19] The solution for both lies in the wisdom to seek the grace to discern the proportions correctly. A rigour of spiritual discernment has always been required in dealing with symbols, most particularly those deemed to enhance a sense of holiness and to signify the sacred. The Church has a long, if not ineffective, history of warning of the dangers.[20]

Despite the risks, images have a long history of traditional use which theology sanctions. Seeing is a form of believing, but also of healing. When the Israelites were visited by serpents, they sought Divine relief. Moses was instructed to set a fiery serpent on a pole so that 'every one that is bitten, when he looketh upon it, shall live' (Numbers 21: 8). Religious images, such as clothing, are sacramentals that depend on the elective affinities of those wearing them to seek a holiness through their use. The religious habit of a monk or nun is a sign of consecration, a testimony to it, and in sociological terms realises a habitus, for a disposition is cultivated to effect the properties of virtue the garment signifies. It becomes a form of protection that conserves a calling. Images made holy impose obligations on those utilising them. Unlike commodities in the culture of postmodernity, there is an expectation that they make a demand on the self. Rituals often serve to manifest this point. Thus, reflecting on consecration ceremonies, Freedberg indicates that

> people do not garland, wash, or crown images just out of habit; they do so because all such acts are symptoms of a relationship between image and respondent that is clearly predicated on the attribution of powers which transcend the purely material aspect of the object.[21]

Images edify by providing a basis of imitation. Through temporal means they invoke a sense of the invisible. If properly used they effect what Nichols notes as a 'transfiguration by grace', an entry into that which might be unattainable through other means. The cultivation of this taste, this wish to see God, is illuminated by artistic representations of the face of Christ on icons. Thus Nichols suggests

> that it is the splendour of the divine meaning shining in the form of Christ that moves us, transforming our sensibility and habitual vision of things. Only so can we come to 'image' that face of God in Jesus by a responding love, ourselves transfigured by grace.[22]

A symbol embodies a transparency that exceeds the expectations of the observer. As Jasper notes, it 'catches what would otherwise stream out of us and be lost in the void. The symbol shows what would, without it, remain completely hidden to us'. Use of symbols demands a suspension of belief in the literal aspects of their appearance. This removes an impediment, and facilitates access to a paradox, of seeing the intangible properties symbols embody.[23]

The intricate task of discerning the sacred basis of symbols involves a journey without presumption. But a characteristic of modernity is that of using symbols *with* presumption. Modernity proclaims the right to manufacture, where man can make any image of himself to maximise the actualisation of his talents. This reaching for commodified symbols involves a belief in their unambiguous nature. But religious symbols only realise their basis in conditions that respect their intrinsic ambiguity, the concealing and revealing they embody, a property that demands a searching. Philosophy has a role for Jaspers, of cultivating understanding, of making 'one ripe for the experience' of reading cyphers. These can be decoded to infer, however indirectly, the existence of God.[24]

This gives philosophy (and sociology when its reflexivity is turned to theological matters) a task of increasing awareness of God. If sociology is to succeed in its theological calling, it can enhance understanding and appreciation of what is already known within culture. The sacred properties it discerns in the social can be returned to the original rites to work out a deeper appreciation of their sacramental basis. Theologians can draw on sociological forms of reflexivity to understand the solemnising of rites, the seeking of their endowment with holiness and their place in a culture of postmodernity whose messages suggest otherwise. Sociology provides theology with some brilliant instruments for resisting modernity. It suggests a respect for distance, and reverence, for the sacredness of ritual, but above all the need for a habitus, a cultivation of discernment.

This relates to Jasper's point that seeking and finding require restraint and constraint, a journeying that cannot be rushed, a point well understood in the context of the cultivation of monastic spirituality. Learning to understand symbols forms part of a monastic journey, where the young novice seeks in humility, a fear of God, a passage that calls for the disciplining of youthful impetuosity.[25]

The issue of deciphering symbols relates to an inclination, a disposition embodied in the term habitus, which is central to Bourdieu's sociology of culture. In dealing with matters of grace, that belong to charisma, Weber noted that with routinisation, foms of recruitment and training of novices were required. He went to add 'charisma can only be "awakened" and "tested"; it cannot be "learned" or "taught"'.[26] This relates to the cultivation of disposition, an awakening of a sense of grace, a sensibility of the holy, and the nurturing of spiritual sight to see with eyes of faith. It is an especially important but strangely neglected task to cultivate amongst the young, those proximate to priests and monks, boys who are altar servers and choirboys, if the issue of vocations is to be taken seriously.

There is a crisis of reproduction of clergy. Among many other factors, there has been a failure to attend to the sources of recruitment well understood in monastic and clerical traditions – the altar servers. Few priests have not been altar servers. This secret apprenticeship into a vocation, a conversion of disposition from boy to man to priest, relates to a form of reproduction set badly at risk by the recent permission for girls to serve. The damaging implications of this concession have not been understood.

If as much attention was given to the nurture of spiritual capacities amongst choirboys as to musical expertise, the prospects for an enchantment of a religious dimension to culture would be greatly enhanced by their witness and perhaps later vocations. Intense liturgical experience, often combined with a sense of grace reaches deeply and formatively into a nascent self in this role whose growth needs to be carefully nurtured. Unfortunately, the Anglican report *Heritage and Renewal* on Cathedrals made no reference to the cultivation of spiritual needs in the section on the choir schools[27] and only seemed to understand the role of the choirboy in terms of sexism and its eradication.[28] Indeed, the yearly *Choir Schools Today* seems devoid of any reference to religious matters, being largely concerned with tours, recordings and school events.

These issues might seem beside the point were it not for the importance of the issue of disposition expressed by the term habitus in Bourdieu's approach to sociology of culture. This complex term has critical implications for his understanding of the relationship between the actor and the cultural field. But more crucially it exposes a debt to theology.

For Bourdieu, the term habitus serves to resolve problems of structure and action, subjectivity and objectivity in transactions. It relates to dispositions to engage, to relate, to render things durable in transactions so that one has the feel for the game peculiar to a particular field. In his case, these games can be liturgical, but also educational, aesthetic, and cultural. Indeed, habitus can be applied to any field. It is a disembodied form of analysis, where dispositions serve in terms of maximising advantage in a game of power.

Bourdieu masks his own biographical preferences. His own reflexivity seems an instrument to effect that concealment. Thus, there is a property of smoke-screen in the Delphic nature of his prose style that makes him unnecessarily difficult to read. He defends his prose as necessarily complex, given the nature of inquiry into cultural field. The complexity of the prose protects the analytical purity of the study and prevents 'the reading from slipping back into the simplicities of the smart essay or the political polemic'.[29] Yet there is a biographical masking in his prose that qualifies his reflexivity that is intentional. He justifies his anonymity by claiming that

> by revealing certain private information, by making bovaristic confessions about myself, my lifestyle, my preferences, I may give ammunition to people who utilize against sociology the most elementary weapon there is – relativism.[30]

His route into the centre of French life through the Provinces and Algeria lends a quality of identification with the marginal whose peripheral status he seeks so often to redeem and to recentre in his sociological analysis. His own journey might give biographical reasons for his defensiveness when operating as the professor of sociology at the College de France, in Paris. But there are other factors that excite curiosity about his masking and these relate to Catholicism. In an unusual biographical aside, Bourdieu refers to his life as a boarder in a public school and cites Flaubert as saying that 'anyone who has not known boarding school by age of ten knows nothing about society'.[31] Clearly, his childhood made a mark, but were there Catholic elements in it? Robbins has argued that there is an element of zealous iconoclasm in Bourdieu's work, which some are tempted to apply against him. But this might misunderstand, for as Robbins notes there a strong ethical imperative behind Bourdieu's sociology which is designed to keep alive a prelapsarian vision of human relations.[32]

There are too many Catholic aspects to Bourdieu's sociology to be accidental. Compared to commonly pallid, theologically deaf Anglo-American sociologists, Bourdieu's metaphors are uncommonly red bloodedly Catholic. His notion of symbolic power draws heavily on the rhetoric of sacramental theology. Phrases such as transubstantiation and consecration litter his work. There might be something for saying that Bourdieu sees no distinction between theology and culture, but this would be a fine reading. Yet he does argue in a phrase that is more than an ironical aside that 'the sociology of culture is the sociology of the religion of our time'.[33]

It would be tedious to cite too many examples, but the following illustrate a style or rhetoric where the metaphor is decidedly Catholic. An issue arises over how far one can press the model he draws on to analyse his own analysis to draw out its theological implications? For instance, in a discussion of the market of symbolic goods, Bourdieu notes

> by defending cultural orthodoxy or the sphere of legitimate culture against competing, schismatic or heretical messages, which may provoke radical

demands and heterodox practices among various publics, the system of conservation and cultural consecration fulfils a function homologous to that of the Church.[34]

In *Distinction*, referring to Kant's notion of taste of reflection, Bourdieu feels this gives culture a property of the sacred. Thus, he adds 'cultural consecration does indeed confer on the objects, persons and situations it touches a sort of ontological promotion akin to a transubstantiation'.[35] The capacity to consecrate, to name and to confer, forms a crucial ingredient of power for agents and institutions in their use of cultural capital, the basis of which is disguised and placed beyond redress in some mystifying manner. Demystifying this power lies behind much of Bourdieu's analysis of culture. By dealing in mystifications, indirectly, as against those who sell directly in the cultural marketplace, intellectuals take on priestly powers by their capacity to sacralise ideas. In so dominating they

> are the predestined bearers of the eschatological hopes which, insofar as they support their 'inner-worldly asceticism' and their sense of 'mission', are the true opium of the intellectuals. The analogy with religion is not artificial: in each case the most indubitable transcendence with respect to strictly temporal interest springs from the immanence of struggles of interest.[36]

Finally, in *Homo Academicus*, he points to the new kinds of validation for cultural protagonists, their clubs where quasi-official newspaper commentaries are found that constitute 'reading which is the evening prayer of the active intellectual'.[37] Theological and sociological resonances emerge in the Bourdieu's term habitus.

Bourdieu uses the term habitus to refer to the growth in sensibility of membership of the field. In his study of French university life, where power and influence are mapped in masterly fashion, Bourdieu uses the term habitus to refer to an aggregation that reproduces a collective defence of a professorial body. This emerges as 'the product of the sort of social conservation instinct that is the *habitus* of the members of a dominant group'.[38] Habitus refers to what is durable through accumulation of tradition, a mentality which members of a group acquire through habitual engagement in the field which comes to signify their cultural capital. It also draws attention to what it is reasonable to know, what is embodied in the social that relates to a quality of being 'at home' in a field. Johnson has suggested that Bourdieu sees habitus as representing a 'theoretical intention' a resource that effects structures within a field that is itself structured. Significantly, Johnson goes on to add that it also refers to a 'feel for the game' a knowing how to enact in a way that is not necessarily calculated nor does it follow conscious obedience to rules. Habitus points to what is durable in biography, 'the result of a long process of inculcation beginning in early childhood, which becomes a "second sense" or a second nature'.[39]

The issue of awakening and testing religious sensibilities relates to a slightly eccentric notion of the term oblate in *Homo Academicus*. In Bourdieu's account, the term refers to lucky survivors, victims of their elite status who in being so consecrated come to a passive ignorance of any other cultural world, apart from life in the academy. There is an intensity of loyalty to the habitus of the academy felt by those of humble origin given a place of rank within its assembly.[40] The monastic use of the term referred to boys donated to the monastery, who grew within it, knowing only heavenly realities, a world of liturgy and theology, within a Gothic cage. Many of the very great medieval minds grew into wisdom and holiness through this route.[41] The term is ambiguous in that it refers to those marginal to secular life by their appropriation into monastic culture, but it also signifies adults who are borderline to the life of the monastery, but who for different reasons cannot or do not have a fully committed vocation to the life, such as Huysmans, who researched the issue heavily for one of his final novels *The Oblate*, that was in reality devoted to his own biographical plight in Catholicism.[42]

Bourdieu found the notion of habitus in Panofsky's *Gothic Architecture and Scholasticism*. For Bourdieu, the term habitus relates to acquired dispositions, to the actor being the social agent, the practical operator of the construction of structures that take on objective qualities.[43] Maher aptly suggests that habitus offered Bourdieu a means of escape from a structuralism that had no subject and from a subject that had no structure. In an interview with Maher, Bourdieu recollects that when translating Panofsky in 1967, he was struck by the connection between the structure of the space of the Church, the Gothic Cathedral, and the structure of the *summa* of Aquinas.[44]

A sense of this search that relates to a habitus appears in Pieper's account of the sacred. In asking what makes a building a church, Pieper suggests they are consecrated to a purpose as shelters, repositories, within which the sacred is to be found. They create expectations, arenas marked apart for listening to the Divine. But the spaces within the Church are also marked for purpose, as in the sanctuary, where liturgical rules govern ritual contact and the manifestation of sacred properties that affirm the purpose of the building. Pieper was seeking a connection between the invisible quality of the sacred and its tangible expression in architectural form.[45]

Habitus relates to an opening to the sacred, one that has medieval roots. Codd has explored the notion of habitus in terms of the habit forming force of Scholasticism, designed to lead to a cultivated disposition towards objects that manifested to the senses the basis of the belief.[46] Panofsky saw the connection between Gothic art and Scholasticism in terms of something more concrete than a parallel. He had in mind a genuine cause and effect relationship emerging through diffusion, spread through a mental habit that could be reduced to the Scholastic sense of a 'principle that regulates the act'.[47] Architecture became a habit, a basis, of theological clarification a point understood by Suger by the principle of transparency. The basis of faith was to be made clear to the senses in a manner that also harmonised with imagination and reason. The sense of hierarchy displayed in the Cathedral, in its carving and in its the liturgical order, owed much to the angelic ranking in the Pseudo-Dionysius, who so much influenced Suger.[48] Bourdieu refers to Denys the Areopagite to illustrate the correspondence between a hierarchy of values and of being, to point to the notion of perfect correspondence between differing orders.[49] Panofsky encapsulates this correspondence embodied in the notion of habitus when he suggests that

> in its imagery, the High Gothic cathedral sought to embody the whole of Christian knowledge, theological, moral, natural, and historical, with everything in its place and that which no longer found its place, suppressed.[50]

Guardini had also admired medieval anthropology for its firmer richer hold on reality than was possible for modern man and his anthropological counterpart. A sense of hierarchy was an earthly reflection of angelic heavenly orders.[51] The richness of sacred symbolism became a measure for reading the medieval world in terms of evidences of Divine life. No disconnection was to be admitted in symbols blessed and shaped to ring true.

Nefarious rather than pious purposes operate in Bourdieu's approach to symbols. They are instruments of dissimulation, where forms of disavowal and misrecognition secure a mystification that can be translated into the cash nexus. They assist the economic and political accumulation of cultural capital.[52] Whereas sacred symbols necessitate a disinterest for survival in their use, symbols in Bourdieu's account require an interest, a structural awareness of position which has to be regulated to maximise domination. His approach to symbols presupposes the detachment of morality from habitus thus marking a separation from its theological roots. The notion of habitus or disposition used by Aquinas refers to Aristotle's

special category of the term, of *having on*, which is expressed in the 'relation which holds between a man wearing clothes and the clothes he is
wearing'. Habitus refers also to moral qualities.[53] The notion of a religious
habit signifies a sign of consecration, a moral aspiration for the wearer, a
witness the observer might discern.

Bourdieu's uses the term habitus to refer to 'practice in its humblest
form' in rituals and in the mundane tasks of everyday life. Later, he goes
on to define habitus as

being the social embodied, it is 'at home' in the field it inhabits, it
perceives it immediately as endowed with meaning and interest.[54]

The notion of habitus relates to strategies of the game, the self-understanding
of the actor in a space of possibilities as to what might be won. It denotes
the implicit *modus operandi* of a particular field, the objectified consensus
as to what constitutes it and how to play in it. These strategies become
second nature as habitus relates to what is generative in the structure of the
field. It is what lies below the surface of the social transaction that bears
on a sense of place in the field. Secondly, habitus relates to a property of
embodiment in terms of the cultural properties appropriated to realise an
identifiable position in a contested field, a point Bourdieu pursues in relation to Flaubert's public recognition as a writer.[55] Thirdly, habitus signifies
a career of grasping and integrating connections as in the imagery of the
Cathedral and its occupants. This relates to the recognition of what is seen
in belief and practice, the tacit understandings of those used to the expend-
iture of symbolic capital to survive play on a sacred field. Habitus relates
to careers of understanding and the accumulation of tacit knowing unavailable to outsiders. Thus a monk who was a choirboy is steeped in psalms
and liturgical practice. It is perhaps the only space or field where he can
play himself to the full, for that is the only game he knows by the nature
of his vocation. His habitus makes him unavailable to other dispositions,
which he treats as unsignified unwarranted intrusions. There is a property
of imitation in habitus, a reciprocity in disposition and its accomplishment.
This is understood in monastic life which is after all a field for searching
for God with its own strategies for survival. In this setting, habitus is the
form of finding the self before God and being consecrated into the implications of that search. Clearly, habitus has important religious implications,
for it seems to integrate acting with believing and its means of realisation.
Will needs to be harnessed to disposition.

A crucial dimension in Bourdieu's writing is the link between symbolic
and cultural capital, and the habitual capacity to decipher. It relates to
forms of knowing how to cope with the indeterminate. This presupposes

a consciousness of possibilities, a knowing what to do, that suggests similarities with notions of stocks of knowledge in the context of ethnomethodology. For Bourdieu, this tacit knowing relates to marking distinctions, indices and qualities of judgement of taste. Self-evident forms of taste have a naturalised property that gives them an implicit protection, rendering them in someway above categorisation and judgement. These forms relate to the inequality of recognition and the forms of misrecognition that naturalise and perpetuate these differences in distinctions that matter.

Habitus is a remarkably ambiguous term being about the determinate and indeterminate. In one setting it is about the problem of classification and being classified, of structuring and being structured, that governs inequalities in the use of symbolic capital between classes.[56] It is about the power to define and this links it to the field of cultural production. But it also has a circular quality, one of a self-fulfilling prophecy, a property of hope rising above adversity.[57]

The theological debts embodied in the opaque term habitus permit its application in the religious field in a way that links sociology with culture. It generates a point of connection, an expectation of the need to cultivate a disposition to act, but in what field? This issue arises in the division between academic theology and that form of theology where faith is linked to praxis. More especially it gives a social surround, a cultural ambit, a setting to Kelsey's notion of habitus discussed in Chapter 3. But it does more than indicate what is theologically desirable. It suggests what is analytically missing that might connect structure to belief and action in the field in an academic theology that disavows such a connection. It begs questions as to what is *not* fleshed out in an academic theology removed from a site of enactment, a congregational or communal setting for the realisation of belief. Academic theology has stipulated that no games of belief that would draw on a habitus dealing in strategies of faith can be played on its site lest its non-confessional witness be compromised. But as suggested earlier, this non-confessional status deludes, for in proclaiming a detachment from the symbolic capital of ecclesial culture, academic theology permits itself to be implicated in that of the secular academy. The issue is not about the denial of habitus, but of affiliation to which form: secular and academic or sacred and ecclesial?

The symbolic resources of the university, its graduation ceremonies and examinations, sustain a hidden agenda of privilege, a form of misrecognition of the mapping of the site, where position is a function of unequal access to cultural capital.[58] This hidden agenda also accounts for the unequal mapping of academic subjects within the culture of the university.[59]

By abdicating access to the originals of the metaphors of consecration and transubstantiation, academic theology denudes itself of the means of securing its autonomy, the protection of its own distinctive symbolic capital, its right to name these terms in the context of its own habitus in its own field of cultural reproduction. Robbins suggests that Bourdieu having accepted that religious practice sustains class divisions, wished 'to show that religious work involved the imposition and consecration of dualistic thinking'.[60] Perhaps, the most important lesson Bourdieu teaches theology is to understand its power, the need to selectively use its symbolic and cultural capital, and to *believe* in its social instruments, for if it does not, then others will not follow.

In Bourdieu's analysis of academic culture, the issue arises of affiliation to a form of consecration and transmutation. Although he does not deal with the subject, Bourdieu suggests an ironic fate for academic theology, which thought it had escaped from the mysterious and non-rational powers of ecclesial culture, and its tyranny of symbols, only to find itself under an equivalent secular agenda that draws on the distinctive requirements of a university cultural capital, if power is to be secured. Bourdieu argues that the transmutation of social truth into academic truth is not just a game of writing, but involves a social alchemy, which secures a symbolic efficiency and the exercise of power. There is a self-confirming, self-selecting property to this task for oblates, those seeking a place in the university field. Like the altar server, grasping the mysteries of the priesthood in a 'magical circle of perceptions', the university oblate seeks the equivalent of a magical power that operates beyond the mechanism. But the exercise of symbolic power presupposes belief in its basis for as Bourdieu suggests

we only ever preach to the converted. The power of the academic euphemism is absolute only when it works on agents selected in such a way that the social and academic conditions of their production dispose them to recognize it absolutely.[61]

Why is Bourdieu so valuable for understanding the link between theology and culture through sociological lens? His central importance lies in what it *permits* theology to say in culture, a licence granted on the basis of what sociology says elsewhere about the cultural. Perversely, Bourdieu uses a sacerdotal language to speak of culture, which liberal theologians with a misguided account of its basis of reproduction spurn in the interests of 'reason' 'relevance' and what they *think* is self-evident about matters cultural. Bourdieu's significance lies not only in the area of theological metaphors harnessed to sociological purpose, but also in the notion of habitus, which permits disposition to believe to be inserted into the rhetoric of sociology itself in its dealings with other parts of culture. The value of Bourdieu's account is that it draws attention to the symbolic capital which theologians need to preserve to secure autonomy in a contested marketplace if they are to make a prophetic mark. Whereas secularisation speaks of a marginalisation of the sacred, Bourdieu gives it a fighting chance, one that is not fatalistic, but which characterises the basis of his sociology of culture as a whole. By *not* entering the marketplace, theology risks having its symbolic capital misappropriated, a failure of conservation that permits pastiche and imitation by other symbol brokers to occur with impunity.

There is a strand of bad faith in Bourdieu, the implication that the symbolic capital of belief cannot speak for itself but has to spoken for. This is a grey area, one that points to the mystery of grace emerging through deficient sociological analysis. But it could be retorted that the failure of analysis is an inadmissible presumption, given the Church's wish for a dialogue with sociology, but more importantly its evident failure to connect to contemporary culture, signified in falling attendance figures and the marginalisation of the message which seems to confirm the tenets of secularisation. What theologians might dislike intensely about Bourdieu is his appropriation of what they have jettisoned, the apparatus of the sacerdotal, deemed vain irrelevant superstitions by liberals, but in his hands, devious instruments for the maintenance of power. The obvious question to ask is: if these sustain the basis of power in cultural fields in general, why can the same analysis not be used to *recover* a means of 'successful' reproduction of religious belief, Catholicism, in a society which seems to have lost its grammar book of faith?

There are three important strands in Bourdieu in relation to religion. Firstly, his concern is with the reproduction of belief, an approach that relates to Weber's interest in charisma, enchantment and the means through religious legitimacy is secured. Bourdieu shares with Weber a concern with power and domination, the manifestation of priestly mystification in the reproduction of belief. But Bourdieu reformulates Weber's approach to sociology of religion in terms of symbolic interaction. Bourdieu wishes to examine the structure of objective relations between agents in the religious field. This leads him to argue that this structure 'determines both the form their interactions may assume and the representation they may have of these interactions'. Bourdieu does not contest the specifically religious interests of this field, but examines these in the context of the function of legitimation of positions. What is at stake in the competition for religious power 'is the *monopoly of the legitimate exercise of the power to modify, in a deep and lasting fashion, the practice and world-view of lay people,* by imposing on and inculcating in them a particular *religious habitus*'.[62] Religious legitimacy, for Bourdieu, involves the mobilisation of a symbolic force to secure position in the objective structure. All the power of religious agents over the laity derives from the structure of symbolic power that constitutes their relationships. This point is understood in the tension between the charismatic prophet and the routinising and bureaucratising Church, which is organised to secure a monopoly of authority against his competition for believers. A monopoly of power is maintained though the capacity to impose a systematisation on belief, through ritual and practical instruments – such as catechisms and breviaries – and these sustain the structure religion serves to reproduce.[63]

Secondly, there is a sacramental strand running through Bourdieu's approach to culture. Because enchantment relates to the intangible, to properties of aura, grace, and social magic that elicit curiosity and a sense of mystery, it carries properties of vulnerability. Enchantment seems to embody a powerlessness. The very ambiguity of its properties suggests a reading into elusiveness, one that accentuates the definiteness of disenchantment. But the value of Bourdieu's approach to culture is to suggest that indefiniteness has a property of unaccountability, a mysterious ability to name, to consecrate, that is above redress. This power reaches a perfection in a theological context.

In their dealings with culture, some theologians fail to realise that a sacramental theology shapes secular forms of understanding of culture and ritual. Thus, a sacramental theology lies behind Austin's notion of performative utterances where actions are believed to realise what they signify. This *ex opere operato* theological approach has been explored by Skorupski in his analysis of operative ceremonies.[64] Bourdieu expands this notion of sacramental efficacy, its mysterious capacity to recategorise, into a basis for understanding culture, but in terms of a power to disguise and to conceal forms of legitimation and domination.

Some radical forms of theology seek to escape, or to deny any forms of legitimation and domination, thus proclaiming a world few sociologists can understand. By a magic of proclamation, what is endemic is denied. But the approach of Weber and Bourdieu does allow for an issue of grace in reproduction. Sociology's main contribution to theology is to force it to examine the servicing of the sacramental in relation to its cultural and symbolic capital. This calls for a rebuilding and conservation of symbolic and cultural capital within the religious field, again, underlining the ironic point that sociological interventions into theology tend to lead back to orthodox and traditional considerations.

Thirdly, Bourdieu's concern is with the capacity of agents to transfigure, to consecrate in the market, to secure monopoly of position and power in the reproduction of culture. For Bourdieu, mystifications disguise advantages. But mystifications are ambiguous in that they enable and disable. In one reading they signify barriers to comprehension, thus effecting exclusion, but in another they elicit curiosity and represent an enticement for inclusion. The appropriation of mystification to regulate boundaries and to deploy symbolic capital in a way that enhances power and advantage is crucial to Bourdieu's understanding of culture and strategies that govern its fields of play. This ambiguous property of mystification engenders a curiosity that begs attention. It points to an aura of interest, a social magic that surrounds secular acts of consecration.

Theologians will flee at the mention of magic in liturgical accounts, because of its instrumental overtones and the superstition with which it is linked. But Bourdieu means something wider. He is speaking of what attracts, the sensibility that nurtures the habitus of those engaged in the ritual transaction. Social magic points to what is distinctive about the field, the novelty it engenders and the awe it occasions that entices and attracts. It is linked to an experiential sense of grace, of being acted on that is magical. Thus, a young boy after serving his first mass might describe the event as 'brilliant'. Properties of social magic, of aura need to be protected, for here theology and sociology collude for different reasons. Both affirm the living nature of the rite. For the sociologist, the living nature of the social bond needs to be affirmed. For the theologian, the living rite is a condition of sacramental validity. Word has to be fused to action, for no detachment is permitted. For differing reasons, theologians and sociologists are aware of the fragility of the social basis of aura and the need to defend the precarious basis of its realisation.

Benjamin was worried about the destruction of aura in terms of the unique phenomenon of distance. The issue of distance was related to a property of unapproachability and the awe a work of art generated. In his defence of aura, Benjamin refers to a contextualisation of works of art that is defensive. It is the removal of objects of art from ritual to politics, to mass representation and reproduction that worries Benjamin. These processes seem to signify the liquidation of aura. Thus he suggests

> the contextual integration of art in tradition found its expression in the cult. We know that the earliest art works originated in the service of a ritual – first the magical, then the religious kind. It is significant that the existence of the work of art with reference to its aura is never entirely separated from its ritual function. In other words, the unique value of the 'authentic' work of art has its basis in ritual, the location of its original use value.[65]

The capacity of technology to detach the image and sound of rite from its ritual frame of enactment points to a problem of defence of symbolic capital peculiar to the cultural field of religion.

The beauty of the voices that Claudel and Huysmans heard, that effected their conversion to Catholicism, can now be reproduced on record and tape. The sound is removed from the ritual frame, where all senses are catered for in a live performance open to a multitude of inferences. Reception in the bath is now a substitute for the discipline of the pew and the reverence imposed by collective attention. Technology has undermined ecclesial monopoly over the use of its symbolic and cultural capital, but also has distorted its impact in a way some might not realise. The substitution of endless forms of reproduction through technology, a hermeneutic problem of appropriation in a multitude of disconnected settings, for the unique, authentic setting of the work of art, has effected a withering of aura, a point that worried Benjamin who had in mind the Cathedral and choir in his examples.[66] The emancipation of artistic practices from rite objectifies them in a way that also makes them suitable for exhibition and spectacle without commitment. They present to the flâneur rather than to the pilgrim. Personal contact is destroyed and with it obligation, the need to develop a habitus of engagement. As Benjamin aptly noted 'the public is an examiner, but an absent-minded one'.[67] It has somehow lost the means of engagement even though it seems to desire it.

These issues arise in the case of televised programmes, such as BBC's 'Songs of Praise', which attracts millions in excess of those attending Church. This exemplifies the phenomenon of believing and belonging, a rupture accentuated by the eccentric choice of sites of praise by the producer of the series in 1994–5, many of which were in secular settings, the inference being that worship and Church setting *could* be detached. But these programmes exercise an unaccountable tyranny. A capricious producer can present rite without any form of accountability to ecclesial culture; the mass media can invent traditions such as 'the choirgirl of the year'; and it can demand that religious broadcasting be tailored to the needs of multicultural tolerance and representation, thus inventing by its own authority, its own brand of implicit religion, its own broad church of the air. Although it will be denied, the notion is presented that attendance at television services is a substitute for going to Church. As Lapointe notes, in the televising of mass, 'communication is now essentially established around the ritual, by watching the ritual unfolding, instead of *through* the ritual itself'.[68] A further problem arises over the appropriation of religious music to the concert hall. The Early Music movement is obsessed with authenticity of pitch, instrument and score, but does not raise the issue of the religious authenticity of what is produced. Mixed choirs and concerts, all add to the sense that this music is spectacle without engagement. One is almost surprised to find a Byrd mass performed in its intended eucharistic setting with a choir of men and boys in a Catholic Church.[69]

Bourdieu argues that the artistic field requires the need to perceive and to appreciate positions in a social space where possibilities are enhanced or restricted.[70] Autonomy can be illusory or can be well founded and secured through a capacity to exercise symbolic violence, to sustain the tacit basis of power. Symbolic violence is exercised in the control of naming and representing canons of taste and cultural judgement. Disinterest in aesthetic products which are valued for their inherent qualities of beauty, can serve to mask economic interests, which are disguised and disavowed. Naked monetary interest prostitutes aesthetic values that speak of the intangible. The miracle of cultural production in dealing with aesthetics is the way the monetary basis of its transactions, which might pollute, is kept proximate but distant. It is present but in some mysterious manner seems absent. This has to be the case if a link between the aesthetic and the cash nexus is to be secured, for the latter has a subtractive effect on the former. Guiding through these antinomial pitfalls gives prestige and power to experts who decipher the symbolic basis of transactions and keep them running between the definite and the indefinite. The routinisation of contradiction within the production of culture has its roots in an understanding of the genesis and structure of the religious field.

In Bourdieu's analysis, there is a quality of grace conferred in the link between the artist and his dealer, and the writer and his publisher. The reputation of the artist is given an incalculable aura that comes from association with a charismatic dealer or publisher, whose access to symbolic capital opens out a space of possibilities for advancement and recognition. In a field concerned with the production of belief, where bad faith is all too possible, a process of conversion and legitimacy is required which the dealer secures for his protégé. This process requires a capacity to handle antinomies, between the visible and the invisible, the aesthetic and the monetary, where exposure can lead to incredibility. Discussing Flaubert and the French Literary Field, Bourdieu examines the mask of convention and its fear of being exposed. Citing a saying of Saint Bernard, 'quae plus latent, plus placent', Bourdieu notes that

> the more a work hides, the greater the pleasure. The more the writings are able to suggest, veiling what they are unveiling, the greater is the specifically literary effect that they produce and that the objectification tends to destroy.[71]

This process of collective misrecognition, a vital tool in the magician's craft, relates to the acquisition of symbolic capital. Dissimulation is combined with expertise in mapping the contours of the field, a skill, a quality of habitus which the artist seeks in the dealer who takes on priestly powers. These relate 'to the production of the work of art as a sacred, consecrated object, the product of a vast operation of *social alchemy*'.[72] Cultural objects are redefined and are given an allure. A quality of social magic, an aura, is bestowed that makes them attractive. Power in the field of artistic production is based on the capacity to consecrate objects in terms of an aesthetic process that surmounts the tension between the disinterest so necessary to convey credible judgement, and the tacit interest needed to maintain and to maximise monetary profits. Disavowal of the 'economy' to maximise the accumulation of symbolic capital involves coping with a process of contradiction, an antinomy, to secure the production of belief. This process has its origins in Bourdieu's earlier examination of the religious field where a quality of mimesis, of routinely surmounting contradictions, can be found. The production of religious belief, involves 'the most specific (but not ultimate) principle of *ideological alchemy* by which the transfiguration of social relations into supernatural relations operates and is therefore inscribed in the nature of things and thereby justified'.[73] This process of rendering plausible that which could be otherwise deemed to be implausible involves a practice of conversion inherent in sociological understandings of the representations of the holy.[74] Bourdieu's analysis points to an ironic outcome in debate on secularisation. His understanding of culture suggests that the capacity to sacralise in the secular, forms a basis of power to shape and to regulate cultural fields, which theologians seeking to adjust the sacred to the secular, have radically misunderstood. Bourdieu's interests are *not* theological but form part of his project of a sociological reflexivity. This gives greater potency to his insights and the lessons they suggest for theologians.

A central question in Bourdieu's work is: who is the beneficiary of the mystification and the right to name? This relates to an ambiguous concept of Bourdieu: *illusio*. In one sense it means belief in the game, the effective investment to play it, the recognition of what is at stake;[75] in another sense it refers to the uninvolved spectator who sees it as an illusion, a self-deception that generates a hermeneutic of suspicion.[76] *Illusio* has to be related to *doxa*, the form of belief that raises the game above question for the believers.[77] Bourdieu is too clever to avoid the suspicion that sociology is its own form of *doxa*, that it simply substitutes one form of commonsense, that of the actor, for the mystifications of the sociologist and his trade.[78] The truth of rite in sociological and theological terms lies somewhere between Bourdieu's notion of letting go to invest, to link the self to the transaction, in the fulfilment of a reflexivity, and the way doing is a form of saying that implicates the actor in the ritual and what it proclaims, in the way Rappaport has explored.[79] By merging *illusio* into *doxa*, theologians can begin to understand how liturgical games can be reproduced in an otherwise sceptical culture.

Matters might rest inconclusively there if Bourdieu had not written on sociology and liturgy, or if he had not written on the issue of belief and the sociologist. His essays capture the dilemmas of sociological sight in a manner that is not hostile to Catholicism. From his writings, Bourdieu has read too much theology to be indifferent to it. An untranslated essay by Bourdieu, 'Sociologists of belief and beliefs of sociologists' suggests some unexpected resonances that leave one puzzled as to his theological position – if any.[80]

In speaking to sociologists of religion, Bourdieu emphasises his dislike of the inquisitorial questioning of social determinants of cultural production that seems to mask a resentment. His concern is with a sociology of sociology that is a liberating, intellectual and personal instrument, one concerned with the mastery of social impulses. In answering the question whether sociologists of religion can participate in the religious field, he indicates with difficulty, because of incompleteness of information, for the location of production of the field is unclear (the inference being this belongs to issues of grace, to a theology to which sociology has not access). Differences do matter which the indifferent observer might not feel.[81] Bourdieu returns to a theme of objectification and argues that

> one can belong to the religious field and produce a scientific sociology of religion as long as one is aware of this allegiance and of its effects and not try to conceal them – most importantly to oneself. The sociology of sociologists is not motivated by polemical or juridical intentions; it simply aims at revealing some of the most powerful social impediments to scientific production.[82]

The knowing of these social impediments and responsibility for their basis gives a special calling to the sociologist dealing with religious belief. But in going through the act of knowing to find these impediments, the reflexivity of the sociologist involves a peculiar journeying, a discerning that is the result of passages others need not make. This lends a peculiarity to the theological vision of a sociologist, a stress in perspective all the more perplexing for emerging from a reflexivity surprised by grace. Such a reflexivity isolates in what it pronounces. To fellow sociologists, who do not share this theological vision, these are acts of folly. To theologians, they also embody a scandal of presumption. For whichever side, the sociologist is likely to be misunderstood. The sociologist has always to work from an intense almost neurotic feel of the social and its detail, and perhaps has to suffer panic at threats of envelopment without apparent theological relief. A scruple about the social, seeing too much of the mechanism of reproduction, is exasperated by theological positions that see too little. Yet, the sociologist is at the cutting face of culture, where the wager between belief and disbelief is played. This suggests there is a witness of some theological sort in his utterances.

On the religious field, the sociologist sees the dilemma of seeking to believe. Thus Bourdieu asks

> but more profoundly, how can one not see that the dialectic of inner experience and social image is only the visible aspect of the dialectic of faith and bad faith (in the sense of a lie to oneself, individual or collective) which is the basis of the game of masks, the game of mirrors, and the game of masks in front of mirrors, and which aims to provide individuals and groups constrained to the interested repression of worldly interests (economic but also sexual) with circuitous routes to an irreproachable spiritual satisfaction?[83]

The implication of the above passage is that one has to pass through the religious field, for there is no other route, whatever the risks. But this passing in the service of a pure sociological reflexivity risks its own misunderstandings which theology can call to account.

Bourdieu tends to relate religious habitus to ideology, to its masking function of disguising relationships of domination and power when more complex theological and sociological considerations apply, if a fullness of understanding of what is structured in the field is to be understood. Thus, he states 'in every conjuncture, the structure of relations between the religious field and the field of power controls the configuration of the structure of relations constitutive of the religious field'.[84] But in using power to understand the distinctive configurations of the religious field at play there are some misunderstandings of its holy games.

Firstly, Bourdieu gives a reductionist understanding of symbols, conceiving them only in terms of their functional use where their indeterminacy is doomed to yield only one effect – the advancement of power. This needs qualification in the case of liturgical games on the religious field. The habitus cultivated to play signifies a feel for that mysterious game as its actors wander between the sacred and profane in thickets of symbols that might yield the holy or the unholy. In this setting symbols are equivocal to the degree to which they have significance for this game. Seeking their transcendence forms the goal of the game. If condemned to being unequivocal, they are denied their mysterious characteristics that form the curiosity which habitus develops and which lies as the basis of their reproduction. Bourdieu understands this point when he refers to the label charisma as designating symbolic properties and the efficacy that accrues to the religious agents as they adhere to 'the *symbolic power that confers on them the ability to believe in their own symbolic power*'.[85] Of course in theological terms, this symbolic power is an expression of grace conferred in sacramentals that signify what they effect for the actors in their own endeavours to seek the holy and to represent it in their lives. Central to the notion of charisma in Weber's and Bourdieu's account is the notion of social recognition, a process that relates to habitus but also to discernment of gift. Secondly, in liturgical games, actors invert power relationships, so that the weakest in one reading have the strongest theological claims for recognition. The washing of the feet of the youngest boys who serve at the Maundy Thursday mass of the Last Supper signifies this point.

In his introduction to the two essays dealing with the social conditions for effectiveness of ritual discourse and on rites of institution, Bourdieu points to the need for sociology to develop a theory of effect where an authorised way of seeing the social world constructs the reality of that world. Symbolic capital is useful in proportion to its recognition. There is self-validating property to the use of symbols and their capacity to transform. Thus, Bourdieu suggests that 'the mystery of performative magic is thus resolved in the mystery of ministry . . . in the alchemy of *representation* . . . through which the representative creates the group which creates him'.[86]

Following an extensive sociological and anthropological tradition, Bourdieu treats with sympathetic understanding the sense of betrayal felt by some Catholics at some of the shortcuts and experiments in liturgy after Vatican II. His essay on ritual discourse is framed by quotations from deeply affronted Catholics worried at what is violated in their liturgical habitus. Bourdieu felt that 'the outraged faithful are not wrong when they associate the anarchic diversification of ritual with a crisis in the religious institution'. Bourdieu sees a crisis of recognition and authority that has wider implications than the small world of liturgical enactments when he asserts

> that is why the crisis of religious language and its performative efficacy is not limited as is often believed, to the collapse of a world of representations: it is part of the disintegration of an entire universe of social relations of which it is constitutive.[87]

Reminding liturgists of what they had lost in the pursuit of simplicity and relevance, Bourdieu looks at rituals of social magic in the context of authority and performative utterance.[88] Namings are acts of social magic in institutions that change structure and perception of their basis. They operate like sacraments by effecting what they proclaim. Belief is the condition of the cultural effectiveness of rite. It is this loss of faith in the authority of the cultural apparatus of rite, the symbolic capital that underpins its basis, and the habitus that yields it manifestation on the religious field, that suggests that secularisation was accelerated in the past three decades by internal ecclesial misreadings of culture.

There is an implication in Bourdieu which liberal theologians will view with distaste, which Thompson notes, that the myriad of symbolic devices – the robes, the wigs, the ritual expressions and respectful references (of judiciary) are not irrelevant distractions, but are the mechanisms of speaking with authority.[89] In a point that can be related to religious clothing, Bourdieu indicates the way the process of symbolic efficacy transforms the person consecrated by transforming the representations others have of him. Thus, to institute 'is to *signify* to someone what he is and how he should conduct himself as a consequence'.[90] Bourdieu wants to assert, '"become what you are": that is the principle behind the performative magic of all acts of institution'.[91]

A modernity coming to a fullness of a sense of futility and despiritualisation has only one option – to seek forms of enchantment. As Bauman suggests

> all in all, postmodernity can be seen as restoring to the world what modernity, presumptuously had taken away; as a *re-enchantment* of the world that modernity tried hard to *dis-enchant*.[92]

This is to return to an ambition at the heart of Weber's worries over disenchantment and the calculation, which Simmel saw as coming to characterise the tragedy of culture. Weber regarded charisma as the antidote to rationality, the nonrational enchantment that would break free from the deadening clutches of disenchantment. There is an acknowledged sacramental dimension to Weber's approach to charisma which has been neglected, and to which Bourdieu has drawn attention.

Weber's notion of disenchantment embodies a fatalism, a belief that an 'age of enchantment and charisma, was dead buried by bureaucratic domination and scientific'. This pessimism must be related to his biography and his sense of bleakness felt during the First World War.[93] Gerth and Mills noted that Weber liked to refer to Schiller's phrase the 'disenchantment of the world'. They go on to add that rationalisation is to be measured negatively in terms of the degree to which 'magical elements of thought are displaced, or positively by the extent to which ideas gain in systematic coherence and naturalistic consistency'.[94] In this study, the issue of disenchantment relates less to the pervasiveness of calculation and the indispensability of bureaucracy than to its subtractive property in relation to enchantment. There is a fated property to this process, that disenchantment inevitably wins.

Enchantment is a property of what is incomplete, what seems to resist an ordered sociology. For Weber, recognition of the gift of grace, of charisma is central to its sociological basis. Recognition confirms the gift of charisma but also effects its sociological basis in understanding the legitimacy and domination it effects.[95] Weber is concerned with issues of reproduction in a way that has sacramental implications, however imperfectly understood. The fact that he does refer to sacraments in his writings on charisma might surprise. There is a received image of Weber's notion of charisma as solely relating to exotic prophetic individuals, the John the Baptists, operating on the fringes of society with no successors and no mechanism of transmission of their gifts to their heirs. In Weber's writings, charisma is ambiguous for in one form it expresses a capacity to rupture routine, but in another it presupposes routine to reproduce its basis.

Weber recognised the charisma of office, that its transmission occurs through ritual means, where 'personal charisma may be totally absent'.[96] Weber had two forms of charisma in mind, one which did refer to extraordinary properties inhering in an individual or an object. But the other form related to what may be artificially produced in the individual through extraordinary means. These relate to belief, to folk religions.[97] This second form echoes his earlier stipulation that the external course of religious behaviour could only be understood from the 'viewpoint of the religious behaviour's "meaning"'.[98] Symbolic aspects of belief also arise in Weber's approach to religion, together with a recognition of the significance of ritual in the transmission of grace in the context of sacraments. Weber's Lutheran background emerges in his inconsistent approach to sacraments. At some points, these are seen as forms of magic, but at others, in more conventional terms, as tangible expressions of grace. For him, such participation in sharing links also to a Divine life.[99] But Weber's most important point, on prospects of re-enchantment in the present argument, relates to his comment on the evolution of dealings with the supernatural, where 'magic is transformed from a direct manipulation of forces into a *symbolic activity*'. This sweeping away of naturalism, with a movement into decipherment coincides with a realisation that sacred beings cannot be grasped in a concrete sense, but only indirectly. Their transcendental existence is normally 'accessible only through the mediation of symbols and meanings and which consequently appears to be shadowy and sometimes outright unreal'. He goes on to add that real events are symptoms or symbols that point to the need to influence spiritual powers. This insight of Weber relates to the evolution of religion, from primitive understandings of seeking to connect to spirits of the dead. But it also points to the proliferation of symbolic acts and the uncertainties these generate. For Weber, 'all areas of human activity were drawn into this circle of magical activity'.[100]

Weber moves between magic and theology in mapping out a sociology of religion. This intermingling does not preclude definite theological comments emerging. Thus, for Weber, Jesus 'set up the most tremendous requirements for salvation; his doctrine has real aristocratic qualities'. It is noticeable that this discussion of Christ is set up in the context of His indifference to the world.[101]

The sociological understandings of the link between enchantment and culture are tenuous and recent. Schneider argues that 'enchantment is itself an index of our pragmatic incompetence: we can only "buy" wonder, so to speak in its currency'.[102] The move in sociology towards hermeneutics, less in terms of treating alien objects, such as religious beliefs in terms of suspicion, and more to seek a depth of understanding that relates to contextual decipherment, has important implications for its treatment of enchantment. It permits a softer approach, one geared to understanding and implication, rather than to explanation and a fixation on the explicit. A rather more humble sociology, geared to self-policing and characterised by a concern with the social procedures for enablement emerges in dealings with enchantment in culture.

The issue of the accountability of the sociologist, both to biography and insight, relates to an issue of choice. This is not to resuscitate unprofitable debate on value free sociology, or to suggest that a value disposition allows a sociologist to say anything so that analysis is simply a set of subjective projections. It is rather to call the sociologist to account for what is implicated in the sociological act of understanding. A particular form of knowing emerges that involves a contradiction between a heightened sensibility of context and its limits, and the absence of limitations in sociological forms of knowing. If sociology is to succeed, it must become aware of itself and the judgements that emerge in its analytical ventures in understanding. Sociology enables and disables; it enchants and disenchants; and it contextualises and decontextualises. As Bourdieu has aptly indicated, 'just as it de-naturalizes, so sociology de-fatalizes'.[103]

Schneider correctly argues that the rapid expansion of sociology between 1970–90 precluded it from reflecting on its basis as a professional symbolic community with a distinctive frame of reference for dealing with culture. Sociology became entrapped in an increasingly competitive market for funding and legitimacy with the result that proposals for research, geared to funding bureaucracies, were safe, predictable, but had remarkably low theoretical yields. Certainly, they were not geared to deal in the opaque area of the enchantment of culture.[104] This requires inexpensive reflection, but removed from the process of the bureaucratisation of sociology that produces its own version of methodological disenchantment in the pursuit of analytical exactitude.

If habitus and reflexivity can be applied to Bourdieu's approach to culture, something more than an exercise in sociology of knowledge emerges.[105] Biography points to an issue of disposition, as to which thread of argument is to be pulled through culture, that signifying the secular, or a strand that indicates the sacred. This insight can be turned against secularisation to suggest that it is neither natural nor fated. Secularisation can be turned inside out, to be treated as a cultural convention whose other side is the sacred. All sociology can indicate is the mechanism of reproduction that can produce either. The habitus of the sociologist, up to recently so masked, begs questions as to what is being sought in the account, as discussed in Chapter 2. 'The demands of the day' and the demon within, which Weber noted, might drive the sociologist back to the original of the habitus where the link between the scholastic and Gothic might be found. The notion of seeing as a form of believing can make the sociologist no longer a stranger before the rites of the Cathedral, but somebody who grasping their habitus appropriates it to his own. A reflexivity that moves from sociology to spirituality relates to questions of uncommon grace, issues that link theology to culture. The aridness of sociological theorising, its unfocused rambling concerns, its journeying through a literature but never arriving, will always beg questions. It is a myth to think that there is some typicality in sociological journeying, for all passages on the map are individual. In his journeying, the vocation of the sociologist is to be accountable for the integrity of his reflexivity and the nurture of a habitus that marks the tools of his trade. Temptation to move in a theological direction has become less irresistible, as a reflexive sociologist explores further issues of social ecology and the need to conserve spiritual gifts of enchantment that preserve the humanity of culture. The ingredients that bear on theology are apparent increasingly in the sociological agenda emerging from understandings of culture. Beauty, ethics, judgement all intermingle in the issue of culture, but they do so in a way that diminishes the difference between fieldwork in sociology and in theology. This leads back to von Balthasar. His theology of aesthetics has a sociological underpinning, a recognition of its basis but also of what is required to transcend its limitations.

As indicated earlier, von Balthasar did use and understand sociology with exceptional insight. Even more singular is his appreciation of Georg Simmel, the sociologist whose ghost lies behind postmodernity. Von Balthasar had a deep respect for Georg Simmel and cites him frequently in a number of his works. Having the advantage of reading him in German, von Balthasar regarded Simmel not so much as a sociologist as 'the religious philosopher of life and theoretician of art' in the context of a discussion of Bergson and Nietzsche.[106] It was the spiritual aspects of his interest in culture that concerned von Balthasar.

Simmel dabbled with a range of knowledge, not only in sociology, philosophy, aesthetics, but also in literary and spiritual fields. His circles in Berlin, his interest in Nietzsche, Stefan George and his connections with the Webers, point to a man whose breath of interest gave him a concern with the ultimate issues of meaning that overlapped with theology in a way a secularised sociology has seen fit to ignore.

The issue of culture is given a characteristically fragmented treatment in his work. Like Weber, Simmel was concerned with the lag between appreciation of the tangible, the commodification of objects that subtracted from subjective sensibilities, and capacities to enhance and to refine. Cultural refinement lies in increasing value beyond natural performance. The commodification of culture diminishes this process.[107]

Von Balthasar suggests that Simmel was aware of the debt that he owed to the Christian era, but that he was a post-Christian thinker coming to terms with a Church dogma seemingly dead for ever. For von Balthasar, Simmel was the one thinker operating at the end of the Christian and idealist periods who struggled to find a new and contemporary expression of individuality, one that dealt with human uniqueness and who sought the answer to the question 'Who am I'.[108] Von Balthasar was fascinated with Simmel's concern with unity and diversity, put in more crude terms, the relationship between the individual and culture, form and context. The self-defeating basis of culture, as understanding increased, fascinated Simmel and was expressed in terms of form, a point that interested von Balthasar who characterised it as the tension operating between the unity of the whole and unity of the individual.[109] Von Balthasar regarded Simmel as 'working towards an affirmation that will embrace the whole of everyday life, with its divine and nondivine aspects in a single, religious attitude'.[110]

Von Balthasar reminds sociology of a theological past it seems to have forgotten, one exemplified in Simmel, who struggled with the issue of the loneliness, of an interior life coping with a technological civilisation that had become its master. Von Balthasar finds Simmel riddled with worry over tragedy, the self-destructive nature of a culture that admits no exception, a pessimism he finds perplexing. But what is pessimistic in sociology, exemplified by Simmel, is redemptive in von Balthasar's theology. This marks a fundamental difference of understanding and expectation between sociology and theology about how their actors come to belief. The sociologist is the stranger, who speaks for the fragmented from a position equally so and coming from the outside, describes the cultural landscape theologians wish to engage. But theologians, knowing in faith, need not attend to the way belief is constructed in a culture. If holy, they see it as a gift of grace, where understanding of its social construction is downplayed lest it seem a product of human manufacture. Construction is what is already accomplished; it just needs faith to be added, an assumption sociology cannot share. It can share with the notion of faith, but has to seek the means of construction otherwise it faces disciplinary redundancy. This difference in perception accounts for the tragedy of culture that lies in the mutuality of misunderstanding between the theologian and the sociologist.

For the sociologist, an unremitting gloom, a melancholy, a disenchantment, a malaise, anomie, and the tragedy of culture, mark an inductive sketch of lives of quiet desperation lived behind the glitter of postmodernity. The pastiches so played with, the blasphemy so lightly entered, are all part of an emptying in culture, a state of despiritualisation that can only sink into vacuity, a nihilism, and for some of the young who overindulge in drugs, sex, a willed death.

For the theologian, such as von Balthasar, the beauty and glory of God shines above the shambles. He comes to culture, to its tragedy, with a sense of drama, of faith, that is deductive from revelation. So reading over Simmel's notion of the tragedy of culture, he finds it destructively pessimistic. Yet in this context, both the sociologist and the theologian find a mutuality between decay and redemption. The sociological reading is harsher, because it lacks the grace of redemption; the theological message is softer because it is inhibited by charity and the belief that all will be well. The theologian presumes what the sociologist cannot assume. If sociology gives a witness, it is in the trivial, in the military manoeuvres on the cultural field, that require the cultivation of a habitus, ceremonies that heal, that do not fragment, and the blessedness that comes from a commonality of purpose. Thus, for the sociologist, seeking signs of hope is an act of unquiet desperation.

These can be found. One sign of hope is the revival of religious orders, presenting a 'conservative image', but in reality representing radical reinventions. They relate to a condition of postmodernity, but radically seek to transcend its basis. They signify the prospect of a new St Benedict, not a charismatic figure, but the reinvention of religious life that he might recognise, one that does not modernise, but signifies a revolt against modernity and an irresistible resistance to its basis. This relates to a long pattern in Church history of renewal, and counter-Reformation. This capacity to reinvent points to a wider process which Hobsbawm noted of 'a process of formalization and ritualisation, characterized by reference to the past, if only by imposing repetition'.[111]

If culture is to survive, to maintain a link with the theological then the condition of its front line, its contemplative monastic orders, is a matter of first importance. As Weber noted, amongst believers, 'the monks are the elite troops of religious *virtuosi*'.[112] These lives are not pointless escapes, but men and women with definite purposes central to the life and health of the Church. Their importance was well expressed by Weber who noted that

> as the exemplary religious individual, the monk was the first *professional*, at least in those orders that practiced rationalized asceticism, most of all the Jesuit order.

Living a life of continuous self-control and discipline over what did not serve his vocation, the monk

> was predestined to serve as the principal tool of bureaucratic centralization and rationalization in the church and, through his influence as priest and educator, to spread corresponding attitudes among the religious laymen.[113]

In the self-inflicted period of fragmentation in the misguided notion of modernisation in the Spirit of Vatican II, when many nuns and monks left in the 1970s, when going back to their habits, to a spirituality of disinterested prayer and charity, to a disciplined communal living, seemed improbable, as one former nun noted, like trying to put toothpaste back in the tube, the signs of a new generation buying new tubes, reviving these supposedly discredited forms of life in the 1990s is remarkable. It is as if those who fled into the new religious movements in the 1980s, are showing signs of a recovery of nerve and returning to traditional forms of religious life, to find the wisdom of their ancestors not in the East but in the West, within European culture. This is not to discredit those orders that did modernise, and those who stayed, rather it is to point to new signs, however unexpected their shape, which can be discerned, which any sociologist would notice. It is foolish to dismiss these movements on the basis of a pop sociology, that its entrants seek authoritarian structures and are misguided conservatives. These movements tell much about a theological response to a cultural condition, that seemed terminal, but clearly is not. They also speak of what bright young people are seeking which some theologians fail to recognise.

The signs are slender, but there is a social phenomenon abroad, however fledgling, that is significant. Like the issue of Churches that are expanding, that are definite in their demands, however much they are written off as conservative or fundamentalist, religious orders that show similar characteristics, seem to move against the diffuse grains of postmodernity with success. A definiteness that speaks against a culture of fragmentation elicits novices.[114] Although representing a minority organisation in the USA that split with the majority Leadership Conference of Women Religious, the Conference of Major Superiors of Women Religious represents 10,000 women with 10 per cent in formation, far in excess of those orders that liberalised, many of whom now face extinction.[115] New Religious Communities of men and women have numerous problems of recognition, less so in wider society, which is indifferent, and more so within sections of the Church, which again indicates the sham nature of liberalism. Despite these difficulties, some of these orders thrive.[116]

Perhaps the most remarkable sign of a shift is the Community of Saint Jean, founded by five students at the University of Fribourg in Switzerland. In 1975, they asked their Dominican professor of philosophy, Fr Marie-Dominique Phillipe to guide them. Formed by the Cistercians, this order, which stresses a contemplative life, has a definite habit, and a structured way of life and service, and is flooded with novices and with young professed. They combine study with prayer, the main influences being Scholastic and represent a conjunction of faith and theological reflection that nurtures a spirituality, a sense of habitus, which academic theology at a secular university totally fails to signify. These shaven grey habited young monks and wimpled nuns, clearly about business, represent an image supposedly disappeared, but seemingly flourishing, thus signifying new hopes in a sea of sociological pessimism.[117]

In this context, Huysmans was the prototype for journeying from the abyss, where all was emptied. Snatched by grace, he moved by surprise into Catholicism, and with all the misunderstandings generated by this most unlikely of converts, he stayed to the end, never quite joining, but certainly never thinking of departing, a holy oblate who saw too much. In this regard, his movement as a flâneur in Baudelaire's sense, seeing as a man returned from the sick bed to life, makes sense, so that his awe at the transparent innocence of the choirboys at Chartres, the Benedictine nuns he encountered, and the Trappist monks who helped in back to Catholicism, were all part of a journeying, the spiritual cultivation of a habitus, a discernment of grace in others. He could see painfully, but could not quite imitate, as he was denied the monastic vocation he so much wanted. He came to discern what was obscured. This was an unexpected sight for a man, a pioneering critic of French Impressionism and in the school of Zola, for whom ethnography was everything and for whom form had endless possibilities for description. Form is where sociology and theology meet to find a mutuality.

In all dealings with culture, sociology and theology have contrasting meanings over the issue of form. This is exemplified in differences between Simmel and von Balthasar. For Simmel, form serves as a focal point of sociological interest in handling types of social exchange. It acts as an artificial device, a means of encapsulating diverse types of sociability whose characterising content eludes sociological definition. This marks a limitation which sociology has to accept, that all life is encapsulated within forms, but these carry a price of increasing an element of reification, an instrumental objectifying property that distorts the spirit or content of culture. The issue of a spiritual malaise forms part of Simmel's approach to culture.

Reflecting on the struggle between life and form, individuality and standardisation, Simmel pointed to the likelihood of numbers satisfying their religious needs through mysticism. This reflected two points: firstly that 'the forms which channel religious life by means of a series of specific objective images no longer do justice to that life'; and secondly that 'religious longings are not thereby killed, they merely seek other paths and goals'.[118] This echoes earlier comments on the notion of secularisation. Simmel expresses a problem facing a Catholicism seeking to engage with the contemporary world when he suggests that

one of the most profound spiritual dilemmas of innumerable modern men is that although it is impossible to preserve the traditional church religions any longer, the religious impulse still exists. No amount of 'enlightenment' can destroy it, for it can only rob religion of its outer garment, not its life. The intensification of religious life to the point of complete self-sufficiency, the transformation, as it were, of 'faith' from a transitive into an intransitive concept, is a tempting way out of the dilemma, but one which in the long run perhaps involves no small degree of self-contradiction.[119]

In his essay on the tragedy of culture, Simmel is concerned with the dualism between subject and object that runs between the self and the culture it seeks to cultivate. In short, the tragedy of culture lies in the way 'an ability to amass goods unorganically' becomes 'profoundly incommensurate with the form of personal life'.[120] Experience becomes privatised, and the individual is placed on the margin, disembodied from a vision of life that would harmonise a fractured sense of sensibility. Innumerable tragedies occur in this radical contrast between subjective life, finite in time, manifested in a social form and a content that embodies the 'timelessly valid' but which needs to be objectified if it is to be known. The concept of culture is lodged in the middle of this dualism.[121]

Central to Simmel's argument is that objective spiritual forms, such as religion, law and technology, that embody virtues, have to be cultivated, but in the process of so doing, they can become reified. This leads to a paradox with tragic implications. To realise their fullness as objective spiritual forms, they risk becoming 'completely alien and crystallized into self-sufficient independence'. As the capacity to cultivate increases, these forms take on a diversity that exceeds the capacity of the self (the soul) to assimilate. They take on a life of their own that masks and dwarfs the spirituality they were supposed to embody initially and to be servants of in their initial cultivation. Thus, for Simmel the tragedy of culture 'frequently . . . appears as if the creative movement of the soul seems to be dying from its own product'.[122] This point takes on a particular poignancy in the context of postmodernity and the technological capacity in computers to make any image – with impunity. Oakes suggests that for Simmel, the consequences of the tragedy of culture lie in the ossification, proliferation and fragmentation of forms of culture. What makes a diverse culture possible, also destroys it and therein is its tragedy. The result is a subjective narcissistic culture, an endless retreat before diversity.[123]

For Simmel, the tragedy in culture lies in destructive forces which the actor faces in the excess between form and content. The actor confronts a galaxy of objectified entities that generate desires, inadequacies and relationships he cannot master but from which he cannot withdraw. The dilemma of modern man relates to

> his sense of being surrounded by an innumerable number of cultural elements which are neither meaningless to him nor, in the final analysis, meaningful. In their mass they depress him, since he is not capable of assimilating them all, nor can he simply reject them, since after all, they do belong *potentially* within the sphere of his cultural development.[124]

The notion that culture in its growth in a division of labour, of cultivation and refinement, carries a self-destructive illusory quality is for Simmel its tragic aspect. Writing in the last year's of his life, Simmel reflecting on the crisis of culture, seemed to echo a point of Guardini that as ends of life were subordinated to means, and as the objective products of culture developed independently of norms, both conspired to estrange subjective culture and to exceed its capacities of understanding. This led to a restlessness, a covetousness and a craving for pleasure that resulted in illusion and deception as 'people seek personal values on a plane where they are simply not be found'.[125] Although his spiritual ideas were agnostic, perhaps more sympathetic to Christianity than many realise, Simmel's conclusion is gloom-ridden as he speaks of a crisis, deeply familiar and intelligible, but consciously for all, as it is 'the crisis of our own soul'.[126]

Many of these themes of choice that exhaust, have been noted in Huysmans' *Against Nature*, but also in von Balthasar's approach to tragedy where the hero falls within a horizon of meaning or meaningless, where a gamble is made that fails. In his wager, 'having established tiny islands of meanings', the actor risks seeing 'them founder in an infinite ocean of meaninglessness'.[127]

Arguing against Steiner, von Balthasar denies that Christianity is in some distinctive way quasi-tragic. He asserts that 'the Christian is not automatically an optimist; he is exposed to the risk of freedom and hence to the danger of tragic failure'.[128] But von Balthasar points to another paradox in the context of secularisation, that tragedy is often related to nobility, to heroic qualities, as they face the incomprehensible.[129] Notions of nobility have switched from those associated with those martyred for truth to those dying of doubt. Yet, human life becomes most invaluable when it juxtaposed to a divinity that is deemed not to exist.

Von Balthasar is not writing about tragedy, or about dramatic wagers for their intrinsic literary or sociological value. His purpose is manifestly theological, to witness to the redemptive. Amongst his many aims is to break the self-defeating circle of the tragedy of culture which Simmel has proposed. Such a purpose is implicit in his writings. For von Balthasar, form is bound into content in an indissoluble manner. An unresolvable sociological problem can be converted into a basis for theological illumination. At this juncture the wager of faith emerges in the opacity of culture, where any meaning is possible and the meaningless is not impossible. At this point on the map, the sociologist enters the realm of choice in an antinomy of form between the objective and a subjective sense of the divine, where his discipline can speak no more.

For von Balthasar, form relates to what is limitless, what is indissoluble, what can mirror properties of God with a spiritual eye that 'transcends the questionableness of men's own choices and self-evaluation'. What matters is what is revealed of the glory of Christ in a form that bears imitation. Von Balthasar goes on to add that

the exterior of this form must express and reflect its interior to the world
in a credible manner, and the interior must be confirmed, justified, and
made love-worthy in its radiant beauty through the truth of the exterior
that manifests it.[130]

Only a fool would use sociology to cross to Canaan's side. Stuck with
a map that seems a maze, reflecting the condition of postmodernity, the
sociologist seems like the tourist in Ireland told by a native that to make
his intended journey it would be best not to venture from here. But this
is beside the point, for all the sociologist can give witness to is the contextual basis of belief, the need for its construction and reproduction.
Clearly, further study is required of the reflexive basis of the reproduction
of religious belief. There is for example a startling gap between the incorporation of sociological assumptions into police culture, and its virtual
absence in clerical culture. This is not to suggest that holiness would be
increased in someway through sociological means, but rather that a greater
understanding of possibilities of engagement with culture would emerge.
A understanding of the site of belief would be enhanced. This would not
exempt any liturgical, monastic or clerical actors from the injunction

> do not delude yourself into thinking God can be cheated: where a man
> sows, there he reaps; if he sows in the field of self-indulgence he will
> get a harvest of corruption out of it; if he sows in the field of the Spirit
> he will get from it a harvest of eternal life. (Galatians 6: 7–8)

A culture of postmodernity has not changed the thrust of this text. Perhaps
the sociologist's tale for the theologian with ears to hear is that play in
culture is still in the context of Pascal's wager, that the coin is still spinning and that prospects of enchantment are still possible.

Notes and References

1 Sociology, Culture and Religious Belief: Some Reflections

1   Marshall Berman, *All That Is Solid Melts Into Air. The Experience of Modernity* (London: Verso, 1983) pp. 34–6.
2   Edward Rutherfurd, *Sarum* (London: Arrow Books, 1988) pp. 555–8.
3   Mark R. Schwehn, *Exiles from Eden: Religion and the Academic Vocation in America* (New York: Oxford University Press, 1993) p. 104.
4   Ibid., pp. 116–17.
5   Johann Wolfgang von Goethe, *Faust*, tr. Phillip Wayne (London: Penguin, 1949) part I , p. 43.
6   Ibid., pp. 55–6.
7   Barbara Beaumont (ed. and tr.), *The Road from Decadence. From Brothel to Cloister. Selected Letters of J. K. Huysmans* (London: The Athlone Press, 1989) p. 148.
8   J. K. Huysmans, *En Route*, tr. W. Fleming (Cambridge: Dedalus, 1989) p. 231.
9   Max Weber, *Economy and Society*, vol. I (London: The University of California Press, 1978) p. 567.
10 Peter L. Berger, *A Rumour of Angels*, 2nd edn (New York: Anchor Books, 1990) pp. xii–xiii.
11 Rowan Williams, 'Postmodern Theology and the Judgement of the World' in Frederic B. Burnham, (ed.), *Postmodern Theology. Christian Faith in a Pluralist World* (San Francisco: HarperCollins, 1989) p. 103.
12 David Martin, *Tongues of Fire. The Explosion of Protestantism in Latin America* (Oxford: Basil Blackwell, 1990) pp. 288–93.
13 Peter L. Berger, *A Far Glory. The Quest for Faith in an Age of Credulity* (New York: Doubleday, 1993) p. 12.
14 Ibid., p. 10.
15 Derek Jennings, 'Shedding an effortless superiority', *The Times*, 27th January 1992.
16 *The Times*, 27th June 1988.
17 Pierre Bourdieu, *In Other Words. Essays towards a Reflexive Sociology*, tr. Matthew Adamson (Cambridge: Polity Press, 1990) p. 28.
18 Pierre Bourdieu and Loïc J. D. Wacquant, *An Invitation to Reflexive Sociology* (Cambridge: Polity Press, 1992) p. 157.
19 Andrew Greeley, foreward to George A. Hillery, Jr, *The Monastery. A Study in Freedom, Love, and Community* (Westport, Connecticut: Praeger, 1992) p. xvi. See also Helen Rose Fuchs Ebaugh, *Women in the Vanishing Cloister: Organizational Decline in Catholic Religious Orders in the United States* (New Brunswick, New Jersey: Rutgers University Press, 1993) and Laurie Felknor (ed.), *The Crisis in Religious Vocations. An Inside View* (New York: Paulist Press, 1989).
20 Quoted in Richard A. Schoenherr and Lawrence A. Young, *Full Pews and Empty Altars. Demographics of the Priest Shortage in the United States Catholic Dioceses* (Wisconsin: University of Wisconsin Press, 1993) p. 351.

21   John Paul II, *Crossing the Threshold of Hope*, tr. Jenny and Martha McPhee (London: Jonathan Cape, 1994) p. 102.
22   Peter L. Berger, *A Far Glory*, p. 126.
23   Charles Davis, 'Theology in Seminary Confinement', in *The Downside Review*, vol. 81, no. 265, October 1963, p. 307.
24   Hans Urs von Balthasar, *A Short Primer for Unsettled Laymen*, tr. Mary Skerry (San Francisco: Ignatius Press, 1985) pp. 11–5.
25   See Antony Archer, *The Two Catholic Churches. A Study in Oppression* (London: SCM Press, 1986) which first drew attention to the way the middle class were beneficiaries of efforts to renew in a modernising and pluralistic manner. For a considered reflection on the implications of the book, see the special issue, 'Class and Church; After Ghetto Catholicism', *New Blackfriars*, vol. 68, no. 802, February 1987.
26   See for example Dermot A. Lane, 'Faith and Culture: The Challenge of Inculturation', in his edited, *Religion and Culture in Dialogue. A Challenge for the next Millennium* (Dublin: The Columba Press, 1993) pp. 11–39.
27   Grace Davie, *Religion in Britain since 1945: Believing Without Belonging* (Oxford: Blackwell, 1994).
28   Dean M. Kelley, *Why Conservative Churches are Growing* (New York: Harper & Row, 1972).
29   Wade Clark Roof and William McKinney, *American Mainline Religion. Its Changing Shape and Future* (New Brunswick, New Jersey: Rutgers University Press, 1987) p. 19.
30   Ibid., pp. 20–1.
31   Ibid., p. 170.
32   Peter L. Berger, *A Far Glory*, p. 59.
33   Cited and discussed in Wade Clark Roof and William McKinney, *American Mainline Religion*, p. 241.
34   Bill McSweeney, *Roman Catholicism. The Search for Relevance* (Oxford: Basil Blackwell, 1980) p. 168.
35   Ibid., p. 170.
36   Eric Hobsbawm and Terence Ranger (eds), *The Invention of Tradition* (Cambridge: University Press, Canto edition, 1992).
37   Linda Colley, *Britons. Forging the Nation 1707–1837* (London: BCA, 1992) p. 18.
38   Eamon Duffy, *The Stripping of the Altars. Traditional Religion in England 1400–1580* (London: Yale University Press, 1992). For an orthodox Catholic account of Anglicanism, see Aidan Nichols, *The Panther and the Hind. A Theological History of Anglicanism* (Edinburgh: T. & T. Clark, 1993).
39   Cited in Ian Ker, *John Henry Newman. A Biography* (Oxford: Oxford University Press, 1988) p. 585.
40   Romano Guardini, *The End of the Modern World: A Search for Orientation*, tr. Joseph Theman and Herbert Burke (London: Sheed & Ward, 1957) p. 119.
41   George A. Lindbeck, 'The Church's Mission to a Postmodern Culture', in Frederic B. Burnham, (ed.), *Postmodern Theology*, p. 52.
42   Jonathan Sacks, *The Persistence of Faith. Religion, Morality and Society in a Secular Age* (London: Weidenfeld & Nicolson, 1991) p. 19.
43   Ibid., p. 103.

44   Anthony Giddens, *The Transformation of Intimacy. Sexuality, Love & Eroticism in Modern Societies* (Cambridge: Polity Press, 1992) p. 203.
45   Lawrence A. Scaff, *Fleeing the Iron Cage: Culture, Politics, and Modernity in the Thought of Max Weber* (Berkeley: University of California Press, 1991) p. 138.
46   Ibid., pp. 199–200.
47   Ibid., pp. 226–7.
48   Ibid., p. 232.
49   For a useful overview of the significance of these thinkers, see Madan Sarup, *An Introductory Guide to Post-structuralism and Postmodernism* (London: Harvester Wheatsheaf, 1988).
50   Alain Touraine, *Return of the Actor. Social Theory in Postindustrial Society*, tr. Myrna Godzich (Minneapolis: University of Minnesota Press, 1988).
51   Ulrich Beck, Anthony Giddens, Scott Lash, *Reflexive Modernization. Politics, Tradition and Aesthetics in the Modern Social Order* (Cambridge: Polity Press, 1994).
52   Keith Tester, *Media, Culture and Morality* (London: Routledge, 1994) p. 3.
53   Pierre Bourdieu, *In Other Words*, p. 188.
54   Dirk Käsler, *Max Weber. An Introduction to his Life and Work*, tr. Phillipa Hurd (Cambridge: Polity Press, 1988) p. 93.
55   Gordon Marshall, *In Search of the Spirit of Capitalism. An Essay on Max Weber's Protestant Ethic Thesis* (London: Hutchinson, 1982) p. 67.

2   'To be or not to be': The Sociologist's Dilemma

1   Pierre Bourdieu and Loïc J. D. Wacquant, *An Invitation to Reflexive Sociology* (Cambridge: Polity Press, 1992) p. 241.
2   See British Sociological Association (BSA) Newsletter, November 1993.
3   Thomas S. Kuhn, *The Structure of Scientific Revolutions*, 2nd edn (Chicago: The University of Chicago Press, 1970) pp. 198–204.
4   Stewart Clegg, 'How to become an internationally famous British social theorist', in *The Sociological Review*, vol. 40, no. 2, May 1992, pp. 576–98. The idea for his essay comes from a study by Lambert of the elevation of Derrida into a 'cultural icon' in academic circles.
5   Alison Lurie, *Imaginary Friends* (London: Heinemann, 1967).
6   There are notable exceptions. See for example: the appendix 'On intellectual craftsmanship' in C. Wright Mills, *The Sociological Imagination* (New York: Grove Press, 1961) pp. 195–226; Phillip E. Hammond (ed.), *Sociologists at Work: Essays on the Craft of Social Research* (New York: Doubleday, 1967); and Jennifer Platt, *Realities of Social Research. An Empirical Study of British Sociologists* (Falmer: Sussex University Press 1976). These studies are often reflections on methodology and the biography of research strategies that defer to 'official' notions of how findings ought to be constructed in sociology.
7   See for example Jocelyn Cornwell, *Hard-earned Lives: Accounts of Health and Illness from East London* (London: Tavistock, 1984) especially Chapter 1, 'The Study: Research Methods and Theoretical considerations', pp. 1–22. Most research manuals warn against interviewer involvement as effecting bias in response, but the advantage of Cornwell's study, being engaged in

common-sense constructions of illness, is that a sense of involvement is conveyed that enhances the authenticity of the study.

8   Nigel Barley, *The Innocent Anthropologist. Notes from a Mud Hut* (London: Penguin, 1986).

9   Judith Aldridge, 'The Textual Disembodiment of Knowledge in Research Account Writing', in *Sociology*, vol. 27, no. 1, February 1993, pp. 53–66.

10 Clifford Geertz, *Works and Lives. The Anthropologist as Author* (Cambridge: Polity Press, 1989) p. 82.

11 Judith Okely, 'Anthropology and autobiography. Participatory experience and embodied knowledge', in Judith Okely and Helen Callaway (eds), *Anthropology and Autobiography* (London: Routledge, 1992) p. 24.

12 Paul Ricoeur, 'The model of the text: meaningful action considered as a text', in Paul Ricoeur, *Hermeneutics and the Human Sciences: Essays on Language, Action and Interpretation*, tr. John B. Thompson (Cambridge: Cambridge University Press, 1981) pp. 197–221, see especially pp. 220–1.

13 Clifford Geertz, *Works and Lives*, pp. 132–3. The issue of the relationship of the sociologist, as author, to his text, his tribe, is further complicated if the ritual itself takes on textual properties. This occurs when rites, such as liturgies take on reductionist qualities of 'playing too much by the book' so that the sociologist has to seek what to amplify of the social in ritual. This dilemma has been observed by Aidan Kavanagh in his essay 'Textuality and Deritualization: The Case of Western Liturgical Usage', in *Studia Liturgica*, vol. 23, 1993, pp. 70–7.

14 Clifford Geertz, *Works and Lives*, p. 145.

15 Anthony P. Cohen, 'Self-conscious anthropology', in Judith Okely and Helen Callaway, (eds), *Anthropology and Autobiography*, pp. 223–4. See also pp. 229–31.

16 Liz Stanley, 'On Auto/biography in Sociology', in *Sociology*, vol. 27, no. 1, February 1993, pp. 42–5.

17 Pierre Bourdieu and Loïc J. D. Wacquant, *An Invitation to Reflexive Sociology*, p. 236.

18 Gregory Baum, *Theology and Society* (New York: Paulist Press, 1987) pp. 219–27.

19 Alvin Gouldner, *The Coming Crisis of Western Sociology* (London: Heinemann, 1971) pp. 4–5.

20 Ibid., pp. 493–500.

21 Friedrich H. Tenbruck, 'The Cultural Foundations of Society', in Hans Haferkamp, (ed.), *Social Structure and Culture* (New York: Walter de Gruyter, 1989) p. 33.

22 R. G. Collingwood, *An Autobiography* (Oxford: Oxford University Press, 1970) Chapter V, 'Question and Answer', pp. 29–43.

23 Robert K. Merton, 'Some Thoughts on the Concept of Sociological Autobiography', in Matilda White Riley (ed.), *Sociological Lives* (Newbury Park, California: Sage Publications, 1988) pp. 19–20.

24 S. F. Nadel, *The Foundations of Social Anthropology* (London: Cohen & West, 1951) p. 50.

25 Scott Lash, 'Reflexivity and its Doubles: Structure, Aesthetics, Community', in Ulrich Beck, Anthony Giddens, Scott Lash, *Reflexive Modernization. Politics Tradition and Aesthetics in the Modern Social Order* (Cambridge: Polity Press, 1994) p. 136 see also pp. 135–43.

26 Ibid., pp. 153–6. See also p. 165 where Lash shows a certain coolness to ethnomethodology. The issue of becoming, as a social accomplishment, of passing in a role with credibility, characterises ethnomethodology. For a curious example, see the account of Garfinkel's study of 'Agnes' and her secret apprenticeship in Douglas Benson and John A. Hughes, *The Perspective of Ethnomethodology* (London: Longman, 1983) pp. 16–23.
27 Pierre Bourdieu and Loïc J. D. Wacquant, *An Invitation to Sociology*, pp. 36–44.
28 Ibid., pp. 258–60.
29 Robert Slesinski, 'Postmodernity and the resources of the Christian East', in *Communio*, vol. 17, no. 2, Summer 1990, p. 231. Von Balthasar asserted that 'he who can no longer pray is incapable even of beginning a dialogue with one of the world's religions'. See *Convergences: To the Source of Christian Mystery*, tr. E. A. Nelson (San Francisco: Ignatius Press, 1983) p. 14.
30 Patrick McNamara, 'Teaching the Sociology of Religion as a Reflective Enterprise', in *Social Compass*, vol. 41, no. 3, 1994, pp. 329–38.
31 Peter Winch, *The Idea of a Social Science and its Relation to Philosophy* (London: Routledge & Kegan Paul, 1963) pp. 87–8.
32 Kieran Flanagan, *Sociology and Liturgy: Re-presentations of the Holy* (London: Macmillan, 1991).
33 Jean-Luc Marion, *God without Being*, tr. Thomas A. Carlson (Chicago: University of Chicago Press, 1991) p. 178.
34 George A. Hillery, Jr, *The Monastery. A Study in Freedom, Love and Community* (Westport: Praeger, 1992). In this study, the terms love or agapé are alternative words for charity.
35 Peter Winch, *The Idea of a Social Science*, p. 87.
36 Edward Shils, *The Calling of Sociology and Other Essays on the Pursuit of Learning* (Chicago: The University of Chicago Press, 1980) p. 53. Although Jewish and an agnostic, Shils struck up a friendship with John Paul II and seems to have seen him regularly.
37 E. E. Evans-Pritchard, *Theories of Primitive Religion* (Oxford: Clarendon Press, 1965) p. 121.
38 Ibid., pp. 14–17.
39 J. K. Huysmans, *En Route*, tr. W. Fleming (Cambridge: Dedalus, 1989) pp. 92–5. Durtal's appreciation of these women's voices was unusual as he had very definite views that the upper parts should be sung by boys. See p. 52.
40 Alasdair MacIntyre, *After Virtue. a Study in Moral Theory*, 2nd edn (London: Duckworth, 1985).
41 Charles Taylor, *Sources of the Self. The Making of the Modern Identity* (Cambridge: Cambridge University Press, 1992).
42 Romano Guardini, *The End of the Modern World: A Search for Orientation* (London: Sheed & Ward, 1957) p. 99. For a wider discussion of this point, see pp. 95–100.
43 Ibid., p. 106.
44 Ibid., p. 108.
45 Anthony Giddens, *Modernity and Self-Identity. Self and Society in the Late Modern Age* (Cambridge: Polity Press, 1991) p. 9.
46 Ibid., pp. 207–8. See also Phillip A. Mellor, 'Reflexive traditions: Anthony Giddens, high modernity and the contours of Contemporary Religiosity', in *Religious Studies*, vol. 29, 1993, pp. 111–27. Most of this article is

geared to religious studies rather than to the implications of reflexivity for
theology.

47   Oscar Wilde, 'The Critic as Artist', in *The Works of Oscar Wilde* (London:
Galley Press, 1987) pp. 982–3.

48   Paul Heelas, 'The Sacralization of the Self and New Age Capitalism', in
Nicholas Abercrombie and Alan Warde (eds), *Social Change in Contemporary Britain* (Cambridge: Polity Press, 1992) p. 146.

49   Ibid., p. 161. See also his essay 'The New Age in Cultural Context; the
Premodern, the Modern and the Postmodern', in *Religion*, vol. 23, 1993,
pp. 103–16.

50   Anthony Giddens, *The Consequences of Modernity* (Cambridge: Polity Press,
1990) p. 21. Money, experts and forms of *symbolic tokens* that act as the
media interchange effect this process of disembedding.

51   Ibid., p. 49.

52   Charles Taylor, *Sources of the Self*, p. 521.

53   Ivan Illich, *Medical Nemesis. The Expropriation of Health* (London: Calder
& Boyars, 1975). Pain and death are examined in the context of his notion
of 'Structural Iatrogenesis'. See pp. 93–108 and 122–50.

54   Susan Sontag, *Illness as Metaphor* (London: Penguin, 1983).

55   See for example: Sue Scott and David Morgan (eds), *Body Matters: Essays
on the Sociology of the Body* (London: The Falmer Press, 1993); Mike
Featherstone, Mike Hepworth and Bryan S. Turner (eds), *The Body. Social
Process and Cultural Theory* (London: Sage, 1991); and Chris Shilling, *The
Body and Social Theory* (London: Sage Publications, 1993).

56   George Steiner, *Real Presences* (London: Faber and Faber, 1989) p. 3.

57   Peter L. Berger, Brigitte Berger and Hansfried Kellner, *The Homeless Mind*
(London: Penguin, 1973) especially chapter 3, 'Pluralization of Social Life-
Worlds', pp. 62–77. This discussion operates in the context of the link
between the pluralisation and privatisation of religion.

58   Ulrich Beck, *Risk Society. Towards a New Modernity*, tr. Mark Ritter (London: Sage Publications, 1992) p. 98. For another discussion of the implications of risk in relation to the outcomes of decision makers, see Niklas
Luhmann, *Risk: A Sociological Theory*, tr. Rhodes Barrett (Berlin: Walter
de Gruyter, 1993).

59   Ulrich Beck, *Risk Society*, p. 113.

60   Ibid., p. 136.

61   Ibid., p. 214. Again, following other sociologists, Beck sees faith in progress
as the secular religion of modernity, so that the productive forces of business and science have taken the place of God and the Church.

62   See Beck's reply to criticisms of his position, 'Self-Dissolution and Self-
Endangerment of Industrial Society: What Does This Mean?', in Ulrich Beck,
Anthony Giddens, Scott Lash, *Reflexive Modernization*, pp. 174–83.

63   Scott Lash and John Urry, *Economies of Signs and Space* (London: Sage,
1994).

64   Anselm Straus (ed.), *George Herbert Mead on Social Psychology* (Chicago:
Chicago University Press, 1956) Part VI, pp. 199–246. See also John D.
Baldwin, *George Herbert Mead. A Unifying Theory for Sociology* (Newbury
Park, California: Sage Publications, 1986) pp. 106–22.

65   Charles Taylor, *Sources of the Self*, pp. 309–14.

66 Quoted in David Frisby, *Fragments of Modernity. Theories of Modernity in the Work of Simmel, Kracauer and Benjamin* (Cambridge: Polity Press, 1988) p. 29.
67 Keith Tester, *The life and times of post-modernity* (London: Routledge, 1993), p. 127.
68 Robert Bellah *et al.*, *Habits of the Heart. Individualism and Commitment in American Life* (New York: Harper & Row, 1985) p. 75.
69 Ibid., p. 84.
70 Joanne Finkelstein, *The Fashioned Self* (Cambridge: Polity Press, 1991) p. 173.
71 Ibid., p. 187.
72 Blaise Pascal, *Pensées*, tr. A. J. Krailsheimer (London: Penguin, 1966) p. 356.
73 Robert Bellah *et al.*, *Habits of the Heart*, p. 127.
74 Joanne Finkelstein, *The Fashioned Self*, see especially pp. 89–95.
75 Christopher Lasch, *The Culture of Narcissism. American Life in An Age of Diminishing Expectations* (New York: W. W. Norton & Company, 1991).
76 Joanne Finkelstein, *The Fashioned Self*, Chapter 7, 'The Self as Sign', pp. 177–93.
77 Erving Goffman, *Stigma. Notes on the Management of Spoiled Identity* (London: Penguin, 1968).
78 Joanne Finkelstein, *The Fashioned Self*, pp. 173–9.
79 Oscar Wilde, 'The Truth of Masks', in *The Works of Oscar Wilde*, p. 1017.
80 Richard Ellmann, *Oscar Wilde* (London: Hamish Hamilton, 1987) p. 303.
81 Oscar Wilde, *The Picture of Dorian Gray*, in *The Works of Oscar Wilde*, p. 21.
82 Ibid., p. 165.
83 Ibid., pp. 102–4.
84 Jerusha Hull McCormack, *John Gray, Poet, Dandy, and Priest* (Hanover: University Press of New England, 1991) p. 10.
85 Ibid., pp. 38–9.
86 Ibid., pp. 107–8.
87 Ibid., p. 192.
88 Oscar Wilde, *The Picture of Dorian Gray*, p. 101.
89 J. K. Huysmans, *Against Nature*, tr. Robert Baldick (London: Penguin, 1959), p. 36.
90 Kieran Flanagan, 'J. K. Huysmans: The First-Postmodernist Saint?', in *New Blackfriars*, vol. 71, no. 838, May 1990, pp. 217–29. The comment about choice between the revolver and the cross was made in a review by Barbery d'Aurevilly of *Against Nature* which was compared to Baudelaire's *Les Fleurs du mal*. The reviewer indicated that Baudelaire had chosen the foot of the cross and wondered would Huysmans make the same choice. See Robert Baldick, *The Life of J. K. Huysmans* (Oxford: Clarendon Press, 1955) pp. 90–1.
91 J. K. Huysmans, *La Bas* (London: Dedalus, 1986) pp. 49 and 53.
92 Barry Smart, *Postmodernity* (London: Routledge, 1993) pp. 28–32.
93 Claude Pichois, *Baudelaire*, tr. Graham Robb (London: Hamish Hamilton, 1989) epilogue, pp. 365–6. Inconveniently, Baudelaire linked symbolism with modernity, but hated religious ritual, whereas Huysmans despised

modernity but did link symbolism with religious ritual. The significance of Baudelaire in modern thought is indicated by the two studies of his life and work by two who have made equally significant contributions. See Jean-Paul Sartre, *Baudelaire*, tr. Martin Tunrell (New York: New Directions, 1967) especially pp. 56–61 for comments on his religious attitudes. See also Walter Benjamin, *Charles Baudelaire. A Lyric Poet in The Era of High Capitalism*, tr. Harry Zohn (London: Verso, 1983).

94   Richard Ellmann, *Oscar Wilde*, p. 548.
95   Jerusha Hull McCormack, *John Gray, Poet, Dandy and Priest*, p. 109.
96   Charles Baudelaire, 'The Painter of Modern Life', in *The Painter of Modern Life*, tr. Jonathan Mayne (London: Phaidon Press, 1964) pp. 1–40. See especially pp. 12–13.
97   Patrice Bollon, *Morale du Masque. Merveilleux, Zazous, Dandys, Punks, etc.* (Paris: Éditions du Seuil, 1990).
98   Quoted in Graeme Gilloch, 'The Heroic Pedestrian or the Pedestrian Hero? Walter Benjamin and the Flâneur', in *Telos*, no. 91, Spring 1992, p. 116.
99   George de Huszar, 'Nietzsche's theory of decadence and the transvaluation of all values', in *Journal of the History of Ideas*, vol. 6, no. 3, June 1945, p. 267.
100   J. P. Stern, *Nietzsche* (London: Fontana, 1978) pp. 120–1.
101   Johann Wolfgang von Goethe, *Faust*, tr. Phillip Wayne (London: Penguin, 1959) part II, p. 77.
102   Christopher Marlowe, *Doctor Faustus*, David Bevington and Eric Rasmussen (eds) (Manchester: Manchester University Press, 1993) pp. 115–16.
103   Ibid., p. 138.
104   Paul Tillich, *Theology of Culture* (New York: Oxford University Press, 1959) p. 28.
105   Kieran Flanagan, *Sociology and Liturgy*, pp. 105–14.
106   Thomas À Kempis, *The Imitation of Christ*, tr. Leo Sherley-Price (London: Penguin, 1952) p. 149. See also the section on the evils of vain curiosity, pp. 126–7.
107   Jean Leclercq, *The Love of Learning and the Desire for God: a Study of Monastic Culture*, tr. Catherine Misrahi, 3rd edn (New York: Fordham University Press, 1982) Chapter 9, 'Monastic Theology'. Leclercq regards religious knowledge in this setting as knowledge of the self and of God. See pp. 220–2.
108   J. K. Huysmans, *En Route*, p. 313.
109   Alice Walker, *Possessing the Secret of Joy* (London: Jonathan Cape, 1992).
110   Bryan S. Turner, *Religion and Social Theory* (Newbury Park, California: Sage Publications, 1991) p. 246.
111   Chris Rojek, *Ways of Escape. Modern Transformations in Leisure and Travel* (London: Macmillan, 1993).
112   Max Weber, *From Max Weber. Essays in Sociology*, tr. H. H. Gerth and C. Wright Mills (eds) (New York: Oxford University Press, 1958) pp. 155–6.
113   Quoted in Edward C. Jandy, *Charles Horton Cooley. His Life and his Social Theory* (New York: Octagon Books, 1969) p. 233.
114   J. K. Huysmans, *Against Nature*, pp. 219–20.

3 Theology and Culture: An Ambiguous Encounter

1   Bryan S. Turner, *Orientalism, Postmodernism and Globalisation* (London: Routledge, 1994) pp. 185–6.

2   Jean-Paul Willaime, 'Le Croire, l'acteur et le chercheur. Introduction au dossier "Croire et Modernite",' in *Archives de Sciences Sociales des Religions*, vol. 81, Janvier–Mars, 1993, p. 11.

3   John Finney, *Finding Faith Today. How does it happen?*, Swindon: British and Foreign Bible Society, 1992, Chapter 4, 'Factors leading to faith', especially pp. 43–7.

4   William James, *The Varieties of Religious Experience* (New York: Longmans, Green, & Co., 1902) p. 210.

5   David Martin, 'Profane Habit and Sacred Usage', in *Theology*, vol. 82, no. 686, March 1979, pp. 83–4.

6   Andrew Louth, *Discerning the Mystery. An Essay on the Nature of Theology* (Oxford: Clarendon Press, 1989) see especially Chapter VI, 'Living the Mystery', pp. 132–47.

7   Henri J. M. Nouwen, *Behold the Beauty of the Lord. Praying with Icons* (Notre Dame, Indiana: Ave Maria Press, 1987) Chapter III 'The Icon of the Savior of Zvenigorod. Seeing Christ', pp. 45–56. See also Michael Quenot, *The Icon. Window on the Kingdom*, tr. a Carthusian Monk (London: Mowbray, 1992).

8   Nesteros to Cassian quoted in Wulstan Mork, *The Benedictine Way* (Petersham, Massachusetts: St. Bede's Publications, 1987) p. 33.

9   This was a continual theme in von Balthasar's writings from as early as 1948 or before. See Bede McGregor and Thomas Norris (eds), *The Beauty of Christ. An Introduction to the Theology of Hans Urs von Balthasar* (Edinburgh: T. & T. Clark, 1994) p. 5. For an important essay that reflects on this theme see Aidan Nichols, 'The Habit of Theology and how to aquire it', in *The Downside Review*, vol. 105, no. 361, 1987. Nichols cites a comment of von Balthasar that all theology should be 'theology on one's knees' and that if one has to chose between a praying and non-praying theologian, the former is to be followed as a decided preference. See pp. 257–8.

10   Hans Urs von Balthasar, *The Glory of the Lord. A Theological Aesthetics*, vol. I, *Seeing the Form*, tr. Erasmo Leiva-Merikakis (Edinburgh: T. & T. Clark, 1982) pp. 286–7.

11   Ibid., p. 75.

12   John Orme Mills, 'The Introduction of Two Minds', in David Martin, John Orme Mills and W. S. F. Pickering (eds), *Sociology and Theology: Alliance and Conflict* (Brighton: The Harvester Press, 1980) p. 5.

13   Timothy Radcliffe, 'Relativizing the Relativizers: a theologian's assessment of the role of sociological explantion of religious phenomena and theology today' in ibid., pp. 161–2.

14   David A. Fraser and Tony Campolo, *Sociology Through the Eyes of Faith* (London: Apollos, 1992) p. 309.

15   Garrett Green, 'The Sociology of Dogmatics: Niklas Luhmann's Challenge to Theology', in *The Journal of the American Academy of Religion*, vol. 4, no. 1, 1982, p. 20.

16   Ibid., pp. 23–4. A similar theme is pursued in Kieran Flanagan, *Sociology*

and Liturgy: Re-presentation of the Holy (London: Macmillan, 1991). Chapter 6 'Holy and Unholy Rites: Lies and Mistakes in Liturgy', pp. 150–85.

17 Niklas Luhmann, 'Society, Meaning, Religion – Based on Self-Reference', in *Sociological Analysis*, vol. 46, no. 1, 1985, p. 9.

18 See Colleen McDannell and Bernhard Lang, *Heaven. A History* (London: Yale University Press, 1988) and the special issue on hell in *New Blackfriars*, vol. 69, no. 821, November 1988. In Catholicism, at least, matters have been considerably re-adjusted with a new emphasis on traditional notions of heaven and hell. See the *Cathechism of the Catholic Church* (London: Geoffrey Chapman, 1994) article 12, pp. 233–41.

19 Niklas Luhmann, 'Society, Meaning Religion', p. 15.

20 Zygmunt Bauman, *Intimations of Postmodernity* (London: Routledge, 1992) p. 209.

21 Ibid., p. 143.

22 John Milbank, *Theology and Social Theory. Beyond Secular Reason* (Oxford: Basil Blackwell, 1990) pp. 380–1.

23 Richard H. Roberts, 'Transcendental Sociology? A Critique of John Milbank's *Theology and Social Theory. Beyond Secular Reason*', in *Scottish Journal of Theology*, vol. 46, 1993, pp. 527–35. See also Kieran Flanagan, preface and 'Sublime Policing: Sociology and Milbank's City of God', in a special issue of *New Blackfriars*, vol. 73, no. 861, June 1992, pp. 302–4 and pp. 333–41. As far as one is aware, the only main sociology journal review it received was mine in *The British Journal of Sociology*, vol. 44, no. 2, June 1993, pp. 360–1.

24 Richard H. Roberts, 'Transcendental Sociology', p. 534.

25 David Martin, *The Breaking of the Image. A Sociology of Christian Theory and Practice* (Oxford: Basil Blackwell, 1980) p. 1.

26 Peter L. Berger, *The Social Reality of Religion* (London: Penguin, 1973) Appendix II 'Sociological and Theological Perspectives, pp. 181–90.

27 Robin Gill, 'Sociologists and Theologians: A Comparison', in *Sociological Focus*, vol. 23, no. 3, August 1990, pp. 167–75.

28 Arnold Nash, 'Some Reflections upon the Sociological Approach to Theology', in *International Yearbook for the Sociology of Religion*, vol. 2, 1966, see especially p. 197.

29 Peter L. Berger, 'A Sociological view of the Secularization of Theology', in *Journal for the Scientific Study of Religion*, vol. 5, 1966, p. 10.

30 Ibid., p. 13.

31 Avery Dulles, *The Craft of Theology. From Symbol to System* (Dublin: Gill and Macmillan, 1992) pp. 160–3.

32 Ibid., Chapter 6, 'Tradition as a Theological Source' pp. 87–104.

33 Hans Frei, *Types of Christian Theology*, George Hunsinger and William C. Placher (eds) (New Haven: Yale University Press, 1992) p. 22.

34 Peter L. Berger, *A Rumour of Angels*, 2nd edn (New York: Anchor Books, 1990) p. 32.

35 Hugh Montefiore, *The Church Times*, 7th January 1994.

36 Alister E. McGrath, *The Renewal of Anglicanism* (London: SPCK, 1993) Chapter 2, 'A Lost Generation', pp. 37–53.

37 Ibid., p. 122.

38 George Lindbeck, *The Nature of Doctrine: Religion and Theology in a*

Postliberal Age (Philadelphia: The Westminster Press, 1984). The 'cultural linguistic' arguments of this book appealed more to theologians than to sociologists, few of whom use or know of this pivotal work. For an extended treatment of this study see the special issue of *Modern Theology*, vol. 4, no. 2, January 1988.

39 Alister E. McGrath, *The Renewal of Anglicanism*, p. 132.

40 Ibid., p. 164.

41 David Lodge, *Paradise News* (London: Penguin, 1992) pp. 35–6.

42 Thomas Aquinas, *Summa Theologiae* (London: Eyre & Spottiswoode, 1964) vol. 1, p. 3.

43 Ibid., p. 33.

44 Ibid., vol. 23, p. 145.

45 Ibid., vol. 39, p. 15.

46 Ibid., p. 29.

47 Ibid., p. 107.

48 John Paul II, *Veritatis Splendor* (Vatican City: Libreria Editrice Vaticana, 1993) p. 133.

49 Joseph Ratzinger, '*Communio*: a program', in *Communio*, vol. 19, no. 3, Fall 1992, pp. 436–49.

50 Aidan Nichols, *The Shape of Catholic Theology* (Edinburgh: T. & T. Clark, 1991) pp. 341–355.

51 Matthew L. Lamb 'Inulturation and Western culture: the dialogical experience between gospel and culture', in *Communio*, vol. 21, no. 1, Spring 1994, pp. 139–40.

52 *Instruction on the Ecclesial Vocation of the Theologian* (London: CTS/ Veritas, 1990) p. 9.

53 Brian Wicker, *Culture and Liturgy* (London: Sheed and Ward, 1963) p. 39.

54 *Pastoral Constitution on the Church in the Modern World* (*Gaudium et Spes*) in Austin Flannery (ed.), *Vatican II. The Conciliar and Post Conciliar Documents*, Dublin: Dominican Publications, 1975, Chapter II, 'Proper Development of Culture', pp. 958–68.

55 Ibid., pp. 966–7. Little attention was paid by the document to the role of sociology in constituting the culture theology was to understand. The expectation that sociology, with other behavioural sciences, was to nurture 'a purer and more mature living of the faith' has never been properly understood or confronted as a theological issue.

56 Catherine Bell, 'The Authority of Ritual Experts', in *Studia Liturgica*, vol. 23, 1993, pp. 98–120. For a general overview of the sociological and cultural implications of liturgy see M. Francis Mannion, 'Liturgy and the Present Crisis of Culture', in *Worship*, vol. 62, no. 2, March 1988, pp. 98–123.

57 Enda McDonagh, 'The Church in the Modern World (*Gaudium et Spes*)' in Adrian Hastings (ed.), *Modern Catholicism: Vatican II and After* (London: SPCK, 1991) p. 101. Referring to the Holocaust, McDonagh does note that in *Gaudium et Spes*, a 'sense of the tragic is largely missing from its worldview as the cross is from its theology'. See p. 110.

58 Dermot A. Lane, 'Faith and Culture: the Challenge of Inculturation', in Dermot A. Lane (ed.), *Religion and Culture in Dialogue. A Challenge for the next Millenium* (Dublin: The Columbia Press, 1993) p. 34.

238 *Notes and References to pp. 72–5*

59   Urban T. Holmes, 'Liminality and Liturgy', in *Worship*, vol. 47, no. 7, 1973, pp. 386–7.
60   Crispian Hollis, 'Mass media: the language of our culture', in *Briefings*, 14 October 1993, p. 12.
61   Bernard Lambert, '*Gaudium et Spes* and the Travail of Today's Ecclesial Conception', in Joseph Gremillion (ed.), *The Church and Culture since Vatican II. The Experience of North and Latin America* (Notre Dame, Indiana, University of Notre Dame Press, 1985) p. 37.
62   *Gaudium et Spes*, in Austin Flannery (ed.), *Vatican II. The Conciliar and Post Conciliar Documents*, p. 910.
63   Joe Holland, 'The Cultural Vision of Pope John Paul II: Toward a Conservative/Liberal Postmodern Dialogue', in David Ray Griffin, William A. Beardslee and Joe Holland, *Varieties of Postmodern Theology* (New York: State University of New York Press, 1989) pp. 111–13.
64   Gregory Baum, *Theology and Society* (New York: Paulist Press, 1987) pp. 51. This comment arises in the context of labour. Baum refers to the notion of commodity fetishism (not a term of John Paul II). This is a process that bears amplification and reflects a mutual interest of theology and sociology in dealing with culture, a point developed later in this study.
65   Reproduced in Joseph Gremillion (ed.), *The Church and Culture since Vatican II*, p. 200.
66   Ibid., p. 317.
67   W. J. Hill, entry on theology in *New Catholic Encyclopaedia* (Palatine, Illinois: J. Heraty, 1981) vol. 17, 1978, p. 652.
68   John Paul II, *Centesimus Annus*, London: Catholic Truth Society, 1991, p. 38.
69   Ibid., p. 41.
70   Michael P. Hornsby-Smith, *Roman Catholics in England: Studies in Social Structure since the Second World War* (Cambridge: Cambridge University Press, 1987) and *The Changing Parish. A study of Parishes, Priests, and Parishioners after Vatican II* (London: Routledge, 1989). Hornsby-Smith has made an incalculable contribution to the growth of a sociology of Catholicism in the United Kingdom.
71   Julien Potel, *L'Église Catholique en France. Approches Sociologiques* (Paris: Descelée de Brouwer, 1994).
72   For a useful discussion of the origins and significance of the term, see volumes 7–10 of *Inculturation. Working papers on Living Faith and Cultures* edited by Arij A. Roest Crollius (Rome: Pontifical Gregorian University, 1986 and 1987). See also Kieran Flanagan, 'Theological pluralism: a sociological critique', in Ian Hamnett (ed.), *Religious Pluralism and Unbelief. Studies Critical and Comparative* (London: Routledge, 1990) especially pp. 99–102. The term inculturation can be used in an uncritical sociological manner as a form of consciousness raising for indigenous cultures and as a means of escaping Eurocentrism. See for example Aylward Shorter, *Evangelization and Culture* (London: Geoffrey Chapman, 1994) especially pp. 32–8.
73   Giancarlo Collet, 'From Theological Vandalism to Theological Romanticism? Questions about a Multicultural identity of Christianity', in Norbert Greinacher and Norbert Mette (eds.), *Christianity and Cultures. Concilium* (London: SCM Press, 1994) p. 34.

74   John Webster, 'Locality and Catholicity: Reflections on and the Church', in *Scottish Journal of Theology*, vol. 45, no. 1, 1992, p. 5.

75   Gregory Baum, 'Two Question Marks: Inculturation and Multiculturalism', in Norbert Greinacher and Norbert Mette (eds), *Christianity and Cultures*, p. 102.

76   *Catechism of the Catholic Church*, p. 198.

77   Ibid., pp. 274–5.

78   Thomas Day, *Why Catholics Can't Sing. The Culture of Catholicism and the Triumph of Bad Taste* (New York: Crossroad, 1993).

79   Matthew L. Lamb, 'Inculturation and Western culture: the dialogical experience between gospel and culture', pp. 132–44.

80   Press release of Matthew Fox, a former Dominican and creation theologian on joining the American Episcopal Church, 15th April 1994.

81   Christina Scott, *A Historian and his World. A Life of Christopher Dawson 1889–1970* (London: Sheed & Ward, 1984) p. 206.

82   David Lowenthal, *The Past is a Foreign Country* (Cambridge: Cambridge University Press, 1985). For a useful appreciation of the French sociologist Danièle Hervieu-Léger and her book *La religion pour mémoire*, see Grace Davie, 'Religion and modernity: A French Contribution to the Debate', in Kieran Flanagan and Peter Jupp, (eds), *Postmodernity, sociology and religion* (London: Macmillan, 1996).

83   Zoltan Alszeghy and Maurizio Flick, *Introductory Theology* (London: Sheed and Ward, 1982) pp. 40–1.

84   Ibid., p. 63.

85   Ibid., pp. 70–1.

86   Ibid., pp. 90–1.

87   Owen Chadwick, *The Secularization of the European Mind in the 19th Century* (Cambridge: Cambridge University Press, 1990).

88   Zoltan Alszeghy and Maurizio Flick, *Introductory Theology*, pp. 129–30.

89   Paul Tillich, *Theology of Culture* (New York: Oxford University Press, 1959) pp. 42–3.

90   Ibid., pp. 57–8.

91   Ibid., p. 60.

92   H. Richard Niebuhr, *Christ and Culture* (New York: Harper & Row, 1975) pp. 241–9.

93   Ibid., p. 69.

94   Ibid., pp. 107–15.

95   Ibid., p. 135.

96   Ibid., p. 212.

97   Ibid., pp. 222–4.

98   Max Weber, *The Protestant Ethic and the Spirit of Capitalism*, tr. Talcott Parsons (London: Unwin University Books, 1930) p. 40. Weber's somewhat equivocal views on Catholicism, the issue of its rights and expansion in higher education in relation to a Protesant conception of German culture, have been discussed by Gary A. Abraham, 'Context and prejudice in Max Weber's thought: criticisms of Wilhelm Hennis', in *History of the Human Sciences*, vol. 6, no. 3, August 1993, pp. 1–17. See also in ibid. the reply of Hennis, pp. 19–23.

99   Avery Dulles, *The Craft of Theology*, p. 22. The remainder of chapter 2 on theology and symbolic communication is of relevance.

240   Notes and References to pp. 83–91

100 Peter L. Berger, *A Far Glory. A Quest for Faith in an Age of Credulity* (New York: Doubleday, 1993) pp. 139–40.
101 Rohit Barot (ed.), *Religion and Ethnicity: Minorities and Social Change in the Metropolis* (Kampen-the Netherlands: Kok Pharos, 1993).
102 Paul Morris, 'Judaism and pluralism: the price of "religious freedom"', in Ian Hamnett (ed.), *Religious Pluralism and Unbelief*, pp. 179–201.
103 Kieran Flanagan, 'Theological pluralism: a sociological critique', in Ian Hamnett (ed.), *Religious Pluralism and Unbelief*, p. 89.
104 Gavin D'Costa, 'The End of "Theology" and "Religious Studies"', in *Theology*, vol. 99, no. 788, March 1996.
105 This discussion is summarised from Aidan Nichols, *The Shape of Catholic Theology*, pp. 263–310.
106 Pauline Matarasso (ed. and tr.), *The Cistercian World. Monastic Writings of the Twelfth Century* (London: Penguin, 1993) p. 154.
107 Jean Leclerq, *The Love of Learning and Desire for God: a Study of Monastic Culture*, 3rd edn (New York: Fordham University Press, 1982) pp. 217–24.
108 J. Huizinga, *The Waning of the Middle Ages*, tr. F. Hopman (London: Penguin, 1955) p. 148.
109 For a discussion of the significance of the Pseudo-Denys in a wider context see Hans Urs von Balthasar, *The Glory of the Lord. A Theological Aesthetics*, vol. II, *Studies in Theological Style: Clerical Styles*, tr. Andrew Louth, Frances McDonagh and Brian McNeil (Edinburgh: T. & T. Clark, 1984) pp. 144–210. See also Paul Rorem, *Biblical and Liturgical Symbols within the Pseudo-Dionysian Synthesis* (Toronto: Pontifical Institute of Mediaeval Studies, 1948).
110 J. K. Huysmans, *The Cathedral*, tr. Clara Bell (Cambridge: Dedalus, 1989). It would difficult to find an equivalent work that marries interior spiritual sensibility to aesthetic reflection. The book endeavours to capture and to decipher the mysteries of the Gothic, Chartres in this case, in the fullness of its theological and symbolic implications. To some extent, the book is a model for this study and its treatment of habitus and the religious field.
111 Aidan Nichols, *The Shape of Catholic Theology*, pp. 321–3.
112 Pierre Bourdieu, *Homo Academicus*, tr. Peter Collier (Cambridge: Polity Press, 1988) p. 63.
113 John Kingman, *Truth in the University. The E. H. Young Lecture* (University of Bristol, 1993).
114 See Andrew Wernick, *Promotional Culture. Advertising, Ideology and Symbolic Expression* (London: Sage, 1991) chapter 7 'The promotional university', pp. 154–80.
115 See Gavin D'Costa, 'The End of "Theology" and "Religious Studies"', section I 'on (not) doing theology in the University'.
116 See David Bebbington, 'The Secularization of British Universities since the Mid-Nineteenth Century', in George M. Marsden and Bradley J. Longfield, (eds), *The Secularization of the Academy* (New York: Oxford University Press, 1992) pp. 259–77.
117 George M. Marsden, 'The Soul of the American University: A Historical Overivew' in ibid., pp. 35–6.
118 Robert Wood Lynn, ' "The Survival of Recognizably Protestant Colleges": Reflections on Old-Line Protestantism, 1950–1990', in ibid., pp. 170–4.

119 D. G. Hart, 'American Learning and the Problem of Religious Studies' in ibid., pp. 219–20.
120 Ursula King (ed.), *Turning Points in Religious Studies. Essays in Honour of Geoffrey Parrinder* (Edinburgh: T. & T. Clark, 1990) pp. 302–4.
121 Adrian Cunningham, 'Religious Studies in the Universities. England' in ibid., pp. 29–31.
122 Daniel Cere, 'Newman, God and the Academy', in *Theological Studies*, vol. 55, 1994, pp. 5–9.
123 Ibid., p. 15.
124 Phillip Gleason, 'American Catholic Higher Education, 1940–1990: The ideological context', in George M. Marsden and Bradley J. Longfied (eds), *The Secularization of the Academy*, pp. 234–58.
125 Reproduced in *Briefings*, 21 July 1994, p. 9.
126 Ibid., p. 4.
127 David F. Ford, *A Long Rumour of Wisdom. Resdescribing Theology* (Cambridge: Cambridge University Press, 1992) p. 27.
128 Ibid., pp. 12–13.
129 *Report on the Organisation of the Permanent Civil Service* in *Papers relating to the re-organization of the Civil Service, 1854–55* [1870] XX. See also Edward Hughes, 'Civil Service Reform 1853–5', *Public Administration*, vol. 32, 1854, pp. 17–51.
130 David H. Kelsey, *Between Athens and Berlin. The Theological Education Debate* (Grand Rapids, Michigan: William B. Eerdmans Publishing Company, 1993) p. 34. Kelsey notes the way this links to Newman's idea of habits of learning and the virtues these secure for character.
131 Kieran Flanagan, 'The Godless and the Burlesque: Newman and the other Irish Universities', in James D. Bastable (ed.), *Newman and Gladstone Centennial Essays* (Dublin: Veritas Publications, 1978) pp. 239–77.
132 John Henry Newman, *The Idea of a University* (New York: Doubleday, 1959) p. 96.
133 Ibid., pp. 124–6.
134 David H. Kelsey, *To Understand God Truly. What's Theological about a Theological School* (Louisville, Kentucky: Westminster/John Know Press, 1992) p. 110.
135 Ibid., pp. 135–42.

4 The Disappearance of God: The Secularisation of Sociology

1 Keith Tester, *The Life and Times of Post-modernity* (London: Routledge, 1993) pp. 73–8.
2 Zygmunt Bauman, *Intimations of Postmodernity* (London: Routledge, 1992) pp. xxiv.
3 David Lyon, *The Steeple's Shadow: on the Myths and Realities of Secularization* (London: SPCK, 1985) p. 20.
4 Blaise Pascal, *Pensées*, tr. A. J. Krailsheimer (London: Penguin, 1966) p. 150.
5 George Steiner, *Real Presences* (London: Faber & Faber, 1989) pp. 24–7.
6 Zygmunt Bauman, *Hermeneutics and Social Science. Approaches to Understanding* (London: Hutchinson, 1978) pp. 172–3.

7   See for example Don Martindale, *The Nature and Types of Sociological Theory* (Boston: Houghton Mifflin, 1960).

8   James A. Beckford, *Religion and Advanced Industrial Society* (London: Unwin Hyman, 1989) p. 6.

9   Hubert Dreyfus and Paul Rainbow, 'Can there be a Science of Existential Structure and Social Meaning', in Craig Calhoun, Edward LiPuma and Moishe Postone, (eds), *Bourdieu. Critical Perspectives* (Cambridge: Polity Press, 1993) p. 41.

10   H. Stuart Hughes, *Consciousness and Society. The Reorientation of European Social Thought 1890–1930* (New York: Random House, 1958) pp. 342–3.

11   Roger Martin du Gard, *Jean Barois*, tr. Stuart Gilbert (London: The Bodley Head, 1950) p. 318.

12   Ibid., pp. 342–51.

13   See preface by W. S. F. Pickering to Robert Hertz, *Sin and Expiation in Primitive Societies*, tr. Robert Parkin (Oxford: British Centre for Durkheimian Studies, 1994) pp. 5–12.

14   D. G. Charlton, *Secular Religions in France 1815–1870* (Oxford: Oxford University Press, 1963) pp. 92–3.

15   Wolf Lepenies, *Between Literature and Science: the Rise of Sociology*, tr. R. J. Hollingdale (Cambridge: Cambridge University Press, 1988) pp. 41–2.

16   Henri de Lubac, *The Drama of Atheist Humanism*, tr. Edith M. Riley, (London: Sheed and Ward 1949) pp. 158–9. See also Hans Urs von Balthasar, *The Theology of Henri de Lubac. An Overview*, tr. Susan Clements (San Francisco: Ignatius Press, 1991) especially Chapter 3, 'The Two "Atheisms"', pp. 45–59.

17   John Milbank, *Theology and Social Theory. Beyond Secular Reason* (Oxford: Basil Blackwell, 1990) p. 56.

18   Ibid., p. 52.

19   Wolf Lepenies, *Between Literature and Science: the Rise of Sociology*, p. 71.

20   Ibid., Chapter 8, 'Hostility to science and faith in poetry as a German ideology', pp. 203–19.

21   Guy Oakes, introduction in *Georg Simmel. Essays on Interpretation in Social Sciences*, tr. Guy Oakes (Manchester: Manchester University Press, 1980) p. 37.

22   Dirk Käsler, *Max Weber. An Introduction to his Life and Work*, tr. Phillipa Hurd (Cambridge: Polity Press, 1988) pp. 74–94.

23   William H. Swatos, Jr. and Peter Kivisto, 'Weber as "Christian Sociologist"', in *Journal for the Scientific Study of Religion*, vol. 30, no. 4, December 1991, pp. 347–62.

24   Martin Albrow, *Max Weber's Construction of Social Reality* (London: Macmillan, 1990) p. 45.

25   Max Weber, *From Max Weber: Essays in Sociology*, tr. H. H. Gerth and C. Wright Mills (eds) (New York: Oxford University Press, 1958) pp. 153–5. See also David Owen, *Maturity and Modernity: Nietzsche, Weber and Foucault, and the Ambivalence of Reason* (London: Routledge, 1994) pp. 113–22. See also the essay by Robert K. Merton, 'Puritanism, Pietism and Science' in his *Social Theory and Social Structure* (New York: The Free Press, 1968 edition) pp. 628–60.

26   Lawrence A. Scaff, *Fleeing the Iron Cage: Culture, Politics and Modernity in the Thought of Max Weber* (Berkeley: University of California Press, 1991) p. 151.

27   Ibid., p. 225.

28   C. Wright Mills, *The Sociological Imagination* (New York: Grove Press, 1961) pp. 171–2.

29   Emile Durkheim, *Suicide*, tr. John A. Spaulding and George Simpson (New York: The Free Press, 1966).

30   This has been a widely discussed theme in the history of sociology. See for example Geoffrey Hawthorn, *Enlightenment and Despair. A History of Sociology* (Cambridge: Cambridge University Press, 1976) Chapter 9, 'History Ignored' pp. 191–216. Swatos has suggested that there was nothing specifically Protestant about American sociology but that it did assimilate the dominant culture of Protestantism in its period of formation in the late nineteenth century. Its development involved a shift from religious sociology to sociology of religion as a mere specialism (and hence into the secularisation of the discipline). See William H. Swatos, Jr., 'Religious Sociology and the Sociology of Religion in America at the Turn of the Twentieth Century: Divergences from a Common Theme', in *Sociological Analysis*. vol. 50, no. 4, 1989, pp. 363–75. Comments on the expansion of sociology in the late nineteenth century make reference to Protestant influences on seminal figures such as William Sumner, Albion Small, and Charles Horton Cooley. These figures brought rural Protestant Mid-Western values to the study of urban and industrial life and gave early American sociology a concern with moral progress, a worry that became often a crusade of outsiders on what seemed the unAmerican activities and customs of city life. See Roscoe C. Hinkle, Jr, and Gisela J. Hinkle, *The Development of Modern Sociology. Its Nature and Growth in the United States* (New York: Random House, 1954) pp. 3–4 and 7–14.

31   James A. Beckford, *Religion and Advanced Industrial Society* (London: Unwin Hyman, 1989) p. 51. See also pp. 49–55.

32   Phillip Abrams, *The Origins of British Sociology, 1834–1914* (Chicago: University of Chicago Press, 1968).

33   Ian Hamnett, 'A Mistake about Error', in *New Blackfriars*, vol. 67, no. 788, February 1986, pp. 69–78.

34   A. H. Halsey, 'Provincials and Professionals: The British Post-War Sociologists', in *LSE Quarterly*, vol. 1, no. 1, March 1987, pp. 43–74.

35   Wolf Lepenies, *Between Literature and Science: the Rise of Sociology*, chapters 5–6, pp. 145–95.

36   Christopher G. A. Bryant and Henk A. Becker (eds), *What Has Sociology Achieved?* (London: Macmillan, 1990). See chapters in relation to France, Germany and Holland.

37   John Westergaard and Ray Pahl, 'Looking backwards and forwards: the UCG's review of sociology', in *The British Journal of Sociology*, vol. 40, no. 3, 1989, pp. 374–91. See also John Eldridge, 'Sociology in Britain; A Going Concern', in Christopher G. A. Bryant and Henk A. Becker (eds), *What has Sociology Achieved?*, pp. 157–78.

38   James V. Spickard, 'Texts and Contexts: Recent Trends in the Sociology of Religion as Reflected in US textbooks', in *Social Compass*, vol. 41, no. 3, 1994, pp. 313–28.

39   Karel Dobbelaere, 'CISR, An Alternative Approach to Sociology of Religion in Europe: ACSS and CISR Compared', in *Sociological Anlaysis*, vol. 50, no. 4, 1989, pp. 377–87.

40   Gregory Baum, 'Sociology and Salvation: Do We Need a Catholic Sociology?', in *Theological Studies*, vol. 50, 1989, p. 721.

41   Loretta M. Morris, 'Secular Transcendence: from ACSS to ASR', in *Sociological Analysis*, 1989, vol. 50, no. 4, pp. 329–49.

42   Peter Kivisto, 'The Brief Career of Catholic Sociology', in ibid. pp. 351–61.

43   Max Weber, *From Max Weber: Essays in Sociology*, pp. 153–4.

44   Gregory Baum, 'Sociology and Salvation: Do we Need a Catholic Sociology?', pp. 742–3.

45   Stanislav Andreski, *Social Sciences as Sorcery* (London: Penguin, 1974) pp. 31–2.

46   James Beckford, 'The Insulation and Isolation of the Sociology of Religion', in *Sociological Analysis*, vol. 46, no. 4, 1985, p. 350. For an overview of British research in sociology of religion, see Roy Wallis and Steve Bruce, 'Religion: the British contribution', in *The British Journal of Sociology*, vol. 40, no. 3, 1989, pp. 493–520.

47   James A. Beckford, *Religion and Advanced Industrial Society*, pp. 13–17.

48   Friedrich Nietzsche, *The Will to Power*, Walter Kaufmann (ed.) tr. Walter Kaufmann and R. J. Hollingdale (New York: Random House, 1968) p. 33.

49   Bryan Wilson, *Religion in Sociological Perspective* (Oxford: Oxford University Press, 1982) p. 149.

50   Bryan Wilson, 'Reflections on a Many Sided Controversy', in Steve Bruce (ed.), *Religion and Modernization. Sociologists and Historians Debate the Secularization Thesis* (Oxford: Clarendon Press, 1992) p. 210.

51   Stephen L. Carter, *The Culture of Disbelief: How American Law and Politics Trivialize Religious Devotion* (New York: Basic Books, 1993) p. 60.

52   Quoted in ibid., p. 81.

53   Franco Ferrarotti, *Faith without Dogma. The Place of Religion in Postmodern Societies* (New Brunswick: Transaction Publishers, 1993) p. 141.

54   George Steiner, *Real Presences*, p. 178.

55   Blaise Pascal, *Pensées*, p. 66.

56   Alasdair MacIntyre, *After Virtue. A Study in Moral Theory*, 2nd edn (London: Duckworth, 1985) pp. 11–12.

57   Ibid., pp. 26–7. See also Lawrence A. Scaff, *Fleeing the Iron Cage*, pp. 127–33; Martin Albrow, *Max Weber's Construction of Social Theory*, Chapter 3, 'The Nietzschean Challenge', pp. 46–61 and Georg Stauth, 'Nietzsche, Weber, and afirmative sociology of culture', in *European Journal of Sociology*, vol. 33, 1992, pp. 219–47.

58   Friedrich Nietzsche, *Ecce Homo*, tr. R. J. Hollingdale (London: Penguin, 1979) especially pp. 114–15.

59   Ibid., p. 50.

60   Zygmunt Bauman. *Modernity and the Holocaust* (Cambridge: Polity Press, 1991) pp. 218–21.

61   Thomas Aquinas, *Summa Theologiae*, vol. 11 (London: Eyre & Spottiswoode, 1964) p. 223. See also question 83 on freewill, pp. 237–49.

62   Gianni Vattimo, *The End of Modernity. Nihilism and Hermeneutics in*

Post-modern Culture, tr. Jon R. Snyder (Cambridge: Polity Press, 1991) pp. 99–103.

63 Fyodor Dostoyevsky, *The Brothers Karamazov*, tr. David Magarshack (London: Folio Society, 1964) p. 285.

64 Robert W. Friedrichs, *A Sociology of Sociology* (New York: The Free Press, 1970). Theological metaphors riddle this work as it endeavours to characterise the relationship between sociology and its moral responsibilities.

65 Steven Connor, *Theory and Cultural Value* (Oxford: Blackwell, 1992) p. 102.

66 Stjepan G. Mestrovic, *The Coming Fin de Siècle. An Application of Durkheim's Sociology to Modernity and Postmodernism* (London: Routledge, 1992) pp. 210–11.

67 Ibid., p. 19.

68 Huston Smith, 'Secularization and the Sacred: The Contemporary Science', in Donald R. Culter (ed.), *The Religious Situation: 1968* (Boston: Beacon Press, 1968) p. 595.

69 David Martin, 'The secularization issue; prospect and retrospect', in *The British Journal of Sociology*, vol. 42, no. 3, September 1991, p. 466.

70 Ian Hamnett, 'Sociology of Religion and Sociology of Error', in *Religion*, vol. 3, Spring 1973, pp. 1–12.

71 Danièle Hervieu-Léger, 'Religion and Modernity in the French Context: For a New Approach to Secularization', in *Sociological Analysis*, vol. 51, 1990, p. 24.

72 For some recent reflections on French religious orders, see Paul Lebeau, *La vie religieuse. un chemin d'humanité* (Bruxelles: Vie consacrée, 1992).

73 See Roger Finke, 'An Unsecular America', in Steve Bruce (ed.), *Religion and Modernization* (Oxford: Clarendon Press, 1992) pp. 145–69.

74 Rodney Stark and Laurence R. Iannaccone, 'A Supply-Side Reinterpretation of the "Secularization" of Europe', in *Journal for the Scientific Study of Religion*, vol. 33, no. 3, 1994, p. 249.

75 Walter Daniel, *The Life of Aelred*, in Pauline Matarasso (ed. and tr.), *The Cistercian World. Monastic Writings of the Twelfth Century* (London: Penguin, 1993) p. 153.

76 Rodney Stark and Laurence R. Iannaccone, 'A Supply-side reinterpretaton of the "secularization" of Europe', pp. 241–3.

77 J. Huizinga, *The Waning of the Middle Ages* (London: Penguin, 1955) see especially chapter 23, 'The Advent of the New Form', pp. 307–18.

78 Franco Ferrarotti, *Faith without Dogma*, p. 78.

79 Hans Blumenberg, *The Legitimacy of the Modern Age*, tr. Robert M. Wallace (Cambridge, Mass.: The MIT Press, 1985) p. 104.

80 Ibid., pp. 111–12.

81 Franco Ferrarotti, *Faith Without Dogma*, pp. 127–30.

82 Ibid., p. 136.

83 Ivan Illich, *Medical Nemesis. The Expropriation of Health* (London: Calder & Boyars, 1975) p. 94.

84 Ibid., p. 108.

85 See for example the dialogue between Ivan and Alyosha over the suffering of innocent children and the issue of the existence of God in Fyodor Dostoyevsky, *The Brothers Karamazov*, pp. 266–95.

86   Zygmunt Bauman, *Modernity and the Holocaust*, p. ix.
87   Wolf Lepenies, *Between Literature and Science: the Rise of Sociology*, chapter 15, pp. 334–49.
88   Peter L. Berger, *The Social Reality of Religion* (London: Penguin, 1973) chapters 6–7, pp. 131–73.
89   Peter L. Berger, *The Heretical Imperative. Contemporary Possibilities of Religious Affirmation* (London: Collins, 1980) pp. 10–11.
90   Ibid., pp. 183–4.
91   Robert Wuthnow, *Rediscovering the Sacred. Perspectives on Religion in Contemporary Society* (Grand Rapids, Michigan: Wm. B. Eerdmans, 1992) pp. 29–30.
92   Anthony Giddens, *The Consequences of Modernity* (Cambridge: Polity Press, 1990) p. 43. See also pp. 93–100.
93   Ibid., pp. 79–80.
94   Anthony Giddens, *Modernity and Self-Identity. Self and Society in the Late Modern Age* (Cambridge: Polity Press, 1991) pp. 46–7 and 204.
95   Ibid., p. 207.
96   Anthony Giddens, *The Consequences of Modernity*, pp. 15–16.
97   Joseph Leo Koerner, 'Hans Blumenberg's style', in *History of the Human Sciences*, vol. 6, no. 4, November 1993, pp. 8–9.
98   Bruce Krajewski, 'The musical horizon of religion: Blumenberg's *Matthauspassion*', in ibid., pp. 91–2.
99   Donald R. Kelley, 'Epimetheus restored', in ibid., pp. 97–107.
100 Quoted in Hans Urs von Balthasar, *The Glory of the Lord. A Theological Aesthetics*, vol. II (Edinburgh: T. & T. Clark, 1982) p. 79.
101 Kieran Flanagan, *Sociology and Liturgy: Re-presentations of the Holy* (London: Macmillan, 1991) pp. 89–105.
102 Zygmunt Bauman, *Intimations of Postmodernity*, p. 217 and p. 204.
103 See Tom Nairn, *The Break-Up of Britain. Crisis and Neo-Nationalism*, London: New Left Books, 1977, pp. 359–63 and Benedict Anderson, *Imagined Communities. Reflections on the Origin and Spread of Nationalism* (London: Verso, 1983) Chapter 9, pp. 141–7.
104 Walter Benjamin, *Charles Baudelaire. A Lyric Poet in the Era of High Capitalism*, tr. Harry Zohn (London: Verso, 1983).
105 Gary Smith, (ed.), *On Walter Benjamin. Critical Essays and Recollections* (Cambridge, Massachusetts: The MIT Press, 1991) pp. 329–66.
106 David McLellan, *Simone Weil. Utopian Pessimist* (London: Macmillan, 1989).
107 Walter Benjamin, *Iluminations*, tr. Harry Zohn (New York: Schocken Books, 1969) pp. 257–8.
108 Gershom Scholem, 'Walter Benjamin and His Angel', in Gary Smith (ed.), *On Walter Benjamin*, p. 65. See also Christine Buci-Glucksmann, *Baroque Reason. The Aesthetics of Modernity*, tr. Patrick Camiller (London: Sage Publications, 1994) pp. 39–51. In his introduction, Turner suggests the importance of Benjamin 'lies with his presentation of not a sociology, but a theology of modernity', p. 34. See also Kieran Flanagan, *Sociology and Liturgy*, pp. 89–97.
109 Gershom Scholem, 'Walter Benjamin and His Angel', See pp. 65–6 for reference to the connection between Baudelaire, Benjamin and his interest in Satanism.

110 Ibid., pp. 83–5.

111 Jurgen Habermas, 'Walter Benjamin: Consciousness-Raising or Rescuing Critique', in Gary Smith (ed.), *On Walter Benjamin*, p. 114.

112 Robert Alter, *Necessary Angels. Tradition and Modernity in Kafka, Benjamin and Scholem* (Cambridge, Massachusetts: Harvard University Press, 1991) p. 115. Alter goes on to add that the image of the angel invoked in Benjamin's essays relates to 'the iconography of tradition' one that defines more sharply 'the disasters of secular modernity – the erosion of experience, the decay of wisdom, the loss of redemptive and now in 1940, the universal reign of mass murder'. See pp. 115–16.

113 Ibid., p. 119.

114 George Steiner, *After Babel. Aspects of Language and Translation*, 2nd edn, (Oxford: Oxford University Press, 1992).

115 Irving Wohlfarth, 'On Some Jewish Motifs in Benjamin', in Andrew Benjamin (ed.), *The Problems of Modernity. Adorno and Benjamin* (London: Routledge, 1989) pp. 161–2. John Paul II is not alone in his regard for the wiles of Satan in maintaining an invisibility for Wohlfarth notes that Baudelaire felt that 'one of the devil's most insidious ruses is to persuade us that he does not exist'. See p. 162.

116 Ibid., pp. 180–1.

117 Louis Dupré, *Passage to Modernity: an Essay in the Hermeneutics of Nature and Culture* (New Haven: Yale University Press, 1993).

118 Hans Blumenberg, *The Legitimacy of the Modern Age*, p. 5.

119 Ibid., p. 74.

120 David McLellan, *Karl Marx. Early Texts* (Oxford: Basil Blackwell, 1971) pp. 68–9.

121 Barry Smart, *Postmodernity* (London: Routledge, 1993) pp. 29–32. See also Umberto Eco, *Art and Beauty in the Middle Ages*, tr. Hugh Bredin (New Haven: Yale University Press, 1986).

122 Hans Blumenberg, *The Legitimacy of the Modern Age*, p. 380.

123 Kieran Flanagan, *Sociology and Liturgy*, pp. 105–14.

124 Ibid., pp. 174–85.

125 Hans Blumenberg, *The Legitimacy of the Modern Age*, pp. 237–8.

126 Ibid., pp. 282–3.

127 Hans Urs von Balthasar, *Theo-drama. Theological Dramatic Theory*, vol. II: *Dramatis Personae: Man in God*, tr. Graham Harrison (San Francisco: Ignatius Press, 1990) p. 226.

128 Hans Blumenberg *The Legitimacy of the Modern Age*, p. 346.

129 Ibid., p. 405. Some of these issues are explored in Kieran Flanagan, 'Postmodernity and culture: sociological wagers of the self in theology', in Kieran Flanagan and Peter Jupp (eds), *Postmodernity, Sociology and Religion* (London: Macmillan, 1996).

130 Ibid., p. 355.

131 Ghostly warnings to the curious are a theme in the stories of M. R. James. See for example, '"Oh, whistle, and I'll come to you, my lad"' and 'A warning to the curious' in *The Ghost Stories of M. R. James* (London: Edward Arnold, 1974) pp. 120–50 and 561–87.

132 Hans Blumenberg, *The Legitimacy of the Modern Age*, p. 492.

133 Karl Jaspers, *The Great Philosophers* (London: Rupert Hart-Davis, 1966) p. 166.

134   Hans Blumenberg, *The Legitimacy of the Modern Age*, pp. 498–9. See also Karl Jaspers, *The Great Philosophers*, pp. 120–4.

135   Hans Blumenberg, *The Legitimacy of the Modern Age*, p. 409. For a useful, brief, if not unexpected appreciation of Blumenberg, see Alex Callinicos, *Against Postmodernism*. A Marxist Critique (Cambridge: Polity Press, 1989) pp. 27–8.

136   Larry Shiner, 'The Concept of Secularization in Empirical Research', in *Journal for the Scientific Study of Religion*, 1967, vol. 6, no. 2, pp. 212–16.

137   Yves Lambert, 'From Parish to Transcendent Humanism in France', in James A. Beckford and Thomas Luckman (eds), *The Changing Face of Religion* (London: Sage Publications, 1991) pp. 49–63.

138   Quoted in Aidan Nichols, *Scribe of the Kingdom. Essays on Theology and Culture*, vol. 1 (London: Sheed & Ward, 1994) p. 16.

139   Georg Simmel, 'A contribution to the sociology of religion', in *The American Journal of Sociology*, vol. 60, no. 6, May 1955, p. 8.

140   Agnes Heller and Ferenc Fehér, *The Postmodern Political Condition* (Cambridge: Polity Press, 1991) p. 11.

141   Edward Robinson, *Icons of the Present: Some Reflections on Art, the Sacred and the Holy* (London: SCM, 1993) p. 65.

142   Agnes Heller and Ferenc Fehér, *The Postmodern Political Condition*, p. 7.

5   Concealing and Revealing: The Cultural Prospects of Belief

1   The introduction of a girls' choir to the Cathedral tradition might seem innocuous, but is not. An editorial in *The Times*, 17th July 1993 pointed to the 'real' agenda of the move, that this opened out music scholarships to public schools for girls as well as boys. The reasons for the change were educational and secular and had little to do with the issue of the sacred.

2   See the account of the report in *The Times*, 18th October 1991.

3   Wolfgang Fritz Haug, *Commodity Aesthetics, Ideology and Culture* (New York: International General, 1987) p. 161.

4   See the introduction to the symposium of book reviews on culture by Richard A. Peterson, 'Symbols and Social Life: The Growth of Cultural Studies', in *Contemporary Sociology*, vol. 19, no. 4, July 1990, pp. 498–500. For the reviews, see pp. 500–523. See also Michèle Lamont and Robert Wuthnow, 'Betwixt and Between: Recent Cultural Sociology in Europe and the United States', in George Ritzer (ed.), *Frontiers of Social Theory. The New Syntheses* (New York: Columbia University Press, 1990) pp. 287–315.

5   Cited in George W. Stocking, 'Matthew Arnold, E. B. Tylor and the Uses of Invention', in *American Anthropologist*, vol. 65, 1963, p. 783. See also Edward B. Tylor, *Anthropology* (Michigan: The University of Michigan Press, 1960). As might be expected numerous efforts have been made by anthropologists to characterise and to define culture. See for example: Bronislaw Malinowski, *A Scientific Theory of Culture* (New York: Oxford University Press, 1960) especially chapter 4, 'What is culture?', pp. 36–42; Audrey I. Richards, 'The Concept of Culture in Malinowski's Work', in Raymond Firth (ed.), *Man and Culture. An Evaluation of the Work of Bronislaw Malinowski* (New York: Harper & Row, 1964) pp. 15–31; and Ruth Benedict, *Patterns of Culture* (London: Routledge & Kegan Paul,

1961) pp. 15–40. For an invaluable overview of the term culture, see the entry in Raymond Williams, *Keywords. A Vocabulary of Culture and Society* (London: Fontana, 1976) pp. 76–82.

6   A. L. Kroeber, *Anthropology: Culture Patterns and Processes* (New York: Harcourt, Brace & World, 1963) p. 9.

7   See for example Derek Freeman, *Margaret Mead and Samoa. The Making and Unmaking of an Anthropological Myth* (Cambridge, Mass.: Harvard University Press, 1983); and Michael Herzfeld, *Anthropology through the Looking-Glass. Critical Ethnography in the Margins of Europe* (Cambridge: Cambridge University Press, 1989).

8   Roy Harvey Pearce, *Savagism and Civilization. A Study of the Indian and the American Mind* (Baltimore: the Johns Hopkins Press, 1967) chs 3 and 5, pp. 76–104 and 135–68.

9   Christopher Herbert, *Culture and Anomie: Ethnographic Imagination in the Nineteenth Century* (Chicago: The Chicago University Press, 1991).

10 Richard J. Bernstein, *Beyond Objectivism and Relativism: Science, Hermeneutics and Praxis* (Oxford: Basil Blackwell, 1983).

11 The rise and fall of debate on deviance and its central influence on sociology and its relationship with culture has been well covered in Colin Sumner, *The Sociology of Deviance. An Obituary* (Buckingham: The Open University, 1994). His thesis relates to the way sociological notions of culture, deviance in this case, aids in a society's task of self-recognition. By 1975, that need to equate culture and deviance in this sector of sociology had passed.

12 See for example Rosamund Billington, Sheelagh Strawbridge, Lenore Greensides and Annette Fitzsimmons, *Culture and Society. A Sociology of Culture* (London: Macmillan, 1991).

13 See Raymond Williams, *Culture* (London: Fontana, 1981). Chapter 1 'Towards a Sociology of Culture', pp. 9–32, represents an important attempt to respond to the sense of convergence emerging from the different subdivisions of sociology and anthropology. Any reference to Englishness and culture, must also refer his *Culture and Society* (London: The Hogarth Press, 1990). This book, first published in 1958, has had a seminal influence on English academic thought.

14 The estrangement many sociologists seem to feel from English culture marks a curious contrast with equivalent relationships in France and Germany. Unlike these counterparts, English sociologists do not seem to embody the English spirit of culture. Indeed, they feel not so much isolated from their culture as expelled from it.

15 Quoted in Shmuel N. Eisenstadt, 'Introduction: Culture and Social Structure in Recent Sociological Analysis', in Hans Haferkamp (ed.), *Social Structure and Culture* (New York: Walter de Gruyter, 1989) p. 6.

16 James Lydon, *Ireland in the later Middle Ages* (Dublin: Gill & Macmillan, 1973) pp. 93–7.

17 Michael Richter, *Medieval Ireland. The Enduring Tradition* (London: Macmillan, 1988) pp. 166–7.

18 Brian Friel, *Making History* (London: Faber & Faber, 1989) p. 28.

19 T. S. Eliot, *Notes towards the Definition of Culture* (London: Faber & Faber, 1962) p. 107.

20   Matthew Arnold, *Culture and Anarchy* (Cambridge: Cambridge University Press, 1960) p. 27.
21   George W. Stocking, 'Matthew Arnold, E. B. Tylor, and the Uses of Invention', p. 784.
22   Matthew Arnold, *Culture and Anarchy*, p. xiii.
23   Ibid., pp. 44–51.
24   Clifford Geertz, *The Interpretation of Cultures* (London: Fontana, 1993) ch. 1, 'Thick Description: Toward an Interpretative Theory of Culture', pp. 3–30. See also his essay 'Religion as a Cultural System', in Donald R. Cutler, (ed.), *The Religious Situation: 1968* (Boston: Beacon Press, 1968) pp. 639–88.
25   Clifford Geertz, *The Interpretation of Cultures*, p. 444.
26   See Mark A. Schneider, 'Culture-as-text in the work of Clifford Geertz', in *Theory and Society*, vol. 16, 1987, pp. 809–39.
27   Ann Swidler, 'Culture in Action: Symbols and Strategies', in *American Sociological Review*, vol. 51, no. 2, April 1986, p. 273.
28   Mike Featherstone, 'Towards a Sociology of Postmodern Culture', in Hans Haferkamp (ed.), *Social Structure and Culture*, pp. 150–1.
29   Ibid., p. 167.
30   Zygmunt Bauman, *Modernity and Ambivalence* (Cambridge: Polity Press, 1991) p. 186.
31   Scott Lash and John Urry, *Economies of Signs and Space* (London: Sage, 1994), pp. 3–6.
32   George Ritzer, *The McDonaldization of Society: an Investigation Into the Changing Character of Contemporary Social Life* (Newbury Park, California: Pine Forge Press, 1993).
33   Scott Lash and John Urry, *Economies of Signs and Space*, p. 16.
34   Wolfgang Fritz Haug, *Commodity Aesthetics, Ideology and Culture*, pp. 110–12.
35   Ibid., p. 117.
36   Angela McRobbie, *Postmodernism and Popular Culture* (London: Routledge, 1994).
37   Keith Tester, *Media, Culture and Morality* (London: Routledge, 1994) pp. 76–7.
38   Ibid., p. 4.
39   Ihab Hassan, 'The Culture of Postmodernism', *Theory, Culture and Society*, vol. 2, no. 3, 1985, pp. 123–4. See also Douglas Kellner, 'The Postmodern Turn: Positions, Problems, and Prospects', in George Ritzer (ed.), *Frontiers of Social Theory* (New York: Columbia University Press, 1990) pp. 255–86.
40   Fredric Jameson, 'Postmodernism, or The Cultural Logic of Late Capitalism', *New Left Review*, vol. 146, July–August, 1984, p. 85.
41   Agnes Heller and Ferenc Fehér, *The Postmodern Political Condition* (Cambridge: Polity Press, 1991) p. 9.
42   Ihab Hassan, 'The Culture of Postmodernism', p. 121.
43   Blaise Pascal, *Pensées* (London: Penguin, 1966) p. 218.
44   Charles Jencks, *What is Post-Modernism?* 3rd edn (London: Academic Editions, 1989) p. 55.
45   Steven Connor, *Postmodernist Culture. An Introduction to Theories of the Contemporary* (Oxford: Basil Blackwell, 1989) p. 19.

46 Charles Jencks, *What is Post-Modernism?* pp. 42–3.
47 Jean-François Lyotard, *The Postmodern Condition: A Report on Knowledge*, tr. Geoff Bennington and Brian Massumi (Manchester: Manchester University Press, 1984) pp. xv–xvi.
48 Ibid., p. 79.
49 Ibid., p. 26.
50 Barry Smart, 'On the disorder of things: sociology, postmodernity and the "end of the social" ', in *Sociology*, vol. 24, no. 3, August 1990, pp. 397–416.
51 Mike Featherstone, 'Towards a Sociology of Postmodern Culture', pp. 153–5.
52 Jean-François Lyotard, *The Postmodern Conditon*, p. 41.
53 Georg Stauth and Bryan S. Turner, 'Nostalgia, Postmodernism and the Critique of Mass Culture', in *Theory, Culture and Society*, vol. 5, nos 2–3, June 1988, pp. 523–4. See also Bryan S. Turner (ed.), *Theories of Modernity and Postmodernity* (London: Sage, 1990) Part II, 'Nostalgia and Modernity', pp. 31–87.
54 Alex Callinicos, *Against Postmodernism. A Marxist Critique* (Cambridge: Polity Press, 1989) pp. 3–6.
55 Ibid., pp. 162–171. See also his essay 'Reactionary Postmodernism?', in Roy Boyne and Ali Rattansi (eds), *Postmodernism and Society* (London: Macmillan, 1990) pp. 97–118.
56 Mike Featherstone, 'Towards a Sciology of Postmodern Culture', pp. 160–1.
57 Fredric Jameson, 'Postmodernism, or The Cultural Logic of Late Capitalism', p. 83.
58 Romano Guardini, *The End of the Modern World: A Search for Orientation* (London: Sheed & Ward, 1957) p. 62.
59 Fredric Jameson, 'Postmodernism, or the Cultural Logic of Late Capitalism', p. 66.
60 David Harvey, *The Condition of Postmodernity. An Enquiry into the Origins of Cultural Change* (Oxford: Basil Blackwell, 1989) p. 287.
61 Ibid., p. 292.
62 Paul Blanquart, ' "Post-Marxism" and "Post-Modernity": What is the Church's Presence?', in Claude Geffre and Jean-Pierre Jossua, (eds), *The Debate on Modernity, Concilium* (London: SCM Press, 1992) p. 117.
63 Johan Van der Vloet, 'Faith and the postmodern challenge', in *Communio*, vol. 17, no. 2, Summer 1990, pp. 132–40. This special issue was devoted to Christianity and the question of postmodernity, illustrating how rapidly some theologians have moved in to confronting the issues it raises. The gap between *Communio* theologians and debate on culture is showing promising signs of increased understandings in a way that moves in a sociological direction.
64 Wolfgang Fritz Haug, *Commodity Aesthetics, Ideology and Culture*, pp. 124–6.
65 Christopher Marlowe, *Doctor Faustus* (Manchester: Manchester University Press, 1993), A text, pp. 173–4.
66 Ibid., B text, p. 253.
67 Ibid., A text, p. 144.
68 Ibid., A text, p. 197.

69   Introduction by John Jump (ed.), *Marlowe: Doctor Faustus* (London: Macmillan, 1969) pp. 13–15.
70   Jean-François Lyotard, *The Postmodern Condition*, p. 77.
71   Ibid., pp. 78–81.
72   Karl Jaspers, *Leonardo, Descartes, Max Weber*, tr. Ralph Manheim (London: Routledge & Kegan Paul, 1965) p. 189.
73   Ibid., pp. 256–74.
74   Pierre Bourdieu, 'Genesis and Structure of the Religious Field', in *Comparative Social Research*, vol. 13, 1991, pp. 1–44.
75   Pierre Bourdieu, 'Legitimation and Structured Interests in Weber's Sociology of Religion', in Sam Whimster and Scott Lash (eds), *Max Weber, Rationality and Modernity* (London: Allen & Unwin, 1987) pp. 119–36.
76   Pierre Bourdieu, 'Authorized Language. The Social Conditions for the Effectiveness of Ritual Discourse', in *Language and Symbolic Power*, tr. Gino Raymond and Matthew Adamson (Cambridge: Polity Press, 1991) pp. 107–16.
77   Derek Robbins, *The Work of Pierre Bourdieu* (Milton Keynes: Open University, 1991) pp. 98–100.
78   John B. Keane, *The Field* (Cork: Mercier Press, 1991).
79   Eric Binnie, 'Friel and Field Day', in John P. Harrington (ed.) *Modern Irish Drama* (New York: W.W. Norton, 1991) pp. 564–70. See also Ulf Dantanus, *Brian Friel. A Study* (London: Faber & Faber, 1988) pp. 206–9.
80   Elmer Andrews, 'The Fifth Province', in Alan Peacock (ed.), *The Achievement of Brian Friel* (Gerrards Cross, Bucks.: Colin Smythe, 1993) p. 30.
81   Quoted in Richard Pine, *Brian Friel and Ireland's Drama* (London: Routledge, 1990) p. 13.
82   Ibid., p. 5.
83   Brian Friel, *Translations* (London: Faber & Faber, 1981). See also J. H. Andrews, *A Paper Landscape: the Ordnance Survey in Nineteenth-century Ireland* (Oxford: Clarendon Press, 1975).
84   Richard Pine, *Brian Friel and Ireland's Drama*, p. 31.
85   Kieran Flanagan, 'Brian Friel: A Sociological Appreciation of an Irish playwright', in *Contemporary Review*, vol. 266, no. 1551, April 1995, pp. 199–209.
86   George Steiner, *After Babel. Aspects of Language and Translation.* 2nd edn (Oxford: Oxford University Press, 1992).
87   Victor Turner, *The Ritual Process. Structure and Anti-Structure* (London: Routledge & Kegan Paul, 1969) chs 3 and 5, pp. 94–130 and 166–203.
88   Zygmunt Bauman, *Modernity and Ambivalence*, p. 15.
89   Ibid., p. 174.
90   Ibid., pp. 26–39.
91   Ibid., ch. 4, 'A Case Study in the Sociology of Assimilation I: Trapped in ambivalence', pp. 102–59.
92   *The Observer*, 9th October 1994.
93   Scott Lash and John Urry, *Economies of Signs and Space* (London: Sage, 1994) p. 29.
94   Karl Marx, *Capital*, vol. 1, tr. Samuel Moore and Edward Aveling (London: George Allen & Unwin, 1946) p. 41.
95   Ibid., p. 43.

96   Ibid., p. 51.

97   Georg Simmel, *The Philosophy of Money*, 2nd edn, tr. Tom Bottomore and David Frisby (London: Routledge, 1990) p. 238.

98   Pauline Matarasso (ed.) tr., *The Cistercian World. Monastic Writings of the Twelfth Century* (London: Penguin, 1993) pp. 56–7. For a critique of the links between monasticism and economic formations, that qualifies Weber's thesis, see Hana Friedrich Silber, 'Monasticism and the "Protestant Ethic": asceticism, rationality and wealth in the Medieval West', in *The British Journal of Sociology*, vol. 44, no. 1, March 1993, pp. 103–23.

99   Karl Marx, *Early Writings*, tr. T. B. Bottomore (New York: McGraw-Hill, 1964) p. 192.

100 Georg Simmel, *The Philosophy of Money*, p. 236.

101 Ibid., p. 7.

102 Ibid., p. 69.

103 Ibid., pp. 114–22.

104 Ibid., pp. 128–30.

105 Ibid., p. 280.

106 Ibid., pp. 344–6.

107 Ibid., pp. 400–9.

108 Ibid., p. 457.

109 Ibid., pp. 448–52.

110 Ibid., pp. 459–63.

111 Ibid., p. 476.

112 Ibid., pp. 483–4.

113 Andrew Wernick, *Promotional Culture: Advertising, Ideology and Symbolic Expression* (London: Sage, 1991).

114 Wolfang Fritz Haug, *Commodity Aesthetics, Ideology and Culture*, p. 118. See also Daniel Miller, *Material Culture and Mass Consumption* (Oxford: Basil Blackwell, 1991).

115 Theodor W. Adorno, 'Theses Against Occultism', in *Telos*, no. 19, Spring 1974, pp. 9–12. One might also note the comment of Adorno that the 'more cheerful the spirituality, the more mechanistic' (p. 10) a point that applies to Evangelical assemblies seeking instant spiritual 'success' as indicated by spirit and conversion.

116 Theodor W. Adorno, 'The Stars Down to Earth: the Los Angeles Times Astrology Column' in ibid., pp. 82–4.

117 Theodor W. Adorno and Max Horkheimer, *Dialectic of Enlightenment*, 2nd edn, tr. John Cumming (London: Verso, 1986) pp. 152–4. See also Theodor W. Adorno, *The Culture Industry* (London: Routledge, 1991) ch. 3, 'Culture Industry reconsidered', pp. 85–92.

118 Mike Featherstone, *Consumer Culture and Postmodernism* (London: Sage, 1991) pp. 112–13.

119 Theodor W. Adorno and Max Horkheimer, *Dialectic of Enlightenment*, p. 139.

120 Ibid., p. 130.

121 Lawrence A. Scaff, 'Modernity and the tasks of a sociology of culture', in *History of the Human Sciences*, vol. 3, no. 1, 1990, pp. 94–5.

122 Mike Featherstone, *Consumer Culture and Postmodernism*, pp. 113–22.

123 Daniel Bell, *Sociological Journeys. Essays 1960–1980* (London: Heinemann,

1980) Chapter 17, 'The Return of the Sacred? The Argument on the Future of Religion', p. 353. See also chapter 14, 'Beyond Modernism, Beyond Self', pp. 324–54. Any excursion into understanding the interface between theology and culture through sociological lenses must be indebted to these two pioneering essays.

124 John O'Neill, 'Religion and Postmodernism: The Durkheimian Bond in Bell and Jameson', in *Theory, Culture and Society*, vol. 5, nos 2–3, June 1988, p. 493.

125 For a commentary on this phenomena, see Katharine Le Mee, *Chant. The Origins, Form, Practice, and Healing Power of Gregorian Chant* (London: Rider, 1994).

126 *Heritage and Renewal. The Report of the Archibishops' Commission on Cathedrals* (London: Church House Publishing, 1994) p. 3.

127 Ibid., p. 136.

128 David Lowenthal, *The Past is a Foreign Country* (Cambridge: Cambridge University Press, 1985).

129 Ibid., p. 362.

130 Ibid., p. 399.

131 Kevin Walsh, *The Representation of the Past. Museums and Heritage in the Post-modern World* (London: Routledge, 1992) p. 113. See also Patrick Wright, *On Living in an Old Country* (London: Verso, 1985).

132 John Urry, *The Tourist Gaze. Leisure and Travel in Contemporary Societies* (London: Sage, 1990) p. 85.

133 Ibid., p. 129.

134 Lawrence A. Scaff, 'Modernity and the tasks of a sociology of culture', p. 98.

135 Simon Winchester, 'An Electronic Sink of Depravity', *The Spectator*, 4th February 1995, pp. 9–11.

6 To Canaan's Side: Crossing Culture in Theological and Sociological Safety

1 Eamon Duffy, *The Stripping of the Altars. Traditional Religion in England 1400–1580* (London: Yale University Press, 1992).

2 Grace Davie, *Religion in Britain since 1945: Believing without Belonging* (Oxford: Blackwell, 1994) p. 84.

3 See for example, David Chaney, *The Cultural Turn. Scene-setting Essays on Contemporary Cultural History* (London: Routledge, 1994).

4 Michael Richards, *A People of Priests. The Ministry of the Catholic Church* (London: Darton, Longman & Todd, 1995) pp. 1–2. Richards was editor for some time of the influential journal *The Clergy Review*. He notes the crisis of confidence in the clergy in the 1960s and 1970s and that a new generation has not come forward to replace those who left. The drop in the numbers being ordained has been catastrophic in the countries that most sought to radicalise the Spirit of Vatican II, such as in France, the USA, parts of Germany and in particular in the Netherlands, where a shell of what went before now operates. This property of self-destruction underlines the fatal misreading of culture made in the late 1960s, the effects of which still

resonate, with little signs of understanding how radical is the rethinking of theology required in relation to culture.

5   Eileen Barker, 'New lines in the supra-market: How much can we buy?', in Ian Hamnett (ed.), *Religious Pluralism* (London: Routledge, 1990) pp. 31–42.

6   Louis Dupré, 'Spiritual Life in a Secular Age', in Mary Douglas and Steven Tipton (eds), *Religion and America. Spiritual Life in a Secular Age* (Boston: Beacon Press, 1983) p. 12.

7   Ibid., pp. 7–10.

8   Kieran Flanagan, *Sociology and Liturgy: Re-presentations of the Holy* (London: Macmillan, 1991) see especially chapter 11, 'Apophatic Liturgy: Representing the Absent in Rite', pp. 288–320.

9   See Marc Ouellet, 'Hans Urs von Balthasar: Witness to the integration of faith and culture', in *Communio*, vol. 18, no. 1, Spring 1991, pp. 111–26. For some general appreciations of his work, see: Aidan Nichols, 'Balthasar and his Christology', in *New Blackfriars*, July/August 1985, vol. 66, no. 781/782, pp. 317–24; John O'Donnell, *Hans Urs von Balthasar* (London: Geoffrey Chapman, 1992); Medard Kehl, 'Hans Urs von Balthasar: A Portrait', in Medard Kehl and Werner Loser (eds), *The von Balthasar Reader*, tr. Robert J. Daly and Fred Lawrence (Edinburgh: T. & T. Clark, 1982) pp. 3–54; John Riches, *The Analogy of Beauty. The Theology of Hans Urs von Balthasar* (Edinburgh: T. & T. Clark, 1986); Louis Roberts, *The Theological Aesthetics of Hans Urs von Balthasar* (Washington, DC: The Catholic University of America Press, 1987), and Bede McGregor and Thomas Norris (eds), *The Beauty of Christ. An Introduction to the Theology of Hans Urs von Balthasar* (Edinburgh: T. & T. Clark, 1994).

10   Peter Henrici, 'Hans Urs von Balthasar: A Sketch of His Life', in David L. Schindler (ed.), *Hans Urs von Balthasar: His Life and Work* (San Francisco: Ignatius Press, 1991) p. 7 and p. 31.

11   Gregory W. H. Smith, 'Snapshots "sub specie aeternitatis"': Simmel, Goffman and formal sociology', in *Human Studies*, vol. 12, nos. 1–2, 1989, pp. 19–57.

12   Kieran Flanagan, 'Postmodernity and culture: sociological wagers of the self in theology', in Kieran Flanagan and Peter Jupp (eds), *Postmodernity, Sociology and Religion* (London: Macmillan, 1996).

13   Joseph Ratzinger, 'Homily at the funeral liturgy for Hans Urs von Balthasar', in *Communio*, vol. 15, no. 4, Winter 1988, p. 512.

14   Hans Urs von Balthasar, *Test Everything: Hold Fast to What is Good*, tr. Maria Shrady (San Francisco: Igantius Press, 1989) pp. 25–6.

15   Pierre Bourdieu and Alain Darbel, *The Love of Art. European Art Museums and their Public*, tr. Caroline Beattie and Nick Merriman (Cambridge: Polity Press, 1991) p. 1.

16   Ibid., p. 46.

17   Hans Urs von Balthasar, *The Glory of the Lord. A Theological Aestetics*, vol. 1 (Edinburgh: T. & T. Clark, 1982) p. 156.

18   J. Huizinga, *The Waning of the Middle Ages* (London: Penguin, 1955) pp. 168–71.

19   Ibid., pp. 254–7.

20   Ibid., pp. 160–1.

21   David Freedberg, *The Power of Images. Studies in the History and Theory of Response* (London: The University of Chicago Press, 1991) p. 91.

22   Aidan Nichols, *The Art of God Incarnate. Theology and Image in Christian Tradition* (London: Darton, Longman & Todd, 1980) p. 146.

23   Karl Jaspers, *Truth and Symbol*, tr. Jean T. Wilde, William Kluback and William Kimmel (New York: Twayne Publishers, 1959) pp. 38–40.

24   Ibid., p. 79 and as a whole, chapter 4, 'The Ascent to the Reading of the Cypher-Script', pp. 65–79.

25   Wulstan Mork, *The Benedictine Way* (Petersham, Massachusetts: St Bede's Publications, 1987) pp. 17–20.

26   Max Weber, *Economy and Society*, vol. 1 (London: University of California Press, 1978) p. 249.

27   *Heritage and Renewal. The Report of the Archbishop's Commission on Cathedrals* (London: Church House Publishing, 1994) pp. 44–5.

28   Ibid., pp. 52–3. Little is known about gender and the social construction of religious belief especially in relation to children. For an original insight into the feminisation of religious belief in relation to education, see Mairi Levitt, 'Sexual Identity and religious socialisation', in *The British Journal of Sociology*, vol. 46, no. 3, September 1995, pp. 529–536. She draws attention to the degree to which boys are far more likely to cease attending church than girls by the age of 12. There is evidence of this process of displacement in the virtual collapse of all male choirs in Anglican Churches between 1960 and 1990. When they went mixed, the boys left, and by degrees no children were in the sanctuary. Levitt draws attention to the degree to which there is an unrecognised crisis over the place and extent of *male* practice in church going and participation which a concern with equality of opportunity has obscured. Anyhow, theologians are endeavouring to accommodate to feminism just as a male countermovement is emerging. See for example, Michael S. Kimmel, 'Reading Men: Men, Masculinity, and Publishing', essay reviews on male studies in *Contemporary Sociology*, vol. 21, no. 2, March 1992, pp. 162–71.

29   Pierre Bourdieu, *Distinction. A Social Critique of the Judgement of Taste*, tr. Richard Nice (London: Routledge, 1986) p. xiii. See also Richard Jenkins, *Pierre Bourdieu* (London: Routledge, 1992) pp. 162–72.

30   Pierre Bourdieu and Loïc J. D. Wacquant, *An Invitation to Reflexive Sociology* (Cambridge: Polity Press, 1992) p. 203.

31   Ibid., p. 205.

32   Derek Robbins, *The Work of Pierre Bourdieu* (Milton Keynes: Open University, 1991) p. 177.

33   Pierre Bourdieu and Loïc J. D. Wacquant, *An Invitation to Reflexive Sociology*, pp. 86–7.

34   Pierre Bourdieu, *The Field of Cultural Production. Essays on Art and Literature* (Cambridge: Polity Press, 1993) p. 122. In his approach to culture, Bourdieu is concerned with the right to consecrate, to render mysterious and hallowed, and thus to place above scrutiny.

35   Pierre Bourdieu, *Distinction*, p. 6.

36   Ibid., p. 317.

37   Pierre Bourdieu, *Homo Academicus* (Cambridge: Polity Press, 1988) p. 124.

38   Ibid., p. 150.

39 Introduction by Randal Johnson to Pierre Bourdieu, *The Field of Cultural Production*, p. 5.
40 Pierre Bourdieu, *Homo Academicus*, pp. xxvi and 100–1.
41 For an account of the notion of the child oblate, with its strengths and weaknesses, see Patricia A. Quinn, *Better than The Sons of Kings. Boys and Monks in the Early Middle Ages* (New York: Peter Lang, 1989).
42 J. K. Huysmans, *The Oblate*, tr. Edward Perceval (London: Kegan Paul, Trench, Trubner & Co. Ltd., 1924).
43 Pierre Bourdieu, *In Other Words. Essays towards a Reflexive Sociology* (Cambridge: Polity Press, 1992) pp. 12–13.
44 Cheleen Mahar, 'Pierre Bourdieu: The Intellectual Project', in Richard Harker, Cheleen Mahar, Chris Wilkes (eds), *An Introduction to the Work of Pierre Bourdieu* (London: Macmillan, 1990) pp. 34–5.
45 Josef Pieper, *In Search of the Sacred*, tr. Lothar Krauth (San Francisco: Ignatius Press, 1991) pp. 85–120.
46 John Codd, 'Making Distinctions: The Eye of the Beholder', in Richard Harker, Cheleen Mahar and Chris Wilkes, *An Introduction to the Work of Pierre Bourdieu*, pp. 136–41.
47 Erwin Panofsky, *Gothic Architecture and Scholasticism* (New York: New American Library, 1976) pp. 21–2.
48 *Pseudo-Dionysius. The Complete Works*, tr. Colm Luibheid (London: SPCK, 1987).
49 Pierre Bourdieu, 'Genesis and Structure of the Religious Field', *Comparative Social Research*, vol. 13, 1991, p. 32.
50 Erwin Panofsky, *Gothic Architecture and Scholasticism*, pp. 44–5.
51 Romano Guardini, *The End of the Modern World: A Search for Orientation* (London: Sheed & Ward, 1957) pp. 30–9.
52 Pierre Bourdieu, *The Field of Cultural Production*, p. 75.
53 Thomas Aquinas, *Summa Theologiae*, vol. 22 (London: Eyre & Spottiswoode, 1964) pp. 4–9.
54 Pierre Bourdieu and Loïc J. D. Wacquant, *An Invitation to Reflexive Sociology*, p. 128. See also pp. 120–8.
55 Pierre Bourdieu, *The Field of Cultural Production*, pp. 161–3.
56 Pierre Bourdieu, *Distinction*, Chapter 3 'The Habitus and the Space of lifestyles' especially pp. 169–70.
57 See for example Pierre Bourdieu, *Homo Academicus*, p. 99. For an earlier and highly significant treatment of the term habitus see Pierre Bourdieu, *Outline of a Theory of Practice*, tr. Richard Nice (Cambridge: Cambridge University Press, 1977) pp. 76–87. One of the best critical discussions of the term appears in Richard Jenkins, *Pierre Bourdieu*, pp. 74–84.
58 Pierre Bourdieu and Jean-Claude Passeron, *Reproduction in Education, Society and Culture*, tr. Richard Nice (London: Sage Publications, 1977) see especially book 1, 'Foundations of a Theory of Symbolic Violence', pp. 1–68.
59 Pierre Bourdieu, *Homo Academicus*. This general thesis forms the basis of this book, one of the most accessible of his works, and also perhaps the most persuasive. It involves the application of sociometrics to institutions and suggests that many positions are not marginal but need to be understood in the structure and mapping of power.

258   *Notes and References to pp. 205–12*

60   Derek Robbins, *The Work of Pierre Bourdieu*, p. 94.
61   Pierre Bourdieu, *Homo Academicus*, p. 208.
62   Pierre Bourdieu, 'Legimitation and Structured Interests in Weber's Sociology of Religion', in Sam Whimster and Scott Lash (eds), *Weber, Rationality and Modernity* (London: Allen & Unwin, 1987) p. 126.
63   Ibid., pp. 132–3.
64   John Skorupski, *Symbol and Theory. A Philosophical Study of Theories of Religion in Social Anthropology* (Cambridge: Cambridge University Press, 1976) Chapter 7, 'Operative ceremonies', see especially pp. 108–14. See also S. J. Tambiah, *A Performative Approach to Ritual* (London: The British Academy, 1981).
65   Walter Benjamin, 'The Work of Art in the Age of Mechanical Production' in *Illuminations* (New York: Schocken Books, 1969) pp. 223–4.
66   Ibid., p. 221.
67   Ibid., p. 241.
68   Guy Lapointe, 'Shattered Liturgical Space: Questions related to the Televising of Sunday Mass in French Canada', in *Studia Liturgica*, vol. 24, 1994, p. 118.
69   Worries have arisen over the performance of secular music in Catholic Churches. A rather inconclusive document was issued on the question in November 1987 by the Congregation for Divine Worship. For a discussion of its principles see *Briefing*, 18th December, 1987, pp. 111–21. The document seems to convey an inadequate understanding of the wider cultural difficulties that affect the issue of secular and sacred music and the need to establish an ecclesial monopoly.
70   Pierre Bourdieu, *The Field of Cultural Production*, p. 64.
71   Ibid., p. 160.
72   Ibid., p. 81.
73   Pierre Bourdieu, 'Genesis and Structure of the Religious Field', p. 5.
74   This forms the central theme of *Sociology and Liturgy*.
75   See Pierre Bourdieu, *Distinction*, p. 86.
76   Hubert Dreyfus and Paul Rabinow, 'Can there be a Science of Existential Structure and Social Meaning?', in Craig Calhoun, Edward LiPuma and Moishe Postone (eds), *Bourdieu. Critical Perspectives* (Cambridge: Polity Press, 1993) pp. 41–2.
77   Pierre Bourdieu and Loïc J. D. Wacquant, *An Invitation to Reflexive Sociology*, pp. 98–9.
78   Ibid., p. 248.
79   Roy Rappaport, 'The Obvious Aspects of Ritual' and 'Sanctity and Lies in Evolution', in *Ecology, Meaning and Religion* (Richmond, California: North Atlantic Books, 1979) pp. 173–246. For comment on these essays see Kieran Flanagan, *Sociology and Liturgy*, pp. 169–73.
80   Pierre Bourdieu, 'Sociologues de la croyance et croyances de sociologues', in *Archives de Sciences Sociales des Religions*, 1987, vol. 63, no. 1, pp. 155–61. I am very grateful to Amy Hawkins, 2nd Year Sociology and Politics, University of Bristol, 1995 for her painstaking translation of this article which is used in this study.
81   Ibid., p. 157.
82   Ibid., p. 160.

83 Pierre Bourdieu, 'Genesis and Structure of the Religious Field', p. 21.
84 Ibid., p. 31.
85 Ibid., p. 20.
86 Pierre Bourdieu, *Language and Symbolic Power* (Cambridge: Polity Press, 1991) p. 106.
87 Ibid., p. 116.
88 Ibid., pp. 119–23. Performative utterances are understood in this context in terms of the capacity to consecrate.
89 Introduction by John B. Thomspon to ibid., p. 9.
90 Ibid., p. 120.
91 Ibid., p. 122.
92 Zygmunt Bauman, *Intimations of Postmodernity* (London: Routledge, 1992) p. x.
93 Arthur Mitzman, *The Iron Cage: An Historical Interpretation of Max Weber*, 2nd edn (New Brunswick, USA: Transaction Books, 1985) p. 225.
94 Max Weber, *From Max Weber. Essays in Sociology*, tr. H. H. Gerth and C. Wright Mills (eds) (New York: Oxford University Press, 1958) p. 51.
95 Max Weber, *Economy and Society*, vol. 1 (London: University of California Press, 1978) pp. 242–4.
96 Ibid., pp. 248–9.
97 Ibid., pp. 400–1.
98 Ibid., p. 399.
99 Ibid., pp. 558–61.
100 Ibid., pp. 403–7. The capacity of the priesthood to sacralise has been well understood in the context of debate on the perpetuation of social inequality. Bourdieu is not the first to notice its implications for culture in general and professional power in particular. See Kingsley Davis and Wilbert E. Moore, 'Some Principles of Stratification', in Reinhard Bendix and Seymour Martin Lipset (eds), *Class, Status and Power. Social Stratification in Comparative Perspective*, 2nd edn (London: Routledge & Kegan Paul Ltd., 1967) pp. 47–53.
101 Max Weber, *Economy and Society*, vol. 1, pp. 630–4.
102 Mark A. Schneider, *Culture and Enchantment* (Chicago: The University of Chicago Press, 1993) p. 202.
103 Pierre Bourdieu, 'The Sociologist in Question', in *Sociology in Question*, tr. Richard Nice (London: Sage Publications, 1993) p. 26.
104 Mark A. Schneider, *Culture and Enchantment*, pp. 183–6.
105 Rogers Brubaker, 'Social Theory as Habitus', in Craig Calhoun, Edward LiPuma and Moishe Postone (eds), *Bourdieu Critical Perspectives*, pp. 212–34.
106 Hans Urs von Balthasar, *The Glory of the Lord. A Theological Aesthetics*, vol. V, *The Realm of Metaphysics in the Modern Age*, tr. Oliver Davies, Andrew Louth, Brian McNeil, John Saward and Rowan Williams (Edinburgh: T. & T. Clark, 1991) p. 414.
107 Georg Simmel, *The Philosophy of Money*, 2nd edn (London: Routledge, 1990) p. 446. The appreciation of Simmel is surprisingly recent. For a negative and distastefully anti-semitic appraisal that accounts for his marginalisation in German academic life, see the letter of a Dietrich Schaefer in Lewis Coser, 'The Stranger in the Academy' in Lewis Coser (ed.), *Georg*

Simmel (Englewood Cliffs, New Jersey: Prentice-Hall, 1965) pp. 37–9. For an accessible biographical account, see David Frisby, *Georg Simmel* (Chichester: Ellis Horwood Limited, 1984) ch. 2 'Life and Context', pp. 21–44. For a recent general appraisal of the breath of his interests, see the special issue of *Theory, Culture and Society*, vol. 8, no. 3, August 1991. See also Lawrence A. Scaff, 'Georg Simmel's Theory of Culture', in Michael Kaern, Bernard S. Phillips and Robert S. Cohen (eds), *Georg Simmel and Contemporary Sociology* (Dordrecht: Kluwer Academic Publishers, 1990) pp. 283–96.

108 Hans Urs von Balthasar, *Theo-Drama. Theological Dramatic Theory*, vol. I,: *Prologomena*, tr. Graham Harrison (San Francisco: Ignatius Press, 1988) pp. 605–25.

109 Ibid., p. 614.

110 Ibid., p. 619.

111 Eric Hobsbawm, 'Introduction: Inventing Traditions', in Eric Hobsbawm and Terence Ranger (eds), *The Invention of Tradition* (Cambridge: University Press, Canto edition, 1992) p. 4.

112 Max Weber, *Economy and Society*, vol. 2, p. 1170.

113 Ibid., pp. 1172–3.

114 See *The Catholic World Report*, February 1993, p. 48. See also Eleace King, *Cara Formation Directory for Men and Women Religious 1993* (Washington, DC, Georgetown University, 1992) especially pp. 14–15. For a rare and valuable study of the process of renewal in religious orders, see James Sweeney, *The New Religious Order. The Passionists in Britain and Ireland, 1945–1990 and the Option for the Poor* (London: Bellew, 1994). Sweeney makes an important point that the crisis in the religious orders since Vatican II is the crisis of Catholicism in microcosm, for issues of charisma, irruption, institutionalisaton and routinisation can be found in their immediate histories. See p. 149.

115 See interview with Mother Vincent Marie Finnegan, chairman of the Council of Major Superiors of Women Religious, in *The Catholic World Report*, February 1993, pp. 41–2 and pp. 52–5. For comment on numbers in formation see p. 53. I am grateful for Mother Vincent Marie for advice on the present state of her own order, the Carmelite Sisters of the Most Sacred Heart of Los Angeles which seems to exemplify the success one has in mind regarding an up turn in religious vocations amongst orders with a definite identity.

116 I am grateful to Fr. Martin Farrell, President of the Fellowship of New Religious Communities for supplying background information on this new trend.

117 I am grateful to Fr. Michael Robertson, Assistant Priest, St. Osmund's Salisbury for bringing me back from France literature on the Community of Saint Jean.

118 P. A. Lawrence, *Georg Simmel: Sociologist and European* (London: Nelson, 1976) Reading Nine, 'The Conflict of Modern Culture', p. 237.

119 Ibid., p. 240.

120 Quoted in Hans von Balthasar, *Theo-Drama*, vol. I, p. 613.

121 Georg Simmel, *The Conflict in Modern Culture and Other Essays*, tr. K. Peter Etzkorn (New York: Teachers College Press, 1968) p. 27.

122 Ibid., pp. 30–1.
123 See the introduction by Guy Oakes, *Essays on Interpretation in Social Science*, pp. 35–46.
124 Georg Simmel, *The Conflict in Modern Culture and Other Essays*, p. 44.
125 P. A. Lawrence, *Georg Simmel: Sociologist and European*, Reading Twelve, 'The Crisis of Culture', p. 255.
126 Ibid., p. 266.
127 Hans Urs von Balthasar, *Theo-Drama*, vol. I, p. 424.
128 Ibid., p. 428.
129 Ibid., p. 434.
130 Hans Urs von Balthasar, *The Glory of the Lord*, vol. I, p. 28.

Bibliography

Abraham, Gary A., 'Context and prejudice in Max Weber's thought: criticisms of Wilhelm Hennis', *History of the Human Sciences*, vol. 6, no. 3, August 1993, pp. 1–17 and reply of Hennis, pp. 19–23.

Abrams, Phillip, *The Origins of British Sociology, 1834–1914* (Chicago: University of Chicago Press, 1968).

Adorno, Theodor W., 'Theses Against Occultism', *Telos*, no. 19, Spring 1974, pp. 7–12.

Adorno, Theodor W., 'The Stars Down to Earth: the Los Angeles Times Astrology Column', *Telos*, 19, Spring 1974, pp. 13–90.

Adorno, Theodor W., and Max Horkheimer, *Dialectic of Enlightenment*, 2nd edn tr. John Cumming (London: Verso, 1986).

Adorno, Theodor W., *The Culture Industry* (London: Routledge, 1991).

Albrow, Martin, *Max Weber's Construction of Social Reality* (London: Macmillan, 1990).

Aldridge, Judith, 'The Textual Disembodiment of Knowledge in Research Account Writing', *Sociology*, vol. 27, no. 1, February 1993, pp. 53–66.

Alszeghy, Zoltan, and Maurizio Flick, *Introductory Theology* (London: Sheed & Ward, 1982).

Alter, Robert, *Necessary Angels. Tradition and Modernity in Kafka, Benjamin and Scholem* (Cambridge, Massachusetts: Harvard University Press, 1991).

Anderson, Benedict, *Imagined Communities. Reflections on the Origin and Spread of Nationalism* (London: Verso, 1983).

Andreski, Stanislav, *Social Sciences as Sorcery* (London: Penguin, 1974).

Andrews, Elmer, 'The Fifth Province', Alan Peacock (ed.), *The Achievement of Brian Friel* (Gerrards, Cross, Bucks: Colin Smythe, 1993) pp. 29–48.

Andrews, J. H., *A Paper Landscape: the Ordnance Survey in Nineteenth-century Ireland* (Oxford: Clarendon Press, 1975).

Aquinas, Thomas, *Summa Theologiae* (London: Eyre & Spottiswoode, 1964) vols. 1, 11, 22, 23, and 39.

Archer, Antony, *The Two Catholic Churches. A Study in Oppression* (London: SCM Press, 1986).

Arnold, Matthew, *Culture and Anarchy* (Cambridge: Cambridge University Press, 1960).

Baldick, Robert, *The Life of J. K. Huysmans* (Oxford: Clarendon Press, 1955).

Baldwin, John D., *George Herbert Mead. A Unifying Theory for Sociology* (Newbury Park, California: Sage Publications, 1986).

Balthasar, Hans Urs von, *The Glory of the Lord. A Theological Aesthetics*, vol. I, *Seeing the Form*, tr. Erasmo Leiva-Merikakis (Edinburgh: T. & T. Clark, 1982).

Balthasar, Hans Urs von, *Convergences: To the Source of Christian Mystery*, tr. E. A. Nelson (San Francisco: Ignatius Press, 1983).

Balthasar, Hans Urs von, *The Glory of the Lord. A Theological Aesthetics*, vol. II, *Studies in Theological Style: Clerical Styles*, tr. Andrew Louth, Frances McDonagh and Brian McNeil (Edinburgh: T. & T. Clark, 1984).

Balthasar, Hans Urs von, *A Short Primer for Unsettled Laymen*, tr. Mary Skerry (San Francisco: Ignatius Press, 1985).

Balthasar, Hans Urs von, obituary *The Times*, 27th June 1988.

Balthasar, Hans Urs von, *Theo-Drama. Theological Dramatic Theory*, vol. I: *Prologomena*, tr. Graham Harrison (San Francisco: Ignatius Press, 1988).

Balthasar, Hans Urs von, *Test Everything: Hold Fast to What is Good*, tr. Maria Shrady (San Francisco: Ignatius Press, 1989).

Baltahasar, Hans Urs von, *Theo-drama. Theological Dramatic Theory*, vol. II: *Dramatis Personae: Man in God*, tr. Graham Harrison (San Francisco: Ignatius Press, 1990).

Balthasar, Hans Urs von, *The Glory of the Lord. A Theological Aesthetics*, vol. V, *The Realm of Metaphysics in the Modern Age*, tr. Oliver Davies, Andrew Louth, Brian McNeil, John Saward and Rowan Williams (Edinburgh: T. & T. Clark, 1991).

Balthasar, Hans Urs von, *The Theology of Henri de Lubac. An Overview*, tr. Susan Clements (San Francisco: Ignatius Press, 1991).

Barker, Eileen, 'New lines in the supra-market: How much can we buy?', Ian Hamnett (ed.), *Religious Pluralism* (London: Routledge, 1990) pp. 31–42.

Barley, Nigel, *The Innocent Anthropologist. Notes from a Mud Hut* (London: Penguin, 1986).

Barot, Rohit (ed.), *Religion and Ethnicity: Minorities and Social Change in the Metropolis* (Kampen-the Netherlands: Kok Pharos, 1993).

Baudelaire, Charles, 'The Painter of Modern Life', *The Painter of Modern Life*, tr. Jonathan Mayne (London: Phaidon Press, 1964) pp. 1–40.

Baum, Gregory, *Theology and Society* (New York: Paulist Press, 1987).

Baum, Gregory, 'Sociology and Salvation: Do We Need a Catholic Sociology?', *Theological Studies*, vol. 50, (1989) pp. 718–43.

Baum, Gregory, 'Two Question Marks: Inculturation and Multiculturalism', Norbert Greinacher and Norbert Mette, *Christianity and Cultures* (London: SCM Press, 1994) pp. 101–6.

Bauman, Zygmunt, *Hermeneutics and Social Science. Approaches to Understanding* (London: Hutchinson, 1978) pp. 172–3.

Bauman, Zygmunt, *Modernity and Ambivalence* (Cambridge: Polity Press, 1991).

Bauman, Zygmunt, *Modernity and the Holocaust* (Cambridge: Polity Press, 1991).

Bauman, Zygmunt, *Intimations of Postmodernity* (London: Routledge, 1992).

Beaumont, Barbara (ed. and tr.), *The Road from Decadence. From Brothel to Cloister. Selected Letters of J. K. Huysmans* (London: The Athlone Press, 1989).

Bebbington, David, 'The Secularization of British Universities since the Mid-Nineteenth Century', George M. Marsden and Bradley J. Longfield (eds), *The Secularization of the Academy* (New York: Oxford University Press, 1992) pp. 259–277.

Beck, Ulrich, *Risk Society. Towards a New Modernity*, tr. Mark Ritter (London: Sage Publications, 1992).

Beck, Ulrich, 'Self-Dissolution and Self-Endangerment of Industrial Society: What Does This Mean?', Ulrich Beck, Anthony Giddens and Scott Lash, *Reflexive Modernization* (Cambridge: Polity Press, 1994) pp. 174–83.

Beck, Ulrich, Anthony Giddens, Scott Lash, *Reflexive Modernization. Politics, Tradition and Aesthetics in the Modern Social Order* (Cambridge: Polity Press, 1994).

Beckford, James, 'The Insulation and Isolation of the Sociology of Religion', *Sociological Analysis*, vol. 46, no. 4 (1985) pp. 347–54.

Beckford, James A., *Religion and Advanced Industrial Society* (London: Unwin Hyman, 1989).

Bell, Catherine, 'The Authority of Ritual Experts', *Studia Liturgica*, vol. 23 (1993) pp. 98–120.

Bell, Daniel, *Sociological Journeys. Essays 1960–1980* (London: Heinemann, 1980).

Bellah, Robert, Richard Madsen, William M. Sullivan, Ann Swidler, and Steven M. Tipton, *Habits of the Heart. Individualism and Commitment in American Life* (New York: Harper & Row, 1985).

Benedict, Ruth, *Patterns of Culture* (London: Routledge & Kegan Paul, 1961).

Benjamin, Walter, *Iluminations*, tr. Harry Zohn (New York: Schocken Books, 1969).

Benjamin, Walter, *Charles Baudelaire. A Lyric Poet in the Era of High Capitalism*, tr. Harry Zohn (London: Verso, 1983).

Benson, Douglas, and John A. Hughes, *The Perspective of Ethnomethodology* (London: Longman, 1983).

Berger, Peter L., 'A Sociological view of the Secularization of Theology', *Journal for the Scientific Study of Religion*, vol. 5 (1966) pp. 3–16.

Berger, Peter L., *The Social Reality of Religion* (London: Penguin, 1973).

Berger, Peter L, Brigitte Berger and Hansfried Kellner, *The Homeless Mind* (London: Penguin, 1973).

Berger, Peter L., *The Heretical Imperative. Contemporary Possibilities of Religious Affirmation* (London: Collins, 1980).

Berger, Peter L., *A Rumour of Angels*, 2nd edn (New York: Anchor Books, 1990).

Berger, Peter L. *A Far Glory. The Quest for Faith in an Age of Credulity* (New York: Doubleday, 1993).

Berman, Marshall, *All That Is Solid Melts Into Air. The Experience of Modernity* (London: Verso, 1983).

Bernstein, Richard J., *Beyond Objectivism and Relativism: Science, Hermeneutics and Praxis* (Oxford: Basil Blackwell, 1983).

Billington, Rosamund, Sheelagh Strawbridge, Lenore Greensides and Annette Fitzsimmons, *Culture and Society. A Sociology of Culture* (London: Macmillan, 1991).

Binnie, Eric, 'Friel and Field Day', John P. Harrington (ed.). *Modern Irish Drama* (New York: W. W. Norton, 1991) pp. 564–70.

Blanquart, Paul, ' "Post-Marxism" and "Post-Modernity": What is the Church's Presence?', Claude Geffre and Jean-Pierre Jossua, (eds), *The Debate on Modernity, Concilium* (London: SCM Press, 1992), pp. 115–23.

Blumenberg, Hans, *The Legitimacy of the Modern Age*, tr. Robert M. Wallace (Cambridge, Mass.: The MIT Press, 1985).

Bollon, Patrice, *Morale du Masque. Merveilleux, Zazous, Dandys, Punks, etc.* (Paris: Éditions du Seuil, 1990).

Bourdieu, Pierre and Jean-Claude Passeron, *Reproduction in Education, Society and Culture*, tr. Richard Nice (London: Sage Publications, 1977).

Bourdieu, Pierre, *Outline of a Theory of Practice*, tr. Richard Nice (Cambridge: Cambridge University Press, 1977).

Bourdieu, Pierre, *Distinction. A Social Critique of the Judgement of Taste*, tr. Richard Nice (London: Routledge, 1986).

Bourdieu, Pierre, 'Legitimation and Structured Interests in Weber's Sociology of

Religion', Sam Whimster and Scott Lash (eds), *Max Weber, Rationality and Modernity* (London: Allen & Unwin, 1987) pp. 119–36.

Bourdieu, Pierre, 'Sociologues de la croyance et croyances de sociologues', *Archives de Sciences Sociales des Religions* (1987) vol. 63, no. 1, pp. 155–61.

Bourdieu, Pierre, *Homo Academicus*, tr. Peter Collier (Cambridge: Polity Press, 1988).

Bourdieu, Pierre, *In Other Works. Essays towards a Reflexive Sociology*, tr. Matthew Adamson (Cambridge: Polity Press, 1990).

Bourdieu, Pierre and Alain Darbel, *The Love of Art. European Art Museums and their Public*, tr. Caroline Beattie and Nick Merriman (Cambridge: Polity Press, 1991).

Bourdieu, Pierre, 'Authorized Language. The Social Conditions for the Effectiveness of Ritual Discourse', *Language and Symbolic Power*, tr. Gino Raymond and Matthew Adamson (Cambridge: Polity Press, 1991) pp. 107–16.

Bourdieu, Pierre, 'Genesis and Structure of the Religious Field', *Comparative Social Research*, vol. 13 (1991) pp. 1–44.

Bourdieu, Pierre and Loïc J. D. Wacquant, *An Invitation to Reflexive Sociology* (Cambridge: Polity Press, 1992).

Bourdieu, Pierre, 'The Sociologist in Question', *Sociology in Question*, tr. Richard Nice (London: Sage Publications, 1993).

Bourdieu, Pierre, *The Field of Cultural Production. Essays on Art and Literature* (Cambridge: Polity Press, 1993).

British Sociological Association (BSA) Newsletter, November 1993.

Brubaker, Rogers, 'Social Theory as Habitus', Craig Calhoun, Edward LiPuma and Moishe Postone, (eds), *Bourdieu Critical Perspectives* (Cambridge: Polity Press, 1993) pp. 212–34.

Bryant, Christopher G. A., and Henk A. Becker (eds), *What Has Sociology Achieved?* (London: Macmillan, 1990).

Buci-Glucksmann, Christine, *Baroque Reason. The Aesthetics of Modernity*, tr. Patrick Camiller (London: Sage Publications, 1994).

Callinicos, Alex, *Against Postmodernism. A Marxist Critique* (Cambridge: Polity Press, 1989).

Callinicos, Alex, 'Reactionary Postmodernism?', Roy Boyne and Ali Rattansi (eds), *Postmodernism and Society* (London: Macmillan, 1990) pp. 97–118.

Carter, Stephen L., *The Culture of Disbelief: How American Law and Politics Trivialize Religious Devotion* (New York: Basic Books, 1993).

Cathechism of the Catholic Church (London: Geoffrey Chapman, 1994).

Cere, Daniel, 'Newman, God and the Academy', *Theological Studies*, vol. 55 (1994) pp. 3–23.

Chadwick, Owen, *The Secularization of the European Mind in the 19th century* (Cambridge: Cambridge University Press, 1990).

Chaney, David, *The Cultural Turn. Scene-setting Essays on Contemporary Cultural history* (London: Routledge, 1994).

Charlton, D. G., *Secular Religions in France 1815–1870* (Oxford: Oxford University Press, 1963).

Class and Church; After Ghetto Catholicism, New Blackfriars, vol. 68, no. 802, February 1987.

Clegg, Stewart, 'How to become an internationally famous British social theorist', *The Sociological Review*, vol. 40, no. 2, May 1992, pp. 576–98.

Codd, John, 'Making Distinctions: The Eye of the Beholder', Richard Harker,

Cheleen Mahar, Chris Wilkes, *An Introduction to the Work of Pierre Bourdieu* (London: Macmillan, 1990) pp. 132–59.

Cohen, Anthony P., 'Self-conscious anthropology', Judith Okely and Helen Callaway (eds), *Anthropology and Autobiography* (London: Routledge, 1992) pp. 221–41.

Collet, Giancarlo, 'From Theological Vandalism to Theological Romanticism? Questions about a Multicultural identity of Christianity', Norbert Greinacher and Norbert Mette (eds), *Christianity and Cultures. Concilium* (London: SCM Press, 1994) pp. 25–37.

Colley, Linda, *Britons. Forging the Nation 1707–1837* (London: BCA, 1992).

Collingwood, R. G., *An Autobiography* (Oxford: Oxford University Press, 1970).

Congregation for Divine Worship report on Concerts in Church, *Briefing*, 18th December, 1987, pp. 111–21.

Connor, Steven, *Postmodernist Culture. An Introduction to Theories of the Contemporary* (Oxford: Basil Blackwell, 1989).

Connor, Steven, *Theory and Cultural Value* (Oxford: Blackwell, 1992).

Cornwell, Jocelyn, *Hard-earned Lives: Accounts of Health and Illness from East London* (London: Tavistock, 1984).

Cunningham, Adrian, 'Religious Studies in the Universities. England', Ursula King (ed.), *Turning Points in Religious Studies. Essays in Honour of Geoffrey Parrinder* (Edinburgh: T. & T. Clark, 1990) pp. 29–31.

D'Costa, Gavin, 'The End of "Theology" and "Religious Studies"', *Theology*, vol. 99, no. 788, March 1996.

Daniel, Walter, *The Life of Aelred*, Pauline Matarasso (ed. and tr.), *The Cistercian World* (London: Penguin, 1993) pp. 152–68.

Dantanus, Ulf, *Brian Friel. A Study* (London: Faber & Faber, 1988).

Davie, Grace, *Religion in Britain since 1945: Believing Without Belonging* (Oxford: Blackwell, 1994).

Davie, Grace, 'Religion and modernity: A French Contribution to the Debate', Kieran Flanagan and Peter Jupp (eds), *Postmodernity, Sociology and Religion* (London: Macmillan, 1996).

Davis, Charles, 'Theology in Seminary Confinement', *The Downside Review*, vol. 81, no. 265, October 1963, pp. 307–316.

Davis, Kingsley and Wilbert E. Moore, 'Some Principles of Stratification', Reinhard Bendix and Seymour Martin Lipset (eds), *Class, Status and Power. Social Stratification in Comparative Perspective*, 2nd edn (London: Routledge & Kegan Paul Ltd., 1967) pp. 47–53.

Day, Thomas, *Why Catholics Can't Sing. The Culture of Catholicism and the Triumph of Bad Taste* (New York: Crossroad, 1993).

Dobbelaere, Karel, 'CISR, An Alternative Approach to Sociology of Religion in Europe: ACSS and CISR Compared', *Sociological Anlaysis*, vol. 50, no. 4 (1989) pp. 377–87.

Dostoyevsky, Fyodor, *The Brothers Karamazov*, tr. David Magarshack (London: Folio Society, 1964).

Dreyfus, Hubert, and Paul Rainbow, 'Can there be a Science of Existential Structure and Social Meaning', Craig Calhoun, Edward LiPuma and Moishe Postone (eds), *Bourdieu. Critical Perspectives* (Cambridge: Polity Press, 1993) pp. 35–44.

Duffy, Eamon, *The Stripping of the Altars. Traditional Religion in England 1400–1580* (London: Yale University Press, 1992).

Dulles, Avery, *The Craft of Theology. From Symbol to System* (Dublin: Gill & Macmillan, 1992).

Dupré, Louis, 'Spiritual Life in a Secular Age', Mary Douglas and Steven Tipton (eds), *Religion and America. Spiritual Life in a Secular Age* (Boston: Beacon Press, 1983) pp. 3–13.

Dupré, Louis, *Passage to Modernity: an Essay in the Hermeneutics of Nature and Culture* (New Haven: Yale University Press, 1993).

Durkheim, Emile, *Suicide*, tr. John A. Spaulding and George Simpson (New York: The Free Press, 1966).

Ebaugh, Helen Rose Fuchs, *Women in the Vanishing Cloister: Organizational Decline in Catholic Religious Orders in the United States* (New Brunswick, New Jersey: Rutgers University Press, 1993).

Eisenstadt, Shmuel N., 'Introduction: Culture and Social Structure in Recent Sociological Analysis', Hans Haferkamp (ed.), *Social Structure and Culture* (New York: Walter de Gruyter, 1989) pp. 5–11.

Eldridge, John, 'Sociology in Britain; A Going Concern', Christopher G. A. Bryant and Henk A. Becker (eds), *What has Sociology Achieved?* (London: Macmillan, 1990) pp. 157–78.

Eliot, T. S., *Notes towards the Definition of Culture* (London: Faber & Faber, 1962).

Ellmann, Richard, *Oscar Wilde* (London: Hamish Hamilton, 1987).

Evans-Pritchard, E. E., *Theories of Primitive Religion* (Oxford: Clarendon Press, 1965).

Featherstone, Mike, 'Towards a Sociology of Postmodern Culture', Hans Haferkamp, (ed.), *Social Structure and Culture* (New York: Walter de Gruyter, 1989) pp. 147–72.

Featherstone, Mike, *Consumer Culture and Postmodernism* (London: Sage, 1991).

Featherstone, Mike, Mike Hepworth and Bryan S. Turner (eds), *The Body. Social Process and Cultural Theory* (London: Sage, 1991).

Felknor, Laurie, (ed.), *The Crisis in Religious Vocations. An Inside View* (New York: Paulist Press, 1989).

Ferrarotti, Franco, *Faith without Dogma. The Place of Religion in Postmodern Societies* (New Brunswick: Transaction Publishers, 1993).

Finke, Roger 'An Unsecular America', Steve Bruce (ed.), *Religion and Modernization* (Oxford: Clarendon Press, 1992) pp. 145–69.

Finkelstein, Joanne, *The Fashioned Self* (Cambridge: Polity Press, 1991).

Finnegan, Mother Vincent Marie, chairman of the Council of Major Superiors of Women Religious, interview, *The Catholic World Report*, February 1993, pp. 41–2 and pp. 52–5.

Finney, John, *Finding Faith Today. How does it happen?* (Swindon: British and Foreign Bible Society, 1992).

Firth, Raymond (ed.), *Man and Culture. An Evaluation of the Work of Bronislaw Malinowski* (New York: Harper & Row, 1964).

Flanagan, Kieran, 'The Godless and the Burlesque: Newman and the other Irish Universities', James D. Bastable (ed.), *Newman and Gladstone Centennial Essays* (Dublin: Veritas Publications, 1978) pp. 239–77.

Flanagan, Kieran, 'J. K. Huysmans: The First-Postmodernist Saint?', *New Blackfriars*, vol. 71, no. 838, May 1990, pp. 217–29.

Flanagan, Kieran, 'Theological pluralism: a sociological critique', Ian Hamnett (ed.), *Religious Pluralism and Unbelief. Studies Critical and Comparative* (London: Routledge, 1990) pp. 81–113.

Flanagan, Kieran, *Sociology and Liturgy: Re-presentations of the Holy* (London: Macmillan, 1991).

Flanagan, Kieran, preface and 'Sublime Policing: Sociology and Milbank's City of God', special issue of *New Blackfriars*, vol. 73, no. 861, June 1992, pp. 302–4 and 333–41.

Flanagan, Kieran, review of John Milbank, *Theology and Social Theory*, *The British Journal of Sociology*, vol. 44, no. 2, June 1993, pp. 360–1.

Flanagan, Kieran, 'Brian Friel: A Sociological Appreciation of an Irish playwright', *Contemporary Review*, vol. 266, no. 1551, April 1995, pp. 199–209.

Flanagan, Kieran, 'Postmodernity and Culture: Sociological Wagers of the Self in Theology', Kieran Flanagan and Peter Jupp (eds), *Postmodernity, Sociology and Religion* (London: Macmillan, 1996).

Ford, David F., *A Long Rumour of Wisdom. Resdescribing Theology* (Cambridge: Cambridge University Press, 1992).

Fox, Matthew, press release on joining the American Episcopal Church, 15th April 1994.

Fraser, David A. and Tony Campolo, *Sociology Through the Eyes of Faith* (London: Apollos, 1992).

Freedberg, David, *The Power of Images. Studies in the History and Theory of Response* (London: University of Chicago Press, 1991).

Freeman, Derek, *Margaret Mead and Samoa. The Making and Unmaking of an Anthropological Myth* (Cambridge, Mass.: Harvard University Press, 1983).

Frei, Hans, *Types of Christian Theology* (ed.), George Hunsinger and William C. Placher (New Haven: Yale University Press, 1992).

Friedrichs, Robert W., *A Sociology of Sociology* (New York: The Free Press, 1970).

Friel, Brian, *Translations* (London: Faber & Faber, 1981).

Friel, Brian, *Making History* (London: Faber & Faber, 1989).

Frisby, David, *George Simmel* (Chichester: Ellis Horwood Limited, 1984).

Frisby, David, *Fragments of Modernity. Theories of Modernity in the Work of Simmel, Kracauer and Benjamin* (Cambridge: Polity Press, 1988).

Gard, Roger Martin du, *Jean Barois*, tr. Stuart Gilbert (London: The Bodley Head, 1950).

Geertz, Clifford, 'Religion as a Cultural System', Donald R. Cutler (ed.), *The Religious Situation: 1968* (Boston: Beacon Press, 1968).

Geertz, Clifford, *Works and Lives. The Anthropologist as Author* (Cambridge: Polity Press, 1989).

Geertz, Clifford, *The Interpretation of Cultures* (London: Fontana, 1993).

Giddens, Anthony, *The Consequences of Modernity* (Cambridge: Polity Press, 1990).

Giddens, Anthony, *Modernity and Self-Identity. Self and Society in the Late Modern Age* (Cambridge: Polity Press, 1991).

Giddens, Anthony, *The Transformation of Intimacy. Sexuality, Love and Eroticism in Modern Societies* (Cambridge: Polity Press, 1992).

Gill, Robin, 'Sociologists and Theologians: A Comparison', *Sociological Focus*, vol. 23, no. 3, August 1990, pp. 167–75.

Gilloch, Graeme, 'The Heroic Pedestrian or the Pedestrian Hero? Walter Benjamin and the Flâneur', *Telos*, no. 91, Spring 1992, pp. 108–16.

Gleason, Phillip, 'American Catholic Higher Education, 1940–1990: The ideological context', George M. Marsden and Bradley J. Longfied (eds), *The Secularization of the Academy* (New York: Oxford University Press, 1992) pp. 234–58.

Goethe, Joann Wolfgang von *Faust*, tr. Phillip Wayne (London: Penguin, 1949) Part I.

Goethe, Johann Wolfgang von, *Faust*, tr. Phillip Wayne (London: Penguin, 1959) Part II.

Goffman, Erving, *Stigma. Notes on the Management of Spoiled Identity* (London: Penguin, 1968).

Gouldner, Alvin, *The Coming Crisis of Western Sociology* (London: Heinemann, 1971).

Greeley, Andrew, foreward to George A. Hillery, Jr, *The Monastery. A Study in Freedom, Love, and Community* (Westport, Connecticut: Praeger, 1992) pp. xv–xvi.

Green, Garrett, 'The Sociology of Dogmatics: Niklas Luhmann's Challenge to Theology', *The Journal of the American Academy of Religion*, vol. 4, no. 1 (1982) pp. 19–34.

Guardini, Romano, *The End of the Modern World: A Search for Orientation*, tr. Joseph Theman and Herbert Burke (London: Sheed & Ward, 1957).

Habermas, Jurgen, 'Walter Benjamin: Consciousness-Raising or Rescuing Critique', Gary Smith (ed.), *On Walter Benjamin* (Cambridge, Massachusetts: The MIT Press, 1991) pp. 90–128.

Halsey, A. H., 'Provincials and Professionals: The British Post-War Sociologists', *LSE Quarterly*, vol. 1, no. 1, March 1987, pp. 43–74.

Hammond, Phillip E. (ed.), *Sociologists at Work: Essays on the Craft of Social Research* (New York: Doubleday, 1967).

Hamnett, Ian, 'Sociology of Religion and Sociology of Error', *Religion*, vol. 3, Spring 1973, pp. 1–12.

Hamnett, Ian, 'A Mistake about Error', *New Blackfriars*, vol. 67, no. 788, February 1986, pp. 69–78.

Hart, D. G., 'American Learning and the Problem of Religious Studies', George M. Marsden and Bradley J. Longfield (eds), *The Secularization of the Academy* (New York: Oxford University Press, 1992) pp. 219–20.

Harvey, David, *The Condition of Postmodernity. An Enquiry into the Origins of Cultural Change* (Oxford: Basil Blackwell, 1989).

Harvey Pearce, Roy, *Savagism and Civilization. A Study of the Indian and the American Mind* (Baltimore: the Johns Hopkins Press, 1967).

Hassan, Ihab, 'The Culture of Postmodernism', *Theory, Culture and Society*, vol. 2, no. 3 (1985) pp. 119–131.

Haug, Wolfgang Fritz, *Commodity Aesthetics, Ideology and Culture* (New York: International General, 1987).

Hawthorn, Geoffrey, *Enlightenment and Despair. A History of Sociology* (Cambridge: Cambridge University Press, 1976).

Heelas, Paul, 'The Sacralization of the Self and New Age Capitalism', Nicholas Abercrombie and Alan Warde (eds), *Social Change in Contemporary Britain* (Cambridge: Polity Press, 1992) pp. 138–66.

Heelas, Paul, 'The New Age in Cultural Context; the Premodern, the Modern and the Postmodern', *Religion*, vol. 23 (1993) pp. 103–16.

Heller, Agnes and Ferenc Fehér, *The Postmodern Political Condition* (Cambridge: Polity Press, 1991).

Henrici, Peter, 'Hans Urs von Balthasar: A Sketch of His Life', David L. Schindler (ed.), *Hans Urs von Balthasar: His Life and Work* (San Francisco: Ignatius Press, 1991) pp. 7–43.

Herbert, Christopher, *Culture and Anomie: Ethnographic Imagination in the Nineteenth Century* (Chicago: The Chicago University Press, 1991).

Heritage & Renewal. The Report of the Archibishops' Commission on Cathedrals (London: Church House Publishing, 1994).

Hervieu-Léger, Danièle, 'Religion and Modernity in the French Context: For a New Approach to Secularization', *Sociological Analysis*, vol. 51 (1990) pp. 15–25.

Herzfeld, Michael, *Anthropology through the Looking-Glass. Critical Ethnography in the Margins of Europe* (Cambridge: Cambridge University Press, 1989).

Hill, W. J., entry on theology in *New Catholic Encyclopaedia* (Palatine, Illinois: J. Heraty, 1978), vol. 17, pp. 652–7.

Hillery, George A., Jr, *The Monastery. A Study in Freedom, Love and Community* (Westport: Praeger, 1992).

Hinkle, Roscoe C., Jr, and Gisela J. Hinkle, *The Development of Modern Sociology. Its Nature and Growth in the United States* (New York: Random House, 1954).

Hobsbawm, Eric, and Terence Ranger (eds), *The Invention of Tradition* (Cambridge: University Press, Canto edition, 1992).

Holland, Joe, 'The Cultural Vision of Pope John Paul II: Toward a Conservative/Liberal Postmodern Dialogue', David Ray Griffin, William A. Beardslee and Joe Holland, *Varieties of Postmodern Theology* (New York: State University of New York Press, 1989) pp. 95–127.

Hollis, Crispian, 'Mass media: the language of our culture', *Briefings*, 14 October 1993, pp. 10–13.

Holmes, Urban T., 'Liminality and Liturgy', *Worship*, vol. 47, no. 7, 1973, pp. 386–397.

Hornsby-Smith, Michael P., *Roman Catholics in England: Studies in Social Structure since the Second World War* (Cambridge: Cambridge University Press, 1987).

Hornsby-Smith, Michael P., *The Changing Parish. A study of Parishes, Priests, and Parishioners after Vatican II* (London: Routledge, 1989).

Hughes, Edward, 'Civil Service Reform 1853–5', *Public Administration*, vol. 32 (1854) pp. 17–51.

Hughes, H. Stuart, *Consciousness and Society. The Reorientation of European Social Thought 1890–1930* (New York: Random House, 1958).

Huizinga, J., *The Waning of the Middle Ages*, tr. F. Hopman (London: Penguin, 1955).

Hull McCormack, Jerusha, *John Gray, Poet, Dandy, and Priest* (Hanover: University Press of New England, 1991).

Huszar, George de, 'Nietzsche's theory of decadence and the transvaluation of all values', *Journal of the History of Ideas*, vol. 6, no. 3, June 1945, pp. 259–72.

Huysmans, J. K., *The Oblate*, tr. Edward Perceval (London: Kegan Paul, Trench, Trubner & Co. Ltd., 1924).

Huysmans, J. K., *Against Nature*, tr. Robert Baldick (London: Penguin, 1959).

Huysmans, J. K., *La Bas* (London: Dedalus, 1986).
Huysmans, J. K., *En Route*, tr. W. Fleming (Cambridge: Dedalus, 1989).
Huysmans, J. K., *The Cathedral*, tr. Clara Bell (Cambridge: Dedalus, 1989).
Illich, Ivan, *Medical Nemesis. The Expropriation of Health* (London: Calder & Boyars, 1975).
Instruction on the Ecclesial Vocation of the Theologian (London: CTS/Veritas, 1990).
James, M. R., ' "Oh, whistle, and I'll come to you, my lad" ' and 'A warning to the curious', *The Ghost Stories of M. R. James* (London: Edward Arnold, 1974) pp. 120–50 and 561–87.
James, William, *The Varieties of Religious Experience* (New York: Longmans, Green, & Co., 1902).
Jameson, Fredric, 'Postmodernism, or The Cultural Logic of Late Capitalism', *New Left Review*, vol. 146, July–August (1984) pp. 53–92.
Jandy, Edward C., *Charles Horton Cooley. His Life and his Social Theory* (New York: Octagon Books, 1969).
Jaspers, Karl, *Truth and Symbol*, tr. Jean T. Wilde, William Kluback and William Kimmel (New York: Twayne Publishers, 1959).
Jaspers, Karl, *Leonardo, Descartes, Max Weber*, tr. Ralph Manheim (London: Routledge & Kegan Paul, 1965).
Jaspers, Karl, *The Great Philosophers* (London: Rupert Hart-Davis, 1966).
Jencks, Charles, *What is Post-Modernism?*, 3rd edn (London: Academic Editions, 1989).
Jenkins, Richard, *Pierre Bourdieu* (London: Routledge, 1992).
Jennings, Derek, 'Shedding an effortless superiority', *The Times*, 27th January 1992.
John Paul II, *Centesimus Annus* (London: Catholic Truth Society, 1991).
John Paul II, *Veritatis Splendor* (Vatican City: Libreria Editrice Vaticana, 1993).
John Paul II, *Crossing the Threshold of Hope*, tr. Jenny and Martha McPhee (London: Jonathan Cape, 1994).
Jump, John (ed.), *Marlowe: Doctor Faustus* (London: Macmillan, 1969) introduction, pp. 11–21.
Käsler, Dirk, *Max Weber. An Introduction to his Life and Work*, tr. Phillipa Hurd (Cambridge: Polity Press, 1988).
Kavanagh, Aidan, 'Textuality and Deritualization: The Case of Western Liturgical Usage', *Studia Liturgica*, vol. 23 (1993) pp. 70–7.
Keane, John B., *The Field* (Cork: Mercier Press, 1991).
Kehl, Medard, 'Hans Urs von Balthasar: A Portrait', Medard Kehl and Werner Loser (eds), *The von Balthasar Reader*, tr. Robert J. Daly and Fred Lawrence (Edinburgh: T. & T. Clark, 1982) pp. 3–54.
Kelley, Dean M., *Why Conservative Churches are Growing* (New York: Harper & Row, 1972).
Kelley, Donald R., 'Epimetheus restored', *History of the Human Sciences*, vol. 6, no. 4, November 1993, pp. 97–107.
Kellner, Douglas, 'The Postmodern Turn: Positions, Problems, and Prospects', George Ritzer (ed.), *Frontiers of Social Theory* (New York: Columbia University Press, 1990) pp. 255–86.
Kelsey, David H., *To Understand God Truly. What's Theological about a Theological School* (Louisville, Kentucky: Westminster/John Know Press, 1992).

Kelsey, David H., *Between Athens and Berlin. The Theological Education Debate* (Grand Rapids, Michigan: William B. Eerdmans Publishing Company, 1993).

Kempis, Thomas À., *The Imitation of Christ*, tr. Leo Sherley-Price (London: Penguin, 1952).

Ker, Ian, *John Henry Newman. A Biography* (Oxford: Oxford University Press, 1988).

Kimmel, Michael S. 'Reading Men: Men Masculinity and Publishing', *Contemporary Sociology*, vol. 21, no. 2, March 1992, pp. 162–71.

King, Eleace, *Cara Formation Directory for Men and Women Religious 1993* (Washington, DC, Georgetown University, 1992) pp. 1–15.

King, Ursula (ed.), *Turning Points in Religious Studies. Essays in Honour of Geoffrey Parrinder* (Edinburgh: T. & T. Clark, 1990).

Kingman, John, *Truth in the University. The E. H. Young Lecture* (University of Bristol, 1993).

Kivisto, Peter, 'The Brief Career of Catholic Sociology', *Sociological Analysis* (1989) vol. 50, no. 4, pp. 351–61.

Koerner, Joseph Leo, 'Hans Blumenberg's style', *History of Human Sciences*, vol. 6, no. 4, November 1993, pp. 1–10.

Krajewski, Bruce, 'The musical horizon of religion: Blumenberg's *Matthauspassion*', *History of the Human Sciences*, vol. 6, no. 4, November 1993, pp. 81–95.

Kroeber, A. L., *Anthropology: Culture Patterns and Processes* (New York: Harcourt, Brace & World, 1963).

Kuhn, Thomas S., *The Structure of Scientific Revolutions*, 2nd edn (Chicago: The University of Chicago Press, 1970).

Lamb, Matthew L., 'Inculturation and Western culture: the dialogical experience between gospel and culture', *Communio*, vol. 21, no. 1, Spring 1994, pp. 124–44.

Lambert, Bernard, '*Gaudium et Spes* and the Travail of Today's Ecclesial Conception', Joseph Gremillion (ed.), *The Church and Culture since Vatican II. The Experience of North and Latin America* (Notre Dame, Indiana, University of Notre Dame Press, 1985) pp. 31–52.

Lambert, Yves, 'From Parish to Transcendent Humanism in France', James A. Beckford and Thomas Luckman (eds), *The Changing Face of Religion* (London: Sage Publications, 1991) pp. 49–63.

Lamont, Michèle and Robert Wuthnow, 'Betwixt and Between: Recent Cultural Sociology in Europe and the United States', George Ritzer (ed.), *Frontiers of Social Theory. The New Syntheses* (New York: Columbia University Press, 1990) pp. 287–315.

Lane, Dermot A., 'Faith and Culture: The Challenge of Inculturation', Dermot Lane (ed.), *Religion and Culture in Dialogue. A Challenge for the Next Millennium* (Dublin: Columba Press, 1993) pp. 11–39.

Lapointe, Guy, 'Shattered Liturgical Space: Questions related to the Televising of Sunday Mass in French Canada', *Studia Liturgica*, vol. 24, 1994, pp. 109–21.

Lasch, Christopher, *The Culture of Narcissism. American Life in An Age of Diminishing Expectations* (New York: W. W. Norton & Company, 1991).

Lash, Scott and John Urry, *Economies of Signs and Space* (London: Sage, 1994).

Lash, Scott, 'Reflexivity and its Doubles: Structure, Aesthetics, Community', Ulrich Beck, Anthony Giddens and Scott Lash, *Reflexive Modernization* (Cambridge: Polity Press, 1994) pp. 110–73.

Lawrence, P. A., *George Simmel: Sociologist and European* (London: Nelson, 1976).

Le Mee, Katharine, *Chant. The Origins, Form, Practice, and Healing Power of Gregorian Chant* (London: Rider, 1994).

Lebeau, Paul, *La vie religieuse. un chemin d'humanité* (Bruxelles: Vie consacrée, 1992).

Leclercq, Jean, *The Love of Learning and the Desire for God: a Study of Monastic Culture*, 3rd edn, tr. Catherine Misrahi (New York: Fordham University Press, 1982).

Lepenies, Wolf, *Between Literature and Science: the Rise of Sociology*, tr. R. J. Hollingdale (Cambridge: Cambridge University Press, 1988).

Levitt, Mairi, 'Sexual identity and religious socialisation', *The British Journal of Sociology*, vol. 46, no. 3 September 1995, pp. 529–536.

Lindbeck, George, *The Nature of Doctrine: Religion and Theology in a Postliberal Age* (Philadelphia: The Westminster Press, 1984).

Lindbeck, George, special issue of *Modern Theology*, vol. 4, no. 2, January 1988.

Lindbeck, George A., 'The Church's Mission to a Postmodern Culture', Frederic B. Burnham, *Postmodern Theology* (San Francisco: Harper Collins, 1989) pp. 37–55.

Lodge, David, *Paradise News* (London: Penguin, 1992).

Louth, Andrew, *Discerning the Mystery. An Essay on the Nature of Theology* (Oxford: Clarendon Press, 1989).

Lowenthal, David, *The Past is a Foreign Country* (Cambridge: Cambridge University Press, 1985).

Lubac, Henri de, *The Drama of Atheist Humanism*, tr. Edith M. Riley (London: Sheed and Ward, 1949).

Luhmann, Niklas, 'Society, Meaning, Religion – Based on Self-Reference', *Sociological Analysis*, vol. 46, no. 1 (1985) pp. 5–20.

Luhmann, Niklas, *Risk: A Sociological Theory*, tr. Rhodes Barrett (Berlin: Walter de Gruyter, 1993).

Lurie, Alison, *Imaginary Friends* (London: Heinemann, 1967).

Lydon, James, *Ireland in the later Middle Ages* (Dublin: Gill and Macmillan, 1973).

Lyon, David, *The Steeple's Shadow: on the Myths and Realities of Secularization* (London: SPCK, 1985).

Lyotard, Jean-François, *The Postmodern Condition: A Report on Knowledge*, tr. Geoff Bennington and Brian Massumi (Manchester: Manchester University Press, 1984).

MacIntyre, Alasdair, *After Virtue. a Study in Moral Theory*, 2nd edn (London: Duckworth, 1985).

Mahar, Cheleen, 'Pierre Bourdieu: The Intellectual Project', Richard Harker, Cheleen Mahar, Chris Wilkes (eds), *An Introduction to the Work of Pierre Bourdieu* (London: Macmillan, 1990) pp. 26–57.

Malinowski, Bronislaw *A Scientific Theory of Culture* (New York: Oxford University Press, 1960).

Mannion, M. Francis, 'Liturgy and the Present Crisis of Culture', *Worship*, vol. 62, no. 2, March 1988, pp. 98–123.

Marion, Jean-Luc, *God without Being*, tr. Thomas A. Carlson (Chicago: University of Chicago Press, 1991).

Marlowe, Christopher, *Doctor Faustus* (eds) David Bevington and Eric Rasmussen (Manchester: Manchester University Press, 1993).

Marsden, George M., 'The Soul of the American University: A Historical Overview', George M. Marsden and Bradley J. Longfield (eds), *The Secularization of the Academy* (New York: Oxford University Press, 1992) pp. 9–45.

Marshall, Gordon, *In Search of the Spirit of Capitalism. An Essay on Max Weber's Protestant Ethic Thesis* (London: Hutchinson, 1982).

Martin, David, 'Profane Habit and Sacred Usage', *Theology*, vol. 82, no. 686, March 1979, pp. 83–95.

Martin, David, *The Breaking of the Image. A Sociology of Christian Theory and Practice* (Oxford: Basil Blackwell, 1980).

Martin, David *Tongues of Fire. The Explosion of Protestantism in Latin America*, (Oxford: Basil Blackwell, 1990).

Martin, David, 'The secularization issue; prospect and retrospect'. *The British Journal of Sociology*, vol. 42, no. 3, September 1991, pp. 465–74.

Martindale, Don, *The Nature and Types of Sociological Theory* (Boston: Houghton Mifflin, 1960).

Marx, Karl, *Capital*, vol. 1, tr. Samuel Moore and Edward Aveling (London: George Allen & Unwin, 1946).

Marx, Karl, *Early Writings*, tr. T. B. Bottomore (New York: McGraw-Hill, 1964) p. 192.

Matarasso, Pauline (ed. and tr.), *The Cistercian World. Monastic Writings of the Twelfth Century* (London: Penguin, 1993).

McDannell, Colleen and Bernhard Lang, *Heaven. A History* (London: Yale University Press, 1988).

McDonagh, Enda, 'The Church in the Modern World (*Gaudium et Spes*)', Adrian Hastings (ed.), *Modern Catholicism: Vatican II and After* (London: SPCK, 1991) pp. 96–112.

McGrath, Alister E., *The Renewal of Anglicanism* (London: SPCK, 1993).

McGregor, Bede and Thomas Norris (eds), *The Beauty of Christ. An Introduction to the Theology of Hans Urs von Balthasar* (Edinburgh: T. & T. Clark, 1994).

McLellan, David, *Simone Weil. Utopian Pessimist* (London: Macmillan, 1989).

McNamara, Patrick, 'Teaching the Sociology of Religion as a Reflective Enterprise', *Social Compass*, vol. 41, no. 3 (1994) pp. 329–38.

McRobbie, Angela, *Postmodernism and Popular Culture* (London: Routledge, 1994).

McSweeney, Bill, *Roman Catholicism. The Search for Relevance* (Oxford: Basil Blackwell, 1980).

Mellor, Phillip A., 'Reflexive Traditions: Anthony Giddens, High Modernity and the Contours of Contemporary Religiosity', *Religious Studies*, vol. 29 (1993) pp. 111–27.

Merton, Robert K., 'Puritanism, Pietism and Science', his *Social Theory and Social Structure* (New York: The Free Press, 1968 edn) pp. 628–60.

Merton, Robert K., 'Some Thoughts on the Concept of Sociological Autobiography', Matilda White Riley (ed.), *Sociological Lives* (Newbury Park, California: Sage Publications, 1988) pp. 17–21.

Mestrovic, Stjepan G., *The Coming Fin de Siècle. An Application of Durkheim's Sociology to Modernity and Postmodernism* (London: Routledge, 1992).

Milbank, John, *Theology and Social Theory. Beyond Secular Reason* (Oxford: Basil Blackwell, 1990).

Miller, Daniel, *Material Culture and Mass Consumption* (Oxford: Basil Blackwell, 1991).

Mitzman, Arthur, *The Iron Cage: An Historical Interpretation of Max Weber*, 2nd edn (New Brunswick, USA: Transaction Books, 1985).

Mixed cathedral choirs, editorial in *The Times*, 17th July 1993.

Montefiore, Hugh, *The Church Times*, 7th January 1994.

Mork, Wulstan, *The Benedictine Way* (Petersham, Massachusetts: St. Bede's Publications, 1987).

Morris, Loretta M., 'Secular Transcendence: from ACSS to ASR', *Sociological Analysis* (1989) vol. 50, no. 4, pp. 329–49.

Morris, Paul, 'Judaism and pluralism: the Price of "Religious Freedom"', Ian Hamnett (ed.), *Religious Pluralism & Unbelief* (London: Routledge, 1990) pp. 179–201).

Nadel, S. F., *The Foundations of Social Anthropology* (London: Cohen & West, 1951).

Nairn, Tom, *The Break-Up of Britain. Crisis and Neo-Nationalism* (London: New Left Books, 1977).

Nash, Arnold, 'Some Reflections upon the Sociological Approach to Theology', *International Yearbook for the Sociology of Religion*, vol. 2 (1966) pp. 185–97.

Newman, John Henry, *The Idea of a University* (New York: Doubleday, 1959).

Nichols, Aidan, *The Art of God Incarnate. Theology and Image in Christian Tradition* (London: Darton, Longman & Todd, 1980).

Nichols, Aidan, 'Balthasar and his Christology', *New Blackfriars*, July/August 1985, vol. 66, no. 781/782, pp. 317–24.

Nichols, Aidan, 'The Habit of Theology and how to aquire it', *The Downside Review*, vol. 105, no. 361 (1987) pp. 247–59.

Nichols, Aidan, *The Shape of Catholic Theology* (Edinburgh: T. & T. Clark, 1991).

Nichols, Aidan, *The Panther and the Hind. A Theological History of Anglicanism* (Edinburgh: T. & T. Clark, 1993).

Nichols, Aidan, *Scribe of the Kingdom. Essays on Theology and Culture*, vol. 1 (London: Sheed & Ward, 1994).

Niebuhr, H. Richard, *Christ and Culture* (New York: Harper & Row, 1975).

Nietzsche, Friedrich, *The Will to Power* (ed.) Walter Kaufmann, tr. Walter Kaufmann and R. J. Hollingdale (New York: Random House, 1968).

Nietzsche, Friedrich, *Ecce Homo*, tr. R. J. Hollingdale (London: Penguin, 1979).

Nouwen, Henri J. M., *Behold the Beauty of the Lord. Praying with Icons* (Notre Dame, Indiana: Ave Maria Press, 1987).

O'Donnell, John, *Hans Urs von Balthasar* (London: Geoffrey Chapman, 1992).

O'Neill, John, 'Religion and Postmodernism: The Durkheimian Bond in Bell and Jameson', *Theory, Culture and Society*, vol. 5, nos. 2–3, June 1988, pp. 493–508.

Oakes, Guy, introduction, *Georg Simmel. Essays on Interpretation in Social Sciences*, tr. Guy Oakes (Manchester: Manchester University Press, 1980) pp. 3–94.

Okely, Judith, 'Anthropology and autobiography. Participatory experience and embodied knowledge', Judith Okely and Helen Callaway (eds), *Anthropology and Autobiography* (London: Routledge, 1992) pp. 1–28.

Orme Mills, John, 'The Introduction of Two Minds', David Martin, John Orme Mills and W. S. F. Pickering (eds), *Sociology and Theology: Alliance and Conflict* (Brighton: The Harvester Press, 1980) pp. 1–14.

Ouellet, Marc, 'Hans Urs von Balthasar: Witness to the integration of faith and culture', *Communio*, vol. 18, no. 1, Spring 1991, pp. 111–26.

Owen, David, *Maturity and Modernity: Nietzsche, Weber and Foucault, and the Ambivalence of Reason* (London: Routledge, 1994).

Panofsky, Erwin, *Gothic Architecture and Scholasticism* (New York: New American Library, 1976).

Pascal, Blaise, *Pensées*, tr. A. J. Krailsheimer (London: Penguin, 1966).

Pastoral Constitution on the Church in the Modern World (Gaudium et Spes) Austin Flannery (ed.), *Vatican II. The Conciliar and Post Conciliar Documents* (Dublin: Dominican Publications, 1975).

Peterson, Richard A., 'Symbols and Social Life: The Growth of Cultural Studies', *Contemporary Sociology*, vol. 19, no. 4, July 1990, pp. 498–500.

Pichois, Claude, *Baudelaire*, tr. Graham Robb (London: Hamish Hamilton, 1989).

Pickering, W. S. F., preface to Robert Hertz, *Sin and Expiation in Primitive Societies*, tr. Robert Parkin (Oxford: British Centre for Durkheimian Studies, 1994) pp. 5–14.

Pieper, Josef, *In Search of the Sacred*, tr. Lothar Krauth (San Fancisco: Igantius Press, 1991).

Pine, Richard, *Brian Friel and Ireland's Drama* (London: Routledge, 1990).

Platt, Jennifer, *Realities of Social Research. An Empirical Study of British Sociologists* (Falmer: Sussex University Press 1976).

Poll results on youth and morality, *The Observer*, 9th October 1994.

Potel, Julien, *L'Église Catholique en France. Approches sociologiques* (Paris: Descelée de Brouwer, 1994).

Pseudo-Dionysius. The Complete Works, tr. Colm Luibheid (London: SPCK, 1987).

Quenot, Michael, *The Icon. Window on the Kingdom*, tr. a Carthusian Monk (London: Mowbray, 1992).

Quinn, Patricia A., *Better than The Sons of Kings. Boys and Monks in the Early Middle Ages* (New York: Peter Lang, 1989).

Radcliffe, Timothy, 'Relativizing the Relativizers: a Theologian's Assessment of the Role of Sociological Explanation of Religious Phenomena and Theology Today', David Martin, John Orme Mills and W. S. F. Pickering (eds), *Sociology and Theology: Alliance and Conflict* (Brighton: The Harvester Press, 1980) pp. 151–62.

Rappaport, Roy, 'The Obvious Aspects of Ritual' and 'Sanctity and Lies in Evolution', *Ecology, Meaning and Religion* (Richmond, California: North Atlantic Books 1979) pp. 173–246.

Ratzinger, Joseph, 'Homily at the funeral liturgy for Hans Urs von Balthasar', *Communio*, vol. 15, no. 4, Winter 1988, pp. 512–6.

Ratzinger, Joseph, '*Communio*: a program', *Communio*, vol. 19, no. 3, Fall 1992, pp. 436–49.

Report on the Organisation of the Permanent Civil Service in *Papers relating to the re-organization of the Civil Service*, 1854–55 [1870] XX.

Richards, Michael, *A People of Priests. The Ministry of the Catholic Church* (London: Darton, Longman and Todd, 1995).

Riches, John, *The Analogy of Beauty. The Theology of Hans Urs von Balthasar* (Edinburgh: T. & T. Clark, 1986).

Richter, Michael, *Medieval Ireland. The Enduring Tradition* (London: Macmillan, 1988).

Ricoeur, Paul, 'The model of the text: meaningful action considered as a text', Paul Ricoeur, *Hermeneutics and the Human Sciences: Essays on Language, Action and Interpretation*, tr. John B. Thompson (Cambridge: Cambridge University Press, 1981) pp. 197–221.

Ritzer, George, *The McDonaldization of Society: an Investigation Into the Changing Character of Contemporary Social Life* (Newbury Park, California: Pine Forge Press, 1993).

Robbins, Derek, *The Work of Pierre Bourdieu* (Milton Keynes: Open University, 1991).

Roberts, Louis, *The Theological Aesthetics of Hans Urs von Balthasar* (Washington, DC: The Catholic University of America Press, 1987).

Roberts, Richard H., 'Transcendental Sociology? A Critique of John Milbank's *Theology and Social Theory Beyond Secular Reason*', *Scottish Journal of Theology*, vol. 46 (1993) pp. 527–35.

Robinson, Edward, *Icons of the Present: Some Reflections on Art, the Sacred and the Holy* (London: SCM, 1993).

Roest Crollius, Arij A., (ed.), *Inculturation. Working papers on Living Faith and Cultures*, vols. 7–10 (Rome: Pontifical Gregorian University, 1986 and 1987).

Rojek, Chris, *Ways of Escape. Modern Transformations in Leisure and Travel* (London: Macmillan, 1993).

Roof, Wade Clark and William McKinney, *American Mainline Religion. Its Changing Shape and Future* (New Brunswick, New Jersey: Rutgers University Press, 1987).

Rorem, Paul, *Biblical and Liturgical Symbols within the Pseudo-Dionysian Synthesis* (Toronto: Pontifical Institute of Mediaeval Studies, 1948).

Rutherfurd, Edward, *Sarum* (London: Arrow Books, 1988).

Sacks, Jonathan, *The Persistence of Faith. Religion, Morality & Society in a Secular Age* (London: Weidenfeld and Nicolson, 1991).

Salisbury Cathedral, report of episcopal visit, *The Times*, 18th October 1991.

Sartre, Jean-Paul, *Baudelaire*, tr. Martin Tunrell (New York: New Directions, 1967).

Sarup, Madan, *An Introductory Guide to Post-structuralism and Postmodernism* (London: Harvester Wheatsheaf, 1988).

Scaff, Lawrence A., 'Georg Simmel's Theory of Culture', Michael Kaern, Bernard S. Phillips and Robert S. Cohen (eds), *Georg Simmel and Contemporary Sociology* (Dordrecht: Kluwer Academic Publishers, 1990) pp. 283–96.

Scaff, Lawrence A., 'Modernity and the tasks of a sociology of culture', *History of the Human Sciences*, vol. 3, no. 1 (1990) pp. 85–100.

Scaff, Lawrence A., *Fleeing the Iron Cage: Culture, Politics, and Modernity in the Thought of Max Weber* (Berkeley: University of California Press, 1991).

Schaefer, Dietrich, letter on Simmel, Lewis Coser, 'The Stranger in the Academy', Lewis Coser (ed.), *Georg Simmel* (Englewood Cliffs, New Jersey: Prentice-Hall, 1965) pp. 37–39.

Schneider, Mark A., 'Culture-as-text in the work of Clifford Geertz', *Theory and Society*, vol. 16 (1987) pp. 809–39.

Schneider, Mark A., *Culture and Enchantment* (Chicago: The University of Chicago Press, 1993).

Schoenherr, Richard A. and Lawrence A. Young, *Full Pews and Empty Altars.*

278 *Bibliography*

Demographics of the Priest Shortage in the United States Catholic Dioceses (Wisconsin: University of Wisconsin Press, 1993).

Scholem, Gershom, 'Walter Benjamin and His Angel', Gary Smith, (ed.), *On Walter Benjamin* (Cambridge, Massachusetts: The MIT Press, 1991) pp. 51–89.

Schwehn, Mark R., *Exiles from Eden: Religion and the Academic Vocation in America* (New York: Oxford University Press, 1993).

Scott, Christina, *A Historian and his World. A Life of Christopher Dawson 1889–1970* (London: Sheed & Ward, 1984).

Scott, Sue and David Morgan (eds), *Body Matters: Essays on the Sociology of the Body* (London: The Falmer Press, 1993).

Shilling, Chris, *The Body and Social Theory* (London: Sage Publications, 1993).

Shils, Edward *The Calling of Sociology and Other Essays on the Pursuit of Learning* (Chicago: University of Chicago Press, 1980).

Shiner, Larry, 'The Concept of Secularization in Empirical Research', *Journal for the Scientific Study of Religion* (1967) vol. 6, no. 2, pp. 207–20.

Shorter, Aylward, *Evangelization and Culture* (London: Geoffrey Chapman, 1994).

Silber, Hana Friedrich, 'Monasticism and the "Protestant Ethic": Asceticism, Rationality and Wealth in the Medieval West', *The British Journal of Sociology*, vol. 44, no. 1, March 1993, pp. 103–23.

Simmel, Georg, 'A contribution to the sociology of religion', *The American Journal of Sociology*, vol. 60, no. 6, May 1955, pp. 1–18.

Simmel, Georg, *The Conflict in Modern Culture and Other Essays*, tr. K. Peter Etzkorn (New York: Teachers College Press, 1968).

Simmel, Georg, *Essays on Interpretation in Social Science*, tr. Guy Oakes (Manchester: Manchester University Press, 1980) pp. 35–46.

Simmel, Georg, *The Philosophy of Money*, 2nd edn, tr. Tom Bottomore and David Frisby (London: Routledge, 1990).

Simmel, Georg, special issue, *Theory, Culture & Society*, vol. 8, no. 3, August 1991.

Skorupski, John, *Symbol and Theory. A Philosophical Study of Theories of Religion in Social Anthropology* (Cambridge: Cambridge University Press, 1976).

Slesinski, Robert, 'Postmodernity and the resources of the Christian East', *Communio*, vol. 17, no. 2, Summer 1990, pp. 220–37.

Smart, Barry, 'On the disorder of things: sociology, postmodernity and the "end of the social"', *Sociology*, vol. 24, no. 3, August 1990, pp. 397–416.

Smart, Barry, *Postmodernity* (London: Routledge, 1993).

Smith, Gary (ed.), *On Walter Benjamin. Critical Essays and Recollections* (Cambridge, Massachusetts: The MIT Press, 1991).

Smith, Gregory W. H., 'Snapshots "sub specie aeternitatis": Simmel, Goffman and formal sociology', *Human Studies*, vol. 12, nos. 1–2 (1989) pp. 19–57.

Smith, Huston, 'Secularization and the Sacred: The Contemporary Science', Donald R. Culter (ed.), *The Religious Situation: 1968* (Boston: Beacon Press, 1968) pp. 583–637.

Sontag, Susan, *Illness as Metaphor* (London: Penguin, 1983).

Special issue on George Lindbeck *Modern Theology*, vol. 4, no. 2, January 1988.

Special issue on Hell, *New Blackfriars*, vol. 69, no. 821, November 1988.

Spickard, James V., 'Texts and Contexts: Recent Trends in the Sociology of Religion as Reflected in US textbooks', *Social Compass*, vol. 41, no. 3 (1994) pp. 313–28.

Stanley, Liz, 'On Auto/biography in Sociology', *Sociology*, vol. 27, no. 1, February 1993, pp. 41–52.

Stark, Rodney and Laurence R. Iannaccone, 'A Supply-Side Reinterpretation of the "Secularization" of Europe', *Journal for the Scientific Study of Religion*, vol. 33, no. 3 (1994) pp. 230–52.

Stauth, Georg and Bryan S. Turner, 'Nostalgia, Postmodernism and the Critique of Mass Culture', *Theory, Culture and Society*, vol. 5, nos. 2–3, June 1988, pp. 509–26.

Stauth, Georg, 'Nietzsche, Weber, and afirmative sociology of culture', *European Journal of Sociology*, vol. 33 (1992) pp. 219–47.

Steiner, George, *Real Presences* (London: Faber & Faber, 1989).

Steiner, George, *After Babel. Aspects of Language & Translation*, 2rd edn (Oxford: Oxford University Press, 1992).

Stern, J. P., *Nietzsche* (London: Fontana, 1978).

Stocking, George W., 'Matthew Arnold, E. B. Tylor and the Uses of Invention', *American Anthropologist*, vol. 65 (1963) pp. 783–99.

Strauss, Anselm (ed.), *George Herbert Mead on Social Psychology* (Chicago: Chicago University Press, 1956).

Sumner, Colin, *The Sociology of Deviance. An Obituary* (Buckingham: The Open University, 1994).

Swatos, William H., Jr, 'Religious Sociology and the Sociology of Religion in America at the Turn of the Twentieth Century: Divergences from a Common Theme', *Sociological Analysis*, vol. 50, no. 4 (1989) pp. 36–75.

Swatos, William H., Jr, and Peter Kivisto, 'Weber as "Christian Sociologist"', *Journal for the Scientific Study of Religion*, vol. 30, no. 4, December 1991, pp. 347–62.

Sweeney, James, *The New Religious Order. The Passionists in Britain and Ireland, 1945–1990 and the Option for the Poor* (London: Bellew, 1994).

Swidler, Ann, 'Culture in Action: Symbols and Strategies', *American Sociological Review*, vol. 51, no. 2, April 1986, pp. 273–86.

Tambiah, S. J., *A Performative Approach to Ritual* (London: The British Academy, 1981).

Taylor, Charles, *Sources of the Self. The Making of the Modern Identity* (Cambridge: Cambridge University Press, 1992).

Tenbruck, Friedrich H., 'The Cultural Foundations of Society', Hans Haferkamp (ed.), *Social Structure and Culture* (New York: Walter de Gruyter, 1989) pp.15–35.

Tester, Keith, *The life and times of Post-modernity* (London: Routledge, 1993).

Tester, Keith, *Media, Culture and Morality* (London: Routledge, 1994).

The Presence of the Church in the University and in University Culture, Briefings, 21 July 1994, pp. 2–9.

Tillich, Paul, *Theology of Culture* (New York: Oxford University Press, 1959).

Touraine, Alain, *Return of the Actor. Social Theory in Postindustrial Society*, tr. Myrna Godzich (Minneapolis: University of Minnesota Press, 1988).

Turner, Bryan S. (ed.), *Theories of Modernity and Postmodernity* (London: Sage, 1990).

Turner, Bryan S., *Religion and Social Theory* (Newbury Park, California: Sage Publications, 1991).

Turner, Bryan S., *Orientalism, Postmodernism and Globalisation* (London: Routledge, 1994).

Turner, Victor, *The Ritual Process. Structure and Anti-Structure* (London: Routledge & Kegan Paul, 1969).
Tylor, Edward B., *Anthropology* (Michigan: The University of Michigan Press, 1960).
Urry, John, *The Tourist Gaze. Leisure and Travel in Contemporary Societies* (London: Sage, 1990).
Vattimo, Gianni, *The End of Modernity. Nihilism and Hermeneutics in Postmodern Culture*, tr. Jon R. Snyder (Cambridge: Polity Press, 1991).
Vloet, Johan Van der, 'Faith and the postmodern challenge', *Communio*, vol. 17, no. 2, Summer 1990, pp. 132–40.
Walker, Alice, *Possessing the Secret of Joy* (London: Jonathan Cape, 1992).
Wallis, Roy and Steve Bruce, 'Religion: the British contribution', *The British Journal of Sociology*, vol. 40, no. 3 (1989) pp. 493–520.
Walsh, Kevin, *The Representation of the Past. Museums and Heritage in the Postmodern World* (London: Routledge, 1992).
Weber, Max, *The Protestant Ethic and the Spirit of Capitalism*, tr. Talcott Parsons (London: Unwin University Books, 1930).
Weber, Max, *From Max Weber. Essays in Sociology*, tr. H. H. Gerth and C. Wright Mills (eds) (New York: Oxford University Press, 1958).
Weber, Max, *Economy and Society*, vols. 1 and 2 (London: The University of California Press, 1978).
Webster, John, 'Locality and Catholicity: Reflections on and the Church', *Scottish Journal of Theology*, vol. 45, no. 1 (1992) pp. 1–17.
Wernick, Andrew, *Promotional Culture. Advertising, Ideology and Symbolic Expression* (London: Sage, 1991).
Westergaard, John and Ray Pahl, 'Looking Backwards and Forwards: the UCG's Review of sociology', *The British Journal of Sociology*, vol. 40, no. 3 (1989) pp. 374–91.
Wicker, Brian, *Culture and Liturgy* (London: Sheed & Ward, 1963).
Wilde, Oscar, *The Picture of Dorian Gray*, *The Works of Oscar Wilde* (London: Galley Press, 1987) pp. 18–167.
Wilde, Oscar, 'The Critic as Artist', *The Works of Oscar Wilde* (London: Galley Press, 1987) pp. 948–98.
Wilde, Oscar, 'The Truth of Masks', *The Works of Oscar Wilde* (London: Galley Press, 1987) pp. 999–1017.
Willaime, Jean-Paul, 'Le Croire, l'acteur et le chercheur. Introduction au dossier "Croire et Modernite"', *Archives de Sciences Sociales des Religions*, vol. 81, Janvier-Mars (1993) pp. 7–16.
Williams, Raymond, *Keywords. A vocabulary of culture and society* (London: Fontana, 1976).
Williams, Raymond, *Culture* (London: Fontana, 1981).
Williams, Raymond, *Culture and Society* (London: The Hogarth Press, 1990).
Williams, Rowan, 'Postmodern Theology and the Judgement of the World', Frederic B. Burnham (ed.), *Postmodern Theology. Christian Faith in a Pluralist World* (San Francisco: HarperCollins, 1989).
Wilson, Bryan, *Religion in Sociological Perspective* (Oxford: Oxford University Press, 1982).
Wilson, Bryan, 'Reflections on a Many Sided Controversy', Steve Bruce (ed.), *Religion and Modernization. Sociologists and Historians Debate the Secularization Thesis* (Oxford: Clarendon Press, 1992) pp. 195–210.

Winch, Peter, *The Idea of a Social Science and its Relation to Philosophy* (London: Routledge & Kegan Paul, 1963).

Winchester, Simon, 'An Electronic Sink of Depravity', *The Spectator*, 4th February 1995, pp. 9–11.

Wohlfarth, Irving, 'On Some Jewish Motifs in Benjamin', Andrew Benjamin (ed.), *The Problems of Modernity. Adorno and Benjamin* (London: Routledge, 1989) pp. 157–215.

Wood Lynn, Robert, ' "The Survival of Recognizably Protesant Colleges": Reflections on Old-Line Protestantism, 1950–1990', George M. Marsden and Bradley J. Longfield (eds), *The Secularization of the Academy* (New York: Oxford University Press, 1992) pp. 170–94.

Wright Mills, C., *The Sociological Imagination* (New York: Grove Press, 1961).

Wright, Patrick, *On Living in an Old Country* (London: Verso, 1985).

Wuthnow, Robert, *Rediscovering the Sacred. Perspectives on Religion in Contemporary Society* (Grand Rapids, Michigan: Wm. B. Eerdmans, 1992).

Index

Schneider, Mark A., enchantment and
culture, 217–18
Scholem, Gershom, on Walter
Benjamin's angel, 134–5
Secularisation
as ambiguity in sociology, 101
Peter L. Berger on its crisis,
129–30
Hans Blumenberg's definition, 125
and commodity fetishism, 175
as the cultural displacement of the
sacred, 62–3, 180–3
as de-sacralisation, 143–4, 258
n.69
as faith, 120
Franco Ferrarotti, 125–6
Danièle Hervieu-Léger, 123
and indifference, 125–6
Yves Lambert on the French
experience, 144
and liberal theology, 10–11
David Martin and nationalism, 123
masking of evil, 125–9
money as secular God, 175, 177
as myth, 123–5
and pluralism, 129
and postmodernism, 164
as provocation, 125
of sociology, 103
as 'spiritual anathema', 137
as theft, 125, 177–8
of theology, 61–2
Bryan Turner, 48, 52
Bryan Wilson, 115
Self
and anxiety, 32, 36
as assemblage, 39
Gregory Baum, 24
Robert Bellah, 39
Wolfgang Fritz Haug, 165
George Herbert Mead, 38
and postmodernity, 38–9, 131–2
self-religiosity, 34–5
Simmel on the fluidity of the self, 14
and sociological wagers, 32
the sociologist's, 21–2
Shaw, George Bernard
John Bull's Other Island, xi
on minorities and majorities, 121

Shils, Edward, on sociology and
revelation, 31
Simeon, Brother, fortunate innocence
of knowing, 3
Simmel, Georg
Hans Urs von Balthasar's appraisal,
219–20
culture, 178–9, 219, 224–5
on money, 176–9
on Nicholas of Cusa, 176
religion, 223–5
significance, 156–7
sociology and the fluidity of the
self, 14
sociology and recovery of lost
unity, 14
on spiritual estrangement, 178–9
tragedy of culture, 220, 223–4
Slesinski, Robert, non-praying
theologian, 28
Smith, Huston, on the return of the
sacred, 122
Social magic
as grace, 208
and liturgy, 214–15
and signs, 136
Sociologist
cultural image, 18
as expert, 130
and God's design, 7
moral responsibilities of reflexivity,
24–5, 186–7
as outlaw, 18
as prophet, 119
and religious belief, 28, 31, 103,
212
as scientist and holy, 121
and self-identity, 21–4
as witchdoctor, 113
Sociology
as autobiography, 22, 23, 25, 50
Zygmunt Bauman, 58–9, 133
British sociology, 109–10
and Catholicism, 7–8, 103–5
and decadence, 114
as de-fatalising, 217
Evangelical versions, 56–7
Germany, 105–6
moral condition, 160